A Collection of Abstracts From Otsego County, New York Newspaper Obituaries 1808-1875

As Compiled By
Gertrude Audrey Barber

HERITAGE BOOKS
2008

HERITAGE BOOKS
AN IMPRINT OF HERITAGE BOOKS, INC.

Books, CDs, and more—Worldwide

For our listing of thousands of titles see our website
at
www.HeritageBooks.com

Published 2008 by
HERITAGE BOOKS, INC.
Publishing Division
100 Railroad Ave. #104
Westminster, Maryland 21157

Copyright © 1993 Gertrude Audrey Barber

All rights reserved. No part of this book may be reproduced or transmitted in any form or by any means, electronic or mechanical, including photocopying, recording or by any information storage and retrieval system without written permission from the author, except for the inclusion of brief quotations in a review.

International Standard Book Numbers
Paperbound: 978-1-58549-798-0
Clothbound: 978-0-7884-7111-7

PREFACE

This is a compilation of typed manuscripts by Gertrude Audrey Barber that combines several of her works regarding Otsego County New York obituaries and includes all found for the years 1808 to 1875.

It is to be regretted that Ms. Barber did not include names of surviving relatives of the deceased such as spouses, parents and/or children in her abstractions. For a time I considered going back over the original newspapers and adding this information, but the enormity of the task seemed so overwhelming that it might have taken years before this edition would be ready for publication.

Most of the newspaper issues used by Ms. Barber are available on microfilm through inter-library loan from the New York State Library. Write, giving specifics, to New York State Newspaper Project, New York State Library, Cultural Education Center, Empire State Plaza, Albany, NY 12230, or phone (518) 474-7491 for further information. All those listed below are available from this address.

The *Cooperstown Federalist* is available for the years 1809-1817; OCLC Number 04684065, location E25.

The *Watch-tower* is available 1814 to 1831; OCLC Number 09999283, location E25.

The *Freeman's Journal, and Otsego County Advertiser*, 1817-1819, OCLC Number 11129027, location E25.

There are Otsego County newspapers that Ms. Barber did not use that are available to researchers today through the New York State Library at the above address. They are:

Cherry Valley Gazette, 1818-1820, OCLC Number 09836457, location E25. And the same for 1818-1849, OCLC Number 09836457, location D03, 5-6.

Otsego Republican Press, 1812-1813, OCLC Number 1176202, location E25.

Freeman's Journal, 1819-1820, OCLC Number 09833256, location E25.

The Glimmerglass, 1808-1809, OCLC Number 04684059, location E25.

Impartial Observer, 1808-1809, OCLC Number 04684059, location E25.

The Otsego Farmer and the Otsego Republican, 1911-1972, OCLC Number 10928593, location D 19, 8-4.

The Otsego Farmer, 1885-1910, OCLC Number 16515014, location D 19, 8-4.

Oneonta Star, 1890-1931, OCLC Number 11315545, location D 61, 8-2.

Unadilla Times, 1857-1869, OCLC Number 11593732, location D 05, 7-5. Same publication, 1876-1967, OCLC Number 09992936, location D 05, 7-5.

The Worcester Times, 1914-1933, OCLC Number 10975781, location D 23, 4-2.

I would also urge researchers who have access to the Library of Congress newspaper files in Washington, DC to check there for these newspapers. The Library of Congress does not loan out their microfilm on interlibrary loan. It is also possible that these newspapers are available on a local level in Cooperstown or other Otsego County locations.

We would like to pay tribute to Gertrude Audrey Barber. All we have been able to find out about her is that she at one time worked for the New York Biographical & Genealogical Society in New York City. A check with them reveals no records of her beyond the fact that she was employed by them. She is found in no Who's Who. A check is being done by a New York City friend to try to locate an obituary on her, but is not available at the time we go to press.

Gertrude Audrey Barber was a dedicated woman who left behind her hundreds of manuscripts pertaining to the state of New York comprised of cemetery records, church records, will and newspaper abstracts. None of her works was ever published. I am told that the New York Biographical & Genealogical Society library contains numerous works by her. Many of these typescripts have been filmed by the Latter Day Saints Church and are available through their Local Family History Libraries. It is our pleasure to bring to the public her works pertaining to Otsego County, New York newspaper obituaries in one indexed volume.

Martha & William Reamy,
Editors
Waipahu, Hawaii
March 1993

DEATH NOTICES COPIED FROM THE *COOPERSTOWN FEDERALIST*

From 1808-1812

Cooperstown, Otsego County, New York

Dec. 15, 1808, Otsego, Mrs. ABIGAIL MATHEWSON, aged 59. [1/7/1809]
March 18, 1809, Half Moon, ISAAC S. IRISH of Worcester, aged 24 years. [4/1]
March 21, 1809, Otsego, Mrs. JULIA TANNER. [4/1]
March 28, 1809, Otsego, Mrs. STEPHEN FITCH. [4/22]
April 15, 1809, Otsego, CATHERINE FITCH, dau. [4/22]
April 13, 1809, Otsego, Mrs. ESTHER STEPHENS. [4/22]
Aug. 12, 1809, Otsego, DAVID BOSWELL. [8/19]
Oct. 18, 1809, MARGARET BOWERS, dau. of JOHN M. [10/21]
Dec. 22, 1809, Albany, Hon. WILLIAM COOPER of Cooperstown, aged 55. [12/30]
Jan. 31, 1810, Mrs. SABIN. [2/10]
March 16, 1810, Otsego, EZRA STETSON, aged 18. [3/31]
Nov. 3, 1810, Cooperstown, Mrs. RACHEL MUDGE, aged 45. [11/10]
Nov. 24, 1810, Otsego, JOHN PIER, aged 21. [12/1]
Nov. 24, 1810, Fly Creek, JOHN ADAMS. [12/1]
Dec. 2, 1811 [sic] son of BENJ. BISSELL, aged 12. [12/6/1810]
Dec. 23, 1810, Otsego, POLLY PIER. [1/12/1811]
Dec. 31, 1810, Hartwick, Mrs. BETSEY APLIN. [1/12/1811]
Jan. 20, 1811, Butternuts, POLLY DANIELSON, aged 19. [2/2]
Feb. 23, 1811, Butternuts, Mrs. ELIZABETH MORRIS. [3/2]
July 29, 1811, Cooperstown, WM. COOPER POMEROY, aged 5 months. [8/3]
Sept. 30, 1811, Milford, Mrs. CORNELIA CONKEY, aged 27. [10/12]
Nov. 16, 1811, Philadelphia, RICHARD R. SMITH, first sheriff of Otsego Co., formerly of Cooperstown. [11/30]
Feb. 10, 1812, Middlefield, NOADIAH WHITE, aged 91.
March 9, 1812, Cooperstown, Dr. ELISHA MILLER, aged 72.
March 11, 1812, Cooperstown, Mrs. MARY AVERILL, aged 76.
May 9, 1812, Middlefield, Capt. JOTHAM AMES, aged 68. [5/16]
June 2, 1812, Cooperstown, Mrs. LYDIA HERICK, aged 50. [6/6]
June 17, 1812, Otsego, JOHN NILES. [6/20]
June 25, 1812, Otsego, Mrs. HARMONY BROCKWAY, aged 44. [7/4]

1812, Cooperstown, MARY BRADFORD, aged 13 months. [7/18]
Sept. 11, 1812, Springfield, LOUISA CARY, aged 19. [9/12]
Sept. 22, 1812, Cooperstown, ELISHA TALMADGE. [9/25]
[No date] Pierstown, Mrs. JOHN WILLIAMS. [9/25]
Sept. 29, 1812, Maryland, JABEZ MAPLES of Richfield. [10/2]

DEATH NOTICES COPIED FROM
WATCH TOWER

1828-1831

1828, New Lisbon, OLIVER CAMPBELL, aged 100. [3/24]
March 31, 1828, Albany, JOHN W. YATES, aged 76. [4/7]
April 14, 1828, Burlington, Mrs. ABIGAIL NICKERSON, aged 76. [4/28]
April 27, 1828, Laurens, JOHN BLOOD, aged 85. [5/5]
May 10, 1828, Cooperstown, ELIJAH GARDNER, aged 36. [5/12]
May 10, 1828, Hartwick, WILLIAM MURRAY (Rev. Soldier). [5/19]
May 17, 1828, Garrattsville, SALLY MARIA ROBERTS, aged 6. [5/26]
May 27, 1838, Exeter, Mrs. OLIVE NASH, aged 46. [6/2]
May 17, 1828, Middlefield, ASA RANSOM, aged 47. [6/2]
June 3, 1828, Otsego, Mrs. LOIS LEE, aged 73. [6/9]
June 4, 1828, Hartwick, Dea. PRINCE WEST (Rev. Soldier), aged 93. [6/9]
July 14, 1828, Middlefield, JEREMY S. TITUS, aged 4. [7/21]
July 28, 1828, Milford, THOMAS MUMFORD, aged 26. [8/16]
July 26, 1828, Springfield, son of Capt. DAN. GILCHRIST, aged 4. [8/16]
Aug. 22, 1828, Cooperstown, Mrs. LOUISIANNA PETTE, aged 64. [8/25]
Aug. 21, 1828, Otsego, Mrs. MARCY WILLIAMS, aged 73. [8/25]
Aug. 21, 1828, Cooperstown, JACOB PLATTNER, aged 53. [8/25]
Aug. 27, 1828, Middlefield, JOSEPH L. CRAFTS, aged 4. [9/22]
Sept. 13, 1828, Middlefield, MARIA A. CRAFTS, 11 months. [9/22]
Sept. 17, 1828, Middlefield, GEORGE S. CRAFTS, aged 2. [9/22]
Sept. 19, 1828, Fly Creek, FRANCIS GRISWOLD JARVIS, aged 9. [10/6]
Sept. 30, 1828, Oaksville, JULIA ANN ALDEN, aged 15. [10/6]
Oct. 1, 1828, Edmeston, Mrs. POLLY WALDO, aged 38. [10/13]
Oct. 10, 1828, Milford, JOSEPH RICE, aged 40. [10/13]
Oct. 3, 1828, Garrattsville, SEYMOUR COBURN, aged 21. [10/13]
Oct. 20, 1828, Otsego, ERASTUS CLARK, aged 33. [10/27]
Oct. 28, 1828, Hartwick, JAMES S. BURLINGTON, aged 7. [11/3]
Nov. 23, 1828, Worcester, Mrs. CLARRISSA CHASE. [12/1]

[No date] Otsego, Mrs. SOPHIA B. WARREN, aged 32. [12/8]
Nov. 28, 1828, Decatur, DAVID TRIPPE, aged 61. [12/8]
Dec. 6, 1828, Springwater, HARVEY APLIN, Cooperstown, aged 25. [12/22]
Dec. 14, 1828, Cherry Valley, JOSEPH HUBBARD, aged 76. [12/22]
Dec. 1, 1828, Warren, Dea. JONATHAN BLOOMFIELD, aged 78. [12/22]
[No date] Warren, Mrs. BETSEY EMERSON, aged 25. [12/22]
Dec. 19, 1828, Hartwick, Mrs. ELIZABETH TUCKER, aged 67. [12/29]
Jan. 2, 1829, Plainfield, RICHARD CAMPBELL, aged 26. [1/12]
Jan. 7, 1829, Hartwick, MINERVA ALGER, aged 16. [1/19]
Jan. 12, 1829, Cooperstown, JOHN J. SPARROW, aged 4. [1/19]
Jan. 21, 1829, Cooperstown, Mrs. MARY POTTER, aged 38. [2/2]
Jan. 22, 1829, Cherry Valley, NANCY DAVISON, aged 23. [2/2]
Feb. 14, 1829, Otsego, JARED ALLEN, aged 76. [2/16]
Feb. 11, 1829, Milford, HENRY SCOTT, aged 74. [2/16]
Feb. 22, 1829, Exeter, GEORGE HERKIMER, aged 65. [3/2]
April 25, 1829, Burlington, JEREMIAH MEACHAM, aged 71. [3/23 sic]
March 12, 1829, Springfield, JEREMIAH THURSTON, aged 34. [3/23]
March 26, 1829, Burlington, ENOCH MACK, aged 27. [3/30]
March 24, 1829, Cherry Valley, Mrs. MARGARET CLYDE, aged 44. [4/6]
April 3, 1829, Burlington, son of BENJ. BAKER, infant. [4/13]
May 9, 1829, Exeter, GRIFFITH HUBBARD, aged 53. [5/11]
May 18, 1829, Laurens, Mrs. THANKFUL I. SLOOPER, aged 57. [5/25]
May 23, 1829, Middlefield, GEORGE O. GATES, aged 17. [5/25]
May 23, 1829, Otsego, WILLIAM WALBY, aged 42. [5/25]
May 25, 1829, Milford, OLIVE WELLS RUSSELL, aged 6. [6/8]
June 1, 1829, Otsego, CHARLES BABCOCK, aged 57. [6/8]
June 20, 1829, Otsego, HIRAM W. HALE, aged 30. [6/15 sic]
June 6, 1829, Cooperstown, Mrs. HULDAH BRADFORD, aged 58. [6/15]
June 28, 1829, Cooperstown, Mrs. ELIZA FOOTE, aged 35. [7/6]
July 15, 1829, Hartwick, Mrs. ALMIRA BROWNEL, aged 27. [7/20]
July 15, 1829, Cooperstown, CATHERINE B. FOOTE, 3 months. [7/20]
July 18, 1829, Otsego, Mrs. MARY CURLISS, aged 28. [7/20]
July 15, 1829, Milford, AMASA MILLER, aged 9. [7/20]
July 28, 1829, Cooperstown, STEPHEN FITCH, aged 71. [8/10]
Aug. 2, 1829, Cooperstown, Mrs. JOANNA LUCE, aged 72. [8/10]
Aug. 7, 1829, Worcester, Mrs. FREELOVE WARNER. [8/17]
Aug. 11, 1829, Middlefield, WM. BLAIR, aged 21. [8/17]
Aug. 20, 1829, Otsego, DARIUS WARREN, aged 69. [8/24]

Aug. 29, 1829, Cooperstown, Col. AUGUSTUS RODGERS, aged 36. [8/31]
Sept. 1, 1829, Cooperstown, MARIET METCALF, 14 months. [9/7]
Sept. 24, 1829, Cooperstown, PHILIP CORY, aged 22. [9/28]
Sept. 31, 1829, Edmeston, Mrs. SABRINA MONROE. [9/28]
Oct. 14, 1829, Burlington, ALPHA MILLER, aged 34. [10/19]
Oct. 26, 1829, Springfield, JOSHUA RANSOM, aged 87. [11/2]
Oct. 26, 1829, Otsego, HULDAH BISSELL, aged 25. [11/2]
Oct. 12, 1829, Springfield, MOSES P. GRAVES, aged 19. [11/2]
Nov. 16, 1829, Burlington, Mrs. ESTHER TIFFANY, aged 65. [11/23 sic]
Nov. 21, 1829, WILLIAM F. EATON, aged 1. [11/20 sic]
Nov. 23, 1829, Otsego, Mrs. REBECCA A. TURNER, aged 28. [11/20 sic]
Nov. 28, 1829, Laurens, JOHN A. OTIS, aged 34. [12/7]
Dec. 7, 1829, Edmeston, CHARLES BATES, aged 49. [12/14]
Dec. 5, 1829, Burlington, CHARLES MATHER, aged 27. [12/14]
Dec. 8, 1829, Burlington, Mrs. MEHITABLE RITTER, aged 47. [12/14]
Dec. 17, 1829, Otsego, DANIEL EDDY, aged 28. [12/21]
Dec. 17, 1829, Otsego, WM. WOLCOTT, aged 90. [12/21]
Dec. 12, 1829, Milford, SALMON RUSSELL. [12/21]
Dec. 27, 1830 [sic] Cooperstown, ELIZA D. INGRAHAM, 4 months. [1/4/1830]
Jan. 7, 1830, Exeter, ROBERT JOHNSON, aged 30. [1/11]
Jan. 9, 1830, Burlington, Mrs. HANNAH POPE, aged 88. [1/25]
Jan. 30, 1830, Cherry Valley, Mrs. SABRINA CAMPBELL, aged 53. [2/6]
Jan. 30, 1830, Burlington, ALFRED D. BLAKEMAN, aged 9. [2/6]
Feb. --, 1830, Burlington, WM. ANGEL, aged 88. [2/22]
Feb. 21, 1830, Otsego, MARIAH L. REED, 14 months. [3/1]
March 4, 1830, Richfield, LUCINA BROWN, aged 20. [3/15]
April 15, 1830, Springfield, GEORGIANA CLARK, aged 6. [4/19]
April 8, 1830, Milford, JOHN WATKINS, aged 3. [4/19]
April 4, 1830, Cherry Valley, CATHERINE STEWART, aged 11. [4/19]
April 22, 1830, Burlington, WM. CHURCH, aged 42. [4/26]
May 14, 1830, Cooperstown, DANIEL OLENDORF, aged 75. [5/17]
May 6, 1830, Cooperstown, HELEN ROBISON, aged 6. [5/17]
May 27, 1830, Otsego, Mrs. CONTENT JARVIS, aged 33. [5/31]
May 21, 1830, Butternuts, Mrs. ALVINA A. PIER DANIELSON. [6/7]
June 25, 1830, Burlington, MARY O. DIXON, 8 months. [7/5]
July 9, 1830, Middlefield, SIMEON WOODARD, aged 33. [7/12]
July 10, 1830, Middlefield, Mrs. JERUSHA TITUS, aged 35. [7/12]
July 12, 1830, Otsego, Mrs. OLIVE PRESTON, aged 33. [7/26]

July 23, 1830, Cooperstown, FRANCIS VAN BERGEN, 9 months. [7/26]
Sept. 6, 1830, Cooperstown, Mrs. HARRIET B. STEWART, aged 32. [9/13]
Sept. 5, 1830, Otsego, WAYNE O. BLISS, 19 months. [9/13]
Sept. 12, 1830, Otsego, Mrs. MARCIA M. MORRIS of Troy, aged 23. [9/20]
Sept. 23, 1830, Port Byron, Cayuga Co., NATHAN BATES of Cooperstown, aged 50. [10/11]
Oct. 18, 1830, Cherry Valley, Mrs. LOIS MC LEAN, aged 53. [10/25]
Oct. 31, 1830, Exeter, Mrs. ARMINDA CLARK, aged 61. [11/8]
Oct. 28, 1830, Little Falls, CHARLES W. BABCOCK of Otsego, aged 25. [11/8]
Nov. 29, 1830, Cooperstown, JOHN F. ERNST, aged 51. [11/29]
Nov. 20, 1830, Cooperstown, JOHN PIERCE, aged 2. [12/6]
Nov. 24, 1830, Cooperstown, ALMARADER FITCH, aged 2. [12/27]
Jan. 24, 1831, Cooperstown, HORATIO G. JOHNSON, aged 53. [1/31]
Jan. 23, 1831, Cooperstown, SOPHRONIA GREGORY, aged 6. [1/31]
[No date] Cooperstown, STEPHEN GREGORY, aged 2. [1/31]
Jan. 27, 1831, Middlefield, Mrs. MARY INGLAS, aged 70. [1/31]
Jan. 27, 1831, Exeter, REUBEN SMITH, aged 82. [2/7]
Feb. 2, 1831, Hartwick, Mrs. MARCY CHASE, aged 56. [2/7]
Jan. 27, 1831, Fairfield, Mrs. LOVINA M. ARNOLD formerly of Cooperstown, aged 23. [2/21]
Feb. 17, 1831, Cooperstown, CHAS. CHAPMAN of Auburn, aged 36. [2/21]
Feb. 27, 1831, Oneonta, NIJAH GRIFFIN, aged 63. [3/14]
Feb. 24, 1831, Exeter, Mrs. COMFORT ROBINSON, aged 65.
March 12, 1831, Worcester, SILAS CRIPPEN, aged 74. [3/21]
March 18, 1831, Otsego, Mrs. ELIZA DEWEY, aged 34. [3/21]
March 27, 1831, Red Hook Landing, JOHN S. ELMENDORF, aged 26. [4/4]
April 10, 1831, Hartwick, ISAAC BURCH, aged 19. [4/18]
April 7, 1831, Hartwick, CHESTER KENYON, aged 31. [4/25]
May 1, 1831, Otsego, Mrs. PHOEBE WOODHOUSE, aged 75. [5/9]
May 10, 1831, Cooperstown, EZRA CRANE, aged 71. [5/16]
June 1, 1831, Salisbury, Herkimer Co., ELVIRA GRAHAM of Otsego, aged 17. [6/13]
June 5, 1831, Cooperstown, FRANCIS LYNDE SABIN, aged 2. [6/13]
June 8, 1831, Otsego, EMELINE B. APLIN, aged 2. [6/13]
May 26, 1831, Maryland, Otsego Co., Mrs. MARGARET WALLING, aged 23. [6/13]

June 13, 1831, Cooperstown, KING BINGHAM, aged 45. [6/20]
June 30, 1831, Cooperstown, JUSTUS CRANDAL, aged 34. [7/4]
July 13, 1831, Otsego, Maj. GEORGE PIER, aged 37. [7/16?]
July 17, 1831, New Lisbon, JOHN BELL, aged 100. [7/23]
July 25, 1831, Hartwick, Capt. ZACHARIAH W. SICKLES, aged 76. [8/8]
Aug. 16, 1831, Cooperstown, THEODORE GRAVES, aged 13 months. [8/22]
Aug. 24, 1831, Barnstable, Mass., Col. ARTEMAS SHELDON, aged 53. [9/5]
Aug. 30, 1831, Unadilla, Mrs. ELIZA HOUGH, aged 32. [9/12]

DEATHS

OTSEGO HERALD & WESTERN ADVERTISER, 1795-1821
FREEMAN'S JOURNAL, 1829-1840

Nov. 11, 1795, Charleston, S.C., Major TIMOTHY OLCOTT, son of the late Lieut. Governor of Vermont, aged 19 years.
March 21, 1796, Mrs. WHIPPLE, consort of Mr. BARNEY WHIPPLE of Cooperstown, N.Y. [March --, 1796]
April 13, 1795, in Cooperstown, N.Y., Mrs. ELIZABETH HARPER, consort of Mr. JAMES HARPER. [April --, 1796]
April 8, 1796, WILLIAM POWERS, Esq. of the town of Canaan. [April --, 1796]
[no date of death given] Mr. WILLIAM COX, of Unadilla, N.Y. [May 12, 1796]
[no date of death given] June 16, 1796. Mr. ROBERT MC CURDY [6/16/1796]
June 6, 1796, at Bower's Patent, Mr. JEREMIAH IRONS.
June 23, 1796, at Chamblee, Canada, Col. ELEAZER FITCH, formerly of Connecticut.
Sept. 21, 1796, at Albany, OLIVER L. KER, Esq., son of Rev. NATHAN KER of Goshen.
Sept. 13, 1796, in Orangeburgh District, Mr. HENRY STONEMAN, aged 105 years, a native of Berne, Switzerland.
[no date given] PATRICK GRADY, at Crookhaven, Ireland.[12/8/1796]
Oct. 13, 1796, at Canaan, N.Y., Hon. WILLIAM B. WHITING, Esq.
Dec. 14, 1795, at Prefquile, his Excellency, ANTHONY WAYNE, Com. in Chief of the Federal Army.

Jan. 28, 1797, Capt. THOMAS PORTER.
On April 12, 1797, body of PELEG THORNTON, son of Mr. SAMUEL THORNTON of Burlington, was found, having lain in snow for four months and six days. Death having occurred the previous December from exposure.
April 7, 1797, in the town of Burlington, Mr. SILAS SHOEMAKER. Accidental death.
April 18, 1797, at Hartford, Conn., Rev. ELKANAH WINCHESTER.
[no date given] At Philadelphia, Dr. NICHOLAS WAY. [9/21/1797]
Jan. 7, 1798, Mr. ABRAHAM LIPPET of Hartwick Patent.
Dec. 30, 1797, Mrs. SARAH GOTT of Cooperstown, N.Y.
April 8, 1798 (place not given) Mrs. HAWLEY, wife of the Rev. RUFUS HAWLEY.
April 26, 1798, at Butternuts, Mrs. ANN MUSSON.
Aug. 18, 1798, WILLIAM BASTOW of Cooperstown, N.Y., aged 19, killed by lightning.
Sept. --, 1798, in Philadelphia, Pa., BENJAMIN FRANKLIN BACHE.
Sept. --, 1798, in New York, THOMAS GREENLEAF.
Sept. 29, 1798, at Butternuts, JOHN THORP of Butternuts, aged 54.
Jan. 24, 1799, in Philadelphia, HENRY TAZEWELL, Esq.
Oct. 4, 1799, in Cooperstown, N.Y., Mrs. SARAH WHIPPLE, dau. of ELIJAH WILCOX of North Killingsworth, Conn., aged 29.
Feb. 6, 1800, in New York, HENRY BOWERS, Esq.
March 30, 1800, in Trenton, N.J., Mr. CHARLES SMITH, aged 32. (Lieut. in the Regt. of the U.S. First Regt.)
May 20, 1800, at Boston, Hon. MOSES GILL, Lieut. Gov. & Commander in Chief of Mass.
July 2, 1800, in Cooperstown, N.Y., JOHN CHRISTOPHER HARTWICK (suicide).
July 2, 1800, at Boston, Mr. THOMAS PARKER, aged 50. (Naval officer Rev. War.)
Aug. 28, 1800, Mrs. HANNAH TUBBS of Cooperstown, N.Y.
Sept. 19, 1800, in Oakscreek, near Cooperstown, Mrs. HENRY BOSTWICK (drowned).
Sept. 17, 1800, in Cooperstown, N.Y., Mr. JONATHAN HALL, aged 27.
Dec. 15, 1800, in Cooperstown, N.Y., Mr. NORMAN LANDON, aged 27.
Dec. 18, 1800, Mr. TIMOTHY JOHNSON of Cooperstown, N.Y.
Jan. 3, 1801, at Butternuts, SAMUEL SHAW, aged 48.
May 12, 1801, at New York, DAVID VAN HORNE, Adjutant General.
May 26, 1801, at Schoharie, Mr. PETER I. VROOMAN.

June 16, 1801, NICHOLAS HATTER of German Flats, aged 78.
Aug. 1, 1801, at Schenectady, N.Y., JONATHAN EDWARDS, D.D.
Sept. 23, 1801, Mrs. HANNAH TUBBS of Coopertown, N.Y., aged 77. (See notice of Aug. 28, 1800.)
Sept. 13, 1801, Mrs. MIRIAM MORSE of Burlington, N.Y., aged 39.
Oct. 18, 1801, in Cooperstown, N.Y., ISRAEL GUILD, aged 74.
Dec. 13, 1801, at Trenton, N.J., Mr. RENSSELAER WILLIAMS of Cooperstown.
Sept. 11, 1802, in Albany, N.Y., JOHN I. CUYLER, Esq.
Sept. 11, 1802, at Claverack, N.Y., Maj. Gen. ROBERT VAN RENSSELAER, aged 61.
Sept. 10, 1802, at Poughkeepsie, SOLOMAN SUTHERLAND, Esq., aged 38.
Nov. 4, 1802, in Cooperstown, N.Y., Mrs. SALLY FARLING, aged 30.
April 28, 1803, in Cooperstown, N.Y., Miss SALLY COOK, aged 10.
March 10, 1803, EBENEZER CHENEY of Cooperstown, N.Y.
March 10, 1803, in Cooperstown, N.Y., Mr. AVERY AVERILL, aged 31.
March 12, 1803, in Cooperstown, N.Y., CHARLES MOREHOUSE, aged 17.
April 26, 1803, at Poughkeepsie, N.Y., Hon. ISAAC BLOOM.
June --, 1803, at Holderness, N.H., Hon. SAMUEL LIVERMORE, aged 71.
July 18, 1803, in Pierstown, N.Y., Capt. STEPHEN SMITH.
Aug. 6, 1803, at New Haven, Conn., SAMUEL BISHOP, Esq.
Aug. 1, 1803, at New Haven, Conn., JOHN BISHOP, aged 36, son of SAMUEL BISHOP
Aug. 10, 1803, at Albany, N.Y., Mr. JAMES DOLE, aged 62.
Oct. --, 1803, at Providence, R.I., JOHN BROWN, Esq., aged 68.
June 1, 1804, Mrs. MARGARET MOTT of Cooperstown, N.Y. (accidental death).
Aug. 30, 1804, at Philadelphia, Pa., Rev. JOHN BLAIR LINN, aged 27.
Aug. 30, 1804, near New York, Commodore JAMES NICHOLSON, aged 69.
Aug. 30, 1804, at Poughkeepsie, N.Y., ROBERT H. LIVINGSTON, Esq.
Aug. 30, 1804, in Greene County, N.Y., PETER A. VAN BERGEN.
Dec. --, 1804, in Cooperstown, N.Y., Mrs. MARY JARVIS, aged 75.
Jan. --, 1805, at Norwich, Conn., Mr. SAMUEL BROWN, aged 90.
March 4, 1805, in Cooperstown, N.Y., SAMUEL TUBBS, Esq., aged 72.
April 14, 1805, at Claverack, LAWRENCE HOGEBOOM, Esq., aged 68.
May 3, 1805, at Cherry Valley, N.Y., EPHRAIM HUDSON, Esq., aged 48.

Oct. 19, 1805, at Fly Creek, N.Y., Mrs. DESIRE CARTER.
Oct. 19, 1805, infant child of JAMES AVERILL, Esq. of Cooperstown.
Oct. 24, 1805, at Manheim, Pa., Rev. JOHN FREDERICK ERNST.
Nov. 21, 1805, Mrs. STEPHEN HOLDEN of Hartwick, N.Y. (suicide).
Nov. 15, 1805, CHRISTOPHER BABBIT, aged 76.
Dec. 6, 1805, Mrs. JACOB I. CUYLER of Otego, N.Y., aged 27.
Dec. 14, 1805, Mrs. MARY CLINTON of Cooperstown, aged 57.
Jan. 25, 1806, Mrs. ANNA HINMAN of Hartwick, N.Y., aged 54.
Feb. 18, 1806, in Cooperstown, N.Y., Mrs. PAMELA WORDEN.
Feb. 18, 1806, DAVID D. CHITTENDEN of Worcester, N.Y.
April 17, 1806, DANIEL SHOVE of Middlefield, N.Y.
June 2, 1806, RUFUS HAWKINS of Exeter, N.Y.
July 1, 1806, at Butternuts, N.Y., WILLIAM MUSSON, aged 42 (native of England).
July 3, 1806, in Exeter, N.Y., NATHAN MARVIN (accidental death).
July 28, 1806, in Pittsfield, N.Y., JAMES D. WHITEFORD, aged 25.
Aug. 1, 1806, at Burlington, N.Y., Mrs. NABBY CHAPIN, aged 39.
Oct. 7, 1806, in Cherry Valley, N.Y., JOEL B. POTTER, Esq.
Oct. 1, 1806, at Burlington, N.Y., Mrs. DOLLY BLANCHARD, aged 41.
Oct. 31, 1806, in the town of Hartwick, N.Y., ISAAC MALLERY, aged 57.
Dec. 5, 1806, in Cooperstown, N.Y., Mrs. SALLY HUNTINGTON.
Dec. 13, 1806, in Cooperstown, N.Y., Col. RICHARD CARY.
Jan. 1, 1807, RICHARD EDWARDS, Esq.
Jan. 5, 1807, in Albany, N.Y., ROBERT JOHNSON.
March 10, 1807, Mrs. AMY CLARK of Hartwick, N.Y.
March 14, 1807, in Pittsfield, N.Y., ISAAC NASH, Esq.
March 15, 1807, in Stewart's Patent, in the town of Otsego, Mrs. ABIGAIL HARRIS.
March 25, 1807, in the town of Hartwick, N.Y., Mrs. SALLY BRADFORD.
April 21, 1807, in Cooperstown, N.Y., EPHRAIM HUDSON, aged 15; son of Judge HUDSON of Cherry Valley.
April 29, 1807, JOHN BECKLEY, Esq., aged 50 (native of England).
May 25, 1807, in Albany, N.Y., Mrs. LAURA SPENCER, aged 40.
June 2, 1807, at Plattsburgh, N.Y., Mrs. ELIZABETH ADDAMS, aged 92.
June 7, 1807, JOSEPH SIMONDS, Esq., of Paris, Oneida County, N.Y., aged 30.
July 15, 1807, Mrs. RHEDA BUCKLEY, aged 56.
July 30, 1807, SAMUEL WARD, Jr. of Hartwick, N.Y., aged 17 (drowned).

June --, 1807, in the town of Catherine, Broome County, Col. LUKE BONNEY.
Aug. 30, 1807, in Hartwick, N.Y., Mrs. NANCY SKIFF, aged 25.
Sept. 11, 1807, in Milford, N.Y., Mrs. JERUSHA LEE, aged 43.
Sept. 26, 1807, in the town of Hartwick, LEMUEL CLEVELAND, aged 47.
Oct. 13, 1807, AZRIKIM PIERCE of Otsego, aged 56.
Nov. 6, 1807, at Cherry Valley, N.Y., OZIAS WALDO.
Nov. 12, 1807, at Butternuts, N.Y., ICHABOD B. PALMER, Esq., aged 70.
Nov. 15, 1807, at Norwich, N.Y., SARAH REYNOLDS, aged 52.
Dec. 2, 1807, in Cooperstown, N.Y., Mrs. JOSEPH HOLT.
Jan. 8, 1808, at Cherry Valley, N.Y., Miss SUSAN MILLS, dau. of Col. ROGER MILLS of Canajoharie, aged 23.
Jan. 17, 1808, in the town of Hartwick, Mrs. BETHIAH JACOBS of Hingham, Mass., aged 73.
Jan. 20, 1808, in Hartwick, N.Y., Mrs. ANN HALL, aged 71.
April 2, 1808, in Burlington, N.Y., Mrs. LURIANIA (or LURANA) HUBBEL, dau. of DAVID CHAPIN of Richmond, Mass., aged 24.
May 30, 1808, in the town of Otsego, Mr. WILLIAM DOWSE, aged 89 (native of England).
June 7, 1808, in Hartwick, N.Y., THOMAS HALL, aged 72.
Aug. 16, 1808, in the town of Hartwick, Mrs. SARAH ANN SAYRE, aged 43, formerly of Elizabeth, N.J.
Oct. 21, 1808, at Onondaga, SARAH CATHERINE HOOPER, dau. of JASPER HOOPER, Esq., aged 3 (accidental burning).
March 1, 1809, at Herkimer, GAYLORD GRISWOLD, Esq., aged 42.
March 6, 1809, Mrs. LYDIA WHITING of Norwich, Conn. [4/8]
April 25, 1809, at Scipio, GIDEON FREEMAN, aged 60. [5/20]
April 24, 1809, at Tolland, ERASTUS EDGERTON, aged 22. [5/10]
May 19, 1809, in the town of Otsego, Mrs. PATIENCE MORSE, aged 56. [6/3]
Aug. 7, 1809, at Lebanon, JONATHAN TRUMBULL, Esq., Governor of Conn. [8/19]
June 11, 1809, at Washington, Ky., ANDREW SMALLIE, aged 86. [9/2]
Oct. 18, 1809, year-old dau. of JOHN M. BOWERS of Cooperstown, N.Y. [10/21]
Nov. 12, 1809, in Albany, N.Y., Mrs. ELIZABETH NIELL. [11/18]
Nov. 18, 1809, at Weathersfield, Conn., Col. JOHN CHESTER, aged 60, Rev. Officer. [11/25]

Dec. 22, 1809, in Albany, N.Y., WILLIAM COOPER, Esq., aged 55. [12/30]
In Burlington, N.Y., Mrs. BOLTON, wife of Rev. Mr. BOLTON of that place. [12/25/1809]
Feb. 22, 1810, at Sidney, N.Y., Capt. EDWARD HOWELL, aged 58 [3/3].
March 30, 1810, in Hartwick, N.Y., Mrs. ELIZABETH SMITH, aged 64. [4/7]
March 22, 1810, in Burlington, N.Y., GERSHOM POPE, aged 67. [4/7]
March 23, 1810, in Burlington, N.Y., NATHAN GOFF, Esq., aged 87. [4/7]
May 12, 1810, at Scarsdale, Westchester Co., N.Y., Mrs. SARAH TOMPKINS, aged 72. [4/7]
July 10, 1810, at Stockbridge, Mass., Mrs. EDWARDS (suicide). [7/21]
July 23, 1810, in Cooperstown, N.Y., SALLY DOUBLEDAY, dau. of Capt. SETH DOUBLEDAY, aged 18. [7/28]
Aug. 8, 1810, Hon. JOHN BROOME, Lieut. Gov. of N.Y. [8/18]
Aug. 15, 1810, at New Hartford, Conn., Rev. GIDDEM A. KNOWLTON, aged 51. [9/1]
Sept. 19 1810, in N.Y. City, JAMES CHEETHAM, aged 38. [9/29]
Oct. 15, 1810, at Befont, N.C., Hon. ALFRED MOORE, Esq., aged 55. [11/17]
Oct. 8, 1810, at Richmond, Va., Col. EDWARD CARRINGTON. [11/17]
Oct. 21, 1810, at Norfolk, Va., Commodore SAMUEL NARRON [BARRON?]. [11/17]
Nov. 24, 1810, in Cooperstown, N.Y., JOHN PIER, son of ABNER PIER. [12/1]
Dec. 24, 1810, in Cooperstown, N.Y., ABNER PIER, aged 49. [12/29]
Dec. 31, 1810, in Cooperstown, N.Y., POLLY PIER, dau. of ABNER PIER. [1/12/1811]
Jan. 10, 1811, in town of Hartwick, Mrs. BETSEY APLIN, dau. of ABNER PIER. [1/12]
Jan. 15, 1811, in Cooperstown, N.Y., Mrs. NANCY STEVENS, dau. of ABNER PIER, aged 23. [1/19]
Jan. 31, 1811, at Milford, N.H., WILLIAM WELLS, aged 29. [2/9]
March 16, 1811, TRUMAN SMITH, aged 23, Guard in States Prison. [3/30]
April 13, 1811, in Cooperstown, N.Y., JOHN BURRELL, aged 45. [4/20]
April 24, 1811, in Cooperstown, N.Y., Mr. WARREN, aged 86. [4/27]
April 15, 1811, in Otego, JONATHAN JOHNSON, Esq. [4/27]
Jan. 22, 1811, in Bladen Co., N.C., MARY SUTTON, aged 116. [4/27]

Aug. 7, 1811, at Cobleskill, N.Y., Mrs. MERIAM REDINGTON, aged 58. [8/17]

Sept. 27, 1811, in Cooperstown, N.Y., JEREMY R. ANGEL, aged 14, son of CALEB ANGEL of Exeter, N.Y. [9/28]

Sept. 30, 1811, in Albany, N.Y., ELIZABETH COOPER, dau. of RICHARD COOPER, Esq. of Cooperstown. [10/5]

Dec. 7, 1811, at Richfield, N.Y., Mrs. EUNICE BEARDSLEY, age 47. [12/21]

March 9, 1812, in Cooperstown, N.Y., Dr. ELISHA MILLER of Ballston, aged 72. [3/14]

March 5, 1812, at Herkimer, N.Y., Mr. HOUSEMAN, native of Poland [4/4]

April 17, 1812, at Richmond, Mass., Maj. ASA DOUGLASS of New Canaan, N.Y., aged 72. Rev. Officer. [4/25]

At Southampton twp., Bedford Co., Pa., Mr. AGHOR WORLAY, aged 106. [4/25]

At Great Barrington, Mass., JOHN WHITTY, aged 103 [4/25]

April 22, 1812, at Cherry Valley, N.Y., Maj. JOHN WALTON, aged 49. [5/2]

April 7, 1812, at Belpre, Col. ISRAEL PUTNAM, son of the Rev. patriot, aged 73. [5/2]

May 16, 1812, at Whitestown, HUGH WHITE, Esq., aged 80. [5/9] [sic]

May 9, 1812, at Deruyter, N.Y., SIMEON RIDER. [5/15]

July 11, 1812, at Johnstown, N.Y., MATHIAS B. HILDRETH, Esq., Atty. Gen. of N.Y. [7/25]

Aug. 6, 1812, at Cape Vincent, ALPHEUS CUTLER, aged 30, formerly of Guilford, Vt. [8/29]

Sept. 30, 1812, in DeRuyter, N.Y., Mrs. LUCINDA CAYE, aged 42. [10/10]

Oct. 29, 1812, at Schlosser, N.Y., VINE GRIFFIN, aged 21. [11/14]

Nov. 1, 1812, JOHN PERKINS, aged 63 [11/28]

Dec. 6, 1812, at Cleveland, Ohio, ELEAZER LOOMIS, Jr. [1/9/1813]

Dec. 15, 1812, in Cazenovia, JOSEPH HEWES, aged 19, formerly of Springfield, N.Y. [1/16/1813]

Feb. 18, 1813, in Cooperstown, N.Y., WILLIAM DOWSE, Esq., aged 42. [2/20]

Feb. 17, 1813, in Middlefield, N.Y., OBADIAH DUNHAM, aged 83. [2/20]

Feb. 8, 1813, in New York, WILLIAM FRENCH, formerly of Cooperstown. [2/20]

Feb. 26, 1813, in Cooperstown, N.Y., Mrs. ELIZBETH R. GOODSELL, aged 41. [2/27]
Feb. 26, 1813, at Clermont, Hon. ROBERT R. LIVINGSTON, aged 66. [3/6]
March 2, 1813, in town of Otsego, JACOB PECK, aged 41. [3/6]
Feb. 28, 1813, in Otsego, Mrs. PRISCILLA WEAVER, aged 72. [3/6]
Feb. 27, 1813, in Otsego, DAVID SHIPMAN, aged 84. [3/6]
Feb. 26, 1813, in Otsego, ABIEL THURSTON, aged 21. [3/6]
Feb. 27, 1813, in Otsego, BENAJAH WHIPPLE, aged 44. [3/6]
Jan. 28, 1813, at sea, Lieut. JOHN CUSHING WYLWIN (U.S.N.). [3/13]
March 5, 1813, in Albany, N.Y., RICHARD F. COOPER, Esq., bur. in Cooperstown, N.Y. [3/13]
March 8, 1813, in Cooperstown, N.Y., Mrs. ABIGAIL HUNTINGTON, aged 44. [3/13]
March 4, 1813, in Cooperstown, N.Y., Mrs. SAREPTA HILL, aged 28, formerly of Ellington, Conn. [3/13]
March 13, 1813, in Cherry Valley, CHRISTOPHER ALLEN, aged 27. [3/20]
March 15, 1813, in Cooperstown, N.Y., ISAIAH THURBER, aged 51. [3/20]
March 19, 1813, in Middlefield, N.Y., JAMES INGALLS, Esq. [3/20]
March 25, 1813, in Cooperstown, N.Y., Mrs. SUSAN GRAVES, aged 49. [3/27]
March 24, 1813, MARTHA DEWEY, dau. of ELIZABETH DEWEY of Hartwick, N.Y. [4/3]
April 24, 1813, in town of Otsego, CYRUS THURSTON, aged 25. [5/8]
April 28, 1813, in Otsego, Capt. THOMAS WILLIAMS, aged 33. [5/8]
May 10, 1813, at Springfield, N.Y., RUTH HERRICK of Cooperstown, aged 20. [5/15]
May 9, 1813, at Hartwick, N.Y., Mrs. MARY POTTER, aged 50. [6/12]
May 11, 1813, in town of Otsego, ELIZABETH COMSTOCK, aged 61. [6/12]
July 12, 1813, in Cooperstown, N.Y., ELIHU PHINNEY, aged 58. [7/17]
July 12, 1813, in Cooperstown, N.Y., RICHARD WARD, son of ROBERT WARD, aged 1 year, 8 months. [7/17]
July 13, 1813, in Cooperstown, N.Y., ELIZABETH COOPER, dau. of JAMES COOPER in Cooperstown, N.Y., aged 1 year, 10 months. [7/17]
Aug. 8, 1813, in Cooperstown, N.Y., IRA THURSTON, aged 22. [8/14]
Aug. 12, 1813, in New York, SAMUEL OSGOOD, Esq. [8/21]

Aug. 12, 1813, in East Haven, Conn., ORLANDO BENTON, Esq., of Unadilla, N.Y. [8/21]
Aug. 15, 1813, in Cooperstown, N.Y., ZERVIAH NILES, aged 9. [8/28]
Aug. 2, 1813, in Maryland, N.Y., JOSIAH CHASE, aged 65. [8/28]
Aug. 28, 1813, in Otsego, son of WILLIAM FAIRCHILD, aged 5. [9/4]
Sept. 2, 1813, in Cooperstown, N.Y., Mrs. HANNAH FLINT, aged 28. [9/4]
Sept. 4, 1813, in Albany, N.Y., EZEKIEL BURLINGHAM of Hartwick, N.Y. [9/11]
Sept. 10, 1813, in Cooperstown, LORA BALDWIN, aged 15. [9/11]
Sept. 14, 1813, in Cooperstown, Mrs. THANKFUL THURSTON, aged 63. [9/25]
Oct. 2, 1813, in Cooperstown, Capt. ROSWELL PEABODY. [10/9]
Nov. 9, 1813, in Cooperstown, TRACEY METCALF, aged 45. [11/13]
Nov. 9, 1813, at Hartford, Conn., NOAH WEBSTER, Esq., aged 91. [11/27]
Dec. 1, 1813, in Cooperstown, MARY ROOT, aged 20. [12/4]
Dec. 25, 1813, in town of Otsego, Mrs. MARY METCALF, aged 78. [1/1/1814]
Dec. 30, 1813, in Hartwick, N.Y., Lieut. ABEL CAULKINS, aged 62, formerly of Lisbon, Conn. [1/8/1814]
Jan. 4, 1814, in Otsego, Major MOSES OSTRANDER, aged 50. [1/8]
Dec. 20, 1813, in town of Livingston, Col. ROBERT F. LIVINGSTON, aged 55. [1/8/1814]
At Greenburgh, N.Y., ELIJAH TOMPKINS, brother of the Governor. (Actual date not given.) [1/8]
March 11, 1814, in Laurens, N.Y., DANIEL GRIFFITH, aged 88. [3/19]
March 16, 1814, in Cooperstown, N.Y., JAMES WHIPPLE. [3/19]
Jan. 29, 1814, in Sandwich, Mass., ELEAZER H. PARKER, aged 44. [4/2]
March 26, 1814, in Hartwick, N.Y., Mrs. DOROTHY MIX, aged 52. [4/2]
April 16, 1814, at Oswego, N.Y., STEPHEN MACK, Esq. [4/23]
March 23, 1814, in Pittsfield, N.Y., Dr. JOSEPH O. CONE, aged 57. [5/7]
May 30, 1814, in Cooperstown, Mrs. SIBYL SWEATLAND. [6/1]
June 27, 1814, in Cooperstown, JESSE H. STARR, aged 26 [6/30]
June 27, 1814, in Middlefield, N.Y., ORRIN INGALLS. [6/30]
June 2, 1814, in Cooperstown, MOSES BARNES. [7/7]
July 10, 1814, in Cooperstown, Mrs. PHILLIS SPRAGUE, aged 70. [7/14]
July 21, 1814, in Albany, N.Y., EBENEZER FOOT, Esq. [7/28]

July 13, 1814, at East Bloomfield, N.Y., POLLYDORE B. WISNER, Esq. [7/28]

Aug. 9, 1814, in Otsego, BENJAMIN TODD, aged 28. [8/11]

Aug. 4, 1814, in Milford, N.Y., CALVIN ACKLEY, aged 25. [8/11]

Aug. 20, 1814, in the town of Laurens, WILLIAM HOPKINS, aged 50. [9/1]

July 12, 1814, Brig. Gen. JOHN SWIFT of Palmyra, N.Y. [7/28]

Oct. 8, 1814, in Cooperstown, Mrs. MELISANT WOODHOUSE, aged 28. [10/13]

Oct. 16, 1814, in Cherry Valley, Capt. WILLIAM ALLEN, aged 56. [10/20]

Oct. 16, 1814, in Middlefield, ISAAC GREEN, aged 58. [10/20]

Oct. 14, 1814, in Otsego, SOLOMON CLARK, aged 40. [10/20]

Dec. 1, 1814, in Cooperstown, OLIVER WINEGAR. [12/8]

Dec. 1, 1814, in Cooperstown, Capt. ISAAC WILLIAMS. [12/8]

Feb. 16, 1815, in Cooperstown, N.Y., DANIEL A. CLARK of Pierstown, aged 18. [2/23]

Feb. 27, 1815, in Cooperstown, N.Y., HARRIET GRIFFIN

March 12, 1815, in Cooperstown, DANIEL BOW, aged 27. [3/16]

March 29, 1815, at Hartwick, Mrs. SARAH LYONS, aged 47. [4/6]

June 12, 1815, at Edmeston, N.Y., SUSAN DE FOREST, aged 28. [6/22]

June 15, 1815, in Cooperstown, N.Y., Mrs. AMANDA FULLER, aged 21. [6/22]

Aug. 23, 1815, in Otsego, Mrs. PENELOPE NEWELL. [8/31]

Aug. 31, 1815, in Conn., CHAUNCEY GOODRICH, Esq , Lieut. Gov. of Conn., aged 57. [8/31]

Sept. 29, 1815, in Plainsfield, CALEB BROWN, aged 59. [10/5]

Oct. 8, 1815, in Otsego, Metcalf Hill Settlement, LYDIA METCALF, aged 20. [10/12]

Nov. 1, 1815, at Hartwick, Col. REUBEN ROOT, aged 45. [11/2]

Oct. 27, 1815, in Cooperstown, JOHN LAWRENCE MC NAMEE, aged 4 years, son of LAWRENCE M'NAMEE [sic]. [11/2]

Oct. 31, 1815, in Cooperstown, infant son of ELISHA TAYLOR, aged 3 months. [11/2]

Oct. 27, 1815, at Hartwick, Mrs. MARTHA PIER, aged 33. [11/2]

Oct. 28, 1815, at Hartwick, MARY DAY SPRAGUE, aged 6. [11/2]

Oct. 23, 1815, at Chenango, N.Y., JARED PAGE, aged 60. [11/2]

Nov. 9, 1815, in Cooperstown, Mrs. LOIS METCALF, aged 38. [11/9]

Nov. 7, 1815, at Hartwick, HENRY SPRAGUE, aged 23. [11/9]

Nov. 15, 1815, in Cooperstown, AURELIA LADD of Burlington, N.Y., aged 18. [11/16]

Nov. 19, 1815, in Hartwick, ZEBEDIAH F. COOK, aged 71. [11/23]
Nov. 19, 1815, in Middlefield, SAMUEL CANFIELD, aged 70. [11/23]
[no date given] In Cambridge, N.Y., Mr. SOLOMON CROCKER. [11/23]
Oct. 15, 1815, in Laurens Dist., S.C., SOLOMON NIBLET, aged 141 years, native of England. [11/23]
Nov. 28, 1815, in Cooperstown, PRUDENCE CUMMINGS, aged 14. [11/30]
Nov. 20, 1815, in Claverack, Columbia County, N.Y., CHIRON PENNIMAN (suicide). [12/7]
Dec. 5, 1815, in Cooperstown, WILLIAM TIFFANY, aged 26. [12/7]
Jan. 23, 1816, in Hartwick, Mrs. PHOEBE STEERE. [1/25]
Dec. 19, 1815, in Harrisburg, Pa., HARVEY HUBBARD of Otsego. [1/25/1816]
Jan. 2, 1816, at Clarence, Niagara Co., N.Y., Dr. DANIEL M'CLEARY. [1/25]
Jan. 29, 1816, in Cooperstown, DARIUS LOOMER, aged 42. [2/1]
Jan. 18, 1816, in Bedford, Va., Major JOHN REID. [2/15]
Feb. 7, 1816, in Westford, N.Y., Hon. ROBERT ROSEBOOM, aged 61. [2/15]
July 5, 1815 in Louisiana, Capt. SAMUEL GRIFFITH, aged 49. [3/21/1816]
April 4, 1816, at New Haven, JOHN KENYON, of Hopkinton, R.I. [4/11]
May 24, 1816, in Albany, DUDLEY WALSH. [6/6]
May 24, 1816, in Bennington, Vt., ANTHONY HASWELL, Esq. [6/6]
June 3, 1816, in Cooperstown, ROBERT HENRY. [6/6]
June 6, 1816, in the Creek Agency, Col. BENJAMIN HAWKINS, Indian Agent. [6/6]
July 23, 1816, in Cooperstown, N.Y., Mrs. MINDWELL BOSWORTH, aged 68. [7/25]
June 30, 1816, at Beaufort, S.C., Hon. PAUL HAMILTON, Secy. of Navy. [7/25]
July 10, 1816, in Brunswick Co., Va., Hon. THOMAS GHOLSON. [7/25]
Sept. 9, 1816, in Albany, Gen. HENRY K. VAN RENSSELAER, aged 73. [9/19]
Oct. 11, 1816, at Washington, D.C., Col. TOBIAS LEAR. [10/24]
Oct. 25, 1816, in Middlefield, Mrs. ELIZABETH TEMPLE, aged 27. [10/31]
Nov. 6, 1816, in Morrisania, N.Y., Hon. GOUVERNEUR MORRIS, aged 65. [11/21]

Dec. 11, 1816, in Otsego, NATHAN LUCE, aged 80. [12/12]
Dec. 28, 1816, at Clinton, Oneida Co., Rev. ASEL BACKUS, D.D. [1/9/1817]
Jan. 5, 1817, in Otsego, Mr. PARLEY JOHNSON. [1/9]
Jan. 12, 1817, in Middlefield, CALVIN THOMAS, aged 30. [1/16]
Jan. 27, 1817, in Cooperstown, ASA HARRIS, aged 80. [2/6]
Feb. 9, 1817, Mrs. EMILY HIGBY. [2/13]
May 17, 1817, in Otsego, POLLY HARTSHORN, aged 19. [5/22]
May 30, 1817, in Albany, RICHARD LUSH, Esq. [6/5]
June 7, 1817, in Otsego, ELIPHALET WILLIAMS, aged 46. [6/12]
June 14, 1817, in Burlington, N.Y., Mrs. LUCY COMSTOCK, aged 72. [6/19]
Sept. 13, 1817, in Cooperstown, N.Y., Mrs. ELIZABETH COOPER, aged 65. [9/18]
Dec. 10, 1817, in Cooperstown, HANNAH COOPER, only surviving dau. of RICHARD F. COOPER, Esq., aged 15. [12/11]
Dec. 14, 1817, in Cooperstown, N.Y., Mrs. ARMENIA ROGERS, aged 20. [12/18]
Jan. 1, 1818, in Cooperstown, N.Y., ISAAC COOPER, Esq., aged 37. [1/5]
Dec. 20, 1817, in Cooperstown, N.Y., Mrs. MERCY DOUBLEDAY. [1/5/1818]
Jan. 17, 1818, in Cooperstown, Capt. THOMAS TANNER, Rev. Officer. [1/19]
Feb. 5, 1818, in Cooperstown, ABRAHAM HARTWELL, aged 45. [2/9]
March 19, 1818, in Middlefield, OTHNIEL LUCE, aged 56. [3/23]
April 9, 1818, at Madrid, St. Lawrence Co., N.Y., LEONARD REED, age 14. [5/11]
May 11, 1818. ORA DAGGETT, aged 23. JOSEPH LOOMIS, aged 24. ABRAHAM LOOMIS, aged 34. ASA LORD, Esq., aged 50. EZRA BIGELOW, aged 26. [NOTE: All appear under this date and under this issue. (5/11)]
April 14, 1818, SAMUEL GIBSON of Waddington, formerly of Hamilton (drowned). [5/11]
June 28, 1818, at Butternuts, N.Y., Mrs. CATHERINE PRENTISS, aged 24. [6/29]
June 22, 1818, in Hartwick, MATHEW DARBYSHIRE, Esq., aged 70. [6/29]
July 30, 1818, at Mt. Vernon, N.Y., Mrs. MARIAH CLINTON, wife of Gov. CLINTON. [8/10]
Oct. 30, 1818, in Hartwick, Maj. JAMES BUTTERFIELD, age 64. [11/9]

Dec. 1, 1818, in Butternuts, N.Y., HEZEKIAH DAYTON, Exq., aged 62. [12/14]
Oct. 30, 1818, in Sherburne, N.Y., HART BENEDICT, aged 16. [12/14]
Jan. 17, 1819, in Middlefield, Miss MELISSA CHELES, aged 18. [1/25]
Jan. 10, 1819, in Cooperstown, BETSEY CLARK, dau. of ABEL CLARK, aged 17. [1/25]
Feb. 11, 1819, in Cooperstown, SETH COOK, aged 37. [2/15]
Feb. 5, 1819, in Albany, N.Y., Mrs. HANNAH VAN BUREN, aged 36, wife of MARTIN VAN BUREN. [2/15]
March 1, 1819, in Westford, N.Y., Mrs. BETSEY PHELPS, aged 43, late of Colchester, Conn. [3/8]
March 19, 1819, in Cherry Valley, Mrs. MARY DIELL. [3/29]
April 13, 1819, at Westport, Mass., PELEG TRIPP, aged 20. [5/3]
May 7, 1819, at Westford, N.Y., Mrs. FANNY HOWE, aged 33, dau. of Dr. TIMOTHY PARKER of Decatur. [5/10]
April 20, 1819, at Columbus, Ohio, Mrs. LUCIA WILLIAMS, dau. of WM. GARRETT, Esq. of Otsego Co., aged 24. [5/17]
May 12, 1819, in Cooperstown, N.Y., WM. MARVIN, aged 24. [5/17]
June 12, 1819, at Jamaica, L.I., Mrs. MARY KING, aged 50. [6/14]
June 27, 1819, in Hartwick, N.Y., RACHEL ANN SPRAGUE, dau. of Maj. JOSEPH SPRAGUE, aged 12. [7/5]
July 1, 1819, at Baltimore, Md., Gen. LEVIN WINDER, aged 63. [7/5]
June 28, 1819, at Trenton, N.Y., Gen. MELANCTON LLOYD WOOLSEY of Plattsburgh, aged 61. [7/5]
Aug. 17, 1819, in Hartwick, AMOS WINSOR, Esq., aged 77. [8/23]
Aug. 19, 1819, in Exeter, N.Y., EDWARD, son of Rev. DANIEL NASH, aged 4 years. [8/23]
July 28, 1819, in Otsego, FRANCIS HENRY, aged 3 years. [8/23]
Aug. 14, 1819, PRISCILLA HENRY, aged 17. (Both above children of SAMUEL HENRY.) [8/23]
Sept. 2, 1819, in Cooperstown, HELEN MARIA BRADFORD, dau. of GEO. W. BRADFORD, aged 1. [9/6]
Sept. 7, 1819, in Middlefield, ASAPH POTTER, aged 62. [9/13]
Sept. 8, 1819, in Cooperstown, ELLEN, infant dau. of GEORGE POMEROY. [9/13]
Aug. 11, 1819, at Chicago, JAMES F. WHITE, aged 20, formerly of Cooperstown. [9/27]
Oct. 19, 1819, in Cooperstown, WILLIAM COOPER, Esq., aged 34. [10/25]
Oct. 10, 1819, in Pittsfield, N.Y., GARDNER M. CARPENTER, aged 27. [10/25]

Nov. 7, 1819, at Northampton, CALEB STRONG, late Gov. of Mass. [11/15]
[No date] at Bennington, Vt., JONATHAN ROBINSON. [11/15]
[No date] in Georgia, Governor WILLIAM RABUN--Gov. of Ga. [11/15]
Nov. --, 1819, in Cooperstown, N.Y., JAMES AVERILL, Sr., aged 85. [11/15]
Nov. 24, 1819, in Cooperstown, N.Y., Capt. EDWARD THURSTON, aged 80. [11/29]
Dec. 19, 1819, in Cooperstown, BEZALEAL WRIGHT, aged 78. [12/20]
Dec. 15, 1819, in Cherry Valley, N.Y., JOHN R. WHITAKER. [12/20]
Dec. 1, 1819, in Waterford, Mrs. HULDAH GALPIN. [1/3/ 1820]
Jan. 9, 1820, in Seneca, Ont. Co., N.Y., VALENTINE BROTHER, Esq. [1/17]
Jan. 3, 1820, at Buffalo, Mrs. MARY HOLT, aged 48. [1/24]
Feb. 6, 1820, in Cooperstown, Mrs. POLLY THURBER, aged 53. [2/7]
Jan. 7, 1820, in Lowville, N.Y., Rev. STEPHEN PARSONS, aged 71. [2/21]
March 12, 1820, in Cherry Valley, Mrs. HANNAH HUDSON, aged 52. [?] [3/13]
May 21, 1820, in Cooperstown, WIGGLESWORTH BURDITT, aged 45. [5/22]
May 6, 1820, at Bethlehem THEOPHILUS EATON, late of Albany. [5/22]
March 8, 1820, at Tangier, Morocco, U.S. Counsul, JAMES SIMPSON. [5/22]
May 22, 1820, in Cooperstown, SOPHIA WILLIAMS, aged 24. [5/29]
May 27, 1820, in Otsego, JOHN HINDS, aged 50. [6/5]
May 8, 1820, at New Lisbon, Elder DANIEL BOLTON, aged 69. [6/19]
Aug. 13, 1820, in Cooperstown, LUCIA LUCRETIA, dau. of Col. RUSSELL WILLIAMS, aged 13 1/2 months. [8/21]
Aug. 28, 1820, in Geneva, N.Y., SARAH ANN HASKELL, formerly of Cooperstown. [8/21]
July 10, 1820, near Fort Jackson, W. W. BIBB (Gov. of Alabama), age 40. [8/21]
July 31, 1820, at Homes Ville, Miss., SAMUEL GRIFFIN, Jr., Esq., late of Otsego Co. [9/11]
Aug. 17, 1820, at Culpepper Court House, Va., Gen. EDWARD STEVENS, Rev. Officer. [9/11]
At Lawrens Dist., N.C., SOLOMON NESBIT, aged 143 years. Native of England and came to the U.S. in 1696. [9/11]
Sept. 5, 1820, in Cherry Valley, MARY MC GOWN, aged 20. [9/18]

Sept. 15, 1820, in Middlefield, CYRENUS COOK. [9/25]
Sept. 10, 1820, in Albany, Mrs. CATHERINE VAN VECHTEN, aged 55. [9/25]
Sept. 13, 1820, in Troy, OBADIAH PENNIMAN, aged 44, formerly of Albany. [9/25]
Sept. 29, 1820, in Cooperstown, Mrs. MARY FOOTE, aged 31. [10/2]
Oct. 25, 1820, near Whitehall, N.Y., HENRY FRANCISCO, aged 134 years, native of England. [11/13]
Nov. 20, 1820, at Little Falls, JOHN M'ARDLE, aged 50. [11/13]
Nov. 4, 1820, Mrs. HANNAH R. RIVERA, of Rhode Island, aged 100. [11/13]
Dec. 14, 1820, in Schoharie, GILES HUBBARD, Esq., aged 24. [12/25]
Dec. 16, 1820, at Washington, D. C., NATHANIEL HAZARD, Esq., [1/1/1821]
Dec. 20, 1820, (place not given), JESSE SLOCUM, Esq., aged 37. [1/1/1821]
Dec. 25, 1810 [sic], at Washington, D.C., Hon. JAMES BURRILL, Jr., of R.I. [1/8/1820]

FREEMAN'S JOURNAL, 1819-1840

Oct. 18, 1819, at Poughkeepsie, N.Y., Hon. MATHIAS B. TALLMADGE.
Oct. 18, 1819, in Albany, N.Y., Mr. JOHN STAFFORD.
Sept. 30, 1819, in Hudson, N.Y., GROSVENOR E. WILLIAMS, aged 18.
Sept. 1, 1819, in Franklin, Missouri township, Dr. WILLIAM BALDWIN, U.S.N.
Oct. 19, 1819, in Cooperstown, N.Y., WILLIAM COOPER, Esq., aged 37. [10/25]
Oct. 2, 1819, at Settle's Hill town of Guilderland, GEORGE REELMAN, aged 112 years. [10/25]
Nov. 11, 1819, in Cooperstown, JAMES AVERELL, Sr., aged 85. [11/15]
Nov. 7, 1819, at Northampton, Mass., Hon CALEB STRONG. [11/15]
[No date] at Bennington, Vt., JONATHAN ROBISON, Esq. [11/15]
[No date] at Warwick, Mass., Dr. MEDAD POMEROY, aged 63. [11/15]
[No date] at Hadley, Mass., Mrs. SYBIL DICKINSON. [11/15]
Sept. 17, 1819, at Mobile, Ala., Mrs. MARY AUGUSTA LEWIS, aged 31. [11/22]
Nov. 14, 1819, at Stratford, Conn., WM. SAMUEL JOHNSON, L.L.D., aged 94. [11/29]

[No date] in Brunswick, Me., Rev. JESSE APPLETON, D.D., aged 47. [11/29]
Nov. 10, 1819, in Hudson, N.Y., Hon. ROBERT JENKINS. [11/29]
[No date] at Lyme, Conn., Mrs. MARY NOYES, aged 51. [11/29]
Nov. 10, 1819, in Utica, N.Y., HENRY CUDENARD, aged 55. [11/29]
[No date] in Norwich, Conn., Mrs. MARY L. HUNTINGTON, aged 46. [11/29]
Nov. 29, 1819, in Elizabethtown, Gen. GAUTIER, aged 102. [11/29]
[No date] in Long Island, SAMUEL JONES, Esq., aged 80. [12/6]
[No date] in York Dist., S.C., WILLIAM HENRY, aged 104. [12/6]
[No date] in New York, ANSON CLARKE, formerly of Del. Co., aged 43. [12/6]
Feb. 8, 1820, at North Haven, Rev. BENJAMIN TRUMBULL, D.D. [2/14]
[No date] at Albany, JOHN VAN SCHAICK, Esq., aged 47. [3/6]
[No date] at Waterford, N.Y., JOHN T. CLOSE, Esq., aged 46. [3/6]
Feb. 16, 1820, in Cincinnati, O., Dr. SAMUEL WILLARD. [3/20]
March 4, 1820, in Otsego, Mrs. ABIGAIL HENRY, aged 43. [3/20]
[No date] at Tonawanda, Pa., Dr. JOHN GOODRICH, formerly of Middlefield, N.Y. [3/27]
March 24, 1820, at Richfield, N.Y., Mrs. POLLY JONES, aged 23. [4/3]
May 11, 1820, at Lansingburgh, DAVID ALLEN, Esq., aged 47 [5/22]
May 27, 1820, in Otsego, JOHN HINDS, aged 50. [6/5]
June 20, 1820, at Middlefield, Mrs. SARAH EATON, aged 67. [6/26]
June 30, 1820, at Cooperstown, N.Y., Mrs. NAOMI WOOD. [6/26]
July 10, 1820, in Richfield, N.Y., Capt. IVORY HOLLAND, aged 80, Rev. Officer. [7/17]
July 7, 1820, at Albany, N.Y., HENRY GUEST, Jr., aged 61. [7/17]
July 27, 1820, at Middlefield, N.Y., JAMES VAN SLYKE, aged 75. [7/31]
July 22, 1820, at Milford, N.Y., EDWARD BROWN, son of JOSEPH MERRIAM, Esq., aged 12. [7/31]
July 29, 1820, at Decatur, N.Y., Mrs. SALLY SEAWARD, aged 74. [8/7]
Aug. 5, 1820, in Cooperstown, N.Y., infant son of JONAH FOSTER. [8/7]
Aug. 10, 1820, in Cooperstown, N.Y., EDGAR, infant son of GEORGE POMEROY, Esq. [8/14]
July 25, 1820, at Otaroga, Md., Major ASA EMMONS. [8/14]
Aug. 18, 1820, in Cooperstown, N.Y., infant child of AARON FITCH. [8/21]
Sept. 19, 1820, at Milford, N.Y., Maj. LEMUEL SARGEANT, aged 78, Rev. Officer. [9/25]

[No date] at Milford, Dr. MORRIS HUGHES. [12/23]
[No dates] at Washington D.C., Hon. NATHANIEL HAZARD and Hon. JESSE SLOCUMB. Representatives from Rhode Island and North Carolina respectively. [1/1/1821]
Dec. 31, 1820, at West Springfield, Mass., Rev. JOSEPH LATHROP, S.T.D., aged 89. [1/15/1821]
Jan. 17, 1821, at Greenville, Maj. AUGUSTINE PREVOST, aged 77. [2/5]
Feb. 3, 1821, at Westford, N.Y., WILLIAM WEBSTER. [2/12]
March 21, 1821, at Cooperstown, N.Y., JOSEPH S. LYMAN, Esq., aged 36. [3/26]
Feb. 28, 1821, in town of Otsego, Mrs. LUCRETIA POTTER, aged 86. [3/26]
March 8, 1821, at Laurens, Mrs. HANNAH WINDSOR, aged 28. [3/26]
April 3, 1821, in Cooperstown, N.Y., Mr. RECOMPENCE GRAVES, aged 66. [4/9]
April 6, 1821, in Burlington, N.Y., TIMOTHY MORSE, Esq., aged 67. [4/9]
March 29, 1821, in Decatur, N.Y., Mrs. JANE KAPLE, aged 102. [4/9]
April 9, 1821, in Burlington, WARD DIMOCH, aged 26. [5/16]
April 12, 1821, in Cooperstown, Mrs. DEBORAH GOODSELL, aged 45. [4/15]
May 2, 1821, in Cooperstown, N.Y., Mrs. ROXANE GRAVES, aged 31. [5/7]
[No date] in Orange Co., MATTHEW MC KENNEY, aged abt. 70. [5/7]
May 10, 1821, at Hartwick, N.Y., NATHAN DAVISON, Esq., aged 64. [5/14]
[No date] at New York, Mrs. MARY DUANE, aged 85, formerly of Duanesburgh. [5/14]
[No date] at Philadelphia, Pa., JAMES WALL, Esq., aged 81. [5/14]
May 10, 1821, at Westford, N.Y., LEONARD DRAKE, aged 28. [5/21]
May 28, 1821, at Medford, Mass., Hon. TIMOTHY BIGELOW, aged 55. [5/21]
May 27, 1821, at Albany, N.Y., JOHN NICHOLSON, Esq., aged 47. [6/4]
June 11, 1821, at Warren, Herkimer County, Mrs. ESTHER TILDEN, aged 73, formerly of Lebanon, Conn. [issue date not given]
June 8, 1821, in Cooperstown, N.Y., ROBERT L. BOWNE, formerly of Butternuts, aged 56. [issue date not given]
July 2, 1821, in Middlefield, N.Y., Mrs. SARAH GARDNER, aged 28.
[No date] in Michigan Territory, Dr. WM. S. MADISON of Kentucky.
June 30, 1821, at Westford, N.Y., CYTUS BABCOCK, aged 21. [7/9]

June 7, 1821, at Brainerd, Cherokee Nations, Rev. SAMUEL WORCESTER, D.D., of Salem, Mass, aged 50. [7/9]
May 16, 1821, Rev. THOMAS SCOTT, aged 75. [7/9]
July 23, 1821, at North Stonington, Ct., ELIAS S. PALMER, aged 70.
[No date] at Walpole, N.H., Gen. AMASA ALLEN, aged 69, Soldier Rev.
[No date] at Charleston, S.C., HEZEKIAH FLAGG, Esq., late of Cooperstown.
July 18, 1821, at Onondaga, N.Y., MARY GEDDES, aged 19. [8/6]
Aug. 4, 1821, in Western, Oneida County, Gen. WM. FLOYD, aged 81, Rev. Officer. [8/13]
Aug. 15, 1821, in Burlington, N.Y., Hon. JEDEDIAH PECK, aged 74. [8/20]
Aug. 27, 1821, in Cooperstown, N.Y., Mrs. SARAH MUNN, aged 60. [9/3]
Oct. 26, 1821, ROXEY ANN, dau. of Maj. ASA EMMONS, aged 19. [10/29]
Oct. 22, 1821, in Sharon, Schoharie Co., Mrs. SARAH LOWE, aged 90. [11/5]
Oct. 24, 1821, at Burlington, N.Y., Hon. ELIAS BOUDINOT, L.L.D., aged 82. [11/5]
Nov. 9, 1821, at Lyme, Conn., Capt. EZRA LEE, Rev. Officer, aged 72. [12/3]
Nov. 26, 1821, at Hartwick, N.Y., Mrs. SOPHIA WOOD, aged 29. [12/3]
Dec. 3, 1821, at Hartwick, N.Y., ELIPHALET STICKNEY. [12/10]
Dec. 1, 1821, at Philadelphia, Pa., RICHARD FAIRMAN, aged 32. [12/17]
Dec. 24, 1821, Greene, Chenango Co., Mrs. HANNAH HENRY.
Jan. 14, 1822, in Otsego, N.Y., GIDEON NILES. [1/21]
Jan. 4, 1822, in Burlington, N.Y., Mrs. RUTH GARDNER, aged 75. [1/21]
Jan. 10, 1822, at New York, BARENT GARDINIER, Esq. [1/21]
[No date] at Homer, Rev. ELIJAH BACHELOR, aged 49. [1/21]
[No date] at Williamstown, Mass., Dr. SAMUEL PORTER, aged 67. [1/21]
[No date] at Rutland, Vt., Rev. HEMAN BALL, D.D., aged 57. [1/21]
Jan. 5, 1822, in Cherry Valley, N.Y., HUGH MITCHELL, native of Ireland, aged 101 years, 9 months. [1/21]
Jan. 19, 1822, in Maryland, N.Y., RUFUS DRAPER. [1/28]
Jan. 29, 1822, at Plainfield, N.Y., Mrs. POLLY LLOYD, aged 18. [2/4]
Jan. 31, 1822, in Madison, N.Y., WALTER MORGAN, native of England, aged 48. [2/4]

Feb. 1, 1822, in Otsego, Mrs. SALLY WOOD, aged 72. [2/11]

Jan. 17, 1822, in Laurens, N.Y., FLUVIA ARNOLD, aged 22. [2/11]

Feb. 16, 1822, at Middlefield, N.Y., Col. ABNER DUNHAM, aged 48. [2/18]

Feb. 6, 1822, at Edmeston, N.Y., DAVID CHAPIN, Esq., aged 50. [2/18]

Feb. 9, 1822, in Cazenovia, N.Y., Col. JOHN LINCKLAEN, first settler of that village. [2/25]

Jan. 27, 1822, in town of Otsego, N.Y., WILLIAM STOWEL, aged 63. [3/4]

[No date] at Castleton, Vt., Gen. ISAAC CLARK, aged 72, Rev. Officer. [3/4]

[No date] at Haverhill, JOHN WHITING, aged 94. [3/4]

March 8, 1822, in Hartwick, N.Y., JAMES FITCH, aged 54. [3/11]

Jan. 19, 1822, at Harpersfield, Ohio, DANIEL PRENTISS, aged 80. [3/11]

March 2, 1822, at Hartford, Conn., ELISHA SKINNER, aged 68. [3/11]

Feb. 21, 1822, at Worcester, N.Y., ELVIRA CHASE, dau. of SETH CHASE, Esq., aged 15. [3/11]

Feb. 27, 1822, in Burlington, N.Y., NOAH FOX. [3/11]

March 11, 1822, in Butternuts, N.Y., Mrs. ELIZABETH TILLSON, aged 42. [3/25]

March 8, 1822, at Woodbury, Conn., Hon. NATHANIEL SMITH, aged 60. [3/25]

March 24, 1822, at Cherry Valley, N.Y., WILLIAM HENRY SEELYE, son of ISAAC SEELYE, Esq., aged 14. [4/1]

April 21, 1822, in Otsego, SIMEON WATERMAN, aged 81. [4/29]

May 6, 1822, in Otsego, N.Y., JUSTIN CLARK, late of Montrose, Pa., aged 27. [5/13]

May 10, 1822, CYRUS CLARK, Esq., aged 50. (Residence not given.) [5/13]

[No date] at Philadelphia, Pa., Com. THOMAS TRUXTON, U.S.N., aged 68. [5/13]

May 12, 1822, at Unadilla, N.Y., Mrs. LUCY FAIRCHILD, aged 34. [5/20]

[No date] in Cooperstown, N.Y., DELOS, infant son of STEPHEN GREGORY. [5/20]

June 7, 1822, at Johnstown, N.Y., CHARLES COAN, formerly of Cooperstown, aged 32. [6/10]

May 27, 1822, at Litchfield, Conn., HELEN PECK, aged 19. [6/10]

[No date] at Stonington, Conn., ELIJAH PALMER, aged 79. [6/10]

July 2, 1822, in Cooperstown, N.Y., SARAH S., infant dau. of JOSEPH WALTON, Esq. [7/8]

July 6, 1822, in Albany, N.Y., THEODORUS V. W. GRANAH, Esq., aged 63. [7/15]
June 30, 1822, at Fairfield, Conn., Hon. JOSIAH MASTERS of Schaghticoke, N.Y., aged 58. [7/15]
July 23, 1822, at Troy, N.Y., Rev. JONAS COE, D.D. [7/29]
July 28, 1822, at Burlington, N.Y., Mrs. ANNIE PRATT. [8/5]
Sept. 2, 1822, at Lexington, Ky., THOMAS DOUGHERTY, Esq.
Sept. 19, 1822, at Louisville, Kentucky, DANIEL WASHBON of Butternuts, aged 27. [10/28]
Oct. 10, 1822, at Hudson, Ohio, NATHAN PIERSON, aged 60. [10/28]
Dec. 15, 1822, at Fredonia, N.Y., ELIPHALET DEWEY, Esq., aged 37, formerly of Hartwick. [12/30]
Dec. 22, 1822, at Butternuts, Mrs. MABLE GLOVER, aged 56. [1/6/1823]
Dec. 26, 1822, at Albany, N.Y., JOHN TEN BROECK, Esq. [1/13/1823]
[No date] in Philadelphia, Pa., Dr. MICHAEL LEIB. [1/13]
Dec. 31, 1822, at Canandaigua, N.Y., GIDEON GRANGER, Esq. [1/13/1823]
Dec. 28, 1822, at Mansfield, Conn., LUCY EMSWORTH, aged 60. [1/20/1823]
Feb. 3, 1823, at Laurens, N.Y., Mrs. ABIGAIL GILBERT, aged 70.
Jan. 23, 1823, at Albany, N.Y., MOSES I. CANTINE, Esq., aged 40. [1/20]
March 12, 1823, in Danube, Herkimer Co., RICHARD VAN HORNE, aged 53. [3/24]
March 11, 1823, in Otsego, Mrs. PHEBE LENT, aged 39. [3/24]
Feb. 27, 1823, at Richfield, Mrs. DAVID TAFT. [3/24]
April 1, 1823, in Fly Creek, near Cooperstown, ELIZA ROCKWELL, aged 21. [4/7]
April 13, 1823, at Milford, N.Y., IRA WELLMAN, aged 31. [4/21]
[No date] at Maryland, N.Y., PETER ROMAN, aged 60. [4/21]
May 13, 1823, at Wethersfield, Rev. DAVID PARSONS, D.D., of Amherst, Mass., aged 74. [5/26]
May 16, 1823, at Springfield, HEZEKIAH HAYDEN, aged 47. [5/26]
May 14, 1823, at Canadarago Springs (probably Richfield), ELIZABETH SEWALL, infant dau. of Rev. Mr. HUSE. [5/26]
May 22, 1823, at Scarsdale, N.Y., JONATHAN TOMPKINS, Esq., aged 87. [6/2]
May 25, 1823, in Otsego, N.Y., SAMUEL SHIPMAN, aged 46. [6/2]
June 4, 1823, at Westford, N.Y., Col. NATHAN KINGSLEY, aged 44. [6/16]

June 20, 1823, in Cooperstown, N.Y., JANE CAMPBELL, dau. of ROBERT CAMPBELL, aged 6. [6/23]
June 19, 1823, at Hartwick, ISAAC BISSELL, aged 75. [6/23]
[No date] at Washington, N.Y., ELIPHALET MOSHER, aged 96. [6/23]
July 3, 1823, at New York, Mrs. ELIZA LOOMIS, aged 55. [7/14]
[No date] at Hartford, Conn., Gen. SAMUEL WYLLYS, aged 85. [7/14]
[No date] at Amherst, Mass., Rev. ZEPHANIAH SWIFT MOORE. [7/14]
July 7, 1823, in Otsego, EZEKIEL KELLOGG, aged 75. [7/14]
July 26, 1823, at Exeter, Miss TEMPA PHILLIPS of Cooperstown, age 27. [8/4]
[No date] at Ballston, RALPH HASCALL, Esq., of Essex Co., N.Y., aged 47. [8/4]
[No date] at Canadaigua, N.Y., Maj. WM. SHEPARD, aged 63. [8/4]
Aug. 2, 1823, in Otsego, JOSHUA HALL, aged 73. [8/11]
July 29, 1823, at Delhi, N.Y., JULIET A. SHERWOOD, aged 21. [8/11]
July 31, 1823, at Hartford, Conn., BARZILLAI HUDSON, aged 82. [8/11]
Aug. 5, 1823, in N.Y., FENNIMORE, only son of JAMES COOPER, Esq., aged 1 year, 10 months. [8/11]
July 31, 1823, in Morrisville, N.Y., Mrs. MARY RICE, formerly of Middlefield, aged 43. [8/18]
Aug. 21, 1823, in Cooperstown, N.Y., THOS. SHANKLAND, Esq., aged 58. [8/25]
Aug. 18, 1823, at Farmington, Conn., Hon. JOHN TREADWELL, aged 78. [9/1]
Aug. --, 1823, at Hartwick, N.Y., Rev. HENRY CHAPMAN. [9/1]
Aug. 31, 1823, at Unadilla, N.Y., Dr. WYLLIS EDSON, aged 40. [9/8]
Sept. 3, 1823, at Hartwick, N.Y., JOSHUA COOK, aged 59. [9/8]
[No date] in Ohio, Hon. ELIJAH BOARDMAN of Conn. [9/8]
[No date] at Somers, N.Y., Gen. WM. GREEN, aged 72. [9/8]
[No date] at Pelham, Mass., ADAM JOHNSON. [9/8]
Sept. 10, 1823, at Fly Creek, near Cooperstown, ASAHEL JARVIS, aged 55. [9/15]
Sept. 1, 1823, at Westford, N.Y., MARY DRAPER, aged 74. [9/15]
Sept. 3, 1823, Mr. OLNEY RICE, aged 26. [9/15]
Sept. 30, 1823, at Whitehall Landing, Rev. JOHN COE of Troy, N.Y. [10/13]
Oct. 3, 1823, at Burlington, N.Y., Gen. JOSEPH BLOOMFIELD. [10/13]
Oct. 1, 1823, in Otsego, Mrs. MARY BLAKLEY, aged 41. [10/13]
Oct. 20, 1823, at Hartwick, ROBERT CARR, aged 83. [10/27]
Nov. 3, 1823, at Burlington, AMANDA ANGEL, aged 34. [11/10]

Nov. 17, 1823, in Otsego, SAMUEL DOW, aged 31. [11/10]
Dec. 13, 1823, at New York, Rev. EZRA SAMPSON, aged 76. [12/22]
Dec. 16, 1823, at Clinton, Oneida County, Mrs. MARILLA BROCKWAY, aged 25. [12/29]
Dec. 28, 1823, ELIAS BUTTON of Brookfield, Madison County, aged 105 years. [1/15/1824]
Jan. 1, 1824, at Burlington, MATTHEW DON SILE, aged 21. [1/12]
Jan. 7, 1824, in Cooperstown, N.Y., Mrs. LYDIA COFFIN, aged 63. [1/12]
Dec. 24, 1823, in Troy, N.Y., Hon. AMASA PAINE formerly of Windsor, Vt. [1/12/1824]
Jan. 7, 1824, at Burlington, ELIZA SILL, aged 33. [1/12]
Jan. 11, 1824, at New Lisbon, ELNATHAN NOBLE, aged 72. [1/19]
Jan. 12, 1824, at Butternuts, Mrs. ELINOR JANES, aged 32. [1/19]
Jan. 13, 1824, at New Berlin, HENRY GOODSELL, aged 24. [1/19]
Jan. 26, 1824, in Cooperstown, N.Y., Mrs. SARAH S. STRANAHAN. [2/2]
Jan. 29, 1824, at Laurens, N.Y., SILAS GILBERT, aged 53. [2/9]
Jan. 31, 1824, at Laurens, N.Y., Mrs. SILAS GILBERT. [2/9]
Feb. 7, 1824, in Otsego, N.Y., Mrs. ABIGAIL NEWELL, aged 58. [2/16]
Feb. 7, 1824, at Middlefield, JOHN WAINE, aged 18. [2/16]
Feb. 7, 1824, JAMES ASHLEY, aged 47. [2/16]
Feb. 21, 1824, at Exeter, N.Y., Mrs. HETTA CUSHMAN, aged 25. [3/1]
Feb. 25, 1824, in Hartwick, N.Y., Mrs. THANKFUL APLIN, aged 73. [3/1]
Feb. 28, 1824, at Plainfield, JAMES LLOYD, Esq., aged 33. [3/8]
March 15, 1824, in Otsego, Mrs. HANNAH COLEMAN, aged 80. [3/29]
March 24, 1824, at Burlington, Mrs. HELEN T. SILL, aged 69. [4/12]
March 29, 1824, Dr. RUSSELL DORR, aged 52. [4/12]
April 2, 1824, COOK DIMOCK, aged 27. [4/12]
April 10, 1824, in Cooperstown, N.Y., Dr. CALVIN BEMIS, aged 40. [4/12]
April 13, 1824, in Canajoharie, N.Y., Gen. JOHN KEYS, aged 80. [4/19]
[No date] at Philadelphia, Rev. WILLIAM ROGERS, D.D., aged 73. [4/19]
April 25, 1824, in Fly Creek, Otsego, Mrs. SABRINA MARVIN, aged 48. [5/3]
May 5, 1824, in Philadelphia, Pa., SUSAN DEWITT of Albany, N.Y. [5/17]
April 27, 1824, in Morrisville, Madison County, THOMAS MORRIS, aged 46. [5/17]

May 30, 1824, in Cherry Valley, Miss HOLT, dau. of Maj. LESTER HOLT, aged 18. [5/31]
May 28, 1824, at Attleborough, Mass., JASPER CUMMINGS late of Burlington, N.Y., aged 15. [6/14]
June 18, 1824, at Hartwick, HENRY MALLARY, aged 21. [6/28]
June 30, 1824, at Cherry Valley, HENRY ROSEBOOM, Esq., aged 25. [7/5]
July 12, 1824, at Hartwick, N.Y., Mrs. JULIANA MARGARET MOELLER, aged 76, a native of Germany. [7/19]
July 14, 1824, at New Berlin, N.Y., Rev. ARTHUR FIELD. [7/26]
July 17, 1824, at Schooley's Mt., Rev. PHILIP M. WHELPEY, aged 30. [7/26]
Aug. 10, 1824, in Otsego, Capt. DANIEL ELWOOD, aged 30. [8/23]
Aug. 16, 1824, at Maryland, [N.Y.], ELEAZER TOMPKINS, Esq., aged 56. [8/23]
Aug. 20, 1824, at Middlefield, N.Y., Mrs. REBECCA ROBINSON. [8/23]
Sept. 16, 1824, at Springfield, N.Y., Mrs. MARY GILCHRIST. [9/27]
Oct. 1, 1824, at Butternuts, RUSSELL SKIDMORE, aged 25. [10/11]
[No date] at Richfield, CORNELIUS C. TUNICLIFF, aged 36. [10/11]
Oct. 4, 1824, at Orville, Lt. JOHN LEROW, aged 34. [10/18]
Oct. 23, 1824, in Otsego, Mrs. ALICE ROBERTS, aged 55. [10/25]
Oct. 16, 1824, at Winfield, HOSMER ALLEN, late of Cherry Valley, aged 25. [10/25]
Oct. 9, 1824, at Milford, N.Y., SIMEON BATES, aged 86. [11/1]
Nov. 16, 1824, at Utica, N.Y., MORRIS S. MILLER, Esq., aged 45. [11/22]
Dec. 23, 1824, at Springfield, N.Y., DANIEL RATHBUN. [1/3/1825]
[No date] at Warren, N.Y., BRADLEY STEWART. [1/3/1825]
Jan. 9, 1825, in Cherry Valley, BERNHART HENN, native of Albany, aged 48. [1/17]
Dec. 31, 1824, at Sharon, N.Y., Mrs. MARIA TEN EYCK, aged 29. [1/17/1825]
Jan. 28, 1825, in Cooperstown, N.Y., MOLLY M'DOWELL, aged 26. [1/31]
Feb. 7, 1825, at Herkimer, JABEZ FOX, Esq., aged 35. [1/31-sic]
Feb. 13, 1825, in Otsego, Mrs. TRIPHENIA KNOWLTON, aged 39. [2/21]
Feb. 24, 1825, at Middlefield, N.Y., JOHN VIELE, aged 97. [2/28]
March 5, 1825, in Otsego, LEMUEL WOODHOUSE, aged 72. [3/14]
March 6, 1825, in Butternuts, LUCRETIA DANIELSON, aged 27. [3/14]
[No date or place] ANNA GREGROY, aged 19. [3/14]

March 8, 1825, at Westford, MARGARET ELIZABETH, infant dau. of
    EZRA WILLIAMS, Esq. [3/21]
March 17, 1825, at Milford, FLURIA, dau. of RODNEY ARNOLD, aged
    5. [4/4]
[No date] at Duanesburgh, SARAH F. FEATHERSTONBAUGH, aged 8.
    [4/4]
April 16, 1825, at Hartwick, N.Y., Capt. BILLE WILLIAMS, aged 41.
    [4/18]
May 6, 1825, at Richfield, N.Y., Mrs. JAMES HAWKS. [5/9]
April 26, 1825, at Edmeston, N.Y., Dea. MARTIN LEE, aged 75. [5/9]
May 10, 1825, in Cooperstown, HENRY E. DWIGHT, aged 48. [5/23]
May 26, 1825, at Albany, N.Y., HENRY B. COOK, formerly of
    Cooperstown. [5/30]
May 25, 1825, at Richfield, N.Y., Mrs. LYDIA HAWLEY, dau. of Capt.
    WILLARD EDDY, aged 27. [6/6]
June 6, 1825, Mrs. CAROLINE VAN BENSCHOTEN, aged 75. [6/13]
June 29, 1825, in Cooperstown, WARD GRIFFIN, aged 40. [7/4]
[No date] JEDEDIAH STORY, 15 years 10 months. [7/1/1825]
July 3, 1825, NOAH COFFIN (formerly Nantucket), 63, Cooperstown.
    [7/11]
June 22, 1825, EZEKIEL CLARK, aged 65, Pompey. [7/18]
July 15, 1825, RENSSELAER W. RUSSELL, 22 years. Cooperstown.
    [7/25]
Aug. 10, 1825, Mrs. ELIZABETH PEAK, 31 years. Burlington. [8/15]
Aug. 7, 1825, Mrs. ABIGAIL GASKIN, 36 years. Guilderland. [8/15]
[No date] Mrs. CHRISTINA HUBBARD, 69 years. Claverack. [8/15]
July 29, 1825, CALEB BENTON, Esq., 67 years. Catskill. [8/15]
Aug. 14, 1825, DAVID PIER, 68 years. Otsego [8/22]
Aug. 8, 1825, BENJAMIN BROOKS, 81 years. Butternuts. [8/22]
Aug. 1, 1825, SEWALL SPALDING, 43 years. Plainfield. [8/22]
May 1, 1825, Dr. LLOYD GILBERT, formerly of Cooperstown, 35 years.
    Baton Rouge, La. [8/22]
[No date] ARTHUR BRUCE, 53 years. Utica. [8/15]
[No date] Miss BETSEY CARY, 22 years. Springfield. [8/29]
[No date] Mrs. ANNA TANNER, 82 years. Otsego. [8/24]
Aug. 16, 1825, Mrs. DEBORAH BISHOP, 67 years. Paris, Oneida Co.
    [8/24]
[No date] MARY, wife of Col. SAMUEL YOUNG, Ballston. [8/24]
[No date] SAMUEL JOHNSON, Jr., 25 years. Otsego. [9/2]
Aug. 22, 1825, Major EDWARD CUMPTON, late of Esperance [NY], 72
    years. Auburn. [9/2]

[No date] CYRUS NORTH, 32 years. Walton, Delaware Co. [9/19]
Sept. 16, 1825, in Cooperstown, N.Y., JANE, infant dau. of SAMUEL STARKWEATHER, Esq. [9/19]
Aug. 30, 1825, in Ohio, NATHANIEL FULLER of Mass., aged 67. [9/26]
Sept. 24, 1825, in Springfield, Stewart's Patent, N.Y., RICHARD ELWOOD, aged 75. [10/3]
[No date] in Springfield, N.Y., Mrs. MARY GILCHRIST. [10/3]
[No date] in Albany, Mrs. WALTER COCHRANE, dau. of Hon. PETER SMITH. [10/3]
Sept. 25, 1825, ROBERT B. HEWSON of Albany. [10/3]
Oct. 22, 1825, at Milford, N.Y., NATHAN WALDO, aged 58. [10/31]
Nov. 6, 1825, in Utica, N.Y., ERASTUS CLARK, Esq., aged 58. [11/14]
Nov. 4, 1825, at Boston, Mass., Hon. WM. GRAY, aged 75. [11/14]
[No date] at Byefield, Mass., Rev. ELIJAH PARISH, D.D., aged 63. [11/28]
Nov. 21, 1825, at Middlefield, N.Y., Capt. JOSEPH TEMPLE, aged 78. [11/28]
[No date] in Otsego, N.Y., Mr. CYRUS ALLEN, aged 33. [11/28]
Oct. 16, 1825, in Detroit, Mich. ELISHA ELDRED of Hartwick, 69. [12/5]
Dec. 15, 1825, in Burlington, N.Y., Mrs. LAURA WARNER, aged 37. [12/26]
Dec. 15, 1825, in Otsego, N.Y., WILLIAM WALBEY, aged 58. [12/26]
Dec. 16, 1825, at Milo, Yates Co., SAMUEL SHERMAN, formerly of Otsego, aged 65. [1/2/1826]
[No date] at Tolland, Conn., Gen ELIJAH CHAPMAN, aged 73. [1/2/1826]
[No date] at Albany, ESTES HOWE, Esq., aged 45. [1/2/ 1826]
Dec. 15, 1825, at Charleston, S.C., Rev. HOOPER CUMMINGS, D.D., late of Albany. [1/2/1826]
Dec. 30, 1825, in Cooperstown, MARY MILLER, infant dau. of Rev. F. T. TIFFANY. [1/2/1826]
Jan. 6, 1826, at Pittsfield, N.Y., Mrs. MARGARET RANDALL, aged 41. [1/16]
Jan. 23, 1826, at Cortlandt Village, DANIEL BETTS, Esq., aged 27. [2/6]
[No date] at Auburn, N.Y., Major RICHARD GOODELL, Keeper of State Prison. [2/6]
[No date] at Canajoharie, N.Y., Mrs. ELIZABETH FREY, aged 92. [2/6]
Jan. 30, 1826, at New Berlin, N.Y., JOSHUA GRANT, aged 72. [2/13]
Feb. 11, 1826, in Otsego, Mrs. POLLY CRANE, aged 67. [2/13]

Feb. 11, 1826, at Boston, Mass., Hon. ELIHU LYMAN, aged 44. Brother of JOSEPH LYMAN of Cooperstown. [2/20]
Feb. 21, 1826, in Hartwick, N.Y., Mrs. LIPPET, aged 65. [3/6]
[No date] in Bridgeport, Conn., Dr. THOMAS HOLMAN, formerly of Cooperstown, aged 32. [3/6]
March 9, 1826, in Cooperstown, Mrs. MEHITABLE PHILLIPS, aged 52. [3/13]
March 4, 1826, in Otsego, MINA NEWTON, aged 18. [3/13]
[No date] Shippensport, Kentucky, Aug. --- DANIEL L. HATCH, aged 30. [3/13/1826]
Feb. 23, 1826, in Columbia, Herkimer Co., SAMUEL HATCH, aged 28. [3/13]
March 3, 1826, in Burlington, N.Y., Dea. BENJ. HARRINGTON, aged 59. [3/13]
March 30, 1826. On March 10, 1826, in Milford, GABRIEL FAIRCHILD, aged 42. [3/13?]
March 13, 1826, in Plainfield, ZURIAL CAMPBELL, aged 58. [3/13?]
March 11, 1826, at Richfield, N.Y., Mrs. BETSEY RICHARDS, aged 30. [3/13?]
March 16, 1826, in Burlington, Mrs. ARTEMAS SHELDON, aged 42. [3/13?]
March 7, 1826, in Maryland, N.Y., DAVID BENEDICT. [3/27]
March 15, 1826, in Hudson, N.Y., Gen. SAMUEL EDMUNDS, aged 66. [3/27]
March 31, 1826, in Richfield, N.Y., JAMES HYDE, Esq., aged 55. [4/10]
March 26, 1826, in Otsego, Otsego County, PHONEHAS COOK, Esq., aged 52. [4/10]
April 1, 1826, in Danube, Herkimer Co., GEORGE SWAIN, aged 98. [4/10]
April 16, 1826, at Butternuts, N.Y., Mrs. JONATHAN MOORE, aged 89. [5/1]
March 28, 1826, in Middlefield, JAMES C. YOUNG, aged 24. [5/1]
April 27, 1826, in Cooperstown, CARLTON KOWLISON, aged 38. [5/1]
May 2, 1826, in Otsego, Lieut. BARAKIAH JOHNSON, aged 79. [5/8]
April 6, 1826, in Columbus, N.Y., HARRIET S. FULLER, aged 7, dau. of ELIJAH FULLER. [5/8]
April 25, 1826, in Warren, Herkimer Co., PHILENA HAWLEY, aged 22. [5/8]
May 4, 1826, in Cooperstown, N.Y., LEWIS COMSTOCK, aged 7, son of Capt. MILES COMSTOCK. [5/8]
May 6, 1826, in Hartwick, PHILO POTTER, aged 33. [5/15]

May 2, 1826, in Norwich, Conn., EZEKIEL MAYEEN, aged 27, great-grandson of GREAT UHCAS. [5/15]
[No date] in Batavia, N.Y., Dr. EPHRAIM BROWN, aged 29. [5/22]
May 26, 1826, in Middlefield, Mrs. OLIVE STARR, aged 55. [6/5]
May 29, 1826, in Butternuts, N.Y., ICHABOD DAVIS, aged 42. [6/12]
June 13, 1826, at Williamsburgh, Va., Mrs. ELIZABETH G. WEBB, formerly of Cooperstown, and a few days previous their son, SAMUEL, aged 26 months. [7/3]
June 26, 1826, in Newark, N.J., CALEB S. RIGGS, Esq., aged 64. [7/3]
July 10, 1826, at Burlington, N.Y., ELISHA, infant son of ELISHA CORNING. [7/3 sic, probably 7/17]
July 12, 1826, in Cooperstown, AARON FITCH, aged 39. [7/17]
July 4, 1826, in Cooperstown, FRANCES REBECCA, dau. of CALVIN GRAVES, aged 2. [7/17]
July 15, 1826, in Otsego, Mrs. MARIETTA WILLIAMS. [7/24]
July 12, 1826, Mrs. REBECCA OSBORN, aged 68. [7/24]
July 20, 1826, in Cooperstown, N. Y., infant son of JAMES STOWEL. [7/24]
July 26, 1826, in Cooperstown, BARTLET ROGERS, aged 56. [7/31]
July 28, 1826, in Plainfield, N.Y., VOSE PALMER, aged 64.
June 24, 1826, in Pinckneyville, Miss., Mrs. SARAH FOX, aged 36, resident of Otsego Co. for several years. [8/14]
Aug. 9, 1826, in Springfield, N.Y., MARIA THURSTON, aged 24. [8/21]
Sept. 4, 1826, in Albany, N.Y., THOMAS BRIDGEN, Esq. [no issue given, 9/11?]
Aug. 29, 1826, in Knox, Albany Co., N.Y., Mrs. ANNA ELIZABETH DIETZ, late of Milford, N.Y. [9/11]
Sept. 8, 1826, in Otsego, CHARLES BAILEY, aged 73. [9/25]
Sept. 25, 1826, in Cherry Valley, N.Y., Gen. ELIJAH HOLT of Buffalo, 64 years. [10/2]
[No date] in Lebanon Springs, N.Y., WILLIAM CRAFTS, Esq. [10/2]
Sept. 21, 1826, at New Berlin, Miss SALLY ANGELL, aged 27. [10/16]
Oct. 4, 1826, in Cooperstown, N.Y., WM., son of ELLERY CORY, aged 10. [10/16]
Oct. 21, 1826, in Cooperstown, Mrs. RACHEL SHANKLAND, aged 51. [10/23]
Oct. 17, 1826, in Richfield, N.Y., Mrs. CAROLINE RICHARDS, 23. [10/23?]
Sept. 21, 1826, in Huntsville, ELIZABETH MORSE, aged 19. [10/23?]
Oct. 22, 1826, in Cooperstown, Col. FARRAND STRANAGAN, aged 43. [10/30]

Oct. 2, 1826, in Cleveland, Ohio, ELIZA ANN HOWARD of Ravenna, aged 22, formerly of Sherburne. [10/30]

Oct. 25, 1826, in Springfield, JEHIEL WATTLES, aged 24. [11/6]

Nov. 4, 1826, in Cooperstown, Mrs. CATHERINE OLENDORF, aged 66. [11/13]

Nov. 20, 1826, at Hyde Hall, Springfield, ARTHUR, infant son of GEORGE CLARK, Esq. [no issue given, 11/27?]

Nov. 17, 1826, in Plainfield, N.Y., Elder WILLET STILLMAN, 49. [11/27]

Dec. 6, 1826, in Richfield, N.Y., MENZO, infant son of Capt. DOROS HATCH, aged 11 months. [12/18]

Dec. 19, in New York, JONATHAN LITTLE. [12/25]

Jan. 3, 1827, at Butternuts, N.Y., Mrs. MARY MORRIS, aged 69. [1/8]

Dec. 18, 1826, at Westford, N.Y., FLAVEL WRIGHT, aged 41. [1/8/1827]

Jan. 1, 1827, at Burlington, N.Y., CATHERINE, dau. of Hon. WM. G. ANGEL, aged 7 months. [1/8]

Jan. 5, 1827, at Auburn, N.Y., JAMES FITCH, formerly of Cooperstown. [1/15]

Jan. 2, 1827, at Walton, Delaware Co., GABRIEL NORTH, Esq., aged 71. [1/22]

Jan. 1, 1827, at Columbus, Ohio, JAMES K. CORY, Esq., aged 29. [1/22]

Jan. 16, 1827, at Philadelphia, Pa., Mrs. MARY MORRIS, aged 78. [1/29]

Jan. 18, 1827, in New York, CORNELIUS RAY, aged 72. [1/29]

Jan. 31, 1827, at Burlington, N.Y., DAVID BRAINARD PRATT, aged 22. [2/12]

Jan. 31, 1827, in Cherry Valley, Capt. MATTHEW L. SUTPHEN, aged 32. [2/12]

Jan. 30, 1827, in Richfield, N.Y., WILLIAM TUNNICLIFF, aged 70. [2/12]

Feb. 10, 1827, in Burlington, N.Y., WEALTHY ALLICE, aged 20. [2/19]

Feb. 22, 1827, in Cooperstown, Mrs. ANN LUVINGSTON. [2/26]

Feb. 13, 1827, at Bowman's Creek, Rev. CYRUS DOWNED, aged 28. [2/26]

Feb. 12, 1827, at Cortland Village, DANIEL SMITH, formerly of Cooperstown, aged 22. [2/26]

Feb. 28, 1827, in Plainfield, N.Y., Capt. PERRY CLARK, aged 65. [3/12]

March 1, 1827, in Penn Yan, N.Y., ABRAHAM VOSBURGH, Esq., formerly of Unadilla. [3/12]

March 9, 1827, in Westford, AMOS HEWIT, aged 30. [3/12]

March 20, 1827, at Albany, Dr. ELIAS WILLARD, aged 71. [3/12]

April 9, 1827, at Worcester, Mass., Col. BENJAMIN BEMIS, aged 82. [3/12]
April 15, 1827, in Warren, Herkimer Co., STEPHEN LUDDINGTON, Esq., aged 62. [4/23]
March 28, 1827, in Otsego, LUMAN SAVAGE, aged 55. [4/30]
[No date] in Otsego, SHERMAN WILLIAMS, aged 26. [4/30]
April 9, 1827, in Otego, N.Y., ELIZABETH FREEMAN, aged 17. [4/30]
June 12, 1827, in Columbus, N.Y., DANIEL ALVERSON, aged 27. [6/18]
July 10, 1827, at Cherry Valley, Mrs. HANNAH CRAFTS, aged 42. [7/23]
July 19, 1827, at Fly Creek, Otsego, JOHN ROCKWELL, aged 70. [7/23]
Aug. 7, 1827, at Westford, N.Y., NATHAN POTTER, aged 38. [8/20]
Aug. 11, 1827, at New Berlin, HANNAH LAVINIA, dau. of Col. E. BEVINS, aged 2. [8/20]
Aug. 20, 1827, in Cooperstown, GEORGE, son of ELLERY CORY, aged 3. [8/27]
Aug. 23, 1827, in Cherry Valley, Mrs. DEBORAH WHITE. [8/27]
Aug. 15, 1827, at Franklin, Delaware Co., Mrs. WEALTHY HAZEN, aged 35. [9/3]
Aug. 15, 1827, in Oxford, N.Y., ORLANDO, son of HENRY MYGATT, aged 15. [9/3]
Aug. 16, 1827, in Howard, N.Y., HEZEKIAH M. COLE, aged 38. [9/10]
Aug. 30, 1827, in Hartwick, N.Y., Rev. CHARLES THORP of Brighton, Monroe Co., aged 49. [9/10]
Aug. 7, 1827, at Medina, Orleans Co., JABEN ALDEN, aged 27, formerly of Cooperstown. [9/17]
Sept. 21, 1827, in Burlington, N.Y., ELIJAH ROOD, aged 22. [9/24]
Sept. 13, 1827, at Canajoharie, Col. HENDRICK FREY, aged 93. [9/24]
Sept. 24, 1827, at Cherry Valley, JOHN WALTON, aged 34. [10/1]
[No date] at Oxford, Conn., NATHAN F. BUCKINGHAM of Burlington, N.Y., aged 25. [10/8]
Oct. 8, 1827, in Exeter, HARRY CLARK, aged 26. [10/15]
Oct. 1, 1827, at Richfield, HARVEY BEARDSLEY, aged 24. [10/15]
Sept. 7, 1827, in Mobile, PETER BEARDSLEY of N.Y. State, aged 30. [10/15]
Oct. 14, 1827, Exeter, OCTAVIA SABRINA ROBINSON, aged 15. [10/22]
Oct. 1, 1827, Victor, Ontario County, Deacon JAMES ROBERTS, 67. One of the first settlers of Burlington, N.Y. [10/29]
Oct. 18, Springfield, N.Y., Mrs. RUTH RICHARDSON, aged 66. [10/29]
Oct. 25, 1827, Burlington, N.Y., JOEL SMITH, aged 71. [10/29]

Nov. 5, 1827, Williamstown, Conn., PETER SCHUYLER PUTNAM, Esq. [10/29]
Oct. 25, 1827, Whitesborough, N.Y., Hon. THOMAS R. GOLD. [10/29?]
Oct. 23, 1827, Richfield, THEODORE CAREY, aged 15. [11/19]
Oct. 12, 1827, Springfield, N.Y., ENOCH MORSE, aged 43. [11/19]
Nov. 23, 1827, Bridgewater, JULIA ANN ROBBINS, aged 21. [12/3]
Dec, 24, 1827, formerly of Springfield, [died in] Cynthiana, Ind., Dr. JAMES H. RICHARDSON, aged 32. [12/24]
Jan. 5, 1828, Cherry Valley, CATHERINE CLYDE, aged 24. [1/14]
Jan. 4, 1828, Worcester, Capt. SIMEON J. ANDREWS, aged 83. [1/14]
Jan. 21, 1828, Genoa, N.Y., Capt. ROGER MOORE, aged 89. [1/14]
Nov. 25, 1827, Gloucester, Mass., JOHN ROGERS, Esq., aged 77. [1/14/1828]
Jan. 8, 1828, Oxford, N.Y., HEZEKIAH WHEELER, aged 81. [1/14?]
Jan. 9, 1828, Oxford, MARY WHEELER, aged 84. [1/14?]
Jan. 7, 1828, New Lisbon, Mrs. CLARISSA ANDRUS, aged 47. [1/14?]
Jan. 19, 1828, Middlefield, BENJAMIN GILBERT, Esq., aged 72. [1/28]
Jan. 31, 1828, Otsego, ABEL METCALF, aged 61. [2/4]
[No date] N.Y. City, Mrs. GRACE WEBSTER, wife of Hon. DAN. WEBSTER. [2/4/1828]
[No date] Mamaroneck, JOHN DELANCEY, Esq., aged 75. [2/4/1828]
[No date] Hudson, N.Y., ROBERT J. COFFIN, aged 22. [2/4/1828]
Feb. 10, 1828, Schenectady, Mrs. MARY ANN DUANE, aged 55.
Dec. 25, 1827, Unadilla, Mrs. MARY BUCKLEY, aged 54. Native of Berkshire, Mass. [2/4/1828?]
Feb. 24, 1828, Geneva, Rev. ORRIN CLARK, aged 40. [3/10]
Feb. 23, 1828, Geneva, REBECCA COOK, aged 20, late of N.J. [3/10]
March 17, 1828, New Lisbon, N.Y., OLIVER CANFIELD, aged 100, formerly of New Milford, Conn. [3/10]
March 27, 1828, West Cambridge, Mass. AMOS WHITEMORE, aged 69. (inventor) [4/14]
April 16, 1828, Col. DANIEL POTTER, aged 43, formerly of Hartwick. [4/28]
March 15, 1828, Hartwick, NAOMI POTTER, aged 27. [4/28]
April 14, 1828, Burlington, ABIGAIL NICKERSON, 76. [4/28]
April 12, 1828, Oppenheim, ABRAHAM TAYLOR, aged 72. [5/5]
April 12, Onondaga, N.Y., Rev. CALEB ALEXANDER, aged 72. [5/5]
[No date] Warren, Herkimer Co., DANIEL MINER, aged 36, formerly of Norwich Conn. [5/5/1828]
[No date] Windsor, Vt., Gen. ZEBINA CURTISS, aged 67. [5/5/1828]
April 22, 1828, Canaan, Conn., Maj. JOHN WEBB, aged 71. [5/12]

[No date] Hartwick, N.Y., WILLIAM MURRAY, aged 73. [5/12]
May 2, 1828, Richfield, Mrs. ALICE GIBBS, aged 30. [5/12]
May 10, 1828, Cooperstown, ELIJAH GARDNER. [5/12]
May 20, 1828, Hartwick, N.Y., EDWARD BOND. [5/26]
May 16, 1828, Garretsville, N.Y., SALLY MARIA, dau. of JOHN ROBERTS, aged 6. [5/26]
May 28, 1828, Exeter, N.Y., Mrs. OLIVE NASH. [6/2]
June 4, 1828, Hartwick, Dea. PRINCE WEST, aged 93. [6/16]
May 31, 1828, Farmerville, N.Y., LAURA HENRY, aged 24. Formerly of Otsego Co. [6/30]
June 28, 1828, Hartwick, Mrs. J.R.M. MILLER. [6/30]
June 21, 1828, Albany, SAMUEL BROWNLEY, aged 75. [6/30]
June 12, Herkimer, FREDERICK SMITH, aged 80. [6/30]
June 14, Throg's Neck, Dr. WRIGHT POST, aged 63. [6/30]
July 6, Cherry Valley, Mrs. THEODA H. SEELYE, aged 44. Formerly of Springfield, Mass. [7/14]
July 14, 1828, Middlefield, JEREMY SUMMERS TITUS, son of JEREMY and JERUSHA TITUS, aged 4. [7/21]
July 16, 1828, Fishkill, N.Y., Col. WM. FEW, aged 81. [7/21]
July 18, 1828, Westford, Mrs. OLIVER BIDLACK. [7/21]
July 31, 1828, Jefferson, N.Y., HENRY RIVENBURGH, aged 40. [8/4]
Aug. 5, 1828, Middlefield, Capt. THOMAS RANSOM, aged 91. [8/11]
[No date] Delhi, CHARLES A. FOOTE. [8/11/1828]
July 28, 1828, Milford, THOMAS MUMFORD, aged 96. [8/11]
Aug. 8, 1828, Hartwick, PRINCE WEST, Jr., aged 42. [8/18]
July 29, Starks, Herkimer Co., WILLIAM HASKINS, aged 86. [8/18]
Aug. 21, 1828, Cooperstown, JACOB M. PLATNER, aged 53. [8/25]
Aug. 15, 1828, Decatur, Mrs. BOIS CHESBREW. [8/25]
Aug. 18, 1828, Decatur, DAVID BISHOP. [8/25]
Aug. 22, 1828, Cooperstown, Mrs. MARY WILLIAMS, aged 73. [8/25]
Aug. 22, 1828, Cooperstown, Mrs. LOUISEANNA PETTE, aged 64. [8/25]
Aug. 22, 1828, Springfield, N.Y., Mrs. ANN ROBINSON, aged 50. [9/1]
Aug. 21, 1828, Laurens, SALLY ANN HOAG, aged 20. [9/1]
Aug. 23, 1828, Springfield, N.Y., Mrs. ELIZABETH OLIVER, aged 71. [9/1]
Aug. 24, 1828, New York City, Rev. HENRY J. FELTUS, aged 53. [9/1]
[No date] Colesville, Broome Co., Mrs. SALLY HAYES, aged 50, formerly of Unadilla, N.Y. [9/1]
Aug. 27, 1828, Middlefield, JOSEPH L., son of ALVA S. CRAFTS, aged 4 years, 8 months. [9/8]

Sept. 9, 1828, Cooperstown, Capt. RALPH WORTHINGTON, aged 50. [9/15]
Sept. 10, 1828, N.Y. City, AUGUSTUS H. LAWRENCE, aged 58. [9/15]
[No date] Rome, N.Y., WM. HAWLEY, aged 31. [9/15/1828]
[No date] Sangerfield, Mrs. RUTH WELLS, aged 88. [9/15/1828]
Sept. 4, 1828, Laurens, Mrs. SARAH HOAG, aged 45. [9/15]
Aug. 21, 1828, Laurens, SARAH ANN HOAG, aged 20. [9/15]
Sept. 10, 1828, Laurens, THOMAS HOAG, aged 18. [9/15]
Sept. 11, Unadilla Forks, DELEVAN, son of Capt. CALEB BROWN, aged 11 months. [9/22]
Sept. 8, 1828, Bridgewater, N.Y., ELIJAH W. STEELE, aged 60. [9/22]
Sept. 29, 1828, Hartwick, HEMAN WEST, aged 52. [9/22]
Sept. 17, 1828, Caughnawage, N.Y., Gen. HENRY FONDA, aged 63. [9/22]
Sept. 20, 1828, Rochester, N.Y., ISRAEL CLARK, aged 39, formerly of Cooperstown. [9/22]
Sept. 30, 1828, Oaksville, JULIA ANN ALDEN, aged 15. [10/13]
Oct. 1, 1828, Edmeston, Mrs. POLLY WALDO, aged 38. [10/13]
Sept. 20, 1828, Rochester, N.Y., ISRAEL CLARK, aged 39, formerly of Cooperstown. (repeated) [10/13]
Oct. 2, 1828, Lebanon, N.Y., Maj. PETER KEAN of Elizabethtown, N.J. [10/13]
Oct. 10, 1828, Milford, JOSEPH RICE, aged 40. [10/13]
Oct. 3, Garratsville, SEYMOUR COBURN, 21 years old. [10/13]
Oct. 28, 1828, Hartwick, JAMES S., son of WILLIAM BURLINGTON, aged 7. [11/10]
Nov. 3, 1828, Middlefield, MOSES GRAVES, aged 93. [11/10]
Nov. 14, 1828, Springfield, SAMUEL HUTCHINS, aged 58. [11/24]
Nov. 20, Hartwick, RUSSELL BARTLETT, aged 75, formerly of Cooperstown. [11/24]
Nov. 14, 1828, Claverack, HENRY LIVINGSTON, Esq. [11/24]
Nov. 13, 1828, Hudson, N.Y., WILLIAM E. NORMAN, aged 51. [11/24]
Nov. 23, 1828, Worcester, N.Y., Mrs. CLARISSA CHASE. [12/1]
Nov. 28, 1828, Oxford, N.Y., Maj. SAMUEL LYON, aged 67. [12/8]
Nov. 27, 1828, Cherry Valley, JOHN LOWCOCK, aged 58, native of England. [12/8]
Nov. 28, 1828, Decatur, DAVID TRIPP, aged 61. [12/8]
Dec. 4, 1828, Otsego, SOPHIA B. WARREN, aged 32. [12/8]
Dec. 5, 1828, New York City, ASA FULLER of Little Falls, N.Y. [12/15]
Nov. 26, 1828, Wheeler, NY, Capt. SILAS WHEELER, aged 78. [12/15]
Dec. 15, 1828, Hartwick, Mrs. NAAMAH ELDRED, aged 68. [12/29]

Dec. 19, 1828, Hartwick, Mrs. ELIZABETH TUCKER, aged 67. [12/29]
Dec. --, 1828, Warren, Herkimer Co., Dea. JONATHAN BLOOMFIELD, 73 years. [12/29]
[No date] Mrs. RUTH BINGHAM, aged 25. [12/29]
[No date] THOMAS PADDOCK, aged 75. [12/29]
[No date] Mrs. MARY HARPER, aged 27. [12/29]
[No date] Exeter, N.Y., ANNA ROGERS, aged 78. [1/5/1829]
Jan. 2, 1829, Plainfield, RICHARD CAMPBELL, aged 26. [1/5]
Jan. 12, 1829, Cherry Valley, HANNAH ELIZABETH HENN, aged 17. [1/19]
Jan. 7, 1829, Hartwick, MINERVA ALGER, aged 16. [1/19]
Jan. 17, 1829, New York City, Mrs. HARRIET EDWARDS. [1/19]
Jan. 13, 1829, Cooperstown, JOHN J., son of ERASTUS SPARROWS, aged 5. [1/19]
Jan. 13, 1829, Springfield, Mrs. MEHITABLE AVERILL, aged 90, formerly of Pomfret, Conn. [1/26]
Dec. 27, 1828, Exeter, Mrs. LORINDA WATERMAN, aged 31. [1/26/1829]
Jan. 12, 1829, Little Falls, N.Y., JOHN NOE, late of Elizabethtown, N.J., aged 25. [1/26]
Jan. 21, 1829, Cooperstown, Mrs. MARY POTTER, aged 39. [2/2]
Jan. 22, 1829, Cherry Valley, NANCY DAVISON, aged 22. [2/2]
Jan. 31, 1829, New Lisbon, ABIGAIL WHITE, aged 34. [2/9]
Jan. 29, 1829, Salem, Mass., TIMOTHY PICKERING, aged 84. [2/9]
Dec. 8, 1828, Rio de Janerio, Midshipman CHARLES ROOT, son of Hon. ERASTUS ROOT of Delhi, N.Y., aged 20. [2/16/1829]
Feb. 10, 1829, Cherry Valley, WILLIAM COOK, aged 84. [2/16]
Feb. 10, 1829, Milford, HENRY SCOTT, Esq., aged 75. [2/16]
Jan. 26, 1829, Butternuts, CYRUS AMES, aged 84. [2/16]
Feb. 6, 1829, Kirkland, N.Y., JOSHUA MORSE, aged 78. [2/16]
Feb. 6, 1829, Plainfield, Mrs. BETTY COATS, aged 46. [2/16]
Feb. 14, 1829, Cooperstown, JARED ALLEN, aged 76. [2/23]
Feb. 4, 1829, Bridgewater, Mrs. SALLY MONROE. [2/23]
Feb. 19, Albany, HENRY HOOGEKERK, aged 23. [2/23]
Feb. 21, Middlefield, Mrs. MARY CAMPBELL, aged 83. [3/2]
Feb. 23, Exeter, GEORGE HERKIMER, aged 65. [3/2]
[No date] near the City of Mexico, DANIEL PATCHEN, formerly of Otsego Co. [3/2/1829]
Feb. 11, 1829, Geneva, Rev. HENRY AXTELL, D.D., aged 56. [3/2]
Feb. 14, 1829, Geneva, REBECCA AXTELL, aged 30. [3/2]

March 4, 1829, Duanesburgh, N.Y., GIDEON HOLLIDAY, Esq., aged 54. [3/9]
Feb. 27, 1829, Canajoharie, N.Y., Rev. J. P. GERRTNER. [3/9]
Jan. 31, 1829, Plainfield, FRANCIS SMITH, aged 21. [3/16]
[No date] Bridgewater, N.Y., DANIEL RINGE, aged 68. [3/16]
March 4, 1829, Richfield, MOSES L., son of Col. JOHN DERTHICK. [3/16]
Feb. 26, 1829, Springfield, HENRY DAVY, Sr., aged 54 years. Frozen to death. [3/16]
March 12, 1829, Springfield, JEREMIAH THURSTON, aged 34. [3/23]
Feb. 20, 1829, Milford, Mrs. RUTH MUMFORD, aged 60. [3/23]
Feb. 25, 1829, Burlington, JEREMIAH MEACHAM, aged 71. [3/23]
March 15, 1829, Cherry Valley, JOHN J. ROSEBOOM, aged 54. [3/23]
March 26, 1829, Burlington, ENOCH MACK, aged 27. [3/30]
March 25, Cherry Valley, Mrs. MARGARET CLYDE, aged 45. [4/6]
Feb. 24, 1829, Harpersfield, N.Y., ERASTUS ROOT, M.D., aged 44. [4/6]
March 30, 1829, New Lisbon, RICHARD EMERSON, aged 58. [4/6]
March 22, 1829, Cooperstown, JACOB MANN, Esq., aged 75. [4/6]
April 2, 1829, Otego, BENJAMIN HOWE, aged 84. [4/20]
April 2, 1829, Otego, Mrs. MARY WEAVER, aged 94. [4/20]
March 29, 1829, Ogdensburgh, Hon. NATHAN FORD, aged 65. [4/13]
April 2, 1829, Otego, Mrs. MARY NEFF, aged 43. [4/20]
April 5, 1829, Hartwick, LYDIA YOUNG, aged 51. [4/20]
April 15, 1829, Otsego, Mrs. SARAH WALBY, aged 65. [4/20]
April 6, 1829, Albany, STEWART LEWIS, aged 54. [4/20]
April 12, 1829, Schenectady, Mrs. HARRIET S. COOKE. [4/20]
[No date] Delhi, N.Y., GEORGE SHERWOOD, aged 41. [4/20]
March 29, Adam[s], Jefferson County, EDWARD SALISBURY, aged 103. [4/20]
April 18, 1829, Mt. Upton, GEORGE FENNO, Esq. [4/27]
April 18, 1829, Burlington, MANASSAH BLOSS, aged 69. [4/27]
April 23, 1829, Milford, Mrs. MARGARET HARPER, aged 90. [4/27]
April 20, 1829, Burlington, WILLIAM CLARKE, aged 33. [4/27]
April 20, 1829, Hartwick, Mrs. ABIGAIL COOK, aged 77. [5/4]
April 23, 1829, Chenango Pt., N.Y., Mrs. OLIVE HUSE, late of Ruchfield. [5/4]
April 12, 1829, New Lisbon, OLIVER M. MATHER, aged 83. [5/4]
April 25, 1829, Hartwick, RHODES FRY, aged 75. [5/4]
May 8, 1829, Exeter, GRIFFITH HUBBARD, aged 53. [5/11]
May 1, 1829, Springfield, Mrs. MARY WALBY, aged 35. [5/11]

May 2, 1829, Herkimer, MELCHORT FOLTS, Esq., aged 83. [5/11]
April 23, 1829, Otego, JONATHAN WEAVER, aged 83. [5/11]
May 6, 1829, Cherry Valley, HENRY BUSH, aged 54. [5/18]
May 10, 1829, Stark, Herkimer Co., Mrs. ELEANOR SAWIN, aged 37. [5/25]
May 23, 1829, Cooperstown, WILLIAM WELBY, aged 42. [5/25]
May 18, 1829, Laurens, Mrs. THANKFUL IRENE SLEEPER, aged 57. [5/25]
May 25, 1829, Milford, OLIVE WELLS RUSSELL, aged 7. [6/8]
June 6, 1829, New Hartford, N.Y., Hon. JEDEDIAH SANGER, aged 79. [6/15]
June 1, 1829, Duanesburgh, Mrs. ANNA HERRICK, aged 88. [6/15]
June 17, 1829, ELIZABETH S. LIVINGSTON of Clermont. [6/22]
June 20, Hartwick, HIRAM W. HALE, aged 30. [6/22]
June 4, 1829, Athens, N.Y., CALEB COFFIN, aged 51. [6/22]
June 10, 1829, Utica, JOHN H. LOTHROP, Esq., 59 years. [6/22]
June 7, 1829, Unadilla Forks, N.Y., Mrs. LUCINDA MAXSON, aged 40. [6/22]
June 28, 1829, Cooperstown, Mrs. ELIZA J. FOOTE, aged 35. [7/6]
May 24, 1829, Burlington, CATO FREEDOM, aged 80. [7/6]
July 15, 1829, Cooperstown, CATHERINE BLACQUE, infant dau. of ELISHA FOOTE, Esq., aged 3 months. [7/20]
July 18, 1829, Cooperstown, Mrs. MARY CURTISS, aged 28. [7/20]
July 15, 1829, Milford, AMASA WHEELER, aged 9. [7/20]
July 11, 1829, Warren, N.Y., WILLIAM AVERILL, aged 74. [7/20]
July 4, 1829, Springfield, Mrs. MARY ANN COOK, aged 28. [7/20]
July 15, 1829, New Lisbon, LOUISA NOBLE, aged 20. [7/27]
July 20, 1829, Rochester, ELISHA TAYLOR, aged 43. Late of Cooperstown. [7/27]
July 7, 1829, Norway, Herkimer Co., SETH SMITH, aged 94. [7/27]
July 15, 1829, Richfield, Mrs. LUCINDA HOWES, aged 47. [8/3]
July 16, 1829, Butternuts, MORRIS GOFF, aged 34. [8/3]
Aug. 7, 1829, Worcester, Mrs. FREELOVE WARNER. [8/17]
Aug. 20, 1829, Otsego, DARIUS WARREN, aged 69. [8/24]
Aug. 11, 1829, Middlefield, WM. L. BLAIR, aged 21. [8/24]
Aug. 29, Cooperstown, Col. AUGUSTUS RODGERS, aged 35. [8/31]
Aug. 23, 1829, Schoharie, LEMUEL CUTHBERT, aged 27. [8/31]
Aug. 10, 1829, Mt. Pleasant, N.Y., ROWETTA HENRY, late of Utica. [8/31]
Aug. 9, 1829, Claverack, N.Y., STEPHEN STORM, Esq., aged 80. [8/31]
Aug. 29, 1829, Cooperstown, ELIZABETH ASHLEY, aged 73. [9/7]

Aug. 20, 1829, Unadilla Forks, N.Y., Mrs. LUCY CLARKE, aged 27. [9/7]
Aug. 26, 1829, Canajoharie, WILLIAM BROWNELL, aged 37. [9/7]
Sept. 2, 1829, Richfield, Mrs. NANCY DOW, aged 64. [9/7]
Aug. 31, 1829, Hartwick, CAROLINE CASE, aged 3. [9/14]
Sept. 6, 1829, N.Y. City, Rev. MATHIAS BRUEN. [9/14]
Sept. 7, 1829, Mrs. WILLIAM VAN NESS. [9/14]
Sept. 16, 1829, Otsego, Mrs. ELIZABETH ALLEN, aged 69. [9/21]
Sept. 18, 1829, Otsego, Mr. THEODORUS ALLEN, aged 47. [9/21]
Sept. 12, 1829, Cherry Valley, Col. JAMES CANNON, aged 78. [9/21]
Aug. 6, 1829, Trenton, N.Y., Dr. FRANCIS ADRIAN VAN DER KEMP (Hibernicus called Dr. VAN DER KEMP "The most carried man in America.") [9/21]
Sept. 24, 1829, Cooperstown, PHILIP CORY, aged 22. [9/28]
Sept. 13, 1829, Huntsville, N.Y., Dr. WM. BENEDICT, aged 30. [9/28]
Sept. 5, 1829, Chazy, N.Y., Hon. ROSWELL HOPKINS, aged 73. [9/28]
Sept. 17, 1829, N.Y. City, RICHARD GRANT, Jr., aged 31. [9/28]
Sept. 13, 1829, Butternuts, Capt. THOMAS P. DIXSON. [10/5]
Sept. 14, 1829, Limington, LAZARUS HOWE, aged 104. [10/5]
Oct. 2, 1829, Norwich, Conn., Mrs. LYDIA ANN COLLIER, aged 20, late of Chanango Pt., N.Y. [10/12]
Oct. 14, 1829, Burlington, ALPHA MILLER, aged 34. [10/19]
Oct. 21, 1829, Hartwick, Mrs. MARGARET MILLER, aged 71. [11/2]
Oct. 12, 1829, Springfield, MOSES P. GRACES, aged 19. [11/2]
Oct. 29, 1829, Hartwick, Mrs. POLLY BREWER. [11/2]
Oct. 26, 1829, Springfield, JOSHUA RANSOM, Esq., aged 87. [11/2]
Oct. 18, 1829, Laurens, DANIEL FELLOWS, Esq., aged 40. [11/2]
Nov. 3, 1829, Schoharie, PETER SWART, aged 77. [11/2]
Nov. 8, 1829, Richfield, Mrs. MARY VEBBER, aged 25. [11/23]
Nov. 16, 1829, Burlington, Mrs. ESTHER TIFFANY, aged 65. [11/23]
Nov. 16, 1829, Burlington, infant dau. of NATHANIEL K. SMITH. [11/23]
Nov. 18, 1829, Clinton, N.Y., NOBLE MORSE, aged 40. [11/30]
Nov. 21, 1829, Middlefield, WILLIAM FRANKLIN EATON, aged 1 year, 4 months. [11/30]
Nov. 22, 1829, Otsego, AUSTIN SAVAGE, aged 32. [11/30]
Nov. 15, 1829, Savannah, Ga., ALONZO W. KINSLEY of Albany. [11/30]
Nov. 28, 1829, Laurens, JOHN A. OTIS, Esq., aged 34. [11/30]
Dec. 7, 1829, Edmeston, CHARLES BATES, aged 47. [12/14]
Dec. 5, 1829, Burlington, CHARLES MATHER, aged 27. [12/14]
Dec. 9, 1829, Burlington, Mrs. MAHITABLE RITTER, aged 48. [12/14]

Sept. 10, 1829, Natchez, Miss., ALANSON WILCOX, aged 30. [12/14]
Dec. 17, 1829, Otsego, DANIEL EDDY, aged 28. [12/21]
Dec. --, 1829, Otsego, WILLIAM WOLCOTT, aged 90. [12/28]
Dec. 25, 1829, Edmeston, ADALINE MAYNARD, age 25. [1/4/1830]
Dec. 30, 1829, Cooperstown, infant dau. of Dr. JOHN INGRAHAM. [1/4/1830]
Dec. 27, 1829, N.Y. City, Rev. JOHN M. MASON, aged 60. [1/4/1830]
Dec. 25, 1829, Carlton, N.Y., Capt. HENRY BOWNE, age 78. [1/4/1830]
Jan. 7, 1830, New Berlin, JEREMY GOODRICH, aged 60. [1/11]
[No date] Delhi, N.Y., Hon. EBENEZER FOOTE, age 75. [1/11/1830]
[No date] Henderson, N.Y., Mrs. MARY M'CUMBER. [1/11/ 1830]
[No date] Otsego, ELIZA JANE NOWLIN, aged 4. [1/25/1830]
Jan. 9, 1830, Burlington, Mrs. HANNAH POPE, aged 88, native of Sterling, Conn. [1/25]
Jan. 30, 1830, Burlington, ALFRED D. BLAKEMAN, 9 years. [2/8]
Jan. 20, 1830, Decatur, Mrs. LYDIA S. HOUCK, aged 21. [2/8]
Feb. 3, 1830, Springfield, Mrs. SARAH HOLT, aged 68. [2/8]
March 31, [1830?] Cherry Valley, Mrs. SABRINA CAMPBELL, aged 53.
Feb. 17, 1830, Burlington, WILLIAM ANGELL, 88 years. [2/22]
Jan. 28, 1830, Richfield, a son of WM. HANNAHS, aged 4. [2/22]
Feb. 7, 1830, Richfield, a dau. of WM. HANNAHS, aged 16 months. [2/22]
Feb. 11, 1830, Hartwick, Mrs. HURD, aged 70. [2/22]
Feb. 18, 1830, Middlefield, Mrs. DUNHAM, aged 90. [2/22]
Feb. 19, 1830, Milford, ALEXANDER M'COLLONS, aged 91. [3/1]
Feb. 12, 1830, Oswego, CHARLES PUMPELLY, Jr., 25 years. [3/1]
FEb. 13, 1830, Buffalo, Mrs. MARY SALISBURY, aged 43. [3/1]
Feb. 28, 1830, Sherburne, HARMON BROWN of New Lisbon, aged 19. [3/8]
[No date] Edmeston, Major COLEGROVE, 71 years. [3/8]
Feb. 26, 1830, New Lisbon, Capt. ISAAC GARDNER, 57 years. [3/8]
Feb. 18, 1830, Farmersville, N.Y., Mrs. NANCY HENRY, formerly of Richfield, 89 years. [3/8]
Feb. 26, 1830, Sidney, N.Y., STEPHEN BRADLEY, 72 years. [3/15]
[No date] Middlefield, REUBEN M'COLLOM, 55 years. [3/15]
Feb. 25, 1830, Edmeston, Mrs. ANNA TEN BROECK, aged 71. [3/29]
April 1, 1830, Springfield, N.Y., Dea. JOHN YOUNG, 67. [4/5]
March 31, 1830, Laurens, JOSEPH H. SLEEPER, aged 65. [4/12]
April 8, 1830, Worcester, THOMAS FULLER, aged 75. [4/12]
March 22, 1830, Plainfield, SIMON YOUNG, 10 years. [4/12]
April 2, 1830, Plainfield, LOREN COWDERY, aged 34. [4/12]

April 1, 1830, Cherry Valley, CATHERINE STEWART, aged 11. [4/12]
April 12, 1830, New Lisbon, Mrs. ELIZABETH COPWELL, aged 79. [4/19]
April 6, 1830, Plainfield, N.Y., DENNIS YOUNGS, aged 39. [4/19]
April 15, 1830, Springfield, N.Y., GEORGIANA, dau. of GEORGE CLARKE. [4/19]
March 27, 1830, Sodus, N.Y., STEPHEN STONE, aged 24. [4/19]
April 1, 1830, Butternuts, ISABEL LUCINDA BARNES, aged 7. [4/19]
April 13, 1830, Butternuts, LUCY MIRANDA BARNES, aged 4, both [see above] daus. of WILLIAM BARNES [4/19]
April 19, 1830, Squoit [sic], N.Y., KIRTLAND GRIFFIN, Esq., 78 years. [4/26]
April 15, 1830, Whitesborough, N.Y., WILLIAM G. TRACY, Esq., aged 60. [4/26]
April 18, 1830, Norwich, FRANKLIN R. BOGUE, aged 5. [4/26]
April 7, 1830, Warren, Mrs. CHARLOTTE ALLEN, aged 26, late of East Windsor, Conn. [4/26]
April 22, 1830, Burlington, WM. CHURCH, Esq., aged 42. [4/26]
April 9, 1830, Richfield, EUNICE B. NORTON, aged 19. [5/3]
April 11, 1830, St. Louis, Mo., Dr. JACOB MILLINGTON, late of Herkimer County. [5/10]
May 3, 1830, Butternuts, Mrs. HANNAH GILBERT, aged 45. [5/10]
May 6, 1830, Cooperstown, HELEN ROWLINSON, aged 6. [5/17]
May 14, 1830, Cooperstown, DANIEL OLENDORF, Sr., aged 75. [5/17]
May 17, 1830, Cooperstown, Mrs. NANCY TIFFANY, 68 years. [5/24]
May --, 1830, Fishkill, JACOB VAN BUNSCHOTEN, aged 77. [5/24]
May 21, 1830, Butternuts, Mrs. AVALINE A. (dau. of THOS. PIER) DANIELSON, aged 25. [5/31]
May 27, 1830, Otsego, Mrs. CONTENT JARVIS, 33 years. [5/31]
May 20, 1830, Springfield, SAFRINUS BASINGER, aged 93. [6/14]
May 27, 1830, Middlefield, HAMMOND GRIFFIN of Westford. [6/14]
June 12, 1830, Binghamton, Mrs. ABIGAIL CUSHMAN, aged 53. [6/21]
June 13, 1830, Middlefield, Mrs. AMY CHAPPEL, aged 38. [6/28]
June 22, 1830, Mt. Upton, N.Y., OLIVER H. EVERETT, aged 48. [7/5]
June 23, 1830, New Berlin, Mrs. CLARISSA FIELD, formerly of Norwich, aged 25. [7/5]
June 26, 1830, Unadilla, ROSWELL WRIGHT, Esq., aged 45 years. [7/12]
July 10, 1830, Middlefield, JERUSHA TITUS, aged 35. [7/12]
July 5, 1830, New Lisbon, Mrs. CYNTHIA PERRY, aged 62. [7/12]
July 13, 1830, Middlefield, Mrs. RUBY SHIPMAN, 25 years. [7/19]

July 3, 1830, Durhamville, N.Y., Mrs. SARAH STILLMAN, aged 22. [7/19]

July 10, 1830, Otsego, Mrs. OLIVE PRESTON, aged 33. [7/19]

June 20, 1830, Danube, LUTHER, son of NICHOLAS LAWYER, aged 1. [7/19]

July 12, 1830, Panama, N.Y., Dr. ORRIN JOHNSON of Hartwick, aged 32. [7/26]

Aug. 4, 1830, Farmersville, N.Y., SAMUEL HENRY, aged 63, late of Richfield. [8/16]

Aug. 3, 1830, Exeter, JEREMIAH ROBINSON. [8/16]

Aug. 28, 1830, Westford, ELIJAH WILSON, 88 years. [9/6]

Aug. 31, 1830, Westford, DAVID WILLIAMS. [9/6]

Sept. 5, 1830, Otsego, WAYNE COLLINS BLISS, aged 19 months. [9/13]

Sept. 6, 1830, Cooperstown, Mrs. HARRIET B. STEWART, aged 32. [9/13]

Sept. 10, 1830, Exeter, HELEN, dau. of Dr. J. S. SPRAGUE, aged 1. [9/20]

Sept. 12, 1830, Otsego, Mrs. MARCIA MARIA MORRIS of Troy, aged 23. [9/20]

Sept. 30, 1830, Hartwick, HENRY WILLIAMS, aged 21. [10/11]

Sept. 28, 1830, Port Byron, N.Y., NATHAN BATES of Cooperstown, aged 50. [10/11]

Sept. 29, 1830, Butternuts, ESTHER ANN WHISTON, aged 20. [10/11]

Sept. 28, 1830, Utica, JASON PARKER, aged 67. [10/11]

Oct. 5, 1830, N.Y. City, JOHN NORTH, aged 29, late of Walton, Delaware Co., [10/11]

Oct. 7, 1830, Rome, N.Y., Mrs. ELIZABETH HURLBURT, aged 20. [10/18]

Oct. 18, 1830, Milford, DANIEL FRENCH, aged 59. [10/25]

Oct. 26, 1830, Hartwick, Capt. CLEMENT MILLER, aged 76. [11/1]

Oct. 31, 1830, Exeter, Mrs. ARMINDA CLARK, aged 61. [11/8]

Nov. 20, 1830, Cooperstown, JOHN, son of LEVI H. PIERCE, aged 2. [11/29]

Nov. 11, 1830, Plainfield, MARY Y. BASINGER, aged 16. [11/29]

Nov. 20, 1830, Watertown, N.Y., Mrs. ALIDA BOARDMAN, aged 28. [11/29]

Nov. 28, 1830, Little Falls, CHARLES W. BABCOCK, formerly of Otsego, aged 25. [11/29]

Nov. --, 1830, LUTHER HARTWELL, aged 35. [11/29]

Nov. 29, 1830, Cooperstown, JOHN FREDERICK ERNST, aged 52. [12/6]

Nov. 25, 1830, New Lisbon, JAMES H. DAVIS, son of SOLOMON DAVIS, Esq., aged 3 1/2 years. [12/6]
Nov. 29, 1830, Burlington, HENRY FITCH, Jr., aged 33. [12/13]
Dec. 13, 1830, Springfield, Mrs. ANN CARY, aged 73. [12/27]
Jan. 17, 1831, Middlefield, Mrs. SARAH TEMPLE, aged 82. [1/29]
Jan. 24, 1831, Cooperstown, HORATIO G. JOHNSON, aged 53. [1/31]
Jan. 27, 1831, Middlefield, Mrs. SARAH INGALLS, aged 70. [1/31]
Jan. 27, 1831, Exeter, REUBEN SMITH, aged 82. [2/7]
Feb. 1, 1831, Maryland, N.Y., SALLY S. WITT, aged 28. [2/7]
Feb. 2, 1831, Hartwick, Mrs. MARY CHASE, aged 56. [2/7]
Jan. 27, 1831, Kingston, N.Y., HARRIET S. PARDEE, formerly of Richfield, aged 14. [2/7]
Feb. 5, 1831, Butternuts, Dea. DAN. SEYMOUR, 71 years. [2/14]
Feb. 4, 1831, Cherry Valley, Rev. EPHRAIM HALL, aged 32. [2/14]
Feb. 17, 1831, Cooperstown, CHARLES CHAPMAN, aged 30, late of Auburn. [2/21]
Feb. 8, 1831, Plainfield, NATHANIEL HUSE SAXTON, aged 11. [2/21]
Feb. 15, 1831, Middlefield, HEZEKIAH WALKER, aged 85. [2/28]
Feb. 19, 1831, Kirkland, N.Y., ANN ELIZABETH LENT, aged 1 1/2 years. [3/7]
Feb. 24, 1831, DAVID HENRY [LENT], aged 3 years, 8 months. Children of DAVID LENT. [3/7]
Feb. 20, 1831, Springfield, Mrs. MARY WINSLOW, formerly of Conn., aged 82. [3/7]
Feb. 24, 1831, Exeter, Mrs. COMFORT ROBINSON, aged 66. [3/14]
Feb. 27, 1831, Oneonta, NIJAH GRIFFITH, aged 63. [3/14]
March 7, 1831, Worcester, SILAS CRIPPEN, Esq., aged 74. [3/21]
March 5, 1831, Canajoharie, JOHN TAYLOR, Esq., aged 35. [3/21]
March 11, 1831, Unadilla, JULIA SOPHIA, dau. of CURTIS NOBLE, aged 7. [3/21]
March 10, 1831, Springfield, LUCIA GATES, aged 26. [3/28]
March 28, 1831, Albany, PAUL CLARK, Esq., aged 67. [4/4]
March 19, 1831, Troy, Col. DERICK LANE, aged 76. [4/4]
March 27, 1831, Red Hook Landing, JOHN S., son of EDMUND ELEMDORF, aged 26, [4/4]
March 29, 1831, Garrattsville, DAN. WHEELER, 2 years. [4/18]
April 10, 1831, Hartwick, ISAAC BURCH, Jr., aged 19. [4/18]
April 4, 1831, Edmeston, Mrs. MARY DE FOREST, aged 67. [4/18]
April 7, 1831, Hartwick, CHESTER KENYON, aged 31. [4/25]
April 18, 1831, Westford, Mrs. SUSANNA WITT, 45 years. [4/25]

April 13, 1831, Garrattsville, CHARLOTTE, dau. of G.W.P. WHEELER, 6 months. [5/2]
May 10, 1831, Cooperstown, EZRA CRANE, aged 74. [5/16]
May 13, 1831, Milford, ADON W. BATES, aged 18. [5/23]
May 24, 1831, Rochester, Col. NATHANIEL ROCHESTER, aged 80. [5/30]
May 29, 1831, Oriskany, N.Y., Col. GARRIT G. LANSING, aged 71. [6/6]
May 26, 1831, Maryland, [N.Y.], Mrs. MARGARET WALLING, aged 23. [6/13]
June 1, 1831, Salisbury, Herkimer Co., ELIZA GRAHAM of Hopeville, Otsego Co., aged 17. [6/13]
June 5, 1831, Cooperstown, FRANCIS LYNDE SABIN, aged 2. [6/13]
June 20, 1831, Plainfield, Dr. HENRY DEWEY of Oswego, aged 31. [6/27]
June 13, 1831, Otsego, KING BINGHAM, aged 45. [6/27]
June 30, 1831, Cooperstown, JUSTUS CRANDALL, aged 36. [7/4]
June 29, 1831, Albany, PHILIP S. PARKER, Esq., aged 55. [7/11]
June 11, 1831, Westford, JAMES B. ROE, aged 75. [7/11]
June 23, 1831, Milford, GEORGE BISSELL, aged 26. [7/11]
July 8, 1831, Middlefield, Mrs. PATTY BURKE, aged 56. [7/11]
July 13, 1831, Otsego, GEORGE PIER, aged 37. [7/18]
July 17, 1831, Brookfield, N.Y., CHARLES O. MUNSON, aged 33. [7/25]
July 18, 1831, Springfield, WM. L. TRACY, aged 1 year, 7 months. [8/1]
July 18, 1831, Phelps, N.Y., Mrs. SALLY BENNETT, aged 34. [8/1]
July 20, 1831, New Brunswick, N.J., Mrs. CORNELIA G. KIRKLAND of Utica. [8/1]
July 25, 1831, Hartwick, Capt. ZACHARIAH W. STICKLES, aged 76. [8/8]
July 23, 1831, Springfield, DANIEL MORSE (Dea.), aged 80. [8/8]
Aug. 1, 1831, Utica, MARY E. BENJAMIN, aged 19. [8/8]
Aug. 11, 1831, Gilbertsville, CYNTHIA ANN LUCE, 14 months. [8/15]
Aug. 9, 1831, Exeter, Mrs. ANNA HERKIMER, aged 26 years. [8/15]
Aug. 5, 1831, Schenectady, GEORGE RITCHIE. [8/15]
Aug. 9, 1831, Cherry Valley, MARY HUDSON, aged 36. [8/22]
Aug. 16, 1831, Cooperstown, THEODORE GRAVES, 13 months. [8/22]
Aug. 3, 1831, Canandaigua, BENJAMIN F. DAY, aged 25. [8/22]
Aug. 16, 1831, Ritchfield, JOHN H. ANDRUS, aged 13. [8/22]
Aug. 16, 1831, Whitesborough, N.Y., Mrs. CAROLINE MORRISON. [8/29]
Aug. 27, 1831, Utica, JAMES S. KING, Esq., aged 65. [9/5]

Aug. 20, 1831, Palatine, N.Y., HENRY MARKELL, Esq., aged 30. [9/5]
Aug. 19, 1831, Little Falls, Mrs. FEETER, aged 60. [9/5]
Aug. 30, 1831, Unadilla, Mrs. ELIZA HOUGH, aged 32. [9/12]
[No date] Solon, Cortland Co., Mrs. HARRIET CONVERSE, aged 40. [9/12/1831]
Sept. 9, 1831, Cherry Valley, MORGAN LEWIS BEARDSLEY, aged 26. [9/19]
Sept. 23, 1831, Oxford, N.Y., Mrs. FRANCES M. F. FARMER, formerly of Hartwick. [9/26]
Sept. 22, 1831, Richfield, JOHN PRINGLE, aged 74. [10/3]
Sept. 24, 1831, Oneonta, JACOB DIETZ, Esq., aged 41. [10/3]
Oct. 2, 1831, Hartford, Conn., THOMAS CHESTER, Esq., aged 68. [10/10]
Oct. 4, 1831, Rensselaerville, ASA COLVARD, Esq., aged 64. [10/10]
Oct. 16, New Berlin, NATHAN BEARDSLEY, Esq. [10/24]
Oct. 15, 1831, Burlington, DANIEL DAWLEY, aged 60. [10/24]
Oct. 25, 1831, Cooperstown, JOHN MOLTHER, aged 68. [10/31]
Oct. 14, 1831, Otego, SAMUEL HYATT, aged 73. [11/7]
Nov. 8, 1831, Milford, Mrs. SCOTT. [11/14]
Nov. 21 1831, Schenectady, GEORGE SHEPARD, Esq., late of Butternuts, aged 56. [11/28]
Dec. 5, 1831, Burlington, Mrs. ANNA NICKERSON, aged 42. [12/12]
Dec. 2, 1831, Albany, Maj. Gen. JOHN STILWELL, aged 52. [12/12]
Dec. 14, 1831, Richfield, JOHN WYMAN, aged 41. [12/19]
Dec. 10, 1831, Troy, JOHN CONVERSE. [12/19]
Dec. 17, 1831, Cooperstown, Mrs. SALLY OSBORN, aged 59. [12/26]
Dec. 10, 1831, Westerlo, N.Y., THOMAS SMITH, Esq., aged 59. [12/26]
Dec. 29, 1831, Otsego, JAMES ALLEN, aged 65. [1/2/1832]
Dec. 8, 1831, Exeter, LEVI CASWELL, aged 53. [1/2/1832]
Dec. 12, 1831, SETH HUBBARD, aged 75. [1/2/1832]
Dec. 27, 1831, Middlefield, Mrs. OLIVER CORY. [1/2/1832]
Dec. 13, 1831, Cayuga, THOS. MUMFORD, Esq., aged 61. [1/2/1832]
Dec. 25, 1831, Cooperstown, DAVID FLING, aged 58. [1/2/1832]
Jan. 2, 1832, Hartwick, WALTER CRAFTS, aged 3. [1/9]
Dec. 31, 1831, Worcester, Mrs. RHODA BIGELOW, aged 60. [1/9/1832]
Jan. 4, 1832, Brunswick, N.Y., AUGUSTA ADELINE SINDERLING, aged 5. [1/16]
Dec. 31, 1831, Richfield, ABRAHAM LIGHTALL, aged 93. [1/16/1832]
Jan. 18, 1832, Otsego, Mrs. BARTHENA DOUBLEDAY, aged 69. [1/23]
Dec. 5, 1831, state of Kentucky, MORRISON D. WILCOX, late of Otsego, aged 38. [1/23/1832]

Dec. 30, 1831, Beekmantown, N.Y., Hon. THOS. TREDWELL, aged 88. [1/23/1832]
Jan. 20, 1832, New Lisbon, STEPHEN ABBEY, Esq., aged 60. [1/23]
Jan. 16, 1832, Springfield, JAMES SCHOFIELD, aged 65. [2/6]
Feb. 8, 1832, Cooperstown, Mrs. SARAH BRADFORD, aged 96. [2/13]
Feb. 5, 1832, Richfield, ALONZO HYDE, aged 23; late of Jamestown, N.Y. [2/13]
Oct. 1, 1831, Paris, France, WM. COOPER, son of the late WM. COOPER, Esq. of Cooperstown, aged 22. [2/20/1832]
March 1, 1832, Burlington, COLLINS FITCH, aged 8. [3/12]
March 4, 1832, Otsego, LUCY ALLEN, aged 35. [3/19]
March 13, 1832, Otsego, JARED ALLEN, aged 45. [3/19]
Feb. 27, 1832, Ellisburgh, N.Y., WM. W. WALKER, Jr., late of Plainfield, aged 29. [3/19]
March 21, 1832, Middlefield, PHEBE DAVISON, aged 10. [3/26]
March 25, 1832, Otsego, JOHN RUSSELL, aged 75. [4/2]
March 20, 1832, Otsego, Mrs. AMOS BABCOCK, aged 78. [4/2]
April 2, 1832, Albany, Mrs. EMELINE JONES, late of Richfield, aged 26. [4/9]
April 9, 1832, Burlington, LEVI THOMPSON, Esq., aged 83. [4/16]
March 15, 1832, Philadelphia, ALFRED T. BISHOP, late of Cooperstown, aged 27. [4/16]
April 14, Cooperstown, CATHERINE FRANCES, infant dau. of Dr. J. HANNAH of Milford. [4/23]
March 29, Pittsfield, JOSEPH BRIGGS, Esq., aged 83. [4/23]
April 25, 1832, Otsego, Mrs. LUCY WATERMAN, aged 21. [4/30]
April 24, 1832, Otsego, Mrs. POLLY PIER, aged 39. [4/30]
April 23, 1832, N.Y., Mrs. CATHERINE MARIA CLARK, aged 36. [4/30]
April 17, 1832, Brighton, Monroe Co., HENRY C. THORP, late of Cooperstown, aged 22. [5/7]
April 23, 1832, Cooperstown, Mrs. SOPHIA PECK, aged 62. [5/7]
May 2, 1832, New Lisbon, ALBERT BENNETT, aged 26. [5/14]
May 1, 1832, Delaware Co., Col. JOHN EELLS, aged 77. [5/14]
May 23, 1832, Cooperstown, ELIZA MATILDA, dau. of DUDLEY ADAMS, aged 16 months. [5/28]
May 26, 1832, Otsego, AUGUSTA MARIA POTTER, aged 30. [6/4]
May 28, 1832, Springfield, JOHN GUSTIN, aged 41. [6/4]
May 7, 1832, Columbia, N.Y., Mrs. ISAAC JONES, aged 40. [6/4]
June 3, 1832, Exeter, Dr. JOSEPH WHITE of Cherry Valley, aged 69. [6/11]
June 12, 1832, Richfield, Mrs. LUCY VAUGHN, aged 62. [6/18]

June 1, 1832, Hebron, Conn., DANIEL BROWN, aged 86, late of
   Cooperstown. [6/18]
June 23, 1832, Worcester, Mrs. SUSANNAH GOTT, aged 45. [7/2]
June 24, 1832, Pittsfield, CHAUNCEY WORDING, aged 20. [7/2]
June 27, 1832, Middlefield, MORGAN H. RICE, aged 25. [7/9]
June 23, 1832, Bridgewater, JAMES L. FOX. [7/9]
June 30, 1832, New Berlin, Mrs. SALLY ROSS, aged 34. [7/9]
July 11, 1832, Utica, OLIVER PEABODY, aged 26, late of Otsego. [7/16]
July 20, 1832, Cooperstown, infant son of STEPHEN GREGORY. [7/23]
July 3, 1832, Maryland, Mrs. CORNELIA SLINGERLAND, age 66. [7/23]
July 31, 1832, Middlefield, Mrs. SARAH BABCOCK. [8/6]
July 25, 1832, Cooperstown, DAVID PEABODY, 69 years. [8/6]
July 24, 1832, Otsego, ABEL CLARK, age 66. [8/13]
Aug. 3, 1832, Springfield, Mrs. CAROLINE GREEN, aged 25. [8/13]
July 30, 1832, New Brunswick, N.J., Rt. Rev. JOHN CROSS, 70 years.
   [8/13]
Aug. 10, 1832, Middlefield, Mrs. VIOLET REYNOLDS, aged 52. [8/20]
Aug. 15, 1832, Stanbury, Erie Co., ABEL ENGLISH, aged 80. [9/3]
Aug. 29, Otsego, JAMES LATHROP, Esq., aged 69. [9/3]
Aug. 30, 1832, Cooperstown, SAMUEL HENRY NELSON, infant. [9/3]
Aug. 30, 1832, Richfield, EZRA CARY, aged 48. [9/10]
Aug. 30, 1832, Utica, CHESTER A. GRISWOLD, aged 24. [9/10]
Sept. 2, 1832, Selina, Dr. WM. KIRKPATRICK. [9/10]
Sept. 1, 1832, New York, Hon. WM. H. MAYNARD of Utica. [9/10]
Sept. 8, 1832, Hartwick, WILLIAM DILLINGHAM, aged 72. [9/10]
[No date] Burlington, ELI TIFFANY, aged 27. [9/24]
Sept. 26, 1832, Middlefield, DARIUS MASON, aged 67. [10/1]
Sept. 28, 1832, Cooperstown, FREDERICK, infant son of ORRIN SABIN.
   [10/1]
Oct. 3, 1832, Westford, EBBEN S. ABBOTT, 30 years. [10/8]
Sept. 27, 1832, Milford, Mrs. ELIZABETH FRENCH. [10/8]
Sept. 26, 1832, Lockport, Mrs. LAURA HOWARD, late of Utica, aged 34.
   [10/15]
Sept. 14, 1832, Burlington, ELI TIFFANY, aged 27. [10/15]
Nov. 1, 1832, Springfield, GOLDSBORO COOPER, aged 26. [11/5]
Oct. 21, 1832, Maryland, Mrs. EUNICE WATERS, aged 27. [11/12]
Nov. 4, 1832, Otsego, Mrs. JANE MC KEEN, aged 74. [11/12]
Nov. 13, 1832, Butternuts, CATHERINE FRANCHOT, aged 23. [11/19]
Nov. 17, 1832, Springfield, Dr. DAVID LITTLE, aged 70. [11/19]
Nov. 17, 1832, Springfield, JAMES RICHARDSON, aged 70. [11/19]

Nov. 19, 1832, Cooperstown, JOB COFFIN of Hudson, N.Y., aged 77. [11/26]
Nov. 28, 1832, Otsego, EUNICE KNOWLTON, aged 15. [12/3]
Nov. 17, 1832, Oxford, N.Y., Mrs. JULIA CLAPP, aged 38. [12/3]
Nov. 25, 1832, Delhi, Delaware Co., JOHN DAY DOWNS, late of Havanna, Tioga Co. [12/10]
Dec. 9, 1832, Burlington, Mrs. EMERANDA M. SHELDON VAUGHN, aged 27. [12/17]
Nov. 14, 1832, Greenfield, Pa., Mrs. MARY SHERMAN, late of Otsego, aged 50. [12/17]
Dec. 17, 1832, Hartwick, JOSEPH D. HUSBANDS, Esq., aged 56. [12/24]
Dec. 7, 1832, New Berlin, BARTHOLOMEW COATS, aged 44. [12/24]
Dec. 24, 1832, Burlington, BENJAMIN CUSHMAN, aged 80. [12/31]
Jan. 1, 1833, Hartwick, ANDREW MURDOCK, aged 29. [1/7]
Jan. 31, 1833, New Lisbon, ABIJAH VAIL, aged 64. [2/4]
Jan. 18, 1833, Bainbridge, Col. MOSES G. BENJAMIN. [2/4]
Jan. 25, 1833, Burlington, ENOCH E. PIERCE, aged 21. [2/4]
Feb. 7, 1833, Cooperstown, JANE OLENDORF, aged 4. [2/11]
[No date] Sidney Plains, Mrs. HANNAH REXFORD, aged 24. [2/18/1833]
Feb. 11, 1833, Worcester, Mrs. MARY ATHERTON, aged 83. [2/18]
Feb. 14, 1833, Burlington, CLYDE, infant son of JOSEPH BLANCHARD. [2/18]
Feb. 16, 1833, Jamestown, N.Y., NATHANIEL HAWKS, Esq., formerly of Cherry Valley. [3/4]
Feb. 26, 1833, N.Y. City, Mrs. EMMA C. STROBLE, late of Hartwick, aged 25. [3/4]
March 15, 1833, Richfield Springs, ISAAC SEELYE, Esq., of Cherry Valley, aged 55. [3/18]
March 24, 1833, Springfield, Rev. ANDREW OLIVER, aged 71. [4/1]
March 30, 1833, Middlefield, ROBERT DAVIS, aged 54. [4/8]
April 14, 1833, Cooperstown, MARY WEBB GRACES, aged 6. [4/22]
April 10, 1833, Edmeston, CLARISSA A. RICHARDSON. [4/22]
March 28, 1833, Pittsfield, RUFUS BRIGGS, aged 71. [5/6]
March 28, 1833, New Lisbon, Mrs. POLLY DOWNING, aged 33. [5/6]
May 9, 1833, Hartwick, ALMIRA ELDRED, 8 years. [5/13]
May 28, 1833, Fairfield, Herkimer Co., Hon. SHERMAN WOOSTER, aged 53. [6/3]
May 23, 1833, Otego, Mrs. ANNA FAIRMAN, aged 79. [6/3]
May 31, 1833, Westford, Capt. DAVID ADAMS, aged 77. [6/10]

June 1, 1833, Hartwick, Mrs. ELIZABETH BENJAMIN. [6/10]
June 27, 1833, Richfield, CORNELIUS M. PAUL, aged 34. [7/1]
June 24, 1833, Hartwick, Mrs. HANNAH ADAMS, aged 73. [7/8]
July 4, 1833, Fort Plain, EZEKIEL THORNTON, aged 27. [7/8]
May 24, 1833, in the mid-west, Elder BARZILLAI H. MILES of Otsego, aged 36. (Asiatic Cholera) [7/15]
July 3, 1833, Springfield, LOUISA J. RATHBUN, aged 15. [7/15]
July 14, 1833, Hartwick, JOHN MURDOCK, aged 48. [7/22]
July 18, 1833, Burlington Flats, DELIA HARMONY, KILBOURN, [sic] aged 16. [7/22]
July 1, 1833, Butternuts, SETH B. ANDRUS, aged 31. [7/29]
July 19, 1833, Unadilla, MARY F. OGDEN, aged 16. [8/5]
July 22, 1833, New Lisbon, Mrs. OLIVE BALARD, aged 27. [8/5]
Aug. 1, 1833, Hartwick, EMMA DAVISON, aged 31. [8/5]
Aug. 1, 1833, Hartwick, Mrs. MARY AUSTICK, aged 47. [8/12]
Aug. 7, 1833, Cooperstown, infant son of Dr. FAULKNER, aged 15 months. [8/12]
Aug. 10, 1833, Plainfield, Col. DAN. LOOMIS, aged 75. [8/19]
Aug. 13, 1833, Plainfield, RICHARD COOK, aged 80. [8/19]
Aug. 9, 1833, Warren, ROSELIND SHAW, aged 12. [8/19]
Aug. 18, 1833, New Lisbon, Mrs. JOB HARRINGTON, aged 62. [8/26]
Aug. 23, 1833, Middlefield, Mrs. ELIAS PARSHALL, aged 35. [8/26]
Aug. 23, 1833, Richfield Springs, CHLOE ALLEN, aged 26. [9/2]
Aug. 24, 1833, Buffalo, WM. YOUNG STONE, aged 20, late of Otsego. [9/9]
Aug. 13, 1833, Plainfield, RICHARD COOK, aged 83. [9/9]
Sept. 2, 1833, Hartwick, ELEZER BLISS, aged 89. [9/9]
Sept. 1, 1833, Milford, ADAM DEITZ, aged 41. [9/9]
Sept. 6, 1833, Middlefield, JOHN G. RICE, aged 51. [9/16]
Sept. 8, 1833, Milford, HORACE M. CRANDALL, aged 19. [9/16]
Sept. 15, 1833, Hartwick, AARON BALDWIN, aged 84. [9/23]
Sept. 3, 1833, Montpelier, Vt., GEO. H. PRENTISS, Esq., son of Hon. SAM. PRENTISS, aged 28. [9/23]
Sept. 9, 1833, Havana, Tioga Co., HIRAM COOK, aged 31.
Sept. 26, 1833, Hartwick, Dr. JOHN DAVIS, aged 29. [9/30]
Sept. 22, 1833, Burlington, HIRAM POPPLE, aged 25. [9/30]
Oct. 2, 1833, Otsego, SAMUEL JOHNSON, aged 70. [10/7]
Sept. 23, 1833, Westford, ISAAC BROOKS, aged 23. [10/7]
Sept. 26, 1833, Harpersfield, Dr. STEPHEN FENN, aged 64. [10/21]
Oct. 19, 1833, Cooperstown, Mrs. JANE A. M. AVERELL, aged 28. [10/21]

Oct. 23, 1833, Hartwick, ORIMEL EDSON, aged 41. [10/28]
Oct. 23, 1833, Worcester, JAMES MC COLLUM, aged 37. [10/28]
Nov. 3, 1833, Cooperstown, ELLERY THAYER, aged 14. [11/11]
Nov. 14, Cooperstown, JOHN C. WOODWARD, aged 50. [11/18]
Nov. 14, 1833, Cooperstown, ORREN HOLMES, aged 16. [11/18]
Nov. 11, 1833, Otsego, Mrs. STEPHEN NORTH. [11/18]
Nov. 16, 1833, Fly Creek, JOHN BADGER, aged 60. [12/2]
Nov. 14, 1833, Norwich, Mrs. ALMIRA FARR, aged 26. [12/2]
Nov. 12, 1833, Decatur, HARRISON WESTON, aged 35. [12/2]
Nov. 15, 1833, Decatur, Mrs. HOYT, aged 87. [12/2]
Nov. 16, 1833, Decatur, Mrs. SARAH FERRIS, aged 93. [12/2]
Nov. 24, 1833, Decatur, ROBERT LUYSCOMB, aged 84. [12/2]
Dec. 3, 1833, Wolcott, WM. COMSTOCK, of Laurens, aged 63. [12/16]
Dec. 17, 1833, Laurens, MARY BROWN, aged 3, dau. of JOHN BROWN. [12/23]
Dec. 17, 1833, Pittsfield, OLIVE E. GREEN, aged 16. [12/30]
Jan. 1, 1834, Burlington, ZACHARIAH BUSH, aged 97. [1/13]
Jan. 6, 1834, Exeter, Mrs. CATHERINE RIDER, aged 30. [1/13]
Jan. 12, 1834, Harpersfield, ANN SCHOFIELD, aged 50. [1/20]
Jan. 13, 1834, Catskill, Mrs. ANN V. SMITH of Oswego, aged 24. [1/27]
Jan. 15, 1834, Otsego, JAMES MC KEAN, aged 34. [2/13]
Jan. 20, 1834, Burlington, AMOS RAY, aged 68. [2/10]
Jan. 31, 1834, Laurens, Dr. EZER WINSOR, aged 66. [2/10]
Jan. 30, 1834, Otsego, JOHN BOWEN, aged 78. [2/17]
Feb. 26, 1834, Hartwick, Mrs. HANNAH S. DAVIS, aged 50. [3/3]
Feb. 13, 1834, Edmeston, JONATHAN HUBBY, aged 70. [3/3]
Feb. 11, 1834, Springville, N.Y., HANNAH R. CHURCH, formerly of Warren, aged 19. [3/3]
Feb. 22, 1834, Peru, N.Y., Hon. JONAS PLATT. [3/10]
March 4, 1834, Winfield, Herkimer Co., Mrs. MARY ELDRED, dau. of ISAAC RUSSELL of Cooperstown.
Feb. 24, 1834, Butternuts, Dr. JOHN BURGESS, aged 73. [3/17]
March 11, 1834, Otsego, HARVEY H. APLIN, aged 2. [3/17]
March 3, 1834, Butternuts, ZACHEUS TOBY, aged 100. [3/24]
April 1, 1834, Plainfield, CALVIN HUNTLEY. [4/14]
March 28, 1834, Worcester, STEPHEN R. OLMSTED, aged 52. [4/21]
March 30, 1834, S. Worcester, DAVID SOWLE, aged 45. [4/21]
April 15, 1834, Milford, SARAH M. MC NAMEE, aged 18. [4/28]
April 29, 1834, Burlington, AHETABLE REED, aged 60. [5/5]
April 24, 1834, Hartwick, ERASTUS WRIGHT, aged 57. [5/5]
May 8, 1834, Middlefield, Mrs. HANNAH OLMSTED, aged 87. [5/12]

April 5, 1833 [sic], St. Louis, Mo., ABRAHAM SWARTOUT, late of
   Otsego, aged 23. [5/12/1834]
April 17, 1834, Columbia, Mrs. POLLY HANNAH, aged 49. [5/12]
May 14, 1834, Cooperstown, Col. HARVEY W. BABCOCK, aged 44.
   [5/19]
April 9, 1834, Middlefield, Mrs. DANIEL RICE, aged 80. [5/19]
April 10, 1834, Middlefield, WILLIAM RICE, aged 90. [5/19]
April 10, 1834, Middlefield, Mrs. LYDIA EGLESTON, aged 76. [5/19]
May 23, 1834, Westford, DAVID SMITH, Esq., aged 64. [6/2]
May 25, 1834, PEREZ DRAKE, aged 74. [6/2]
May 26, 1834, WM. THURBER, aged 8. [6/2]
May 22, 1834, Columbus, Capt. ELIJAH PALMER, aged 68. [6/2]
May 21, 1834, Hartwick, ANN PHILLES BAKER, aged 54. [6/2]
June 2, 1834, Cooperstown, MARY, infant dau. of Dr. JOHN HANNAY
   of Milford. [6/9]
June 5, 1834, New Berlin, Mrs. SUSANNAH GAYLY (?), aged 44. [6/16]
June 7, 1834, Pittsfield, Mrs. JANE WILBER, aged 34. [6/16]
June 9, 1834, Otsego, WILLIAM JOHNSON, aged 48. [6/16]
June 17, 1834, Cooperstown, ARNAND LEE, aged 22. [6/23]
June 15, 1834, Springfield, ANDREW F. SHELDON, aged 23. [6/30]
June 22, 1834, New Berlin, AMANDA ELY, aged 21. [6/30]
July 11, 1834, Middlefield, HELEN STEWART, dau. of JOHN M.
   BOWERS, Esq., aged 18. [7/14]
July 18, 1834, Cooperstown, HENRY, son of S. D. SHAW, Esq., aged 18
   months. [7/28]
July 15, 1834, Danube, WM. BUSH, aged 50. [7/28]
Aug. 4, 1834, Cooperstown, GEORGE A., son of ELLERY CORY, aged
   19 months. [8/11]
Aug. 3, 1834, New Berlin, ALEX. GAZLEY, aged 54. [8/11]
Aug. 12, 1834, Otsego, Dr. WM. W. TIFFT, aged 26. [8/18]
Aug. 16, 1834, Otsego, Mrs. ABIGAIL SMITH, aged 45. [8/25]
Aug. 8, 1834, Litchfield, N.Y., Mrs. MARY TOWNSEND, aged 43. [8/25]
Aug. 11, 1834, Otselic, N.Y., Dr. HARVEY BROWN of Brockfield. [8/25]
Aug. 22, 1834, Cooperstown, ROBERT E. THAYER, aged 24. [8/25]
July 23, 1834, Springfield, Mrs. LEVI GRAY, aged 56. [9/1]
[No date] Mrs. ASAHEL GATES, aged 71. [9/1/1834]
Aug. 29, 1834, Oneonta, JULIA MC DONALD, aged 17. [9/8]
Aug. --, 1834, state of Mich., PATRICK MC BRINE, aged 53, late of
   Cooperstown. [9/8]
Sept. 16, 1834, Exeter, JOSEPH WHITE, aged 57. [9/22]
Sept. 14, 1834, Cooperstown, Mrs. MARCY AVERELL, aged 68. [9/22]

Sept. 16, 1834, Middlefield, Cen. [sic], WM. V. A. ROBINSON, aged 25. [9/22]

Sept. 15, 1834, W. Hartwick, F. MARVIN, infant son of NATHANIEL PIERCE. [9/29]

Sept. 21, 1834, Cherry Valley, THEODATUS EDSON, Esq. of Oneonta, aged 36. [9/29]

Oct. 5, 1834, Exeter, THADDEUS DAILY, aged 55. [10/13]

Sept. 2, 1834, Climax, Mich., DAN. ELDRED, late of Otsego, aged 63. [10/3]

Oct. 3, 1834, Davenport, JOSEPH H. GOODRICH, Esq., aged 30. [10/13]

Oct. 6, 1834, Exeter, THADDEUS DAILY, aged 3. [10/27]

Oct. 18, 1834, Toddsville, ALANSON HICOK, aged 26. [10/27]

Nov. 1, 1834, Richfield, Mrs. SUSANNA DUNBAR, aged 61. [11/10]

Nov. 9, 1834, Exeter, Dea. AMES CURTISS, aged 64. [11/17]

Dec. 2, 1834, Edmeston, ALMA M. SEYMOUR. [12/8]

Nov. 30, 1834, New Berlin, Mrs. HANNAH VAIL, aged 38. [12/8]

Nov. 28, 1834, Otsego, MARTHA PATTERSON, aged 46. [12/8]

Dec. 2, 1834, ABNER BALDWIN, aged 78. [12/8]

Nov. 28, 1834, Plainfield, ISEBENDA BAKER, aged 19. [12/8]

Dec. 5, 1834, Butternuts, JOSEPH PEARSALL, aged 94. [12/15]

Dec. 20, 1834, Fort Miller, N.Y., JOSEPH MUNN, aged 79. [12/29]

Dec. 25, 1834, Hartwick, DELIA TRACY DAVISON, aged 1. [12/29]

Dec. 19, 1834, Burlington, ZACHEUS FLINT, aged 74. [12/29]

Dec. 25, 1834, Hartwick, DAVID MAPLES, aged 80. [12/29]

Dec. 26, 1834, Otsego, LUCY NOYES LEWIS, aged 18. [12/29]

Dec. 28, 1834, Claverack, N.Y., PETER MESICK, aged 35. [12/29]

Dec. 28, 1834, Claverack, N.Y., Mrs. PETER MESICK, aged 83. [12/29]

Jan. 28, 1834 [sic], Cooperstown, FENIMORE, son of ABNER GRAVES, aged 3 1/2 months. [1/5/1835]

Nov. 21, 1834, Oneonta, HENRY P. OSBORN, aged 55. [1/5/1835]

[No date] Auburn, N.Y., MARY E. WILLIAMS, of Utica, aged 18. [1/5/1835]

Dec. 16, 1834, Plainfield, PATTY A. HUNTLEY, aged 14. [1/5/1835]

Jan. 19, 1835, Cooperstown, WM. APLIN, aged 54. [1/26]

Jan. 22, 1835, CHARLES DAVIS, aged 1. [1/26]

Dec. 31, 1834, Westford, JOHN MANNING, aged 63. [1/26/1835]

Jan. 26, 1835, Richfield, Dr. THOMAS HOWES, aged 61. [2/2]

Feb. 2, 1835 Guilford, MARY A. SMITH, aged 32. [2/16]

Feb. 4, 1835, Middlefield, Mrs. ANNA ROGERS, aged 63. [2/16]

Feb. 2, 1835, Milford, Mrs. ELIZABETH LOW, aged 94. [2/23]

Feb. 19, 1835, New Lisbon, JAMES HARRIS, Esq., aged 87. [3/2]
Feb. 22, 1835, Oxford, DAVID JOHNSTON MORRIS of Butternuts, aged 17. [3/2]
Feb. 21, 1835, Unadilla, CURTIS NOBLE, aged 60. [3/9]
Feb. 16, 1835, Little Falls, N.Y., JACOB OSBON, aged 43. [3/9]
March 11, 1835, Hartwick, NEHEMIAH BURCH, aged 82. [3/16]
March 18, 1835, Cherry Valley, Dr. DELOS WHITE, aged 50. [3/23]
March 13, 1835, Hartwick, SARRALETTE A. THRALL, age 3, dau. of Dr. F. G. THRALL. [3/23]
March 20, 1835, Springfield, MARILLA WOOD, aged 19. [3/30]
March 22, 1835, LEONARD RICHARDSON, aged 42. [3/30]
March 26, 1835, Middlefield, Mrs. ALICE SPARROW, aged 74. [3/30]
March 19, 1835, Hartwick, WM. MELVIN MONTGOMERY, aged 22 months. [3/30]
March 23, 1835, Maryland, FRANCIS PETERSON, aged 100. [3/30]
March 27, 1835, Cazenovia, N.Y., PERRY G. CHILDS, Esq., aged 56. [4/6]
March 25, 1835, Butternuts, Mrs. EUNICE CHAPIN, aged 76. [4/6]
March 14, 1835, Hartwick, BREWSTER CLARK, aged 64. [4/6]
March 30, 1835, Mrs. RACHEL BARTLETT, aged 81. [4/6]
March 26, 1835, Westford, Mrs. RHODA GALPIN, aged 91. [4/6]
April 1, 1835, Hartwick, HELEN M. MERRELL, 3 years, 6 months. [4/13]
April 5, 1835, Little Falls, Mrs. CATHERINE A. BURWELL. [4/13]
April 6, 1835, Pittsfield, Mrs. LUCY WOODIN, aged 51. [4/20]
April 8, 1835, Hartwick, Mrs. CAROLINE C. PEAK, aged 23. [4/20]
April 6, 1835, Otsego, Mrs. BETSEY P. COONROD, aged 22. [4/20]
April 19, 1835, Springfield, Capt. JOHN COTES, aged 79. [4/27]
April 11, 1835, Canaan, N.Y., WM. LUSK, Esq., aged 91. [4/27]
May 4, 1835, Cherry Valley, Mrs. JANE MAGHER, aged 44. [5/11]
May 5, 1835, Oxford, HENRY MYGATT, aged 51. [5/11]
May 11, 1835, New Lisbon, Mrs. EUNICE ELDRED, aged 72. [5/18]
May 6, 1835, Exeter, JOHN REED, aged 66. [5/18]
May 13, 1835, Otsego, Dr. BEN. JOHNSON, aged 83. [5/18]
[No date] Penn Yan, Yates Co., CHAS. MOSLEY, infant son of CHAS. V. MORRIS of Butternuts, aged 3 years, 4 months. [5/25]
May 17, 1835, Middlefield, IRA REYNOLDS, aged 2 years, 9 months. [5/25]
May 22, 1835, Albany, PETER EDWARD ELEMDORF, Esq., aged 70. [5/25]
May 13, 1835, W. Hartwick, Mrs. ELEANOR COOK, aged 79. [5/25]
May 24, 1835, Worcester, JOSHUA BIGELOW, Esq., aged 69. [6/8]

June 9, 1835, Cooperstown, Mrs. LUCY TOBY, aged 23. [6/15]
June 8, 1835, Norwich, N.Y., Mrs. ROWENA MITCHELL, aged 42. [6/15]
June 16, 1835, Cooperstown, AUGUSTUS MOLTHER, aged 40. [6/22]
June 25, 1835, Otsego, HULDAH E. PARSHALL, dau. of MINER PARSHALL, aged 5. [6/29]
July 12, 1835, Leonardsville, N.Y., Mrs. ABIGAIL LOOMIS, late of Richfield, N.Y., aged 75. [7/20]
July 8, 1835, Springfield, N.J., CORNELIUS SAMMONS, aged 88. [7/20]
July 19, 1835, Richfield, THEODOTIA P. CURTISS, aged 20. [7/27]
July 1, 1835, Maryland, JOHN CHAMBERLAIN, aged 67. [7/27]
July 26, 1835, Cooperstown, Mrs. CLARISSA JOHNSON, aged 50. [8/3]
July 29, 1835, Otsego, MARY JANE BABCOCK, aged 22. [8/3]
Aug. 2, 1835, Cooperstown, MICHAEL MC NELLY, aged 8 years, 6 months. [8/10]
July 31, 1835, Hartwick, FRANCIS MARION PEAKE, 4 months. [8/10]
Aug. 4, 1835, Rensselaerville, N.Y., Mrs. ELIZ. HARRINGTON, nee SCOTT of Milford. [8/10]
July 8, 1835, Jackson, La., Capt. RICH. S. BIRD of Herkimer Co. [8/24]
Aug. 13, 1835, Springfield, SELINDA RATHBUN, aged 38. [8/24]
Aug. 21, 1835, Cooperstown, SARAH JANE GRAVES, aged 20 months, [8/24]
Sept. 4, 1835, New Lisbon, ISRAEL JOHNSON, aged 22. [9/14]
Sept. 6, 1835, Butternuts, Mr. SIMMONS. [9/14]
Sept. 15, 1835, Milford, DAVID L. SAYRE, aged 62. [9/21]
Sept. 13, 1835, Hartwick, CHAS. STEWART, son of Maj. GEORGE H. DERBYSHIRE, aged 11. [9/21]
Sept. 27, 1835, New Berlin, Mrs. ELIZ. FIELD, aged 55. [10/5]
Oct. 6, 1835, N.Y. City, JOHN K. FORRESTER of Cherry Valley, aged 44. [10/19]
Nov. 4, 1835, Springfield (Hyde Hall), N.Y., GEORGE CLARK, Esq., aged 67. [11/19]
Oct. 29, 1835, Cherry Valley, EZEKIEL JOHNSON, aged 64. [11/19]
Oct. 30, 1835, Sherburne, JOHN STEVENSON, aged 58. [11/19]
Sept. 16, 1835, Warren, N.Y., BETSEY KANE MUNDY, aged 19. [11/19]
Nov. 4, 1835, Hartwick, THIRZA LUTHER, aged 15. [11/16]
Nov. 10, 1835, Springfield, EPAPHRAS VIBBARD, aged 61. [11/23]
Nov. 30, 1835, Hartwick, GRIFFIN CRAFTS, Esq., aged 88. [12/7]
Nov. 21, 1835, Burlington, ABIGAIL WALLACE, aged 23. [12/7]
Nov. 28, 1835, Deposit, N.Y., IRA BIXBY, Esq., aged 33. [12/7]

Nov. 19, 1835, State of Ohio, ASABEL CLARK, aged 36. Native of Cooperstown. [12/7]
Nov. 31, 1835, Unadilla, BENJ. BISSELL, aged 36. [12/7]
Dec. 2, 1835, Walton, N.Y., BENJAMIN NORTH, aged 52. [12/21]
Dec. 17, 1835, St. Johnsville, N.Y., JAMES AVERELL, aged 72. [12/21]
Dec. 12, 1835, Cherry Valley, JOHN C. HALL, aged 55. [12/21]
Dec. 26, 1835, Cooperstown, Mrs. SOPHIA GRIFFIN, aged 71. [12/28]
Dec. 22, 1835, Louisville, N.Y., HAN.[?] ALLEN of Hartwick, aged 58. [12/28]
Dec. 19, 1835, Burlington, N.Y., Mrs. DESIRE ANDRUS, aged 84. [12/28]
Dec. 31, 1835, Otsego, Mrs. MERCY ANN WARREN. [1/4/1836]
Dec. 27, 1835, Decatur, CHANEY P. BOORN (BOOM?), aged 21. [1/11/1836]
Jan. 4, 1836, Cooperstown, LOUISE LUCE. [1/11]
Jan. 8, 1836, Warren, JOHN SIMSON, aged 77. [1/18]
Jan. 12, 1836, Hartwick, LEWIS ADAMS, aged 80. [1/25]
Jan. 20, 1836, Springfield, Mrs. NABBY BUTTERFIELD, aged 41. [1/25]
Jan. 16, 1836, Fort Plain, Mrs. MARY PUTNAM HUDSON, late of Cherry Valley, aged 45. [2/1]
Jan. 22, 1836 Norwich, Mrs. ELIZ. EDSON. [2/1]
Feb. 6, 1836, Otsego, SAM. HUNTINGTON, aged 98. [2/15]
Feb. 4, 1836, Milford, ALBERT WAIT, aged 24. [2/15]
Feb. 16, 1836, Cherry Valley, Mrs. JANE CAMPBELL, aged 92. [2/22]
Feb. 7, 1836, Middlefield, Mrs. MARTHA BOYD, aged 56. [2/22]
Feb. 21, 1836, Garratsville, SUSAN GREGORY, aged 22. [2/29]
March 1, 1836, Otsego, Mrs. PAMELA CHAPMAN, aged 36. [3/7]
Feb. 27, 1836, Otsego, NAOMI BADGER, aged 16. [3/7]
Feb. 17, 1836, Attica, N.Y., Mrs. ANNA TANNER, late of Cooperstown, aged 69. [3/7]
March 3, 1836, Edmeston, Mrs. ABIGAIL SHOLES, aged 68. [3/7]
Feb. 10, 1836, So. Worcester, Mrs. ANN HARTWELL, aged 26. [3/7]
Feb. 21, 1836, So. Worcester, Mrs. ELIZ. FREECK, aged 43. [3/7]
March 8, 1836, Cooperstown, MARY ELIZ. CLARK, aged 33. [3/14]
March 1, 1836, Worcester, Ohio, Maj. JOS. SPRAGUE, aged 65. Late of Otsego. [3/14]
March 16, 1836, Middlefield, Mrs. SARAH AMES, aged 88. [3/28]
March 30, 1836, Hartwick, Mrs. HANNAH K. HUGHES, aged 78. [4/4]
March 18, 1836, Otsego, LUCY LOOMIS, aged 25. [4/4]
March 15, 1836, Warren, Mrs. CATHERINE CLELAND, aged 93. [4/4]
April 5, 1836, Otsego, Mrs. MARY WARREN, aged 78. [4/11]

April 4, 1836, Middlefield, Mrs. SARAH DENTON, aged 76. [4/11]
April 4, 1836, S. Bainbridge, Mrs. NANCY JACKSON of Butternuts. [4/18]
April 14, 1836, Middlefield, ANNIE ANTISDEL, aged 26. [4/25]
April 21, 1836, Canaan Centre, N.Y., Mrs. ELIZ. LUSK, aged 58. [5/2]
April 25, 1836, Laurens, ELIZ. FULLER, aged 67. [5/9]
April 26, 1836, Springfield, ARMINDA THAYER, aged 19. [5/9]
June 5, 1836, Milford, PHILENA WALWORTH, aged 20. [6/13]
June 5, 1836, Exeter, Rev. DANIEL NASH, aged 74. [6/13]
[No date] Middlefield, ISAIAH NEWCOMB, Esq. [6/13]
June 2, 1836, Plainfield, N.Y., RUFFLES SPOONER, Esq., aged 71. [6/13]
June 7, 1836, New Lisbon, WELLESLEY WELLINGTON BOWDISH. [6/20]
June 7, 1836, Otsego, ENSIGN REXFORD, aged 72. [6/27]
June 26, 1836, New Lisbon, LYDIA EMERSON, aged 35. [7/4]
June 27, 1836, Hartwick, Mrs. ABIGAIL MALLERY. [7/11]
July 4, 1836, Hartwick, Capt. SAM. MALLERY, aged 59. [7/11]
June 28, 1836, Gorham, Ontario Co., Dea. TIMOTHY SABIN, aged 74, late of Cooperstown. [7/18]
July 23, 1836, Hartwick, Mrs. TRIPHENA GRISWOLD, aged 79. [8/1]
Aug. 3, 1836, Warren, WILLIAM TUNICLIFF, aged 59. [8/8]
Aug. 2, 1836, Cooperstown, Mrs. CLARINDA FISH, aged 25. [8/1]
July 21, 1836, Otsego, Mrs. HANNAH TODD, aged 79. [8/1]
July 26, 1836, Wellsboro, Pa., HEZEKIAH BOWEN, late of Hartwick, aged 58. [8/15]
Aug. 10, 1836, New Lisbon, Mr. FAITHFUL SMITH, aged 66. [8/22]
Aug. 25, 1836, Middlefield, SAMUEL WILSON, aged 82. [9/5]
Aug. 31, 1836, Oneonta, EUNICE ANGEL, aged 47. [9/5]
Sept. 5, 1836, Hartwick, Mrs. ELLEN OVIT, aged 55. [9/12]
Sept. 6, 1336, New Lisbon, RUSSELL G. SMITH, aged 21. [9/12]
Sept. 13, 1836, Springfield, JOHN MC KELLUP, aged 86. [9/19]
Sept. 18, 1836, Hartwick, THEO. P. CARR, aged 2 years, 5 months. [9/19]
Sept. --, 1836, Otego, Mrs. ELIZ. PERSONS, aged 78. [9/19]
Sept. 15, 1836, Ripley, N.Y., Col. WM. C. DIXSON, of Cherry Valley, aged 37. [9/26]
Sept. 25, 1836, Otsego, Mrs. JANE VAN BENSCHOTEN, aged 90. [10/3]
Sept. 18, 1836, Middlefield, THOMAS JACOBUS, aged 28. [10/3]
Sept 26, 1836, Hartwick, HENRY BAKER, Esq. [10/3]
Sept. 25, 1836, Westford, Col. SAMUEL BABCOCK, aged 75. [10/3]

Sept. 10, 1836, Strongville, O. [Ohio?], JAMES H. JOHNSON, aged 22. [10/3]
Sept. 30, 1836, Hartwick, Mrs. MARTHA STERRE, aged 79. [10/10]
Sept. 29, 1836, Otsego, JABEZ HUBBELL, aged 75. [10/10]
Oct. 2, 1836, Exeter, GEORGE SMITH, aged 10. [10/10]
Oct. 2, 1836, Exeter, Mrs. PHILENA ROSE, aged 27. [10/10]
Oct. 4, 1836, Trenton, N.Y., Mrs. LIMA STEVENS, late of Otsego. [10/10]
Oct. 8, 1836, Otsego, Maj. SETH DOUBLEDAY, aged 76. [10/17]
Oct. 10, 1836, Mrs. DOROTHY FLINT, aged 57. [10/24]
Oct. 13, 1836, Milford, NATHANIEL POPE, aged 51. [10/24]
Oct. 15, 1836, Milford, LYDIA POPE, aged 59. [10/24]
Nov. 18, 1836, Exeter, Mrs. LUCY WHEELER, aged 95. [11/28]
Nov. 14, 1836, Laurens, Dr. SALMON HARRISON, aged 69. [11/28]
Dec. 5, 1836, Louisville, N.Y., Mrs. EMELIN M. LOOMIS, aged 23. [12/17]
Dec. 6, 1836, Warren, N.Y., Mrs. SOPHRONIA EASTON of Cedarville, aged 19. [12/17]
Dec. 11, 1836, Geneva, PHILETUS S. PIERCE, aged 20, late of Otsego. [12/26]
Dec. 9, 1836, Maryland, Mrs. OLIVE TUTHILL, aged 68. [1/2/1837]
Dec. 26, 1836, Hartwick, JOHN COCKETT, aged 60. [1/2/1837]
Dec. 10, 1836, Marshall, Mich., E. J. SHELDON, late of Springfield. [1/9/1837]
Jan. 19, 1837, Oaksville, WM. FITCH, late of Auburn, aged 27. [1/23]
Jan. 14, 1837, Springfield, Mrs. MATILDA G. HUTCHINS.
Jan. 24, 1837, Cooperstown, JOSEPH HOLT, aged 68. [1/30]
Jan. 20, 1837, Westfield, N.Y., Capt. JOHN SHIPBOY, formerly of Middlefield, Otsego Co., aged 70. [1/30]
Jan. 23, 1837, Cooperstown, Mrs. PHEBE STOWEL, aged 81. [2/6]
Jan. 22, 1837, Otsego, ELNATHAN BEEBE, aged 64. [2/6]
Jan. --, 1837, Springfield, MARY J. BESANCON, aged 6. [2/6]
Jan. 22, 1837, Otego, Mrs. MARTHA HALL, aged 42. [2/20]
Feb. 4, 1837, Milford, Mrs. ANN DONNELLY, aged 38. [2/20]
Feb. 11, 1837, Winfield, LOUISA POPPLE, aged 2 years, 3 months. [2/20]
[No date] Winfield, FRANCES POPPLE, aged 1 year, 2 months; both daus. of JOHN POPPLE. [2/20]
Feb. 13, 1837, Burlington, N.Y., Mrs. REBECCA HUBBEL, aged 82. [2/27]
Feb. 9, 1837, Sherburne, N.Y., JOS. GUTHRIE, Jr., aged 36. [2/27]
Jan. 4, 1837, Cadiz, Ohio, ELIPHLET DEWEY, Esq., aged 74. [2/27]

Feb. 19, 1837, Hartwick, Mrs. LOISA [sic] CARR, aged 58. [2/27]
Jan. 25, 1857, Canton, Ill., Mrs. NANCY HOOD, aged 44, late of Springfield. [2/27]
March 3, 1837, Hartwick, SYLVENUS WEST, aged 64. [3/13]
March 4, 1837, Springfield, LAURA REED, 2 years, 5 months. [3/13]
Feb. 23, 1837, Middletown, Conn., FRANCES H. NOYES, aged 7. [3/13]
March 9, 1837, Otsego, HELEN WENTWORTH, 1 year, 3 months. [3/20]
March 6, 1837, Havana, Cuba, Maj. GILBERT BISSELL, late of Cooperstown. [4/3]
March 13, 1837, Butternuts, CHRISTOPHER B. GIFFORD, Jr., aged 16. [4/3]
March 31, 1837, Hartwick, STUKELY ELLSWORTH, Esq., aged 67. [4/10]
April 12, 1837, Hartwick, Col. RALPH MC CLINTOCK of Trinidad, aged 54. [4/17]
April 12, 1837, LEVI IRONS, 32 years,m late of Otsego Co. [4/24]
April 22, 1837, Middlefield, HANNAH REYNOLDS GIDNEY, aged 29. [5/1]
May 5, 1837, Cooperstown, Mrs. HULDAH STARR, aged 72. [5/8]
May 5, 1837, Laurens, ABEL HOAG, Esq., aged 77. [5/15]
[No date] Paris, N.Y., ELIZA RHODES, aged 20. [5/22]
March 11, 1837, Cassville, Wis., Col. L. T. DANIELS, late of Otsego Co. [5/22]
May 23, 1837, Cooperstown, EZRA CHAFFEE, aged 34. [5/29]
June 2, 1837, Otsego, Mrs. MERCY STONE, aged 34. [6/12]
July 11, 1837, Cooperstown, Dr. THOMAS FULLER, aged 72. [7/17]
July 4, 1837, Fly Creek, D. MARVIN NORTHRUP, aged 13. [7/24]
July 17, 1837, Rochester, Dr. ANSON COLMAN, aged 42, late of Springfield. [7/24]
July 20, 1837, Hartwick, MATTHEW DERBYSHIRE, aged 11. [7/24]
July 20, 1837, Hartwick, EDWARD PIERCE, aged 2 months. [7/24]
Aug. 3, 1837, Cooperstown, Mrs. ANN GOULD, aged 29. [8/7]
July 29, 1837, Oneonta, HENRY YOUNG of Kentucky, aged 74. [8/14]
Aug. 20, 1837, Hartwick, Mrs. MARY ANN BURCH, aged 54. [8/28]
Aug. 14, 1837, Exeter, Mrs. JULIA ROSE, aged 49. [9/18]
Sept. 10, 1837, Exeter, PARKER M. CHILD, aged 34. [9/18]
Sept. 11, 1837, Exeter, Mrs. SARAH BECKWITH, aged 33. [9/18]
Sept. 9, 1837, Burlington, STELLE J. BLANCHARD, 7 months. [9/18]
Sept. 12, 1837, Cooperstown, HENRY BEADLE, aged 55. [9/25]
Sept. 5, 1837, Springfield, FRANCIS SYKES, aged 74. [10/9]

Sept. 20, 1837, Oneonta, PHILETUS ANGEL, aged 13. [10/9]
Sept. 27, 1837, Norwich, Dr. JONATHAN JOHNSON, aged 67. [10/9]
Sept. 3, 1837, Otsego, AMANDA KELLOGG. [10/9]
Oct. 15, 1837, Springfield, NELSON MORSE, aged 25. [10/23]
Oct. 17, 1837, New Berlin, Mrs. HANNAH MEDBURY, aged 71. [10/23]
July 14, 1837, Texas, Lt. JAMES J. WILLIAMS, formerly of Otsego, aged 28. [10/23]
Oct. 11, 1837, Cohocton, N.Y., EDWIN COOK, aged 22, brother of Mrs. S. CRIPPEN of Cooperstown. [10/30]
Oct. 23, 1837, Hartwick, Mrs. ORDERSON, aged 75. [10/30]
Oct. 20, 1837, Middlefield, Capt. EZRA EATON. [10/30]
Oct. 16, 1837, Pittsfield, Mrs. BETSEY ADAMS, aged 25. [11/6]
Nov. 1, 1837, Richfield, Mrs. ACHSAH TROWBRIDGE, aged 43. [11/6]
Nov. 3, 1837, Westford, Mrs. RHODA ROBERTS, aged 66. [11/6]
Nov. 6, 1837, Otsego, GARRET OLENDORF. [11/20]
Dec. 22, 1837, Middlefield, Mrs. SARAH GRIFFEN, aged 82. [12/25]
Dec. 16, 1837, New Berlin, Mrs. CHARLOTTE BRIGGS, aged 30. [12/25]
Dec. 11, 1837, Warren, N.Y., Mrs. REBECCA TREADWAY, aged 65. [1/1/1838]
Dec. 25, 1837, Cooperstown, FRANCIS L. BURDICK, aged 11 months. [1/1/1838]
Dec. 20, 1837, Middlefield, Mrs. HANNAH HUBBELL, aged 75. [1/1/1838]
Dec. 23, 1837, Plainfield, Mrs. CAROLINE HUNTLEY, aged 23. [1/15/1838]
Jan. 1, 1838, Plainfield, ISAAC STRYLER, aged 22. [1/15]
Jan. 15, 1838, Springfield, Capt. JOS. WOOD, aged 53. [1/22]
Jan. --, 1838, Mohawk Village on Grand River, CATHERINE BRANT, relict of Capt. JOS. BRANT, aged 78. [1/29]
Jan. 28, 1838, Otsego, Mrs. CATHERINE LOOMIS, aged 58. [2/5]
Jan. 15, 1838, Butternuts, Mrs. JULIA A. FRANCHOT, aged 87. [2/5]
Jan. 29, 1838, Decatur, ELMAN BOOM, aged 11. [2/5]
Jan. 20, 1838, Sodus, N.Y., Dr. C. RICHARDSON, aged 65, late of Burlington. [2/5]
Jan. 1, 1838, Ft. Wayne, Ind., ROBERT ORMSTON, aged 16, late of Springfield. [2/12]
Jan. 13, 1838, WILLIAM O. ORMSTON, aged 5. [2/12]
Jan. 8, 1838, Richfield, Maj. ALFORD PORTER, aged 49. [2/19]
Dec. 23, 1837, Peoria, Ill., Lt. WILLIS EDSON, aged 30, formerly of Richfield. [2/26/1838]

Feb. 17, 1838, Cooperstown, JOSHUA STARR, aged 81. [2/26]
Feb. 13, 1838, Exeter, JOHN REED, aged 24. [2/26]
Feb. 9, 1838, Trumansburgh, N.Y., GERSHOM PALMER, aged 66. [2/26]
Feb. 15, 1838, Milford, Capt. ITHAMAR NEWTON, aged 77. [3/12]
Feb. 23, 1838, S. Worcester, MARY W. BECKER, aged 5 months. [3/12]
March 7, 1838, Hartwick, Dr. GEORGE W. ARNOLD, aged 59. [3/12]
March 9, 1838, S. New Berlin, Mrs. SUSAN HARPER, aged 19. [3/19]
March 15, 1838, Hartwick, Mrs. CATHERINE DAVIDSON, aged 89. [3/26]
March 3, Middlefield, JESSE SMITH, aged 57. [3/26]
March 15, 1838, Butternuts, Mrs. NANCY WASHBON, aged 69. [3/26]
March 24, 1838, Oaksville, WILLIAM WILSON, aged 3 years, 6 months. [4/2]
March 19, 1838, Worcester, JACOB STEVER, aged 54. [4/9]
March 21, 1838, Plainfield, Capt. SAM. LATHAM, aged 86. [4/9]
Feb. 22, 1838, New Lisbon, Maj. MARTIN NOBLE, aged 63. [4/9]
March 26, 1838, Whitesboro, N.Y., Mrs. ANTOINETTE E. G. WEST, aged 24. [4/23]
April 10, 1838, Decatur, JUSTUS FERRIS, aged 73. [4/23]
April 2, 1838, Springfield, PETER GILCHRIST, aged 50.
April 10, Otego, MARTHA M. HALL, aged 21. [4/30]
May 3, 1838, Milford, JESSE EDDY, aged 29. [5/7]
April 14, 1838, Juliet, Ill., ROB. SHOEMAKER, Esq., late of Herkimer Co., aged 57. [5/7]
March 28, 1838, Burlington, HARRIET NICKERSON. [5/14]
April 21, 1838, Exeter, JOHN COMMICK, aged 82. [5/14]
May 4, 1838, Pittsfield, N.Y., AULINA M. CLARK, aged 23. [5/14]
April 17, 1838, Edmeston, Mrs. ZERUIAH BENNETT, aged 91. [5/14]
May 16, 1838, Cooperstown, BENJAMIN RUGGLES, aged 42. [5/21]
May 12, 1838, Butternuts, Mrs. ASENATH MOORE, aged 73. [5/21]
May 14, 1838, Guilford, Mrs. CYNTHIA MORGAN, aged 70. [5/21]
May 17, 1838, Otsego, SAMUEL MORRIS, aged 71.
May 17, 1838, Milford, THOMAS BAKER, aged 70. [5/28]
May 4, 1838, Middlebury, Ohio, PATRICK HUMISTON, late of Otsego, aged 47. [5/28]
May 17, 1838, Roxbury, Maj. Gen. OTIS PRESTON, aged 67. [6/4]
May 29, 1838, Norwich, JASON GLEASON, aged 75. [6/4]
May 20, 1838, Otsego, JOS. MAINE, aged 68. [6/4]
May 27, 1838, Little Falls, JOHN H. PRENTISS, 2nd, aged 25. [6/4]
May 20, 1838, N. Adams, DAN. JOHNSON, aged 27. [6/11]
May 28, 1838, Cooperstown, GEORGE JOHNSON, aged 84. [6/11]

May 31, 1838, Plattsburgh, Hon. MOSS KENT, aged 73. [6/11]
June 7, 1838, Burlington Flats, Mrs. MARY WALKER, aged 33. [6/18]
June 9, 1838, New Lisbon, HENRY PERRY, aged 50. [6/18]
June 18, 1838, Cooperstown, EMMA JANE GRAVES, 1 year, 3 months. [6/25]
June 25, 1838, Otsego, Mrs. FANNY WEST, aged 46. [7/2]
June 16, 1838, Otsego, Capt. ADAM HENRY, aged 97. [7/2]
June 22, 1838, Otsego, Mrs. DILLE LUCE, aged 70. [7/2]
June 23, 1838, Westford, BENJ. WHITE, late of Washington, N.Y. [7/2]
July 20, 1838, Hartwick, Sem., [sic] JOHN DAVIDSON, aged 75. [7/23]
July 23, 1838, Cooperstown, Mrs. NANCY GRAVES, aged 44. [7/30]
Aug. 6, 1838, Cooperstown, FRANCIS LATHROP, aged 25. [8/13]
Aug. 3, 1838, Richfield, SAMUEL CHASE, Esq., aged 56. [8/13]
July 31, 1838, Oxford, N.Y., MARY ELIZABETH WILCOX, aged 18. [8/13]
July 15, 1838, Otsego, L. NEWTON, aged 16. [8/13]
Aug. 13, 1838, Edmeston, Mrs. ELECTA BILYEA, aged 34. [8/20]
July 24, Hamburg, N.Y., DAN. LAWRENCE, late of Otsego. [8/20]
July 31, 1838, Leavenworth, Ia., JOHN L. SMITH, Esq., aged 42, late of Otsego. [8/27]
July 11, 1838, Otsego, Mrs. PHILOTHA KELLOGG, aged 82. [8/27]
Aug. 16, 1838, Jordan, N.Y., Mrs. LEVANTIA E. RAYMOND of Otsego. [9/3]
Sept. 6, 1838, Worcester, Mrs. LAURA DUNHAM. [9/17]
Aug. 27, 1838, Richfield, ADELBERT WESTLEY BURNHAM, aged 16 months. [9/17]
Sept. 4, 1838, Cooperstown, Mrs. BETSEY LEWIS, aged 74. [9/10]
Sept. 13, 1838, Milford, Mrs. LOUIS WAKEFIELD, aged 74. [9/24]
Sept. 11, 1838, Middlefield, JOHN PARSHALL, aged 82. [9/24]
Sept. 11, 1838, New Berlin, SILAS A. CONKEY, aged 40. [9/24]
Sept. 18, 1838, Laurens, Col. EGBERT L. HODSKINS, aged 23. [10/1]
Sept. 15, 1838, Otego, LEVI REDFIELD, aged 93. [10/1]
Sept. 20, 1838, Exeter, Mrs. EUNICE MUNSON, aged 57. [10/1]
Sept. 19, 1838, Cleveland, Ohio, LEVI BEBEE, late of Otsego. [10/1]
Sept. 12, 1838, Ottaway, Ill., Capt. HORACE P. JARVIS, late of Cooperstown. [10/1]
Oct. 3, 1838, Middlefield, HERMAN BAILEY, aged 22. [10/8]
Oct. 3, 1838, Cherry Valley, WILLIAM STORY, aged 53. [10/8]
Oct. 4, 1838, Bergen, N.Y., MORRIS SLEEPER, aged 28, late of Laurens. [10/15]
Nov. 1, 1838, West Hartwick, DAVID STOWELL, aged 41. [11/5]

Nov. 6, 1838, Middlefield, HELEN MARIA STILLMAN, aged 14. [11/19]
Dec. 8, 1838, Otsego, Mrs. VOSSICE POTTER, aged 66. [12/17]
Dec. 17, 1838, Otsego, LAURA C. WARREN, aged 17. [12/24]
Dec. 16, 1838, Clinton, N.Y., DAVID LENT of Otsego, aged 54. [12/24]
June 26, 1838 Waterloo, Seneca Co., JAMES VAN HORNE, formerly of Cooperstown, N.Y. [7/9]
July 8, 1838, Middlefield, GEORGE GATES, aged 56. [7/16]
Dec. 26, 1838, Exeter, MARGARET A. FISHER, aged 14. [1/7/1839]
Jan. 6, 1839, Cooperstown, JAMES BRISTOL, aged 35. [1/14]
Dec. 25, 1838, Cooperstown, Mrs. ELIZABETH RUSSELL, aged 69. [1/14/1839]
Dec. 25, 1838, Otsego, THOMAS WELDON, aged 66. [1/14/1839]
Jan. 5, 1839, Otsego, WILLIAM JAY, aged 52. [1/14]
Jan. 15, 1839, Hartwick, Mrs. MARTHA SMITH, aged 28. [1/28]
Jan. 24, 1839, Cooperstown, JAMES ARTHUR PEAK, son of Dr. PEAK. [1/28]
Jan. 26, 1839, Cooperstown, Maj. ELISHA BURLINGHAM, aged 34. [1/28]
Jan. 15, 1839, Burlington Flats, Rev. ISAAC HEYWARD. [1/28]
Jan. 20, 1839, Unadilla, Mrs. BETSEY HOUGH. [2/4]
Jan. 26, 1839, Hartwick, Mrs. RISPA ALGER, aged 69. [2/4]
Jan. 31, 1839, Hartick, WILLIAM ALWORTH, aged 74. [2/4]
Jan. 31, 1839, Milford, SAMUEL BOSTWICK, aged 39. [2/11]
Feb. 8, 1839, Springfield, CARY, son of ROB. WOOD, 12 months. [2/25]
Feb. 19, 1839, Burlington, infant son of JOS. BLANCHARD, 2 months. [3/4]
Feb. 28, 1839, Unadilla, Mrs. MARIA C. SANDS, aged 23. [3/11]
Feb. 22, 1839, Otsego, ZATTO ANDREAS, aged 75. [3/11]
March 11, 1839, Cooperstown, Mrs. LYDIA LUCE, aged 55. [3/25]
March 12, 1839, Milford, CLARA W. BAKER, aged 35. [3/25]
March 21, 1839, Butternuts, HELEN WASHBON, aged 9. [3/25]
March 19, 1839, Cooperstown, Mrs. SYLVANIA SMITH, aged 25. [3/25]
March 19, 1839, Cooperstown, Mrs. SEREPTA WOODWARD, aged 25. [3/25]
March 27, 1839, Cooperstown, Mrs. CAROLINE WINSLOW, aged 27. [4/1]
March 26, Norwich, PEREZ RANDALL, aged 56. [4/1]
Feb. 28, 1839, Lorain Co., Ohio, ISAAC R. CHENEY of Fly Creek, aged 19. [4/1]
March 26, 1839, Richfield, Mrs. HANNAH BEARDSLEY, aged 69. [4/1]
April 20, 1839, Hartwick, Mrs. MARY EDDY, aged 74. [4/16]

April 16, 1839, Hartwick, AMANDA BARKER, aged 17. [4/22]
April 24, 1839, Hartwick, Mrs. MARY CRAFTS, aged 79. [4/29]
March 21, 1839, Butternuts, ASA COYE, aged 72. [4/29]
April 29, 1839, Butternuts, Mrs. JOHN F. NASH, late of Exeter, aged 26. [5/13]
May 16, 1839, Cherry Valley, Maj. JOHN ROSEBOOM, aged 32. [5/27]
May 22, 1839, Middlefield, SAMUEL GRIFFIN, aged 80. [5/27]
May 22, 1839, Milford, JOS. DONNELLY, aged 85. [5/27]
May 31, 1839, Laurens, Mrs. MARY CHATFIELD. [6/3]
June 2, 1839, Butternuts, Mrs. JULIA COPE, aged 37. [6/10]
June 7, 1839, Cooperstown, HARMONT GROAT, aged 70. [6/10]
June 3, 1839, Rochester, Mrs. TERZY THURBER, late of Otsego. [6/17]
June 4, 1839, Fort Plain, MOSES SMITH, aged 24. [6/17]
June 8, 1839, Oneonta, Mrs. EUNICE FAIRCHILDS, aged 63. [6/17]
June 9, 1839, Unadilla, JOHN ROGERS, aged 81. [6/17]
May 28, 1839, Butternuts, Capt. BENJ. DIXON, aged 32. [6/24]
June 22, 1839, Springfield, CATHERINE M. MULKINS, aged 6. [7/1]
June 12, 1839, Exeter, THOMAS BROOKS, Esq., aged 79. [7/1]
June 23, 1839, Exeter, CHRISTOPHER ROTTO, aged 82. [7/1]
June 22, 1839, Otsego, Mrs. SYNTHA TAYLOR, aged 88. [7/1]
June 19, 1839, Otsego, Mrs. MARY HINDS, aged 23. [7/1]
June 27, 1839, Cooperstown, Mrs. SAMANTHA BENNETT, aged 30. [7/8]
June 16, 1839, Centreville, N.Y., Mrs. DEBORAH LATHAM, late of Richfield, N.Y., aged 53. [7/15]
July 4, 1839, S. Worcester, Mrs. SUSAN STEWARD, aged 67. [7/22]
July 15, 1839, Otsego, SARAH T. ROSE, aged 6 months. [7/22]
June 1, 1839, Exeter, JONATHAN ANGEL, aged 81. [7/22]
July 17, 1839, New Lisbon, Mrs. DESIRE STARKEY, aged 56. [7/22]
July 15, 1839, Otsego, DAVID PATTEN, aged 13. [7/29]
July 9, 1839, Decatur, MARY ANN TRIPP, aged 10. [7/29]
July 25, 1839, Springfield, MENZR. SHIPMAN, 19 months. [8/5]
July 30, 1839, Springfield, DAVID MC RORICA, aged 36. [8/5]
July 25, 1839, Otego, Dr. F. B. WHITMARSH, aged 67. [8/5]
Aug. 3, 1839, Otsego, Mrs. FANNY ANDRUS, aged 22. [8/26]
Aug. 10, 1839, Otsego, SUSAN ANDRUS, dau. of above, aged 2 years, 10 months. [8/26]
Aug. 25, 1839, Otsego, Mrs. NANCY BEADLE, aged 52. [9/9]
Aug. 28, 1839, Otsego, Mrs. MARIETTE T. HERRICK, aged 28. [9/9]
Aug. 31, 1839, Exeter, Mrs. MARY A. ROBINSON, aged 36. [9/9]
Sept. 1, 1839, Westford, NATHANIEL HULL, aged 51. [9/9]

Sept. 4, 1839, Westford, Mrs. ELIZABETH BENEDICT, aged 77. [9/9]
Sept. 9, 1839, Burlington, JOS. REED, 2 years, 4 months. [9/16]
Sept. 11, 1839, Cooperstown, GEORGE LEWIS, 5 years, 5 months. [9/16]
Sept. 24, 1839, Otsego, ORLANDO SCRIBNER, 4 years, 11 months. [9/30]
Oct. 1, 1839, Cooperstown, MELINDA BINGHAM, aged 16. [10/7]
Sept. 28, 1839, Milford, JACOB COLLIER, aged 68. [10/7]
Sept. 30, 1839, Cooperstown, JAMES BUTTS, aged 62. [10/7]
Oct. 3, 1839, Cooperstown, PAMELA, dau. of Chief Justice NELSON, aged 8. [10/7]
Sept. 30, 1839, Otsego, LUCINA [sic] L. EDDY, aged 5. [10/7]
Oct. 2, 1839, Otsego, WILLIAM A. COOPER, aged 25. [10/7]
Oct. 4, 1839, Woodside (Cooperstown), FLORA, dau. of SAM. M. BEAL, 7 months. [10/14]
Sept. 30, 1839, Hartwick, CHAS. DAVISON, aged 2. [10/14]
Oct. 5, 1839, Butternuts, Mrs. HARRIET MAXIM, aged 43. [10/14]
Sept. 22, 1839, Wetumpha, Ala., GEORGE W. MAGHER, Esq., late of Cherry Valley. [10/14]
Oct. 11, 1839, Albany, Mrs. CATHERINE BABCOCK of Cooperstown, aged 51. [10/21]
Oct. 5, 1839, Warren, EARL A. MARBLE, aged 27. [10/21]
Oct. 5, 1839, Otsego, LUCIEN B. SCRIBNER, aged 2. [10/21]
Oct. 11, 1839, Springfield, LINUS A. CARROLL, aged 27. [10/21]
Oct. 12, 1839, Otsego, HANNAH ELIZ. TANNER, aged 5. [10/21]
Oct. 12, 1839, Bridgeport, Conn., Mrs. HARRIET MC LEAN BOTSFORD of Cherry Valley, aged 42. [10/21]
[No date] Prairie de Chien, WILLIAM CAMPBELL, aged 27, late of Cooperstown. [10/21/1839]
Oct. 18, 1839, Otsego, MARY ANN TANNER, aged 7. [10/28]
Oct. 28, 1839, Owego, JULIA A., dau. of C. C. NOBLE of Unadilla, aged 2. [11/11]
Oct. 20, 1839, Chicago, Mrs. CATHERINE C. ARNOLD, aged 24. [11/11]
Nov. 12, 1839, Cooperstown, LOUISA GRAVES, aged 3. [11/18]
Nov. 12, 1839, Cooperstown, Mrs. HENRY STACY. [11/25]
Nov. 19, 1839, Cooperstown, HALLEY, son of Chief Justice NELSON, aged 3. [11/25]
Nov. 19, 1839, Cooperstown, MARY ROOT, aged 16 months. [11/25]
Nov. 20, 1839, Otsego, JAMES COOPERNAIL. [11/25]
Nov. 20, 1839, Otsego, JOHN MISSON, aged 88. [11/25]

Dec. 25, 1839, Cooperstown, WM. GARRET WHISTON, aged 16 months. [12/2 sic]
Dec. 19, 1839, Springfield, Dea. GEORGE HOLT, aged 82. [12/2 sic]
Dec. 4, 1839, Sidney, N.Y., Col. WALTER JOHNSTON, aged 86. [12/2 sic]
Dec. 29, 1839, Exeter, MARY ROBBINSON, aged 6. [12/9 sic]
Oct. 2, 1839, Houston, Texas, SETH J. COOK, late of Otsego. [12/9]
Nov. 26, 1839, Claverack, Columbia Co., JOHN I. MILLER. [12/9]
Nov. 29, 1839, Laurens, JOHN BREESE, Jr., aged 62. [12/9]
Dec. 11, 1839, Cooperstown, RUSSELL MALORY, aged 23. [12/16]
Dec. 18, 1839, Cooperstown, Rev. JOS. TREDWELL PERKINS, aged 25. [12/23]
Dec. 17, 1839, Otsego, ZERA TANNER, aged 1. [12/23]
Dec. --, 1839, Hartwick, JANE A. CONVERSE, aged 4. [12/23]
Dec. 21, 1839, Cherry Valley, ALFRED CRAFTS, Esq., aged 57. [12/23]
Dec. 22, 1839, Otsego, EVAN LEWIS HERRICK, aged 3. [12/30]
Jan. 1, 1840, Cooperstown, SEBASTIAN BONY, aged 26. [1/6]
Dec. 20, 1839, Otsego, Mrs. ABIGAIL COONROD, aged 61. [1/6/1840]
Dec. 18, 1839, Exeter, Mrs. SALINDA BRAINARD, aged 57. [1/6/1840]
Dec. 23, 1839, Hartwick, ANNETTE STRANAHAN, 6 months. [1/6/1840]
Dec. 24, 1839, Hartwick, WILLIAM L. MARCY BECKLEY, aged 3 years, 7 months. [1/6/1840]
Dec. 29, 1839, Otego, PETER SCHRAMBLING, aged 76. [1/6/1840]
Jan. 1, 1840, Butternuts, ELIZA N. BOWNE, aged 22. [1/13]
Jan. 9, 1840 Norwich, ELIAS P. PELLETT, aged 36. [1/20]
Jan. 16, 1840, Oaksville, ALMIRA C. CONNIS, aged 27. [1/27]
Jan. 7, 1840, Warsaw, Ky., JULIA A. F. HANNAY of Cooperstown, aged 29. [1/27]
Jan. 6, 1840, Westford, HORACE KELSO, aged 26. [2/3]
Jan. 28, 1840, Cooperstown, CHARLES M. ROTCH of Butternuts, aged 18. [2/3]
Jan. 26, 1840, Davenport, N.Y., Mrs. MARY E. CRANE of Albany, aged 27. [2/3]
Feb. 3, 1840, Hartwick, Mrs. OLIVE CHASE, aged 31. [2/10]
Feb. 8, 1840, Hartwick, CHESTER A. FASSETT, 13 months. [2/17]
Feb. 14, 1840, Cooperstown, HORACE BALDWIN, aged 35. [2/17]
Jan. 28, 1840, Cooperstown, CHARLES M. ROTCH, aged 18. [2/17]
Feb. 5, 1840, Otsego, Mrs. SALLY TODD, aged 53. [2/24]
Oct. 23, 1839, Tecumseh, Mich., JAMES SHOLES of Otsego, aged 44. [2/24/1840]

Feb. 23, 1840, Butternuts, CHAS. BARDWELL JACKSON, aged 8. [3/2]
Feb. 17, 1840, Stark, N.Y., MARIETT PIERCE, aged 6. [3/2]
Feb. 24, 1840, Cooperstown, PHILIP A. ROOF, 15 months. [3/2]
Feb. 14, 1840, Otsego, HANNAH LOOMIS, aged 45. [3/2]
Feb. 24, 1840, Middlefield, Mrs. WAITY NORTH, aged 66. [3/9]
Feb. 14, 1840, Otsego, Mrs. HANNAH LOOMIS, aged 42. [3/9]
Feb. 21, 1840, Middlefield, Mrs. NANCY JONES, aged 69. [3/16]
March 1, 1840, Portlandville, Mrs. CAROLINE SPAFFORD, aged 19. [3/16]
March 13, 1840, Burlington, GERMAN C. FITCH, aged 5. [3/23]
March 14, 1840, Burlington, DELIA L. FITCH, aged 3. [3/23]
March 20, 1840, Columbia, Mrs. MARY MC KEAN, late of Otsego, aged 27. [3/30]
March 24, 1840, Sidney Plains, NATHANIEL HAVENS, aged 83. [4/6]
April 8, 1840, Otego, DANIEL WELLER, Esq., aged 70. [4/13]
April 13, 1840, Cooperstown, CATHERINE A. WOLCOTT, aged 28. [4/20]
April 15, 1840, Cherry Valley, WM. A. KLINE, aged 29. [4/20]
April 7, 1840, Otsego, JUNIA HUMASTON, aged 44. [4/27]
April 16, 1840, New Lisbon, WM. FULLER, aged 77. [4/27]
April 15, 1840, Plainfield, NATHANIEL SPRAGUE, aged 49. [4/27]
April 13, 1840, Plainfield, Mrs. MARY JOSLYN, aged 50. [4/27]
April 21, 1840, Hartwick, Maj. JOS. GRIFFIN, aged 83. [4/27]
April 12, 1840, Westford, SARAH B. COMSTOCK. [4/27]
April 25, 1840, Hartwick, PATTY WHEELER, aged 58. [5/4]
April 30, 1840, Springfield, REBECCA OLIVE, aged 26. [5/11]
April 29, 1840, Springfield, EDWARD CLOVER, aged 22. [5/11]
May 9, 1840, Richfield, OBED EDSON, aged 93. [5/18]
May 15, 1840, Middlefield, Mrs. LOUISA HUTCHINS, aged 17. [5/18]
May 3, 1840, Richfield, HARRIET D. HUTCHINSON, infant. [5/18]
May 17, 1840, Richfield, Elder JOSHUA HAYWARD, aged 58. [5/25]
May 10, 1840, Butternuts, ADELINE E. GILLET, aged 17. [6/1]
June 9, 1840, Worcester, Mrs. NANCY BURNESON. [6/15]
July 2, 1840, Exeter, ELIZA H. COLEMAN, aged 16. [7/13]
July 13, 1840, Milford, Mrs. SALLY BISSELL, aged 63. [7/20]
June 20, 1840, Hartwick, LORENA NORTHRUP, aged 3. [7/20]
June --, 1840, Exeter, POLLY VEBER, aged 37. [7/20]
July 17, 1840, Cooperstown, Mrs. MARTHA HOLT, aged 70. [7/20]
July 17, 1840, Hartwick, Mrs. MARY A. BROWNELL, aged 34. [7/27]
July 2, 1840, Otego, Col. JOHN A. HUBBELL. [7/27]
Aug. 12, 1840, Butternuts, Mrs. LUCY COOKE, aged 64. [8/17]

Aug. 10, 1840, Cherry Valley, JAMES DICKSON, aged 38. [8/17]
Aug. 14, 1840, Pike, Allegany Co., Mrs. WALTER KERR, aged 61, late of Hartwick. [8/17]
July 24, 1840, Franklin, N.Y., Mrs. EUNICE SCHRAMBLING, aged 20. [8/30]
Aug. 28, 1840, Hartwick, JOSEPH LYON, aged 79. [9/7]
Aug. 13, 1840, Richfield Springs, Dr. ED. CHUSEMAN, aged 66. [9/7]
Aug. 20, 1840, Colesville, N.Y., Mrs. LUCIA FORD, aged 26. [9/7]
Sept. 11, 1840, Otsego, SAMUEL VAN BOSKIRK, aged 26. [9/21]
Sept. 12, 1840, Cooperstown, Mrs. OLIVE BARID, aged 42. [9/21]
Sept. 23, 1840, Otsego, JONATHAN POTTER, aged 70. [9/28]
Sept. 20, 1840, New Lisbon, PAULINA THURSTON, aged 16. [9/28]
Sept. 10, 1840, New Lisbon, ABIGAIL DANIELS, aged 30. [9/28]
Sept. 17, 1840, Butternuts, RICHARD V. MORRIS, aged 17. [9/28]
Sept. 24, 1840, Bath, N.Y., Mrs. CLARINDA SHANT, late of Springfield, aged 24. [10/12]
Oct. 10, 1840, Otsego, JOHN PATTEN, aged 43. [10/19]
Oct. 8, 1840, Decatur, EMILY TRIPP, aged 35. [10/19]
Oct. 4, 1840, Fly Creek, EUGENE HINDS, aged 3. [10/19]
Oct. 22, 1840, Milford, Mrs. LYDIA WALWORTH, aged 66. [10/26]
Oct. 17, 1840, Otsego, Mrs. POLLY HINDS, aged 38. [10/26]
Oct. 24, 1840, Cooperstown, Mrs. PHEBE TRACY, aged 50. [11/2]
Oct. 3, 1840, Portland, Ohio, PASCHAL BESANCON, aged 42. Late of Springfield. [11/2]
Nov. 1, 1840, Westford, Mrs. EUNICE DRAKE, aged 78. [11/2]
Sept. 16, 1840, Clinton, Mich., Mrs. SALLY ENSWORTH, aged 53. Late of Otsego Co. [11/2]
Nov. 25, 1840, Flatbush, L[ong] I[sland], JOS. STRONG, Esq., 75, late of Cooperstown. [11/30]
Nov. 29, 1840, Springfield, ANAN HALL, aged 83. [12/14]
Dec. 6, 1840, Westford, Mrs. SALLY BROOKS, aged 52. [12/14]
Nov. 30, 1840, Springfield, DAVID CAMPBELL, aged 50. [12/14]
Dec. 4, 1840, Cooperstown, Mrs. PHEBE CORY, aged 46. [12/21]
Dec. 7, 1840, Burlington, Mrs. AMANDA HART, aged 33. [12/21]
Dec. 17, 1840, Cooperstown, Mrs. MARY WOOD, aged 90. [12/28]
Dec. 4, 1840, Otsego, Mrs. HARRIET E. JOHNSON, aged 24. [12/28]
Dec. 31, 1840, Gilbertsville, Capt. WM. BURGESS, aged 76. [1/4/1841]

DEATHS FROM JAN. 1841 - SEPT. 5, 1862.
TAKEN FROM
THE *OTSEGO HERALD & WESTERN ADVERTISER*
AND *FREEMAN'S JOURNAL.*
VOLUME II.

Dec. 4, 1840, Otsego, Mrs. HARRIET E. JOHNSON, aged 24. [1/11/1841]

Dec. 31, 1840, Gilbertsville, Capt. WILLIAM BURGESS, aged 76. [11/11/1841]

Jan. 5, 1841, Cherry Valley, MOSES BELCHER, aged 38. [1/11]

Nov. 8, 1840, Flint, Mich., Mrs. URIAH SHORT, formerly of Middlefield, aged 41. [1/11/1841]

Jan. 15, 1841, Middlefield, Mr. S. PRATT, aged 57. [2/8]

Jan. 21, 1841, Burlington, N.Y., JOHN HOOD, aged 87. [2/8]

Jan. 22, 1841, Springfield, PHILIP FISK, aged 37. [2/15]

Feb. 2, 1841, Laurens, Gen. FOWLSTON. [2/15]

Feb. 14, 1841, Otsego, Mrs. MERCY PECK, aged 83. [3/1]

Feb. 14, 1841, Gilbertsville, JEREMIAH TOWNSEND, aged 93. [3/8]

March 11, 1841, Plainfield, Mrs. LIVIA CARRIER, aged 59. [3/15]

March 2, 1841, New Berlin, JOHN M. FELLOWS, formerly of Conn., aged 30. [3/15]

Feb. 26, 1841, Springfield, THOMAS VAN HORNE, aged 98. [3/15]

Feb. 26, 1841, Milford, JOSEPH VARS, aged 81. [3/15]

March 6, 1841, Hartwick, Mrs. REBECCA A. LEO, aged 68. [3/15]

March 13, 1841, Middlefield, Mrs. PHIDELIA SAXTON, aged 35. [3/22]

March 13, 1841, Columbus, N.Y., Mrs. CLARISSA CALKIN, aged 74. [3/22]

March 18, 1841, Exeter, Mrs. LYDIA BALDWIN, aged 34. [3/29]

April 2, 1841, Cooperstown, HANNAH H. WHITE, aged 23. [4/5]

March 22, 1841, Hartwick, RACHEL LUTHER, aged 75. [4/5]

Feb. 17, 1841, Brooklyn, CAROLINE E. MORRIS, aged 7. [4/5]

Feb. 27, 1841, New Berlin, Mrs. SALLY WELCH, aged 28. [4/5]

March 20, 1841, Laurens, REBECCA DERBY, age 17. [4/12]

April 3, 1841, Brooklyn, DELVAN RICHARDS, aged 24. [4/12]

March 26, 1841, Middlefield, ALONZO CAMPBELL, aged 39. [4/19]

March 11, 1841, Hartwick, ELIZABETH BENJAMIN, aged 18. [4/19]

March 18, 1841, Laurens, CALEB ASPINWALL, aged 50. [4/19]

April 9, 1841, Hartwick, CHARLES MC HENRY BOTSFORD, aged 4. [4/19]

April 6, 1841, New Berlin, HARVEY P. ENSIGN, aged 29. [4/19]

April 14, 1841, Springfield, MARY SCOLLARD, aged 8. [4/19]
April 13, 1841, Otsego, JOHN SUTHERLAND, aged 7. [4/26]
April 14, 1841, Hartwick, Mrs. ELIZABETH HAWKS, aged 31. [4/26]
April 14, 1841, Milford, HARRIET M. SAYRE, aged 23. [4/26]
April 3, 1841, Hammondsport, WILLIAM D. SMITH, aged 19. Formerly of Cooperstown. [4/26]
April 15, 1841, Cooperstown, Mrs. HANNAH BREWER, aged 35. [4/26]
April 17, 1841, Milford, ORANGE BISSELL, aged 66. [5/3]
April 14, 1841, Exeter, Mrs. MARY BECKWITH, aged 82. [5/3]
April 24, 1841, Hartwick, Mrs. RUTH PERRY, aged 72. [5/10]
April 18, 1841, Springfield, ELIZABETH WELDON, aged 63. [5/10]
April 25, 1841, New Berlin, HORACE HALL, aged 33. [5/10]
May 17, 1841, Otsego, RUFUS FISKE, aged 57. [5/17]
May 17, 1841, Unadilla, Mrs. LYDIA KINGSLEY, aged 30. [5/24]
May 17, 1841, Milford, Mrs. MARTHA BISSELL, aged 45. [5/31]
May 7, 1841, Rush, Monroe Co., JEREMY TITUS, aged 48. [5/31]
May 14, 1841, Troy, Mich., ALANSON PIERSON, aged 37; formerly of Otsego Co. [5/31]
May 11, 1841, Burlington, CORNELIA DIMOCK, 25 years. [5/31]
June 4, 1841, Cooperstown, WILLIAM VAN BOOSKIRK, aged 78. [6/7]
June 9, 1841, Exeter, EMILY HUBBARD, aged 19. [6/14]
May 21, 1841, Burlington, Major JOHN GARRETT, aged 67. [6/14]
June 8, 1841, Oaksville, Mrs. EUNICE HIGBY, aged 48. [6/14]
June 2, 1841, Fly Creek, WILLIAM PLATNER, aged 33. [6/21]
June 18, 1841, Hartwick, Mrs. CHRISTIANA BILLS, aged 89. [6/21]
June 16, 1841, Butternuts, Mrs. EMILY DANIELSON, aged 58. [6/28]
June 20, 1841, Albany, JAMES KING. [6/28]
June 21, 1841, SAMUEL S. LUSH, aged 58. [6/28]
June 13, 1841, Otsego, Mrs. ALMIRA M. COATS, aged 22. [7/5]
June 27, 1841, Macon, Ga., IRA BRAGG of Cooperstown, aged 53. [7/12]
June 25, 1841, Unadilla, SAMUEL BETTS, aged 75. [7/12]
June 24, 1841, Unadilla, SAMUEL GAYLORD, aged 22. [7/12]
July 16, 1841, Springfield, Mrs. PRUDENCE COATES, aged 80. [7/19]
July 26, 1841, Springfield, Mrs. SUSANNA COOK, aged 70. [7/26]
July 25, 1841, Norwich, N.Y., Dr. CHARLES MITCHELL. [8/2]
July 25, 1841, New Lisbon, SARAH E. HARD, aged 13. [8/9]
Aug. 1, 1841, Springfield, RUFUS TRACY, aged 72. [8/9]
Aug. 4, 1841, Fly Creek, EMMA BOWNE, aged 21. [8/16]
Aug. 8, 1841, Butternuts, DAVID A. GILLET, aged 23. [8/16]
Aug. 10, 1841, Hartwick, Mrs. BETSEY MATTHEWSON, aged 83. [8/16]
Aug. 14, 1841, Otsego, DANIEL BOURNE, aged 74. [8/23]

Aug. 2, 1841, Franklin, MARY L. PIXLEY, aged 21. [8/23]
Aug. 29, 1841, Cooperstown, MARY PHINNEY, aged 37. [8/30]
Aug. 12, 1841, Otsego, HENRY COONROD, aged 74. [8/30]
[No date] New London, N.Y., GEORGE CLINTON, aged 28; late of Milford. [9/6]
Aug. 15, 1841, Mt. Clements, Mich., Mrs. ELMIRA COOKE, aged 57. [9/6]
[No date] Cooperstown, Mrs. BETSEY WILLIAMS RICHARDSON, aged 35. [9/6]
Sept. 9, 1841, Laurens, Mrs. SARAH M. DEANS, aged 27. [9/13]
Sept. 14, 1841, Cooperstown, FRANCES E. LOVELAND, aged 2. [9/20]
Sept. 10, 1841, Westford, PAUL GROFF, aged 64. [9/20]
Aug. 30, 1841, Warren, N.Y., SAMUEL ATKINS, aged 29. [9/20]
Sept. 10, 1841, Hartwick, JABEZ PEMBLETON, aged 77. [9/27]
Sept. 17, 1841, Cherry Valley, BENJAMIN B. PROVOST, aged 65. [9/27]
Aug. 21, 1841, Richland, N.Y., DAVID TREADWAY, aged 99. [10/4]
Sept. 20, 1841, Montpelier, Vt., Mrs. LUCRETIA PRENTISS, aged 88 (? age). [[10/4]
Oct. 3, 1841, West Hartwick, RUFUS PETERS, aged 39. [10/11]
Oct. 14, 1841, Cooperstown, A. V. MOORE, aged 31. [10/18]
Oct. 12, 1841, Hartwick, MARY RIPLEY ROSE, aged 21. [10/18]
Oct. 13, 1841, Milford, ISAAC BISSELL, aged 49. [10/25]
Oct. 6, 1841, Louisville, HARRIET COUSE, infant. [11/8]
Nov. 7, 1841, Portlandville, Mrs. OLIVE THORN, aged 19. [11/15]
Oct. 28, 1841, Hartwick Seminary, Col. J. H. DEWEY. [11/15]
Nov. 5, 1841, Worcester, ALBERT HOUGHTON, Esq., aged 27. [11/15]
Oct. 20, 1841, Cherry Valley, Mrs. JERUSHA ELWELL, aged 56. [11/15]
Oct. 23, 1841, Cherry Valley, SAMUEL ELWELL, aged 62. [11/15]
Sept. 29, 1841, Vandalia, Ill., Dr. L. GRIFFITH, Otsego Co. [11/15]
Nov. 11, 1841, Burlington, EREXENA BROWN, aged 19. [11/22]
Nov. 10, 1841, Burlington, ABRAHAM PERSONS, aged 74. [11/22]
Nov. 15, 1841, Richfield, Hon. OBADIAH BEARDSLEY, aged 70. [11/22]
Nov. 15, 1841, Unadilla, Col. DAVID HOUGH, aged 82. [11/22]
Nov. 15, 1841, Hartwick, DAN. M. CHADDON, aged 27. [11/22]
Nov. 17, 1841, Otsego, ELMIRA PATTEN, aged 13. [11/22]
Nov. 20, 1841, Otsego, SAMUEL SHERWOOD, aged 44. [11/29]
Nov. 22, 1841, Cooperstown, SALLY BODEN, aged 40. [11/29]
Oct. 20, 1841, Hartwick, Mrs. ELIZABETH HINMAN, aged 54. [11/29]
Nov. 25, 1841, Garrettsville, BETSEY BUNDY, aged 23. [11/29]
Nov. 30, 1841, N. Bainbridge, Mr. BILLA THURSTON, aged 33. [12/6]
Nov. 13, 1841, Laurens, JAMES BOYDE, Esq., aged 51. [12/6]

Dec. 9, 1841, Otsego, URIAH LUCE, Esq., aged 79. [12/13]
Nov. 20, 1841, Cherry Valley, AMOS JONES, aged 25. [12/13]
Nov. 8, 1841, Westford, ORLO ALLEN, aged 71. [12/13]
Dec. 15, 1841, Cooperstown, ALLEN RECCORD, aged 23. [12/20]
Dec. 5, 1841, Edmeston, Mrs. MARY HENRY, aged 71. [12/20]
Dec. 5, 1841, Adams, N.Y., Mrs. SALLY MAINE. [12/20]
Dec. 11, 1841, Worcester, N.Y., HARRIET M. FULLER, aged 24. [12/20]
Nov. 30, 1841, Middlefield, Mrs. SUSANNA FLING, aged 56. [12/27]
Dec. 14, 1841, Clinton, Mrs. ADELAIDE SMITH, aged 24. [12/27]
Dec. 30, 1841, Cooperstown, DEIDAMA THURSTAN, aged 15. [1/3/1842]
Dec. 27, 1841, Washington, AMY S. BOWNE, aged 18. [1/10/1842]
Jan. 2, 1842, Cooperstown, HEMAN LLOYD, aged 42. [1/10]
Jan. 4, 1842, Cooperstown, HENRY KNOWLTON Jr., aged 23. [1/17]
Jan. 14, 1842, Cooperstown, JOHN S. HANNAY, aged 24. [1/17]
Jan. 11, 1842, Otsego, STEPHEN NORTH, aged 80. [1/17]
Jan. 6, 1842, Cherry Valley, Mrs. MARY S. DUNLAP, aged 27. [1/17]
Jan. 5, 1842, Cherry Valley, Mrs. MARTHA HODSON, aged 41. [1/17]
Jan. 5, 1842, Toldeo, OH, HARVEY S. BRADFORD, of Cooperstown. [1/24]
Dec. 13, 1841, Lancaster, Wisc., ORRIN F. DEWEY of Laurens, aged 23. [1/24/1842]
Jan. 23, 1842, Jacksonboro, Dea. GRANDUS WILSON, aged 48. [1/31]
Jan. 15, 1842, Cooperstown, WILLIAM HOLMES, aged 1 year. [1/31]
Dec. 31, 1841, W. Hartwick, DAVID B. ALVORD, aged 21. [2/7/1842]
[No date] Laurens, CLARK ROCKWELL, aged 22. [2/7/1842]
Feb. 4, 1842, Middlefield, WILLIAM A. COLLINS, aged 34. [2/7]
[No date] Middlesex, N.Y., Mrs. HANNAH JOHNSON, aged 31. [2/7/1842]
Jan. 8, 1842, Jacksonville, Fla., ELIZABETH H. SPAFFORD, aged 26. [2/7]
Feb. 2, 1842, Pittsfield, THEODORE C. DAVIDSON, aged 26. [2/14]
Feb. 2, 1842, Homer, N.Y., ESEK BRADFORD, aged 73. [2/14]
Feb. 12, 1842, Cooperstown, HENRY JONES. [2/14]
Feb. 9, 1842, Utica, Col. EZRA DEAN, aged 62. [2/21]
Feb. 3, 1842, Little Falls, Mrs. BEDE TODD, aged 66. [2/21]
Feb. 15, 1842, Cooperstown, ELISHA FOOTE, Esq., aged 53. [2/28]
Feb. 20, 1842, Otsego, MARY ELIZABETH WARREN, aged 1 year. [2/28]
Feb. 17, 1842, Springfield, FAYETTE REED, aged 17. [3/7]
Feb. 24, 1842, Springfield, FRANKLIN REED, aged 17. [3/7]

Feb. 15, 1842, Hartwick, FANNY WELLS, aged 40. [3/7]
Feb. 17, 1842, Unadilla Forks, BARKER STILLMAN, aged 23. [3/7]
Feb. 26, 1842, Laurens, LUSINA D. JOHNSON, aged 29. [3/7]
March 9, 1842, Hartwick, JOHN WELLS, aged 83. [3/7]
March 6, 1842, Cooperstown, RACHEL ANN PECK, aged 16. [3/7]
March 4, 1842, Cherry Valley, THEO. WILLIAMS, aged 22. [3/7]
March 5, 1842, SARAH E. NELSON, aged 16. [3/7]
March 7, 1842, AURELIA JUDD, aged 17. [3/7]
March 13, 1842, Cooperstown, Dr. H.S. HARPER, aged 42. [3/21]
March 10, 1842, Otsego, MARY MILLER, aged 20. [3/21]
Feb. 27, 1842, Smyrna, N.Y., Hon. ISAAC FOOTE, aged 100. [3/21]
Feb. 13, 1842, Unadilla, Mich., Mrs. SALLY NOBLE. [3/21]
March 15, 1842, Cherry Valley, MARY ANN RILEY, aged 65. [3/21]
March 21, 1842, Butternuts, ZEBA WASHBON, aged 79. [3/28]
March 7, 1842, Bridgewater, Mrs. RACHEL HARRIS, aged 63. [3/28]
March 18, 1842, Cherry Valley, Mrs. MERCY HORTON, aged 97. [3/28]
March 19, 1842, NANCY PHENIX, aged 27. [3/28]
March 21, 1842, Mrs. CATHERINE VAN DYKE, aged 44. [3/28]
March 25, 1842, Exeter, WILLIAM CLARKE, aged 65. [4/4]
March 29, 1842, Otsego, GEORGE TIFT, aged 26. [4/4]
March 26, 1842, Cherry Valley, LEVANTIA WHITE, aged 22. [4/11]
April 7, 1842, Pittsfield, JOSHUA CHASE, aged 37. [4/18]
March 29, 1842, Laurens, SOLOMON ELDRED, aged 60. [4/18]
April 5, 1842, Laurens, JONATHAN FULLER, aged 96. [4/18]
April 8, 1842, Laurens, SUSAN FULLER, aged 58. [4/18]
April 16, 1842, Hartwick, GEORGE P. FIELD, aged 37. [4/25]
April 9, 1842, Laurens, RHODA FULLER, aged 40. [4/25]
April 13, 1842, Pittsfield, SARAH A. ROAD, aged 21. [4/25]
April 17, 1842, Cooperstown, KENNETH CAMPBELL, 14 months. [4/25]
April 11, 1842, Middlefield, DAVID REED, aged 60. [5/2]
April 25, 1842, Cooperstown, HARRIET TIFFANY, aged 10. [5/2]
April 19, 1842, Norwich, BETSEY RANDALL, aged 19. [5/2]
April 18, 1842, Vernon, Oneida Co., Mrs. CHLOE GRIDLEY (Utica), aged 77. [5/2]
May 5, 1842, Hartwick, Mrs. RUTH IRONS, aged 55. [5/2]
April 23, 1842, Hartwick, MARY STEERE, aged 38. [5/9]
May 3, 1842, New Lisbon, HEZEKIAH GREGORY, aged 65. [5/9]
April 26, 1842, Butternuts, HARRIET E. BENTLEY, aged 9. [5/9]
March 23, 1842, Otsego, GEORGE A. TEFFT, aged 26. [5/9]
May 1, 1842, Cherry Valley, Mrs. MARY HUBBARD, aged 88. [5/9]
May 7, 1842, Otsego, LOUISA KNOWLTON, aged 22. [5/23]

April 13, 1842, Limerick, N.Y., Mrs. ALEX. C. MOFFATT, aged 76. [5/30]
May 21, 1842, Middlefield, Mrs. HANNAH ANTISDEL, aged 65. [5/30]
June 6, 1842, Otsego, EPHRAIM PIER, aged 56. [6/13]
June 8, 1842, Middlefield, ELIAS GROAT, aged 45. [6/13]
May 9, 1842, Knoxville, Pa., DAVID BROWN (Otsego Co.), aged 40. [6/13]
May 29, 1842, Evans, Erie Co., ELIZABETH WOOD, aged 25. [6/13]
June 3, 1842, Adams, N.Y., REUBEN P. MAIN (Otsego), aged 79. [6/13]
May 30, 1842, Middlefield, SAMUEL CAMPBELL, aged 25. [6/20]
April 22, 1842, Andover, N.Y., JAMES HANN, Esq., aged 39. [6/27]
June 19, 1842, Troy, JAMES PARSHALL, aged 27. [7/4]
June 2, 1842, Springfield, JOHN WALL. [7/4]
June 14, 1842, Bridgewater, N.Y., DENNISON BROWN, Esq., aged 79. [7/4]
June 28, 1842, Cortlandville, N.Y., NATHANIEL ANTISDALE, aged 69. [7/11]
July 11, 1842, Middlefield, HORACE I. COFFIN, aged 20. [7/18]
July 11, 1842, URILLA SMITH, aged 27. [7/18]
July 6, 1842, Unadilla, Col. DANIEL CONE, aged 62. [7/18]
June 11, 1842, Marshall, Mich., Mrs. CHARLOTTE PEABODY, aged 38. [7/18]
June 11, 1842, Troy, Rev. DAVID BUTLER, D.D., aged 80. [7/18]
June 20, 1842, Otsego, Mrs. ACHSAH NEWELL, aged 49. [7/25]
July 9, 1842, Laurens, Mrs. MARY GARDNER, aged 60. [7/25]
July 20, 1842, Cherry Valley, Mrs. PHEBE C. LOWE, aged 24. [8/1]
July 20, 1842, Ellicottville, N.Y., JOHN H. PRENTISS, aged 8. [8/1]
Aug. 6, 1842, Ft. Plain, HENRY ADAMS BABCOCK, 13 months. [8/15]
Aug. 10, 1842, Cooperstown, REXAVILLE L. FITCH, aged 4. [8/22]
Aug. 6, 1842, Hartwick, MARY A. ELDRED, aged 21. [8/22]
Aug. 19, 1842, Middlefield, JOHN MANCHESTER, aged 73. [8/22]
Sept. 5, 1842, Exeter, Dr. NABOTH BUCKINGHAM, aged 62. [9/12]
Sept. 2, 1842, Hartick, SEYMOUR GAYLORD, aged 5. [9/12]
Sept. 12, 1842, Westford, SAMUEL CRANDAL, aged 50. [9/26]
Sept. 27, 1842, Butternuts, NATHAN LULL, aged 85. [10/10]
Sept. 29, 1842, South Valley, TEN EYCK C. LOW, aged 39. [10/17]
[No date] Decatur, Mrs. CATHERINE GRAFF, aged 34. [10/17]
Oct. 16, 1842, Cooperstown, Mrs. LYDIA EDSON, aged 40. [10/24]
Oct. 27, 1842, Otsego, AMBROSE HYDE, aged 24. [10/31]
Nov. 7, 1842, Decatur, CLARINDA W. BURTON. [11/14]
Nov. 16, 1842, Milford, Mrs. ROXY KIRBY, aged 46. [11/21]

Nov. 5, 1842, Richfield, DANIEL HANNAHS, aged 76. [11/21]
Nov. 1, 1842, Plainfield, RICHARD CARRIER, aged 68. [11/21]
[No date] Oneonta, WILLIAM ANGEL, aged 65. [11/21]
Nov. 6, 1842, Butternuts, Mrs. JANE D. BURGESS. [11/28]
Nov. 22, 1842, Westford, CALEB MILLER, aged 48. [11/28]
Nov. 25, 1842, Hartwick, Deacon ISAAC BURCH, aged 60. [12/5]
Nov. 20, 1842, Otego, JOHN PHILIPS, aged 73. [12/5]
Dec. 3, 1842, Decatur, Mrs. BETSEY LANE, aged 44. [12/12]
Dec. 5, 1842, Hartwick, Rev. CHAUNCEY LANE, aged 80. [12/12]
Dec. 8, 1842, S. Edmeston, Mrs. HELEN M. SPURR, aged 27. [12/19]
Dec. 12, 1842, New Lisbon, Mrs. ABIGAIL COMSTOCK, aged 73. [12/19]
Dec. 13, 1842, Cooperstown, WILLIAM HATCH, aged 28. [12/26]
Dec. 18, 1842, Middlefield, Mrs. TRYPHENA BEEBEE, aged 66. [12/26]
Dec. 19, 1842, Westford, Mrs. MARTHA SNYDER, aged 19. [12/26]
Dec. 13, 1842, Burlington, MINOR SHOLES, aged 81. [12/26]
Dec. 20, 1842, Middlefield, ED. H. PEGG, aged 23. [1/2/1825]
Dec. 27, 1842, Hartwick, ELIPHALET STICKNEY, aged 64. [1/2/1843]
Dec. 29, 1842, Cooperstown, DAVID WATERMAN, aged 65. [1/2/1843]
Dec. 17, 1842, Burlington, ERASTUS FITCH, aged 68. [1/9/1843]
Jan. 5, 1843, Cooperstown, HELEN BURLINGHAM, aged 7. [1/9]
Jan. 5, 1843, Cooperstown, Mrs. MARY DIXON, aged 60. [1/16]
Jan. 6, 1843, Middlefield, Mrs. MARY PRATT, aged 23. [1/16]
Jan. 12, 1843, Middlefield, MARY E. PRATT, infant. [1/16]
Jan. 16, 1843, Hartwick, Mrs. MARY BURCH, aged 52. [1/23]
Dec. 27, 1842, Plainfield, THOMAS DAVIS, aged 52. [1/23/1843]
Jan. 16, 1843, Buffalo, Mrs. MARY SPARROW, aged 45, formerly of Cooperstown. [1/30]
Jan. 17, 1843, New York, CHARLES F. SHANKLAND, aged 30 (Cooperstown). [1/30]
Jan. 19, 1843, Middlefield, IRA GANO, infant. [1/30]
Jan. 27, 1843, Cooperstown, WILLIAM LEWIS, aged 79. [1/30]
Jan. 28, 1843, Hartwick, JEHIEL TODD, aged 82. [2/2]
Feb. 3, 1843, Butternuts, DENNIS ALDRICH, aged 30. [2/2]
Jan. 22, 1843, Laurens, OLIVE TUCKER, aged 44. [2/2]
Jan. 21, 1843, Unadilla, CATHERINE E. KINGSLEY, aged 7. [2/2]
Feb. 1, 1843, Cooperstown, Rev. S. C. HUTCHINS. [2/2]
Feb. 7, 1843, Cooperstown, JOHN MILLER, aged 74. [2/13]
Feb. 9, 1843, Cooperstown, Mrs. CHARITY BATES, aged 64. [2/13]
Feb. 5, 1843, Elmira, Mrs. LUCY HATCH, aged 73, late of Richfield. [2/20]

Aug. 1842, Havanna, Ill., CELINE CHASE, aged 20 (Maryland). [2/20/1843]
Feb. 9, 1843, Otsego, JULIA BOURNE, aged 19. [2/20]
Feb. 20, 1843, Cooperstown, Mrs. CATHERINE SCOTT, aged 43. [2/27]
Feb. 20, 1843, Burlington, HANNAH E. PIERCE, aged 33. [2/27]
Feb. 26, 1843, New Lisbon, Mrs. SODEIMA GILLETT, age 30. [3/6]
Feb. 27, 1843, New Lisbon, Mrs. MYRA C. GREGORY, aged 26. [3/6]
Feb. 21, 1843, Springfield, Mrs. PATTY BASAINGER, aged 58. [3/6]
March 1, 1843, Cherry Valley, JAMES STORY, aged 27. [3/6]
March 7, 1843, Middlefield, LEWIS BARNUM, aged 54. [3/6]
Feb. 5, 1843, Rockford, Ill., Mrs. MARY A. WATERMAN (Cooperstown). [3/6]
Oct. 2, 1842, Illinois, AUGUSTUS J. PREVOST, aged 77 (Westford). [3/6/1843]
March 7, 1843, Cooperstown, SARAH SCOTT, aged 15. [3/13]
Jan. 9, 1843, Richfield, Mrs. EUNICE B. BABCOCK, aged 31. [3/13]
March 3, 1843, West Burlington, Mrs. AZUBAH SMITH. [3/13]
March 13, 1843, Exeter, ALONZO HERKIMER, aged 37. [3/20]
March 13, 1843, Exeter, WILLIAM L. JOHNSON, aged 33. [3/20]
March 11, 1843, Hartwick, AMOS INGALLS, aged 22. [3/20]
March 1, 1843, Pierstown, EUGENIA E. VAN HORNE, aged 8. [3/20]
March 18, 1843, Otego, BETSEY L. HUNT, aged 34. [3/27]
March 16, 1843, ED. AUSTIN, aged 27. [3/27]
March 27, 1843, Otsego, Mrs. SALLY METCALF, aged 70. [3/27]
[No date] Cooperstown, EMILY BOWERS COLLINS, aged 14 months. [3/27]
March 22, 1843, Butternuts, TIMOTHY DONALDSON, aged 92. [4/10]
Feb. 27, 1843, Springfield, N.Y., BILLINGS COATS, aged 74. [4/10]
March 5, 1843, Hartwick, MARY A. FIELD, 16 months. [4/10]
April 8, 1843, Cooperstown, Mrs. AABRINA CRIPPEN, aged 49. [4/17]
April 10, 1843, Pierstown, HOMER BEADLE, aged 58. [4/17]
April 11, 1843, Milford, Dr. JOHN WHITESIDE, aged 50. [4/17]
April 9, 1843, Milford, Mrs. CORNELIA GOODRICH, aged 35. [4/17]
April 7, 1843, Cherry Valley, ANDREW M. HIBBARD, 7 months. [4/17]
March 20, 1843, Fly Creek, WILLIAM ADDAMS, aged 75. [4/24]
April 6, 1843, W. Edmeston, SALMON FARRAR, Jr., aged 36. [4/24]
April 7, 1843, Springfield, N.Y., Capt. WM. BROWN, aged 84. [4/24]
April 13, 1843, Cleveland, OH, JOHN S. BUTTS, aged 10. [5/1]
Feb. 28, 1843, Pierstown, Mrs. LUCY STOCKER, 55 years. [5/1]
April 27, 1843, Cooperstown, JOHN W. DAVIS, aged 38. [5/1]
April 15, 1843, Springfield, Mrs. JULIA A. CRUMB, aged 32. [5/1]

April 27, 1843, Cherry Valley, MARY ANDREWS, aged 50. [5/8]
[No date] Herkimer Co. (Stark), AMANDA ANGEL (Otsego), aged 24. [5/8]
April 11, 1843, Middlefield, MOSES D. RICH, aged 19. [5/8]
May 9, 1843, Hartwick, NATHANIEL L. CARD, aged 42. [5/15]
April 20, 1843, Laurens, JOEL L. FOWLSTON, aged 8 months. [5/15]
May 8, 1843, Springfield, Mrs. LOIS BARRETT, Jr., aged 38. [5/15]
May 9, 1843, Springfield, MARY JANE FIELD, infant. [5/15]
May 27, 1843, Cooperstown, JAMES HETHERINGTON, aged 45. [6/5]
May 23, 1843, Hartwick, Mrs. MARTHA L. FASSETT, aged 57. [6/12]
May 30, 1843, Burlington, Mrs. RUTH BOLTON, aged 66. [6/12]
June 1, 1843, Middlefield Center, SAMUEL N. BARKER, aged 84. [6/12]
June 12, 1843, Otsego, ELISHA BOWEN, aged 51. [6/19]
June 12, 1843, Cooperstown, Mrs. NANCY A. LATHROP, aged 41. [6/19]
June 11, 1843, Hartwick, THOMAS SHADDEN, Jr., aged 18. [6/19]
June 8, 1843, Edmeston, GURDON A. SHOLES, aged 32. [6/19]
June 19, 1843, Pittsfield, Mrs. EUNICE BEARDSLEY. [6/19]
June 1, 1843, Burlington, HARVEY LOOMIS, aged 18. [6/19]
June 4, 1843, Burlington, Mrs. MARIA LOOMIS, aged 43. [6/19]
June 10, 1843, Springfield, JANE F. OLIVER, aged 30. [6/26]
May 1, 1843, Richfield Springs, Mrs. HANNAH JOHNSON, aged 54. [6/26]
June 15, 1843, Decatur, Mrs. MARTHA DAVIS, aged 64. [6/26]
June 4, 1843, Otsego (Metcalf Hill), Mrs. WEALTHY METCALF, aged 49. [7/3]
July 1, 1843, Orego, BENJAMIN EDSON, aged 84. [7/3]
July 3, 1843, Cherry Valley, THOMAS THOMPSON, aged 85. [7/10]
June 20, 1843, Milford, Mrs. FIDEL BRIDGES, aged 42. [7/10]
July 21, 1843, Cherry Valley, Mrs. HANNAH Y. GOODRICH, aged 24. [7/31]
July 12, 1843, Pittsfield, JOHN WHITE, aged 87. [7/31]
Aug. 2, 1843, Cooperstown, Mr. JOHN RUSSELL, aged 71. [8/7]
July 26, 1843, St. Johnsville, TOMPKINS BATES (Otsego), aged 36. [8/7]
Aug. 3, 1843, Burlington, BETSEY BOLTON, aged 34. [8/14]
July 13, 1843, Maryland, N.Y., AMOS SPENCER, aged 84. [8/14]
July 25, 1843, Otsego Co., DIER HASTINGS, aged 72. [8/14]
Aug. 15, 1843, Exeter, Mrs. SALINDA HARDING, aged 31. [8/21]
July 1, 1843, Otsego, TIMOTHY HUMASTON, aged 83. [8/21]
Aug. 18, 1843, Cooperstown, JULIA M. TRACY, aged 29. [8/28]
Aug. 19, 1843, Milford, ATTICUS A. BARTLETT, infant. [8/28]
Aug. 23, 1843, Hartwick, WILLIAM BURCH, aged 19. [9/4]

Aug. 10, 1843, Key West, Fla., LEWIS M. BRAGG, [9/4]
Sept. 1, 1843, Westford, JOHN E. CHESTER, aged 49. [9/4]
Aug. 19, 1843, New Lisbon, NAAMAN JOHNSON, aged 9. [9/4]
Aug. 31, 1843, Cooperstown, Mrs. LOIS GROAT, aged 63. [9/4]
Sept. 7, 1843, Cooperstown, GEORGE ROBERTS, aged 78. [9/11]
Aug. 27, 1843, E. Worcester, JAMES W. LINCOLN, aged 45. [9/11]
Aug. 27, 1843, Springfield, Mrs. SALLY TRACY, aged 73. [9/11]
Aug. 26, 1843, New Lisbon, Mrs. LUCINDA GARDNER, aged 42. [9/11]
Aug. 30, 1843, Pierstown, FREDERICK W. HARVEY, aged 23. [9/11]
Aug. 11, 1843, Westford, TIMOTHY CANFIELD, aged 85. [9/18]
Sept. 1, 1843, Westfield, Chau. Co., Mrs. RUTH STOWELL (Otsego), aged 64. [9/18]
Sept. 16, 1843, Otsego, ABEL H. CRANDALL, aged 31. [9/15]
Sept. 18, 1843, Cooperstown, HORACE K. ROBERTS. [9/15]
Sept. 23, 1843, Springfield, Mrs. SUSAN MAXFIELD, aged 93. [10/2]
Oct. 4, 1843, Cherry Valley, BENJAMIN ALLEN, aged 80. [10/23]
Oct. 14, 1843, Burlington, ALONZO BABCOCK, aged 32. [10/23]
Oct. 22, 1843, Cooperstown, HENRY NEWCOMB, aged 27. [10/30]
Oct. 15, 1843, New Lisbon, Mrs. ELIZABETH WALKER, aged 86. [10/30]
Oct. 11, 1843, Cherry Valley, JONAS HANNAHS, aged 74. [10/30]
Nov. 6, 1843, Cooperstown, Mrs. NANCY WILSON, aged 37. [11/13]
Nov. 4, 1843, Otsego, SELDON WILSON, aged 47. [11/13]
Nov. 3, 1843, Hartwick, SOPHIA NORTHRUP. [11/13]
Oct. 19, 1843, Pittsfield, RICHARD DAVIDSON, aged 54. [11/13]
Oct. 26, 1843, Springfield, ARTHUR DAVIS, aged 8. [11/13]
Oct. 27, 1843, Exeter, Mrs. CHARLOTTE HUMASTON, aged 47. [11/13]
Nov. 6, 1843, Middlefield, Mrs. HANNAH RICH, aged 46. [11/20]
Nov. 13, 1843, Stark, Herkimer Co., FREDERICK BRONNER, aged 83. [11/20]
Nov. 15, 1843, Cleveland, OH, THEODORE CAMPBELL, aged 24 (Cooperstown). [11/27]
Nov. 29, 1843, Cooperstown, MARY MILLER TIFFANY, aged 18. [12/4]
Nov. 10, 1843, Butternuts, SMITH S. OSBORN, Otsego, aged 49. [12/4]
Nov. 25, 1843, Springfield, Mrs. SARAH A. MULKINS, aged 35. [12/4]
Nov. 26, 1843, Otsego, Mrs. ABIGAIL BOWEN, aged 87. [12/4]
Nov. 26, 1843, Cherry Valley, Mrs. AMELIA M. WOODBURN, aged 28. [12/4]
Nov. 24, 1843, Unadilla Forks, Mrs. HAMMISSON BABCOCK, aged 33. [12/18]

[No date] Springfield, SAMUEL WOOD, aged 57. [12/25]
Dec. 17, 1843, Laurens, JAMES RATHBUN, aged 89. [1/15/1844]
Dec. 31, 1843, Laurens, MARYETTE STRAIGHT, aged 18. [1/15/1844]
Dec. 28, 1843, Laurens, Mrs. SARAH HOWLAND, aged 66. [1/15/1844]
Jan. 2, 1844, Burlington, Mrs. ELIZA ANN STEVENS, aged 22. [1/15]
Dec. 28, 1843, Middlefield, Mrs. MARTHA PETTE, aged 58. [1/15/1844]
Jan. 22, 1844, Middlefield, PHICELIA SAXTON, 17 months. [1/29]
Jan. 22, 1844, Milford, GEORGE BABCOCK, aged 65. [1/29]
Jan. 16, 1844, Exeter, Mrs. BETSEY M. CASWELL, aged 27. [1/29]
Jan. 21, 1844, Exeter, Mrs. BETSEY SMITH, aged 52. [1/29]
Jan. 27, 1844, Middlefield, HARRIET HUTCHINS, aged 18. [2/5]
Jan. 30, 1844, Otsego, ELIZA A. VAN HORNE, aged 3. [2/5]
Jan. 21, 1844, Middlefield, Mrs. POLLY CHASE, aged 70. [2/12]
Feb. 5, 1844, Hartwick, NANCY HENNIKER, aged 15. [2/12]
Feb. 4, 1844, Milford, Mrs. MAYETTE SHUTE, aged 25. [2/12]
Jan. 31, 1844, Butternuts, Mrs. JULIA A. BRASEE, aged 35. [2/12]
Feb. 3, 1844, Burlington, Mrs. ABIGAIL GORHAM, aged 34. [2/12]
Feb. 10, 1844, Cooperstown, ANN C. RAYMOND, aged 8. [2/19]
Feb. 8, 1844, Unadilla, Mrs. ANN WILMOT, aged 60. [2/19]
Feb. 13, 1844, Burlington, ELISHA NICKERSON. [2/19]
Feb. 10, 1844, Burlington, Mrs. CATHERINE BECKER, aged 67. [2/19]
Feb. 22, 1844, Springfield, EZRA CARROLL, aged 60. [3/4]
Feb. 28, 1844, Otsego, Mrs. ARUNAH METCALF, aged 70. [3/4]
Feb. 25, 1844, Middlefield, Mrs. HANNAH DENTON, aged 61. [3/11]
Feb. 25, 1844, E. Richfield, Mrs. SARAH BIXBY, aged 77. [3/11]
March 6, 1844, Middlefield, Mrs. ANJULINE WEEKS, aged 30. [3/11]
March 15, 1844, Cooperstown, CHARLES BOTTSFORD, aged 35. [3/18]
March 11, 1844, Otsego, Mrs. PHEBE WOODWARD, aged 70. [3/18]
March 13, 1844, Mrs. NORMA BALL, aged 51. [3/18]
March 14, 1844, Mrs. ANNA BABBITT, aged 40. [3/18]
Feb. 15, 1844, Herkimer, WARREN BURLINGHAM (Otsego), aged 23. [3/18]
March 12, 1844, Burlington, LEMUEL BOLTON, aged 66. [3/18]
March 18, 1844, Middlefield, ROBERT HENNIKER, aged 50. [3/25]
March 2, 1844, Maryland, ELIZA ANN HASTINGS, aged 32. [3/25]
March 22, 1844, Otsego, SAMUEL M. JONES, aged 66. [3/25]
March 11, 1844, Fly Creek, ELIZA ANN WILLIAMS, age 19. [3/25]
March 15, 1844, Hartwick, WILLIAM W. ALMY, aged 1 year. [3/25]
March 19, 1844, Otsego, STEPHEN ST. JOHN, aged 23. [3/25]
March 14, 1844, Plainfield, HASKELL CRUMB, aged 2. [3/25]

March 17, 1844, Schuyler Lake, Mrs. SUSANNA BREWER, aged 53. [3/25]
March 15, 1844, New Berlin, Mrs. ISABEL WHITE, aged 76. [3/25]
March 8, 1844, Cherry Valley, PHEBE E. GLAZIER, infant. [4/1]
March 11, 1844, Maryland, Mrs. PRINDLE, age 93. [4/1]
March 12, 1844, Elmira, Dr. DORASTUS HATCH, (Otsego), aged 84. [4/1]
March 18, 1844, Springfield, Mrs. MARGARET VAN HORNE, aged 58. [4/1]
March 25, 1844, Clarksville, HELEN P. VANHUSEN, infant. [4/1]
[No date] Hartwick, CEYLON WEBB, aged 2. [4/1]
March 24, 1844, Edmeston, Col. ABEL CAULKINS, aged 64. [4/1]
March 24, 1844, Oneonta, JOSIAH NORTHRUP, aged 65. [4/1]
March 27, 1844, Middlefield, MARCIA CORY, aged 38. [4/1]
March 29, 1844, Otsego, Mrs. HANNAH HUMISTON, aged 79. [4/8]
March 20, 1844, Fly Creek, MARY G. OLENDORF, aged 6. [4/8]
March 17, 1844, Laurens, Mrs. PHEBE MYRES, aged 67. [4/8]
April 2, 1844, Cherry Valley, EMMA TRUD, age 11. [4/8]
Feb. 25, 1844, Cherry Valley, MARION A. LEANING, aged 5. [4/8]
Feb. 3, 1844, Cherry Valley, FRANCIS LEANING, aged 2. [4/8]
March 29, 1844, Cherry Valley, LUCY M. JOHNSON, aged 17. [4/8]
April 5, 1844, Plainfield, Mrs. MARY A. SMITH, aged 57. [4/15]
April 7, 1844, Cooperstown, JANE WITHERS, aged 11. [4/15]
April 15, 1844, ALICE A. BOTSFORD, infant. [4/15 sic]
April 15, 1844, CHARLES G. BOTSFORD, aged 43. [4/15 sic]
April 10, 1844, W. Hartwick, Mrs. JOHN CONKLIN, aged 22. [4/22]
April 12, 1844, CATHERINE PIERCE, aged 19. [4/22]
March 25, 1844, Cherry Valley, Mrs. ELIZABETH GNODELL, aged 47. [4/22]
March 10, 1844, Butternuts, GEORGE CARR NILES, aged 24. [4/22]
April 23, 1844, Unadilla, CALVIN GATES, aged 59. [5/6]
April 28, 1844, Burlington, CHARLOTTE BLANCHARD, aged 10. [5/6]
May 7, 1844, Westford, CYRUS E. KING, aged 6. [5/13]
May 13, 1844, Cooperstown, OMAR BODEN, aged 78. [5/20]
May 14, 1844, Cooperstown, MARY E. DAVIS, aged 4. [5/20]
May 7, 1844, Decatur, BARZILLA BROWN, aged 84. [5/20]
May 8, 1844, Worcester, Mrs. ELIZABETH MARKHAM, aged 69. [5/20]
May 23, 1844, Hartwick, ROGER THRALL, aged 79. [6/3]
May 22, 1844, Hartwick, JAMES PROCTOR, aged 36. [6/3]
May 21, 1844, Hartwick, FRANCIS PIERCE, aged 8. [6/3]
April 22, 1844, Milford, Mrs. ELLIPHALLE MARBLE, aged 22. [6/3]

May 12, 1844, Worcester, HOLDEN RICE, aged 69. [6/3]
May 25, 1844, Utica, AUGUSTUS GILBERT, Middlefield, aged 27. [6/3]
May 15, 1844, N. Franklin, HARMON A. STARR, aged 24. [6/3]
May 28, 1844, Cooperstown, LYDIA ANN DAVIS, aged 15 months. [6/3]
[No date] Warrenton, Mass., REUBEN CHAMPION, Otsego, aged 53. [6/10]
June 4, 1844, Milford, Mrs. SYBIL EDDY, aged 61. [6/10]
May 11, 1844, Otsego, ADELINE FILKINS, aged 16. [6/17]
June 8, 1844, Otsego, Mrs. MARGARET SICKLES, aged 90. [6/17]
June 11, 1844, Otsego, Mrs. RHODA TANNER, aged 65. [6/17]
June 13, 1844, Middlefield, ANN E. BLAIR, aged 12. [6/24]
June 17, 1844, Cooperstown, MARY M. BATES, aged 6. [6/24]
June 13, 1844, Herman, St. Lawrence, IRA TANNER, Otsego, aged 77. [6/24]
June 18, 1844, Springfield, Mrs. ROSE SYKES, aged 80. [7/1]
June 19, 1844, W. Hartwick, CEYLINA SWIFT, aged 31. [7/1]
June 27, 1844, Gilbertsville, JOHN BRYANT, aged 54. [7/8]
June 12, 1844, Springfield, MOSES N. HINDS, aged 80. [7/8]
July 3, 1844, W. Hartwick, Mrs. MALVINA A. SHEPARD. [7/15]
July 5, 1844, W. Hartwick, Mrs. MERCY HOPKINS, aged 30. [7/15]
July 10, 1844, Cooperstown, HENRY CRANDALL, aged 12. [7/15]
June 1, 1844, Unadilla Forks, Col. WILLIAM N. MURRAY, aged 35. [7/22]
June 29, 1844, Springfield, WILLIAM L. CENTER, aged 23. [7/29]
Aug. 5, 1844, Milford, MATILDA BROWN, aged 5. [8/12]
Aug. 1, 1844, New Lisbon, SAMUEL JACOBS, aged 56. [8/12]
July 4, 1844, New Lisbon, Mrs. AMY LULL, aged 46. [8/12]
Sept. 7, 1844, Exeter, Mrs. SARAH GOODRICH, aged 38. [9/16]
July 29, 1844, Otsego, Mrs. RACHEL HODGE, aged 63. [9/16]
Sept. 10, 1844, Unadilla, Mrs. HANNAH M. GALLUP, aged 41. [9/16]
Aug. 29, 1844, New Lisbon, JONAS HODSKINS, aged 84. [9/23]
Sept. 5, 1844, New Berlin, LYDIA TULLER, aged 14. [9/23]
Sept. 19, 1844, Otsego, GEORGE GARRATT, aged 56. [9/23]
Sept. 7, 1844, Worcester, JULIA A. ROBINSON, aged 18. [10/7]
Sept. 30, 1844, Laurens, WILLIAM CLARK, aged 50. [10/7]
Sept. 21, 1844, Butternuts, ASSENETH WALKER, aged 38. [10/14]
Oct. 4, 1844, Middlefield, GEORGE PATTEN, aged 24. [10/14]
Oct. 5, 1844, Butternuts, DANIEL NASH, aged 81. [10/14]
Oct. 12, 1844, Hartwick, JOSEPH CRAFTS, aged 82. [10/21]
Sept. 17, 1844, Otego, ELI STARR, aged 50. [10/21]

Oct. 4, 1844, Cherry Valley, Mrs. ELEANOR DICKSON, aged 74. [10/21]
Oct. 14, 1844, Cooperstown, Mrs. SOVINA BATES, aged 27. [10/21]
Oct. 13, 1844, Gilbertsville, Mrs. LOIS DIXON, aged 61. [10/28]
Oct. 20, 1844, Beardstown, Ill., Mrs. OLIVE VAN ALSTINE, aged 23; formerly of Richfield. [11/4]
Oct. 27, 1844, Cherry Valley, Hon. WILLIAM CAMPBELL, aged 76. [11/4]
Nov. 3, 1844, Otsego, JOEL SQUIRES, aged 84. [11/11]
Nov. 4, 1844, Pittsfield, Mrs. NANCY A. CARD, aged 20. [11/18]
[No date] Burlinghton, SHUBARD REED, aged 74. [11/25]
Nov. 24, 1844, Hartwick, Mrs. MARY DAVIDSON, aged 40. [12/2]
Dec. 4, 1844, Hartwick, ELISHA BILLS, aged 93. [12/9]
Dec. 6, 1844, Cooperstown, JAMES BAILEY, aged 93. [12/9]
Nov. 10, 1844, Otsego, MARY F. COMSTOCK, infant. [12/23]
Dec. 10, 1844, New Lisbon, Mrs. JANE ROBINSON, aged 87. [12/30]
Dec. 13, 1844, JAMES PERKINS, aged 60. [12/30]
Dec. 18, 1844, Richfield Springs, Mrs. ALMIRA PLUMB, aged 41. [12/30]
Dec. 27, 1844, Butternuts, MARY A. BLACKMAN, aged 18. [12/30]
Dec. 9, 1844, Westfield, Chaut. Co., WALTER CRAFTS, aged 70. [12/30]
Jan. 9, 1845, Cooperstown, Mrs. UNICE STORY, aged 68. [1/13]
Jan. 1, 1845, Otsego, SELINA RUSSELL, aged 13. [1/13]
Dec. 30, 1844, Laurens, Mrs. BARBARA MYERS, aged 73. [1/13/1845]
Jan. 9, 1844, Springfield, Mrs. MATILDA HAVENS, aged 53. [1/13]
Nov. 23, 1844, Manchester, Mich., WILLIAM STOWEL (Otsego), aged 64. [1/20/1845]
Jan. 8, 1845, Laurens, Mrs. LAURA A. DUNBAR, aged 23. [1/20]
Jan. 7, 1845, Otsego, Mrs. FANNY M. CHAPMAN, aged 24. [1/20]
Jan. 16, 1845, Cooperstown, AIREL SPAFORD, M.D., aged 60. [1/20 & repeated 1/27]
Jan. 13, 1845, Springfield, DANIEL KEYES. [1/27]
Jan. 5, 1845, Springfield, Mrs. JERUSHA GRIGGS, aged 73. [1/27]
Jan. 22, 1845, Fly Creek, JOHN R. MARVIN, aged 41. [1/27]
Jan. 18, 1845, Hartwick, NICHOLAS STEERE, aged 70. [1/27]
Jan. 17, 1845, Hartwick, ZEBA NEWLAND, aged 70. [1/27]
Jan. 26, 1845, Butternuts, ALANSON MOORE, aged 79. [2/3]
Jan. 22, 1845, Burlington, Mrs. LUCY SWEET, aged 67. [2/10]
Jan. 28, 1845, Burlington, Mrs. SOPHIA CHAPIN, aged 35. [2/10]
Feb. 6, 1845, Hartwick, ELLEN J. PETERS, aged 7. [2/10]
Feb. 15, 1845, Springfield, CORNELIUS L. CARY, aged 57. [2/24]
Feb. 14, 1845, Cooperstown, HENRY C. FISH, aged 4. [2/24]

Feb. 15, 1845, Cooperstown, Mrs. LOUISA PECK, aged 26. [2/24]
Feb. 10, 1845, Fly Creek, LEMUEL ANDERS, aged 81. [3/3]
Feb. 23, 1845, SILAS FIELD, Hartwick, aged 21. [3/3]
Feb. 10, 1845, Wash., Ark., ABNER M. HERKIMER (Otsego), aged 25. [3/10]
Feb. 27, 1845, Burlington, ALEX. PARKER, aged 78. [3/10]
Feb. 22, 1845, Otsego, Mrs. POLLY M. HINDS, aged 24. [3/10]
Feb. 25, 1845, Otsego, STEPHEN ALLEN, aged 70. [3/10]
Feb. 26, 1845, Otsego, ISRAEL LOOMIS, aged 79. [3/10]
Feb. 20, 1845, Edmeston, HIRAM H. KEELER. [3/10]
March 1, 1845, Edmeston, ANDREW V. BURDICK, 4 1/2 years. [3/10]
Feb. 19, 1845, Gilbertsville, ROBERT C. GILBERT, aged 17. [3/10]
Feb. 21, 1845, Cooperstown, JOHN C. BARTHOLOMEW, aged 9. [3/10]
March 1, 1845, Cooperstown, Mrs. JAMES BAILEY, aged 88. [3/10]
March 2, 1845, Otsego, Mrs. REBECCA DUNBAR, aged 75. [3/10]
March 7, 1845, Laurens, JESSIE DUNBAR, aged 61. [3/17]
March 4, 1845, Cicero, JOHN W. REYNOLDS of Hartwick, aged 2. [3/17]
March 6, 1845, Cooperstown, MELVILLE ROOF, infant. [3/24]
Feb. 25, 1845, Exeter, SALLY MARIA CARTER, aged 30. [3/24]
March 14, 1845, Richfield Springs, ELIAS BRAMAN, aged 66. [3/24]
March 23, 1845, Cooperstown, Mrs. GERTRUDE PITCHER, aged 21. [3/24]
March 15, 1845, Otsego, DELOS W. EDGET, Jr., aged 4. [3/24]
March 12, 1845, Middlefield, Mrs. PHEBE COMPTON, aged 70. [3/24]
March 11, 1845, Butternuts, HEPSEY A. WHEELER, aged 31. [3/24]
Jan. 5, 1845, Exeter, Mrs. JULIAN SCHAULES, aged 38. [4/7]
March 26, 1845, Exeter, NATHAN BRAINARD, aged 67. [5/7]
March 31, 1845, Middlefield, Mrs. SYLVIA BRADLEY, aged 71. [5/7]
April 5, 1845, Middlefield, ALFRED D. PARSJALL [sic: probably PARSHALL], aged 28. [4/14]
April 7, 1845, Hartwick, JOS. C. HAWLEY, aged 89. [4/14]
April 1, 1845, N.Y., FARRAND S. STRANAHAN (Cooperstown), aged 33. [4/21]
April 13, 1845, Cherry Valley, Mrs. ANN WILSON, aged 45. [4/21]
April 12, 1845, Hartwick, HOPKINS BURLINGHAM, aged 34. [4/21]
April 12, 1845, S. Edmeston, Mrs. SOPHIA MATTERSON, aged 24. [4/21]
April 10, 1845, Pittsfield, BENJ. HALL, aged 83. [4/21]
April 11, 1845, Burlington, LEMUEL HUBBELL, aged 81. [4/21]
April 7, 1845, Springfield, JOHN CARROLL, aged 52. [4/21]
April 11, 1845, Middlefield, THOMAS PRATT, aged 90. [4/21]

April 10, 1845, Unadilla, Mrs. POLLY LATHROP, aged 76. [4/21]
March 15, 1845, Exeter, MARY ANN ROBINSON, aged 4. [4/21]
March 29, 1845, E. Worcester, ELLEN R.GOTT, aged 4. [4/21]
April 9, 1845, Otsego, Mrs. JULIABETH HINDS, aged 22. [4/28]
April 11, 1845, Burlington, LEMUEL HUBBELL, aged 91. [4/28]
March 30, 1845, Burlington, Col. ARCHIBALD RUTHERFORD, aged 73. [4/28]
April 14, 1845, W. Hartwick, THEO. LEVERETT, aged 2. [4/28]
May 1, 1845, Otsego, MINOR PARSHALL, aged 58. [4/28]
April 21, 1845, Butternuts, PAUL BURGESS, aged 59. [5/12]
April 27, 1845, Milford, Mrs. MARIA PLATT, aged 19. [5/12]
May 8, 1845, Cooperstown, Mrs. EMELINE CURTISS, aged 36. [5/12]
May 13, 1845, Springfield, Mrs. DEBBA TRACY, aged 46. [5/19]
May 14, 1845, Otsego, MARY HENRY, aged 73. [5/19]
May 11, 1845, Cobleskill, WM. MYERS (Maryland). [5/19]
May 17, 1845, Middlefield, ELLIOTT GILL, aged 38. [6/2]
May 28, 1845, Hartwick, SALMON COMSTOCK, aged 78. [6/2]
May 26, 1845, Cherry Valley, MATTHEW CAMPBELL, aged 71. [6/2]
Feb. 6, 1845, Edmeston, ELIZABETH S. GREENE, aged 21. [6/9]
March 7, 1845, Edmeston, DAVID GREENE, aged 49. [6/9]
March 18, 1845, Edmeston, Mrs. BETSEY E. GREEN, aged 42. [6/9]
May 8, 1845, Edmeston, DANIEL GREENE, aged 87. [6/9]
March 22, 1845, Edmeston, Mrs. POLLY DAVIS, aged 32. [6/9]
April 28, 1845, Laurens, GARDNER M. CARPENTER, aged 3. [6/9]
May 5, 1845, Laurens, ELENORA CARPENTER, aged 5. [6/9]
June 6, 1845, Cooperstown, Mrs. ELIZABETH CHASE, aged 72. [6/16]
June 10, 1845, Cherry Valley, GEO. K. WILKINS, aged 2. [6/16]
June 16, 1845, E. Worcester, Mrs. ELIZA CHAMPION, aged 75. [6/23]
June 11, 1845, E. Worcester, CALEB THURBER, aged 84. [6/23]
June 18, 1845, E. Worcester, BERTRAND BIGELOW, aged 2. [6/23]
June 24, 1845, Springfield, Mrs. RACHEL KEYES. [6/30]
June 20, 1845, Cherry Valley, SARAH JANE FEAKINS, aged 1. [7/7]
June 23, 1845, Middlefield, GARDNER BLAIR, aged 77. [7/14]
June 29, 1845, Richfield, LAURA WOODBURY, aged 19. [7/14]
July 5, 1845, Cherry Valley, Mrs. ANN BROWN, aged 31. [7/14]
July 7, 1845, Cherry Valley, FRANCIS A. RUDD, aged 2. [7/14]
July 4, 1845, Summit, Schoharie Co., GIDEON LAKE, aged 65. [7/21]
July 8, 1845, Exeter, MARIA D. MOTT, aged 31. [7/21]
July 13, 1845, Cherry Valley, EBENEZER M. HOLDEN, aged 82. [7/28]
July 27, 1845, E. Worcester, Mrs. MARY E. SHELDON, aged 24. [8/4]
July 26, 1845, Cherry Valley, JEROME A.G. WIETING, aged 8. [8/4]

Aug. 1, 1845, Gilbertsville, JOHN LUCE, aged 75. [8/11]
Aug. 5, 1845, Bainbridge, Rev. JOEL CHAPIN, aged 85. [8/11]
July 8, 1845, Exeter, Mrs. ANNA THOMPSON, aged 64. [8/18]
July 8, 1845, Butternuts, SAMUEL HAYNES, aged 62. [8/18]
July 12, 1845, Cooperstown, JAMES I. PAUL, aged 57. [8/18]
Aug. 17, 1845, Laurens, ISAAC CARR, aged 88. [8/25]
Aug. 18, 1845, Pittsfield, Mrs. REBECCA BUTTS, aged 65. [9/1]
Aug. 28, 1845, Middlefield, JAMES MURPHY, aged 79. [9/8]
Sept. 5, 1845, Fly Creek, AMORET L. HOOKER, aged 14 months. [9/15]
Sept. 3, 1845, S. Worcester, Mrs. HANNAH BECKER, aged 32. [9/15]
[No date] Elkhorn, Wisc., WILLIAM SOUTHERLAND, Otsego, aged 20. [9/22]
Sept. 9, 1845, Cherry Valley, RUSSELL SHERMAN, aged 53. [9/22]
Sept. 24, 1845, Cooperstown, HENRY POTTER, aged 15. [9/29]
Sept. 14, 1845, Middlefield, JAMES STOWELL, aged 17. [9/29]
Sept. 8, 1845, Laurens, Mrs. ANNA BUTTS, aged 43. [9/29]
Sept. 2, 1845, Thunder Bay, Mich., Mrs. SILENCE JAN (Hartwick), aged 45. [10/6]
Sept. 27, 1845, Otsego, ERASTUS CROSS, aged 17. [10/6]
Oct. 2, 1845, Burlington Flats, Mrs. BETSEY LUCE, aged 47. [10/11]
Oct. 2, 1845, Butternuts, HENRY BARRETT, aged 2. [10/11]
Oct. 7, 1845, Edmeston, REOLOFF TEN BROEK, aged 77. [10/18]
Oct. 13, 1845, Decatur, Mrs. PHEBE FERRIS, aged 80. [10/18]
Oct. 5, 1845, Laurens, HENRY W. DOUGLASS, aged 26. [10/18]
Oct. 12, 1845, Otsego, ZEBULON GIBBS, aged 72. [10/18]
Oct. 19, 1845, Cooperstown, JOHN W. ROOT, aged 4 months. [10/25]
Oct. 11, 1845, Plainfield, Mrs. CLARINDA COLE, aged 37. [10/25]
Oct. 2, 1845, Springfield, ORAMEL S. REED, aged 22. [11/1]
Oct. 30, 1845, Gilbertsville, Dr. LATHROP, aged 61. [11/8]
Nov. 1, 1845, Decatur, EBEN DAILEY, aged 69. [11/8]
Oct. 26, 1845, Otsego, ALPHONSO BOWEN. [11/8]
Oct. 26, 1845, Hartwick, OLIVER P. FIELDS, aged 16. [11/8]
Oct. 26, 1845, Laurens, Mrs. MARY DEAN, aged 64. [11/8]
Oct. 24, 1845, Hartwick, Mrs. ELIZ. WELLS, aged 76. [11/8]
Nov. 1, 1845, Cherry Valley, WM. FUNK, aged 26. [11/15]
Nov. 8, 1845, Cherry Valley, NOAH COOK, aged 40. [11/15]
Oct. 14, 1845, Westford, JOHN CAMPBELL, aged 74. [11/15]
Nov. 16, 1845, Cherry Valley, JOSEPH CALDER, aged 76. [11/22]
Nov. 14, 1845, Fly Creek, Mrs. MERCY P. LE ROY, aged 53. [11/29]
Nov. 21, 1845, Cherry Valley, MARGARET RICH, aged 21. [11/29]
Nov. 13, 1845, Laurens, JOEL LULL, M.D., aged 45. [11/29]

Dec. 1, 1845, Cooperstown, POLLY HENNIKER, aged 24. [12/6]
Nov. 30, 1845, Springfield, CLARK WOOD, aged 5. [12/13]
Dec. 7, 1845, Cherry Valley, JOSIAH KRAKE, aged 29. [12/13]
Dec. 7, 1845, Cherry Valley, Mrs. CAROLINE KRAKE, aged 25. [12/13]
Oct. 6, 1845, Ohio, JAMES D. WOODWARD (Otsego), aged 21. [12/20]
Nov. 8, 1845, Worcester, ELIZABETH CRIPPEN, aged 86. [12/20]
Dec. 14, 1845, Worcester, DANIEL CRIPPEN, aged 59. [12/20]
Dec. 15, 1845, Springfield, CHRISTOPHER DUTCHER, aged 65. [12/20]
Dec. 19, 1845, Cooperstown, AMBROSE C. PARSHALL, aged 19. [12/28]
Dec. 14, 1845, Middlefield, EUNICE L. REYNOLDS, infant. [12/28]
Dec. 17, 1845, Cherry Valley, ANNA B. CHAMPLIN, infant. [12/28]
Dec. 12, 1845, Laurens, LLOYD GILBERT, aged 22. [1/3/1846]
Jan. 1, 1846, Otsego, AMOS ELLIS, aged 54. [1/3]
Dec. 25, 1845, Westford, DAVID H. KELSO, aged 9. [1/3/1846]
Jan. 5, 1846, Cherry Valley, Mrs. JANE A. LUSK, aged 35. [1/10]
Dec. 12, 1845, Cherry Valley, Mrs. CAROLINE SEELYE, aged 24. [1/10/1846]
Dec. 7, 1845, Springfield, LUKE MC INTYRE, aged 67. [1/10/1846]
Jan. 2, 1846, Cherry Valley, ELIZABETH ANTISDEL, aged 11. [1/10]
Jan. 14, 1846, Cooperstown, GREGORY BURGESS, infant. [1/24]
Jan. 1, 1846, Maryland, EDWARD H. SEGAR, infant. [1/24]
Jan. 12, 1846, Westford, ORRIL WRIGHT, aged 32. [1/24]
Jan. 21, 1846, Westford, Mrs. CAROLINE BECKER, aged 62. [1/24]
Jan. 18, 1846, Westville, WHITNEY JEWELL, aged 72. [1/24]
Jan. 28, 1846, Cooperstown, Mrs. MARY COOPER, aged 34. [1/31]
Jan. 27, 1846, Cooperstown, JAMES WEEKS, aged 60. [1/31]
Jan. 26, 1846, Cherry Valley, JOHN LUSK, infant. [1/31]
Jan. 23, 1846, Colliersville, Maj. PETER COLLIER (Milford), aged 66. [1/31]
Jan. 29, 1846, Middlefield, TAMSON W. EATON, aged 15. [1/31]
Feb. 1, 1846, Middlefield, RACHEL ANN EATON, aged 19. [2/7]
Feb. 2, 1846, Otsego, ISAAC RUSSELL, aged 75. [2/7]
Jan. 23, 1846, Middlefield, REUBEN SMITH, aged 58. [2/7]
Jan. 27, 1846, Schuylers Lake, Mrs. DELOS HUBBARD. [2/7]
Jan. 16, 1847, Burlington, Mrs. DEBORAH MUNROE, aged 80. [2/7]
Jan. 28, 1847, Unadilla, FREDERICK B. ALLEN, infant. [2/7]
Feb. 13, 1846, Otsego, CAROLINE METCALF, aged 20. [2/21]
Feb. 13, 1846, Cooperstown, MARY FANCHER, aged 3. [2/21]
Feb. 16, 1846, Otsego, Mrs. CHLOE SQUIRES, aged 86. [2/21]
Feb. 12, 1846, Exeter, O. P. ROBINSON, aged 19. [2/21]

[No date] Freedom, ICHABOD SMITH (Otsego), aged 66. [2/21]
Feb. 20, 1846, Cooperstown, ANN WILLIAMS, aged 86. [2/28]
Feb. 24, 1846, Cooperstown, JOHN M. BOWERS, aged 74. [2/28]
Feb. 15, 1846, Kalamazoo, Mich., Mrs. SARAH COOPER COMSTOCK, aged 35. [2/28]
Feb. 24, 1846, Cooperstown, MARY E. SOUTHWORTH, aged 42. [2/28]
Feb. 24, 1846, Otsego, Mrs. CATHARINE MALLORY, aged 28. [2/28] [NOTE: This entry repeated in next issue with date of death given as Feb. 21, 1846.]
Feb. 21, 1846, Springfield, DANIEL HEWES, aged 91. [2/28]
Feb. 21, 1846, Middlefield, Mrs. ISABELLA PIERCE, aged 85. [2/28]
Feb. 12, 1846, Springfield, Mrs. CORNELIUS B. VEDDER, aged 45. [2/28]
Feb. 11, 1846, Cherry Valley, JOHN NELSON, aged 76. [2/28]
Feb. 18, 1846, York, Livingston Co., JOSEPH BALDWIN, aged 80. [3/7]
Feb. 14, 1846, Hartwick, THOMAS PIERCE, aged 62. [3/7]
March 10, 1846, Cooperstown, CHARLES COOK, aged 27. [3/14]
March 6, 1846, Otsego, Dr. SAMUEL HICOCK, aged 96. [3/14]
Feb. 18, 1846, Walworth, N.Y., WM. O. HUBBELL (Middlefield), aged 20. [3/28]
March 13, 1846, Middlefield, AMELIA R. COOPER, aged 21. [3/28]
March 28, 1846, Cooperstown, ISAAC FITCH, aged 53. [4/4]
March 26, 1846, Cherry Valley, Mrs. ELIZ. DUNLAP, aged 86. [4/4]
March 25, 1846, Middlefield, DEWITT SMITH, aged 20. [4/4]
April 7, 1846, Cherry Valley, Mrs. ELENOR CAMPBELL, aged 89. [4/11]
March 23, 1846, Worcester, JOEL M. CHAMBERLAIN, aged 52. [4/11]
April 4, 1846, Cooperstown, Mrs. ALICE SCOTT, aged 57. [4/18]
April 10, 1846, Cherry Valley, GEORGE W. RUDD, aged 35. [4/18]
April 1, 1846, Richfield, DANIEL PATCHIN, aged 86. [4/18]
April 13, 1846, Middlefield, Mrs. NANCY HUBBELL, aged 44. [4/25]
April 15, 1846, Cherry Valley, Mrs. SYLVIA LANSING, aged 32. [4/25]
April 14, 1846, Oneonta, ELEANOR C. CLYDE, aged 33. [5/2]
April 23, 1846, Cherry Valley, Mrs. ALICE LITTLE, aged 78. [5/2]
Jan. 24, 1846, Palmyra, Rev. LINUS NORTH (Otsego). [5/2]
April 9, 1846, Hartwick, ISAAC CHASE, aged 73. [5/16]
April 29, 1846, Cooperstown, HARRIET F. MC EWAN, aged 2. [5/16]
May 11, 1846, Jacksonville, WILLARD HUNT, aged 26. [5/23]
May 16, 1846, Cooperstown, MORRIS HOBBY, infant. [5/23]
April 26, 1846, Otsego, HANNAH L. CLYDE, aged 7. [5/23]
May 19, 1846, Cherry Valley, Mrs. MARTHA L. JUDD, aged 23. [5/23]
May 13, 1846, Decatur, NAHUM T. BROWN, aged 18. [5/23]

May 7, 1843, Cherry Valley, GEORGE VAN DYKE, aged 28. [5/23]
May 23, 1846, Burlington Flats, Mrs. CALPHURNIA ARNOLD, aged 32. [5/30]
May 29, 1846, Decatur, HARVEY BOORNE, aged 46. [6/6]
June 3, 1846, Middlefield, Mrs. MARY KELLY, aged 50. [6/6]
June 3, 1846, Hartwick, Eld. NATHAN BUNDY, aged 39. [6/6]
June 2, 1846, Otsego, NATHANIEL HARRIS, aged 65. [6/6]
May 23, 1846, Jacksonville, J. JUDSON GARDNER, aged 30. [6/6]
April 28, 1846, Fly Creek, EMELINE FITCH, aged 19. [6/6]
April 7, 1846, Fly Creek, Mrs. MARY FIELD, aged 75. [6/6]
June 1, 1846, Plainfield, Mrs. DEBORAH SPICER, aged 65. [6/6]
June 6, 1846, Cherry Valley, ELIZABETH FAULKNER, aged 21. [6/13]
June 8, 1846, Middlefield, Mrs. ELIZA ANTHONY, aged 42. [6/13]
June 16, 1846, Laurens, Mrs. MATILDA HOAG, aged 56. [6/20]
June 13, 1846, Otsego, Mrs. MARY LOOP, aged 86. [6/20]
June 24, 1846, Cooperstown, MARY HINMAN, aged 19. [6/27]
June 22, 1846, Cherry Valley, HENRY SUTLIFF, aged 68. [6/27]
June 25, 1846, Cherry Valley, Mrs. LYDIA PEESO, aged 83. [7/4]
July 7, 1846, Cooperstown, FREDERICK FISH, aged 7. [7/11]
June 20, 1846, Hartwick, Mrs. LUVANA MURDOCK, aged 78. [7/11]
June 23, 1846, Westford, Mrs. ABIGAIL HUSON, aged 73. [7/11]
July 19, 1846, Otsego, CLARISSA DOUBLEDAY, aged 19. [8/1]
July 9, 1846, Milford, Mrs. DESIRE FARRINGTON, aged 79. [8/1]
July 10, 1846, Milford, EMMA M. GEORGIA, aged 2. [8/1]
July 28, 1846, Middlefield, EPHRAIM PEAK, aged 76. [8/1]
July 24, 1846, Middlefield, Mrs. MARY ANN SIBLEY, aged 38. [8/1]
Aug. 5, 1846, Cooperstown, Mrs. EUNICE SPAFORD, aged 51. [8/8]
Aug. 20, 1846, Cooperstown, HAMILTON NISH [?] CRIPPEN, infant. [8/22]
Aug. 16, 1846, Cherry Valley, Mrs. MARY REYNOLDS, aged 46. [8/22]
Aug. 17, 1846, Middlefield, CORLIN CLARK, aged 3. [8/22]
Aug. 10, 1846, Metcalf, Mrs. ALSA NEWTON, aged 54. [8/22]
Aug. 5, 1846, Worcester, Mrs. CATHERINE STEVER, aged 25. [9/5]
Aug. 26, 1846, Cherry Valley, PETER RUTT, aged 55. [9/5]
Aug. 29, 1846, Gilbertsville, COLEY STURGES, aged 62. [9/5]
Aug. 5, 1846, Plainfield, Mrs. HANNAH MOFFATT, aged 75. [9/12]
Sept. 5, 1846, Cherry Valley, HARRIET A. CALDER, aged 20. [9/12]
Sept. 7, 1846, RUFUS HIX, aged 67. [9/12]
Sept. 12, 1846, Cherry Valley, BENONI ROSE, aged 72. [9/19]
Sept. 15, 1846, GEORGE W. MC LEAN, infant. [9/19]
Sept. 10, 1846, Westford, DANIEL CLARK, aged 69. [9/19]

Sept. 4, 1846, Cooperstown, JOSEPHINE CARR, infant. [9/19]
Sept. 24, 1846, Otsego, LAURAETTE MC COLLUM, 1 year. [9/26]
Sept. 27, 1846, Milford, RODERICK RICHARDS, aged 64. [9/26]
Sept. 21, 1846, Maryland, Mrs. REBECCA SCOTT, aged 72. [10/10]
Oct. 7, 1846, Otsego, PELEG ROSE, aged 46. [10/17]
Oct. 18, 1846, Cooperstown, GEORGE C. GRAVES, aged 21. [10/24]
Oct. 6, 1846, Otsego, SETH WHIPPLE, aged 54. [10/24]
Oct. 18, 1846, Cherry Valley, ELIZ. CLIFFORD, aged 19. [10/24]
Oct. 13, 1846, Westford, STALEY CASSAART, aged 49. [10/24]
Oct. 1, 1846, Cherry Valley, SARAH A. LUSCOMB, aged 92. [10/24]
Sept. 25, 1846, Burlington, EPHRAIM CHAMBERLAIN, aged 75. [10/24]
Oct. 23, 1846, Burlington Flats, FLORENCE L. ROBINSON, aged 1. [10/31]
Oct. 1, 1846, Hartwick, MARIA E. BISSELL, aged 3. [10/31]
Nov. 28, 1846, Cooperstown, JOSEPH PERKINS, aged 59. [12/5]
Nov. 19, 1846, Maryland, CORNELIUS SCOTT, aged 73. [12/5]
Nov. 21, 1846, Maryland, RUAMY S. SCOTT, aged 37. [12/5]
Nov. 17, 1846, Springfield, ANGELINE CENTER, aged 23. [12/12]
Dec. 4, 1846, Cooperstown, SYLVESTER H. WOODWARD, aged 7. [12/12]
Dec. 2, 1846, Burlington, Col. WASHINGTON G. PARKER, aged 58. [12/12]
Nov. 21, 1846, Cherry Valley, DAN ANTISDEL, aged 41. [12/12]
Nov. 17, 1846, South Valley, LANSON UTMAN, aged 18. [12/12]
Dec. 1, 1846, Middlefield, SAMUEL VAN ETTEN, aged 23. [12/12]
Dec. 2, 1846, Hartwick, Mrs. POLLY TUCKER, aged 29. [12/12]
Dec. 15, 1846, Cooperstown, MARTHA F. NICHOLS, aged 19. [12/19]
Dec. 7, 1846, Otsego, Mrs. ORRA BROOKS, aged 60. [12/19]
Dec. 27, 1846, East Worcester, SILAS DEVOL, aged 58. [1/2/1847]
Nov. 28, 1846, Maryland, Mrs. SYLVINA BABCOCK, aged 84. [1/2/1847]
Jan. 2, 1847, New Lisbon, CROWELL CROSS, aged 82. [1/9]
Dec. 15, 1846, Butternuts, JASON COOKE, aged 43. [1/9/1847]
Jan. 16, 1847, New Lisbon, JOHN GREGORY, aged 65. [1/23]
Jan. 17, 1847, Cooperstown, JOHN SCHOOLCRAFT ERNST, infant. [1/23]
Jan. 8, 1847, Cherry Valley, JAMES WILSON, aged 70. [1/30]
Jan. 23, 1847, Cherry Valley, Mrs. ELENOR DUTCHER, aged 78. [1/30]
Jan. 15, 1847, Richfield, DELOS TUTTLE, aged 29. [1/30]
Jan. 23, 1847, Otsego, HULDAH LOOMIS, aged 26. [1/30]
Jan. 22, 1847, Milford, RUBEN SCOTT, aged 73. [1/30]
Jan. 23, 1847, Hartwick, THOMAS ELDRED, aged 87. [2/6]

Jan. 27, 1847, Burlington, Mrs. LOIS MAPLES, aged 69. [2/6]
Jan. 25, 1847, Fly Creek, ANSON HIGBY, aged 65. [2/13]
Feb. 4, 1847, Middlefield, JULIA E. BOWEN, infant. [2/13]
Feb. 6, 1847, Decatur, Mrs. BETSEY LAMPMAN, aged 44. [2/13]
Feb. 7, 1847, Index, N.Y., EUNICE VIVER, aged 20. [2/13]
Feb. 7, 1847, Cherry Valley, JOHN F. LEWIS, aged 2. [2/13]
Feb. 7, 1847, Cooperstown, JAMES VAN BERGEN, aged 60. [2/13]
Feb. 7, 1847, Decatur, Mrs. MERCY BURT, aged 62. [2/13]
Feb. 7, 1847, Otsego, Mrs. ARMENA RUSSELL, aged 66. [2/20]
Feb. 14, 1847, Otsego, EDWARD LEWIS, Jr., aged 28. [2/20]
Feb. 15, 1847, Cherry Valley, Mrs. MARY COATS, aged 43. [2/20]
Feb. 12, 1847, Cherry Valley, JENETTE CLIFFORD, aged 24. [2/27]
Jan. 20, 1847, Hartwick, THOMAS CHADDON, aged 71. [2/27]
Jan. 25, 1847, Hartwick, DANIEL OLENDORF, aged 67. [2/27]
Feb. 9, 1847, Middlefield, ELIJAH HUBBELL, aged 77. [3/6]
Feb. 26, 1847, Exeter, Dr. JOHN H. GRAY, aged 44. [3/6]
March 4, 1847, Fly Creek, EMMA A. METCALF, aged 1. [3/6]
March 5, 1847, Worcester, GILES CARTER, aged 38. [3/13]
March 1, 1847, Otsego, Mrs. ELISHABA WILLIAMS, aged 67. [3/20]
March 15, 1847, Milford, Maj. ASA EDDY, aged 65. [3/20]
March 7, 1847, Milford, LURANA MORRIS, aged 17. [3/20]
March 21, 1847, Hartwick, SAMUEL SHORT, aged 82. [3/27]
March 26, 1847, Otsego, Mrs. PHEBE SCRIBNER, aged 72. [4/14]
Nov. 8, 1846, Exeter, Mrs. SOPHIA B. CRANDAL, aged 46. [4/13/1847]
March 8, 1847, Waterville, MARY S. CRANDAL, aged 12. [4/13]
March 30, 1847, Middlefield, ALFRED C. SHEPARD, aged 19. [4/13]
March 27, 1847, Middlefield, ALBERT S. MURPHY, aged 4. [4/20]
April 11, 1847, Worcester, Col. BELA JOHNSON, aged 63. [4/20]
April 4, 1847, Hartwick, STEPHEN FIELD, aged 35. [4/20]
April 14, 1847, Cooperstown, Mrs. SAMANTHA SECOR, aged 39. [4/20]
March 25, 1847, Unadilla, EBENEZER GREGORY, aged 50. [4/24]
April 16, 1847, Burlington, Mrs. ELIZ. CUSHMAN, aged 82. [4/24]
April 18, 1847, Cooperstown, HARVEY PERKINS, aged 37. [4/24]
April 21, 1847, Pittsfield, ADELINE COOK, aged 21. [5/1]
May 5, 1847, Richfield, Mrs. DORCAS EDDY, aged 85. [5/8]
April 27, 1847, Otsego, FRANCIS BRAZIE, aged 41. [5/8]
April 22, 1847, Otsego, PETER SMITH, aged 77. [5/8]
May 6, 1847, Cherry Valley, ARCHIBALD MC KELLIP, aged 92. [5/15]
April 16, 1847, Worcester, ALONZO BULLIS, aged 19. [5/15]
May 8, 1847, South Valley, AARON BALDWIN, aged 90. [5/22]
May 10, 1847, Exeter, MARY A. J. WRIGHT, aged 36. [5/22]

May 27, 1847, Cooperstown, M. M. MANCHESTER, aged 38. [5/29]
June 6, 1847, Cooperstown, GEORGE C. STOWELL, aged 24. [6/12]
June 5, 1847, Edmeston, Col. ADIN DEMING, aged 81. [6/12]
June 5, 1847, Hartwick, Mrs. SARAH H. CHADDON, aged 32. [6/19]
June 17, 1847, Otego, Mrs. ELIZA BUNDY, aged 26. [6/26]
June 19, 1847, Middlefield, GEORGE W. REYNOLD, aged 46. [7/3]
June 22, 1847, New Lisbon, JOHN R. BOWDISH, aged 63. [7/3]
June 28, 1847, Middlefield, ROZELTHA A. HOKE, aged 9. [7/3]
June 20, 1847, Hartwick, NOAH EDDY, aged 87. [7/3]
July 4, 1847, Fly Creek, WARREN BABBIT, aged 74. [7/10]
July 3, 1847, Otsego, JOHN REED, aged 70. [7/10]
July 10, 1847, Cooperstown, JULIA K. FAY, aged 21. [7/24]
July 2, 1847, Unadilla Forks, JOHN CHANEY, aged 84. [7/24]
July 15, 1847, Burlington, ELI DIMOCK, aged 74. [7/24]
July 27, 1847, Middlefield, LUCIA T. CORY, aged 21. [7/31]
July 27, 1847, Unadilla, Col. GEORGE H. NOBLE, aged 44. [7/31]
July 30, 1847, Laurens, BROWN WINSOR. [8/7]
July 24, 1847, Otsego, BETSEY M. PEABODY, aged 22. [8/14]
Aug. 3, 1847, Cherry Valley, Rev. STORYES GILBERT, aged 65. [8/21]
Aug. 15, 1847, Milford, JOSEPH MANCHESTER, aged 66. [8/21]
Aug. 9, 1847, Hartwick, Mrs. RACHEL KENDALL, aged 55. [8/21]
June 21, 1847, W. Burlington, Mrs. ELIZABETH L. SMITH, aged 19. [8/21]
July 28, 1847, W. Burlington, ARTEMAS BYRON SMITH, infant. [8/21]
Aug. 14, 1847 (Louisville), Butternuts, BENAJAH DAVIS, aged 75. [8/21]
Aug. 18, 1847, Decatur, JOSHUA IRISH, aged 80. [8/28]
Aug. 30, 1847, Cooperstown, ROBERT CAMPBELL, aged 66. [9/4]
Aug. 22, 1847, Cooperstown, EZRA W. EATON, aged 54. [9/4]
Aug. 27, 1847, Decatur, THOMAS SHAW, aged 80. [9/4]
Aug. 27, 1847, Burlington, CHARLES D. FITCH, aged 5. [9/4]
Aug. 28, 1847, Hartwick, BENONI PIERCE, aged 88. [9/4]
Aug. 25, 1847, Cherry Valley, MOSES LEWIS, aged 88. [9/11]
Aug. 27, 1847, Hartwick, PETER C. BRISTOL, aged 23. [9/11]
Sept. 2, 1847, Fly Creek, CHARLES H. HIGBY, infant. [9/11]
Sept. 3, 1847, Middlefield, ELIZA J. COOPER. [9/11]
Sept. 10, 1847, Laurens, JOHN HUBBARD, aged 90. [9/18]
Oct. 1, 1847, Cooperstown, CHARLES W. BARTLING, infant. [10/9]
Aug. 17, 1847, Milwaukee, Wisc., Mrs. ELIZABETH OAKLEY, aged 53. [10/9]
Oct. 15, 1847, Cherry Valley, GEORGE CLYDE, aged 75. [10/23]
Oct. 25, 1847, Otsego, Mrs. LUCRETIA GILE, aged 71. [10/30]

Oct. 12, 1847, Hartwick, Mrs. POLLY HACKLEY, aged 81. [11/6]
Oct. 24, 1847, Otsego, ISAAC NEWTON RUSSELL, 19 months. [11/6]
Oct. 31, 1847, Otsego, CHARLOTTE P. SCOTT, aged 5. [11/6]
Oct. 20, 1847, Burlington, ELISHA NICKERSON, aged 19. [11/6]
Oct. 30, 1847, Otsego, Mrs. ALSINA EDGET, aged 23. [11/13]
Oct. 31, 1847, Otsego, WALTER F. ADAMS, 1 yr. [11/13]
Nov. 6, 1847, Maryland, Mrs. RUTH CARPENTER, aged 61. [11/13]
Nov. 17, 1847, Otsego, RICHARD DAVIDSON, aged 92. [12/4]
Nov. 20, 1847, New Lisbon, Mrs. MARY BARRAS, aged 64. [12/4]
Dec. 5, 1847, Butternuts, Mrs. PHEBE A. STEERE, aged 42. [12/11]
Dec. 5, 1847, New York, ARTEMAS BISSELL of Hartwick. [12/11]
Dec. 1, 1847, Otsego, JACOB L. CARD, aged 53. [12/11]
Dec. 14, 1847, Cooperstown, Mrs. MERCY A. BROWN, aged 38. [12/18]
Dec. 15, 1847, Cooperstown, Mrs. ANNA BLAIR, aged 67. [12/18]
Dec. 15, 1847, Hartwick, DANIEL CARR, aged 81. [12/18]
Dec. 1, 1847, Otsego, DANIEL L. CARD, aged 53. [12/18]
Jan. 5, 1848, Laurens, ERASTUS FIELDS, aged 17. [1/2]
Nov. 28, 1847, Burlington, STEPHEN WILBER, aged 68. [1/15/1848]
Dec. 14, 1847, New Lisbon, Mrs. ELECTA MC COLLUM, aged 78. [1/15/1848]
Dec. 31, 1847, Burlington, GRIFFIN BRIGGS, aged 19. [1/15/1848]
Jan. 9, 1848, Laurens, JOHN PEAK, aged 67. [1/15]
Jan. 6, 1848, Hartwick, JESSE ROBINSON, aged 75. [1/15]
Jan. 11, 1848, Hartwick, RUTH TRACY, aged 62. [1/22]
Jan. 16, 1848, Worcester, SAMUEL STORRS, aged 20. [1/29]
Jan. 12, 1848, Laurens, DAVID JOHNSON, aged 77. [2/12]
Feb. 13, 1848, Otsego, Mrs. LOIS JOHNSON, aged 89. [2/19]
Jan. 28, 1848, Otsego, Mrs. ELECTA KIBBY, aged 58. [2/19]
Feb. 11, 1848, Richfield Springs, Mrs. CLARISSA THOMPSON, aged 47. [2/19]
Feb. 24, 1848, Edmeston, Mrs. MARTHA DEMING, aged 79. [3/4]
Feb. 25, 1848, Worcester, NATHAN ADAMS, aged 48. [3/4]
Feb. 21, 1848, Decatur, Mrs. NANCY THAYER, aged 61. [3/4]
Feb. 22, 1848, So. Valley, NOAH ADSIT, aged 80. [3/4]
Feb. 10, 1848, Worcester, CHARLES WAIT, aged 50. [3/4]
Feb. 16, 1848, Westford, ABIGAIL WASHBURN, aged 23. [3/4]
Jan. 19, 1848, Worcester, Mrs. NANCY CAMPBELL, aged 30. [3/4]
Jan .13, 1848, Worcester, Mrs. ASENITH THOMPSON, aged 65. [3/4]
Feb. 10, 1848, Dunnville, Canada, Dr. GEORGE M. HOPKINS (Richfield), aged 24. [3/11]
March 12, 1848, Cherry Valley, WILLIAM MC LEAN, aged 74. [3/18]

March 15, 1848, Otsego, JOSEPH STRAIGHT, aged 64. [3/25]
March 15, 1848, Otsego, IDA R. MARVIN, infant. [3/25]
March 20, 1848, Hartwick, DAVID KENDALL, aged 59. [4/1]
March 25, 1848, Cooperstown, JAMES BUTTS, aged 35. [4/1]
March 25, 1848, Hartwick, ALBERT LATIN, aged 8. [4/15]
April 17, 1848, Cooperstown, Mrs. MARTHA BALDWIN, aged 45. [4/22]
April 17, 1848, Pierstown, JOEL S. PATTEN, aged 3. [4/22]
April 18, 1848, Laurens, JULIA C. BOYD, aged 26. [4/22]
April 5, 1848, Hartwick, Mrs. SARAH CAMP, aged 71. [4/22]
April 20, 1848, Warren, JEPTHA S. BINGHAM, M.D., aged 22. [4/28]
April 6, 1848, Butternuts, ANN G. SHAW, aged 4. [4/28]
April 16, 1848, Bainbridge, Mrs. RACHEL BUTTERFIELD, aged 84. [4/28]
April 19, 1848, Bainbridge, Mrs. LUCY DOLTON, aged 27. [4/28]
April 25, 1848, Laurens, Col. GEORGE W. POWELL, aged 37. [5/6]
April 30, 1848, Cooperstown, Mrs. ELIZA RICE, aged 47. [5/13]
May 11, 1848, Butternuts, GEORGE ARNOLD, aged 30. [5/20]
March 13, 1848, Hartwick, Mrs. DIANTHA BUSH, aged 28. [5/20]
May 1, 1848, Hartwick, Mrs. SUSAN COOK, aged 58. [5/20]
May 18, 1848, Hartwick, W. S. BOWDISH, aged 46. [5/27]
May 3, 1848, Fly Creek, VOLNEY ANNAS, aged 29. [6/3]
May 20, 1848, Milford, ALCENA STOCKWELL, aged 15. [6/10]
May 15, 1848, Butternuts, ALONZO G. WINTON, aged 2. [6/10]
June 1, 1848, Jacksonville, HENRY WILBUR, 1 yr. [6/17]
June 10, 1848, Edmeston, HARRIET A. SOUTHWORTH, aged 15. [6/24]
June 11, 1848, New Lisbon, Mrs. BETSEY GROSS, aged 42. [6/24]
June 21, 1848, Fly Creek, Mrs. EMILY AMES, aged 31. [6/24]
June 15, 1848, Otsego, Mrs. NANCY TANNER, aged 35. [6/24]
June 23, 1848, Westford, Mrs. ANNA SMITH, aged 71. [7/1]
June 28, 1848, Oneonta, EGBERT SMITH, aged 9. [7/8]
July 2, 1848, Cherry Valley, JULIA GRAY, aged 17. [7/15]
July 4, 1848, Cherry Valley, ROENA P. PHELON, aged 15. [7/15]
July 3, 1848, Laurens, DANIEL COMSTOCK, aged 59. [7/15]
June 24, 1848, New Lisbon, JAMES MC COLLOM, aged 79. [7/15]
July 11, 1848, New Lisbon, EVERETT CUMMINGS, aged 3. [7/22]
June 24, 1848, New Lisbon, RUSSELL NEARING, aged 27. [7/22]
May 29, 1848, Pierstown, FENNER R. FITCH, aged 2. [7/29]
July 30, 1848, Hartwick, SARAH S. POPE, infant. [8/5]
July 29, 1848, Cooperstown, Mrs. MARY GRAVES, aged 84. [8/5]
July 24, 1848, Middlefield, JOHN M. REYNOLDS, 11 months. [8/12]

Aug. 6, 1848, Otsego, RUBY A. LEWIS, aged 22. [8/12]
Aug. 7, 1848, Pierstown, SARAH S. KELLOGG, aged 20. [8/12]
Aug. 15, 1848, Otsego, ARUNAH METCALF, aged 78. [8/19]
Aug. 5, 1848, Burlington Green, WM. SIDNEY BABCOCK, aged 8. [8/19]
Aug. 3, 1848, Middlefield, FRANCIS J. ELLISON, infant. [8/26]
Aug. 5, 1848, Middlefield, RANSOM E. BRAZIE, infant. [8/26]
Aug. 12, 1848, Middlefield, URIEL B. LOWELL, infant. [8/26]
Aug. 13, 1848, Middlefield, Mrs. BETSEY CROSS, aged 48. [8/26]
Aug. 17, 1848, Middlefield, LOUISA RATHBUN, 16 months. [8/26]
Aug. 18, 1848, Middlefield, MELVILLE J. SHERWOOD, aged 14. [8/26]
Aug. 18, 1848, Cherry Valley, MASON FITCH, aged 67. [8/26]
Aug. 4, 1848, Decatur, JONATHAN THAYER, aged 65. [8/26]
Aug. 22, 1848, Decatur, Mrs. HANNAH FERRIS, aged 53. [8/26]
Aug. 12, 1848, Gilbertsville, THOMAS HOLLIS, aged 44. [8/26]
Aug. 25, 1848, Toddsville, Mrs. CLARISS SHOLES, aged 46. [9/2]
July 29, 1848, Middlefield, AARON P. CORNISH, aged 19. [9/2]
Aug. 30, 1848, Laurens, Mrs. RUTH ROOT, aged 50. [9/9]
Aug. 24, 1848, New Lisbon, Mrs. MARY S. GREGORY, aged 21. [9/9]
Aug. 11, 1848, Springfield, Mrs. JANE HOYT, aged 28. [9/23]
Sept. 5, 1848, Burlington, SYLVESTER REXFORD, aged 59. [9/30]
Sept. 20, 1848, Springfield, JAMES CENTER, aged 23. [9/30]
Sept. 18, 1848, Middlefield Center, DAN. VAN PATTEN. [9/30]
Sept. 14, 1858, Unadilla, FREDERICK A. NOBLE, aged 4. [10/7]
Sept. 27, 1848, Middlefield, PHIDELIA L. SAXTON, 1 yr. [10/7]
Sept. 28, 1848, Springfield, EUNICE KEYS, aged 62. [10/7]
Sept. 19, 1848, Unadilla, STEPHEN V. STERLING, aged 36. [10/7]
Oct. 1, 1848, Gilbertsville, WILLIAM KNAPP, aged 24. [10/7]
Oct. 6, 1848, Otsego, Mrs. ELINOR MARVIN, aged 70. [10/14]
Oct. 8, 1848, Cooperstown, HENRY O. PARKER, aged 19. [10/14]
Oct. 29, 1848, Exeter, LEMUEL F. VEBBER, aged 82. [10/14]
Oct. 2, 1848, Fly Creek, JAMES R. MADDILL (stranger). [10/14]
Sept. 25, 1848, Fly Creek, Dr. E. B. INGALLS, aged 37. [10/14]
Oct. 7, 1848, Butternuts, JOSEPH BOWNE, aged 70. [10/14]
Sept. 23, 1848, W. Burlington, Mrs. PHEBE SIMMONS, aged 35. [10/21]
Sept. 25, 1848, Middlefield, Mrs. SALLY A. STILL, aged 36. [10/21]
Oct. 13, 1848, Butternuts, Mrs. LYDIA BARTON, aged 37. [10/21]
Oct. 9, 1848, Hartwick, SARAH M. RUSSELL, aged 3. [10/28]
Aug. 25, 1848, Hartwick, ASA E. RUSSELL, aged 9. [10/28]
Oct. 27, 1848, Hartwick, ELISHA S. NEAL, aged 19. [11/4]
Oct. 31, 1848, Otsego, Mrs. MARY EDDY, aged 80. [11/4]

Nov. 4, 1848, E. Hartwick, Mrs. HANNERETT HAGGERTY. [11/18]
Nov. 10, 1848, Brookfield, N.Y., Mrs. PATIENCE BRIGGS, aged 91. [11/18]
Nov. 18, 1848, Otsego, TERESSA BROCKWAY, aged 11. [11/25]
Nov. 18, 1848, New Lisbon, ELISHA G. ROCKWELL, aged 24. [11/25]
Nov. 6, 1848, Fly Creek, JULIETTE LE ROW, aged 3. [12/2]
Nov. 22, 1848, Richfield, JAMES MARKHAM, Jr., aged 56. [12/2]
Nov. 22, 1848, Springfield, CHARLES FITCH, aged 54. [12/2]
Nov. 27, 1848, E. Worcester, PHILO J. CHAMPION, aged 19. [12/2]
Dec. 2, 1848, Oneonta, OLIVE EATON, aged 89. [12/9]
Dec. 7, 1848, Laurens, ELIZABETH A. WAKEFIELD, aged 17. [12/16]
Dec. 1, 1848, Milford, Mrs. ABIGAIL JORDAN, aged 54. [12/23]
Dec. 17, 1848, Louisville (Butternuts), Mrs. MARIA JARVIS, aged 49. [12/23]
Dec. 27, 1848, Hartwick, SAMUEL CRAFTS, aged 89. [12/30]
Dec. 16, 1848, Hartwick, NICHOLAS CAMP, aged 94. [12/30]
Dec. 18, 1849, Pittsfield, JOSEPH SEWELL, aged 50. [1/6/1849]
Dec. 25, 1848, Fly Creek, DANIEL BRAINE, aged 55. [1/6/1849]
Jan. 7, 1849, Maryland, Mrs. THOMAS COOPER, aged 103. [1/13]
Jan. 11, 1849, Cooperstown, WILLIAM NILES, aged 68. [1/20]
Jan. 2, 1849, Hartwick, Mrs. PHEBE STEERE FOOTE, aged 27. [1/20]
Dec. 26, 1848, Richfield Springs, CORNELIA BUCKINGHAM, aged 23. [1/27/1849]
Feb. 13, 1849, Cooperstown, Mrs. NANCY PHINNEY, aged 57. [2/17]
Feb. 2, 1849, Otsego, EARL P. BRAMAN, aged 58. [2/17]
Feb. 6, 1849, Exeter, Mrs. MARY MOTT, aged 78. [2/17]
Feb. 8, 1849, Springfield, MARANDA GENTER, aged 22. [2/17]
Jan. 30, 1849, Decatur, Mrs. ISAAC LANE, aged 78. [2/17]
Jan. 26, 1849, Laurens, Mrs. ELIZA S. POWELL, aged 45. [2/17]
Feb. 6, 1849, Oneointa, Mrs. LYDIA A. DEITZ, aged 18. [2/17]
Jan. 24, 1849, New Lisbon, LEANDER NEARING, aged 15. [2/17]
Feb. 13, 1849, Hartwick, JOSEPH HUBBARD, aged 23. [2/24]
Feb. 17, 1849, Middlefield, DANIEL CUMMINGS, aged 72. [2/24]
Feb. 5, 1849, Edmeston, Mrs. WEALTHY DEMING, aged 49. [2/24]
Jan. 17, 1849, Unadilla, ARTHUR W. EMORY, aged 30. [2/24]
Feb. 28, 1849, Middlefield, HENRY BOWEN, aged 69. [3/3]
Feb. 22, 1849, Cooperstown, MARY F. HARDY, aged 3. [3/10]
Feb. 26, 1849, Otego, JULIA A. CHAMBERLIN, aged 7. [3/10]
March 2, 1849, Burlington Flats, Mrs. ABBY ARNOLD, aged 56. [3/17]
March 3, 1849, Cooperstown, Mrs. ELIZABETH HAND, aged 87. [3/24]
Mar. 4, 1849, Cooperstown, Mrs. HELEN A. WOOD, aged 32. [3/24]

March 9, 1849, Worcester, Mrs. HENRIETTA M. BIGELOW, aged 25. [3/24]
March 18, 1849, Burlington Flats, MONROE C. MORRIS, aged 3. [3/31]
March 28, 1849, Cooperstown, FRANCES HENICKER, infant. [3/31]
April 4, 1849, Otsego, SIRAJAH NEWELL, aged 80. [4/14]
March 5, 1849, Hartwick, REUBENS IRONS, aged 80. [4/14]
March 7, 1849, Hartwick, DANIEL KENYON, aged 87. [4/14]
March 12, 1849, Hartwick, RUFUS STEERE, aged 90. [4/14]
March 23, 1849, Hartwick, BETSEY CHAPPEL, aged 30. [4/14]
April 13, 1849, Cooperstown, HENRY W. W. WALSHE. [4/21]
April 15, 1849, Cooperstown, Mrs. HANNAH BOURNE, aged 67. [4/21]
April 18, 1849, Oneonta, JANE F. SHAW, aged 1. [5/5]
[No date] Otsego, Mrs. ANN TUCKER, aged 27. [5/5/1849]
May 4, 1849, Cohoes, N.Y., LAURA A. RUGGLES, aged 19. [5/12]
May 6, 1849, Westford, JOHN SIBLEY, aged 75. [5/19]
[No date] Otsego, SUSAN MOTT, aged 29. [5/19]
May 1, 1849, Richfield, Mrs. RUTH TILLSON, aged 71. [5/26]
May 4, 1849, Worcester, Mrs. BETSEY LAMPMAN, aged 26. [5/26]
April 27, 1849, Milford, Mrs. SARAH BARKER, aged 78. [5/26]
May 21, 1849, E. Springfield, GABRIEL DUTCHER, aged 66. [6/2]
May 25, 1849, Unadilla, WHEELER WEBB, aged 36. [6/9]
May 25, 1849, W. Springfield, JAMES E. FITCH, aged 2. [6/9]
June 4, 1849, Otsego, Mrs. LUCY PIER, aged 82. [6/16]
June 8, 1849, Springfield, Mrs. HANNAH FISH, aged 72. [6/16]
June 5, 1849, Cherry Valley, Dr. JOHN W. WOODBURN, aged 34. [6/16]
June 6, 1849, Middlefield, Mrs. ELIZABETH CUMMINGS. [6/23]
June 30, 1849, Springfield, JOHN B. SCOTT, infant. [7/7]
July 1, 1849, Cooperstown, GEORGE THRALL, age 1 year, 9 months. [7/7]
July 2, 1849, Cooperstown, WHITMORE E. CHAPMAN, aged 38. [7/14]
June 19, 1849, S. Edmeston, ISAAC P. BROWN, aged 81. [7/14]
July 14, 1849, Cooperstown, Mrs. SUSAN BEADLE, aged 63. [7/21]
July 22, 1849, Otsego, LUTHER EDDY, aged 78. [7/28]
July 22, 1849, Otsego, IRVING D. WHIPPLE, aged 2. [7/28]
July 16, 1849, Hartwick, DANIEL A. HEAD, aged 27. [7/28]
June 18, 1849, Hartwick, HELEN A. HEAD, infant. [7/28]
Aug. 5, 1849, Exeter, JOSIAH ROSE, aged 70. [8/18]
June 20, 1849, New Lisbon, FRANCIS HERRINGTON, aged 73. [8/18]
Aug. 12, 1849, Butternuts, ELIZA EILCOX, aged 26. [8/18]
June 15, 1849, Laurens, Dr. ABEL MORSE, aged 70. [8/18]

Aug. 13, 1849, Winfield, NANCY FITCH of Richfield, aged 32. [8/25]
Aug. 25, 1849, Otsego, Mrs. ESTHER SPRAGUE, aged 71. [9/1]
Aug. 26, 1849, Oneonte, Mrs. JULIA L. DERBY, aged 27. [9/1]
Aug. 23, 1849, Otsego, DANIEL PRESTON, aged 90. [9/1]
Aug. 21, 1849, Middlefield, MARCIA OLIVE, aged 15. [9/1]
Aug. 27, 1849, Wellsboro, LUCY N. WOOD, aged 2. [9/1]
[No date] Unadilla, HOWARD WILLIAMS, aged 2. [9/15]
Aug. 29, 1849, Burlington, MATTHEW O. BISHOP, infant. [9/22]
Sept. 16, 1849, Otsego, ELEAZER HALE, aged 79. [9/29]
Sept. 13, 1849, Otsego, CONSTANT SHERMAN, aged 62. [9/29]
Sept. 25, 1849, New Lisbon, MARY JANE STETSON, aged 22. [10/16]
Sept. 29, 1849, Milford, EMILIUS BISSELL, aged 34. [10/16]
Sept. 18, 1849, Otego, RANSON HUNT, aged 81. [10/16]
Sept. 3, 1849, Toddsville, JOHN H. ELDRIDGE, aged 6. [10/16]
Sept. 23, 1849, Hartwick, WILLIAM C. VERRY, aged 26. [10/20]
Oct. 15, 1849, New Lisbon, CHARLES WING, aged 1. [10/20]
Oct. 13, 1849, Laurens, Mrs. SARAH A. LANE, aged 28. [10/27]
Oct. 16, 1849, Unadilla, WILLIAM WILMOT, aged 69. [10/27]
Oct. 16, 1849, Hartwick, LUCY ANN WARD, aged 23. [10/27]
Oct. 31, 1849, Cooperstown, WILLIAM H. SMITH, aged 19. [11/3]
Oct. 29, 1849, Cooperstown, CATHERINE PECK, aged 19. [11/3]
Oct. 31, 1849, Cooperstown, WILLIAM H. SMITH, 19 yeasr. [11/3]
Oct. 23, 1849, Maryland, STEPHEN M. CORNWELL. [11/3]
Oct. 10, 1849, Otego, PETER MIRES, aged 62. [11/3]
Oct. 30, 1849, Otsego, MARY E. HINDS, aged 7. [11/10]
Nov. 21, 1849, Pierstown, ANNA A. WARREN, aged 8. [11/24]
Nov. 14, 1849, Cooperstown, WALTER J. RUSSELL, infant. [12/8]
Dec. 4, 1849, Cooperstown, HELEN SKINNER, infant. [12/8]
Dec. 4, 1849, Springfield, MORTIMER A. HALL, infant. [12/15]
Nov. 11, 1849, Hartwick, EDWARD B. ANGUR, aged 28. [12/22]
Dec. 6, 1849, Cooperstown, ISRAEL P. DUTCHER, aged 17. [12/22]
Dec. 4, 1849, Middlefield, SALLY JONES, aged 48. [12/22]
Jan. 9, 1850, Milford, HELEN M. NEWELL, aged 19. [1/19]
Jan. 3, 1850, Otsego, ISAAC BROWN, aged 61. [1/19]
Jan. 17, 1850, Otsego, EDWIN C. DOUBLEDAY, aged 24. [1/19]
Dec. 19, 1849, Fly Creek, Deacon ALBERT NORTH, aged 60. [1/19/1850]
Jan. 17, 1850, Middlefield, SARAH TRAVERSE of Utica, aged 20. [1/26]
Jan. 23, 1850, New Lisbon, Mrs. HANNAH S. NEARING, aged 23. [1/26]
Jan. 6, 1850, New Lisbon, JAMES EATON, aged 52. [1/26]

Dec. 22, 1849, E. Worcester, ELIZABETH CHAMPION, aged 8. [1/26/1850]
Jan. 19, 1850, Hartwick, Rev. GEORGE H. MILLER, aged 26. [1/26]
Jan. 11, 1850, Oneonta, JAMES YOUNG, aged 90. [1/26]
Jan. 6, 1850, Hartwick, Mrs. XERIAH CLARK, aged 67. [2/2]
Jan. 24, 1850, E. Springfield, DAN L. MARQUISEE, aged 18. [2/2]
Jan. 25, 1850, Schenevus, OSCHER C. DELONG, aged 25. [2/2]
Jan. 10, 1850, Maryland, WILLIAM HAYNES, aged 74. [2/2]
Feb. 10, 1850, Springfield, Mrs. ANN L. CLARKE, aged 67. [2/16]
Feb. 4, 1850, Hartwick, HORACE BISSELL, aged 60. [2/16]
Feb. 11, 1850, Hartwick, RUFUS CASE, aged 67. [2/16]
Jan. 4, 1850, Maryland, CYNTHIA CHAMBERLAIN, aged 24. [2/23]
Feb. 13, 1850, Middlefield, Mrs. AMY MURPHY, aged 43. [3/2]
Feb. 25, 1850, New Lisbon, ABNER E. ROCKWELL, aged 3. [3/2]
Feb. 25, 1850, New Lisbon, EMILY M. ROCKWELL, aged 5. [3/2]
Feb. 25, 1850, Cooperstown, EMMA STILLMAN, infant. [3/2]
Feb. 20, 1850, Cooperstown, CHAS. R. PECK, infant. [3/16]
March 8, 1850, Cooperstown, Mrs. MARY M. PECK, aged 24. [3/16]
March 13, 1850, Pierstown, Mrs. EXPERIENCE PARSHALL, aged 60. [3/16]
March 13, 1850, Hartwick, B. WHEELER CARR, aged 76. [3/16]
March 2, 1850, New Lisbon, LEROY PARKER, aged 15. [3/23]
March 15, 1850, Milford, CLARK BAKER, aged 2. [3/23]
March 11, 1850, Exeter, SELAH K. LOSSEE, infant. [3/30]
March 24, 1850, Laurens, GEORGE CLYDE, aged 5. [4/6]
March 17, 1850, Cherry Valley, RUTH GRAHAM, aged 40. [4/6]
March 30, 1850, Worcester, Dr. U. Y. BIGELOW, aged 56. [4/6]
March 11, 1850, Cherry Valley, MARTHA A. GOULD, aged 15. [4/6]
March 25, 1850, Unadilla, Mrs. HARRIET E. BURLINGAME, aged 23. [4/6]
March 22, 1850, Laurens, Mrs. DESIRE BECKWITH, aged 78. [4/13]
April 5, 1850, Cherry Valley, Mrs. ELIZA BOWMAN, aged 40. [4/13]
April 6, 1850, Cherry Valley, Mrs. NANCY DRAKE, aged 61. [4/13]
April 14, 1850, Middlefield, Col. BELA KAPLE, aged 76. [4/20]
April 10, 1850, Hartwick, LYMAN HARRINGTON, aged 56. [4/20]
April 12, 1850, Cherry Valley, EUGINE CAMPBELL, aged 5. [4/20]
April 17, 1850, Cherry Valley, Mrs. DEBORAH CAMPBELL, aged 71. [4/20]
[No date] Toddsville, EMMOGENE BOLLES, aged 6. [4/20]
April 10, 1850, New Lisbon, JONATHAN TIFFANY. [4/20]
April 8, 1850, New Lisbon, JULIAETTE TIFFANY, aged 6. [4/20]

April 6, 1850, New Lisbon, ELLEN TIFFANY. [4/20]
April 25, 1850, Cooperstown, RICHARD COOLEY, aged 51. [4/27]
April 22, 1850, Laurens, JANE COMSTOCK, aged 10. [4/27]
April 19, 1850, Cherry Valley, JOHN KINGSBURG, aged 68. [4/27]
April 20, 1850, Cherry Valley, PAMELIA DANIELS, aged 8. [4/27]
March 4, 1850, Decatur, KEZIA DEMELT, aged 24. [5/4]
April 18, 1850, Milford, WILLIAM BARNARD, aged 86. [5/4]
April 18, 1850, Clarksville, JAMES PARSHALL, aged 70. [5/11]
April 17, 1850, Morris, Mrs. AMBROSE D. WINTON, aged 32. [5/11]
May 8, 1850, Otsego, Mrs. SARAH RUSSELL, aged 59. [5/11]
May 5, 1850, Otsego, JANNET MC TAVISH, aged 84. [5/25]
March 3, 1850, Sacramento, Calif., JAMES BIRGE, Jr. of Westford, aged 62. [5/25]
May 16, 1850, Cherry Valley, Capt. JEROME CLARK, aged 95. [5/25]
May 9, 1850, Cherry Valley, Mrs. JERUSHA MARKS, aged 41. [6/1]
May 10, 1850, Edmeston, JOANNA PARKER, aged 17. [6/1]
May 13, 1850, Laurens, MARY E. RATHBUN, aged 3. [6/8]
May 28, 1850, Cooperstown, Mrs. MARY RUGGLES, aged 58. [6/8]
June 9, 1850, Cooperstown, Mrs. HANNAH LAMBERT, aged 72. [6/15]
June 6, 1850, Middlefield, Mrs. CATHERINE RIGHTOR, aged 84. [6/15]
June 11, 1850, Otsego, Mrs. MARY RUSSELL, aged 90. [6/22]
June 15, 1850, Milford, BENONI ADAMS, aged 86. [6/22]
June 23, 1850, Otego, DANIEL MARR, aged 60. [6/29]
March 7, 1850, New Lisbon, NANCY M. GROSS, aged 49. [6/29]
June 22, 1850, New Lisbon, MARVIN H. GROSS, aged 27. [6/29]
July 8, 1850, Clarksville, ELIZABETH CAMPBELL, aged 44. [7/20]
July 8, 1850, Edmeston, Mrs. DIANTHE ST. JOHN, aged 70. [7/20]
July 5, 1850, Milford, ALLEN BAKER, aged 57. [7/27]
July 28, 1850, Cherry Valley, JENNETTE MAY, aged 18. [8/3]
July 10, 1850, Laurens, IRA KENYON, aged 77. [8/3]
Aug. 5, 1850, Burlington, MATHEW DORR SILL, aged 23. [8/10]
July 26, 1850, Middle Center, JOHN RICE, aged 70. [8/10]
Aug. 14, 1850, Cooperstown, MARTHA B. WEEKS, aged 21. [8/17]
Aug. 9, 1850, Oneonta, Mrs. CATHERINE YOUNG, aged 60. [8/17]
Sept. 7, 1850, Westville, JULIUS C. HAINES, aged 26. [9/21]
Aug. 31, 1850, Oneonta, Mrs. POLLY GRAHAM, aged 66. [9/28]
Sept. 22, 1850, Hartwick Sem., Mrs. JANE SWACKHAMER, aged 73. [9/28]
Sept. 26, 1850, Toddsville, Mrs. FIDELIA WILSON, aged 40. [10/5]
Sept. 6, 1850, Fly Creek, Mrs. ELIZA GALLUP, aged 38. [10/5]
Sept 20, 1850, Cooperstown, Mrs. JULIA SEELYE, aged 65. [10/5]

Oct. 5, 1850, Oaksville, JASPER SHERWOOD, aged 68. [10/19]
Oct. 29, 1850, Richfield, Mrs. CORNELIA CHAMBERLIN, aged 59. [11/9]
Nov. 5, 1850, Otsego, EMELINE CHAPMAN, aged 14. [11/9]
Sept. 2, 1850, Burlington, Mrs. PHEBE MONROE, aged 18. [11/9]
Oct. 12, 1850, New Lisbon, HARRIET E. HOWELL, aged 11. [11/16]
Nov. 25, 1850, Cooperstown, MARTHA BUSH, aged 4. [11/30]
Nov. 9, 1850, Edmeston, ISABELLA LUN, aged 40. [11/30]
Nov. 22, 1850, Hartwick, JULIA ANN VAN HORNE, aged 33. [11/30]
Oct. 2, 1850, at sea, AMOS M. PERRY (New Lisbon), aged 28. [12/21]
Dec. 9, 1850, Otsego, Mrs. EUNICE WALLEY, aged 87. [12/21]
[No date] E. Worcester, Mrs. HARRIET CHAMPION, aged 33. [12/21]
[No date] Springfield, EUNICE HEWES, aged 15. [12/21]
Dec. 16, 1850, Fly Creek, Mrs. ADA A. CHAPPELL, aged 28. [12/28]
Jan. 1, 1851, Cooperstown, OSCAR W. CHILDS, aged 8. [1/11]
Jan. 8, 1851, Otsego, JULIA WILLIAMS, aged 35. [1/11]
Jan. 8, 1851, Richfield, Mrs. ABIGAIL EDSON, aged 77. [1/18]
Jan. 9, 1851, Otsego, LAURA E. RAYMOND, aged 3. [1/18]
Jan. 9, 1851, Laurens, BURR B. CHAPMAN, infant. [1/18]
Jan. 12, 1851, Middlefield, DELOS MASTERS, aged 18. [1/18]
Jan. 14, 1851, Otsego, EMILY J. WATERMAN, aged 32. [1/18]
Jan. 10, 1851, Otsego, MARY E. ROBERTS, aged 2. [1/18]
Jan. 19, 1851, Cooperstown, ELIZA L. BROWN. [1/25]
Jan. 17, 1851, Clarksville, HENRIETTA M. PARSHALL, aged 6. [1/25]
Jan. 28, 1851, Otsego, ANDREW SCRIBNER, aged 78. [2/1]
Jan. 22, 1851, Hartwick, JOSEPH CAMP, aged 91. [2/1]
Jan. 26, 1851, Cooperstown, ABIJAH FAIRCHILD, aged 93. [2/8]
Feb. 4, 1851, Middlefield, GEORGE F. KIRBY, aged 1. [2/8]
Jan. 25, 1851, Jacksonville, JOHN W. JACOBS, aged 27. [2/8]
Feb. 2, 1851, Westford, MARY BYAM, aged 14. [2/15]
Jan. 26, 1851, Unadilla, SETH ROWLEY, aged 90. [2/15]
Feb. 13, 1851, Butternuts, DAVID GILLET, aged 61. [2/22]
Feb. 23, 1851, Burlington, JOHN A. OLIVER, aged 32. [3/1]
Feb. 19, 1851, Otsego, HELEN L. FREEMAN, aged 4. [3/1]
Feb. 22, 1851, Unadilla, Mrs. HANNAH S. EDSON, aged 25. [3/1]
March 4, 1851, Middlefield, JEME EGLESTON, aged 72. [3/8]
March 4, 1851, Milford, BENJAMIN WESTCOTT, aged 79. [3/8]
March 1, 1851, Hopeville, GUSTAVUS A. HYDE, aged 39. [3/8]
Feb. 24, 1851, Jacksonville, Mrs. CYNTHIA CLARKE, aged 55. [3/15]
March 7, 1851, New Berlin, MARCUS S. WILLARD, aged 63. [3/15]

March 9, 1851, New Lisbon, Col. JOSEPH GARDNER, aged 80 (?). [3/15]
March 10, 1851, Springfield, MARTHA C. WOOD. [3/15]
April 9, 1851, Laurens, Gen. ERASTUS CRAFTS, aged 71. [4/19]
April 11, 1851, Cherry Valley, BENJAMIN DENSLOW, aged 91. [4/19]
March 28, 1851, Oneonta, SARAH ANN HOPKINS, aged 12. [4/19]
April 8, 1851, Cooperstown, Mrs. LEVANTIA HENNIKER, aged 26. [4/12]
March 31, 1851, Decatur, Mrs. SARAH M. LANSING, aged 58. [4/12]
May 6, 1851, Cooperstown, Mrs. NANCY THAYER, aged 64. [5/10]
April 17, 1851, Westford, DAVID A. BEDEAU, aged 25. [5/10]
June 5, 1851, Edmeston, Mrs. AMY SUTHERLAND, aged 48. [6/14]
April 24, 1851, Otsego, Mrs. AMELIA DAVIDSON, aged 59. [6/14]
June 7, 1851, Cooperstown, Mrs. LOVICI CHAFFEE, aged 65. [6/14]
June 10, 1851, Richfield, Mrs. ANNA MC COLLUM, aged 71. [6/21]
June 18, 1851, Cooperstown, CHARLOTTE M. EDWARDS, aged 1. [6/21]
June 3, 1851, Middlefield, Mrs. HARRIET A. WOOD, aged 22. [6/21]
May 17, 1851, Hartwick Sem., JOSEPHINE E. J. BOYD, aged 4. [6/21]
Aug. 21, 1851, Cherry Valley, JOSHUA TUCKER, aged 71. [8/30]
Aug. 20, 1851, Exeter, CALEB ANGELL, aged 83. [8/30]
Aug. 26, 1851, Middlefield, Mrs. BETSEY MORRIS OLENDORF, aged 67. [9/6]
Sept. 8, 1851, Cooperstown, HENRY PHINNEY, aged 2. [9/13]
Sept. 9, 1851, Cooperstown, AGNES S. RUSSELL, infant. [9/13]
Sept. 9, 1851, Edmeston, Mrs. PATTY SMITH, aged 73. [9/20]
Sept. 8, 1851, Springfield, Mrs. CHLOE LAY, aged 70. [9/27]
Sept. 15, 1851, Springfield, LESTER D. KEYES, infant. [9/27]
Sept. 4, 1851, Burlington, Mrs. MATILDA CASLER, aged 33. [10/4]
Oct. 6, 1851, Cooperstown, ELLA F. GRAVES, infant. [10/18]
Nov. 3, 1851, W. Edmeston, BENJAMIN AROLD [sic], aged 63. [11/15]
Nov. 3, 1851, Westford, JOHN JACKSON, aged 97. [11/15]
Nov. 12, 1851, Edmeston, Capt. ISAAC SMITH, aged 82. [11/21]
Nov. 10, 1851, Milford, Mrs. ELIZABETH MARTIN, aged 69. [11/21]
Nov. 23, 1851, Cooperstown, RALPH SHERMAN COFFIN, aged 4. [11/28]
Nov. 23, 1851, Middlefield, JULIA A. BROOKS, aged 11. [11/28]
Dec. 5, 1851, Edmeston, FRANKLIN PARKER, aged 7. [12/12]
Dec. 10, 1851, Middlefield, RHODA ANN BATES, aged 15 months. [12/19]

Dec. 11, 1851, Edmeston, Mrs. SUSANNAH BURLINGAME, aged 77. [12/19]
Dec. 16, 1851, Garrattsville, RUSSELL BENJAMIN, aged 52 [12/19]
Dec. 19, 1851, Cooperstown, KATE WILSON, aged 1. [12/26]
Dec. 13, 1851, Unadilla, Mrs. MARY GANO, aged 72. [12/26]
Dec. 14, 1851, Edmeston, ABRAHAM B. PARKER, aged 28. [1/2/1852]
Dec. 5, 1851, Edmeston, FRANKLIN PARKER, aged 7. [1/2/1852]
Dec. 18, 1851, Edmeston, ABRAHAM PARKER, aged 2. [1/2/1852]
Dec. 16, 1851, Plainfield, WILLIAM H. MURRAY, aged 72. [1/2/1852]
Dec. 10, 1851, S. Hartwick, Mrs. ELIZABETH WEBB, aged 67. [1/2/1852]
Dec. 21, 1851, Burlington, WILLIAM ALEXIS MILLER, aged 24. [1/2/1852]
Jan. 6, 1852, Otsego, Mrs. OLIVE LAKE, aged 55. [1/9]
Jan. 16, 1852, Otsego, LESTER C. DOUBLEDAY, aged 53. [1/23]
Jan. 20, 1852, E. Worcester, PAUL C. CRIPPEN, aged 26. [1/30]
Jan. 25, 1852, Middlefield, DANIEL MUNROE, aged 84. [1/30]
Jan. 28, 1852, Westford, Mrs. SARAH J. BREESE, aged 32. [1/30]
Jan. 20, 1852, Cooperstown, WILLIAM G. EDWARDS, aged 4. [2/6]
Jan. 11, 1852, Oaksville, PETER T. CARR, aged 61. [2/13]
Feb. 7, 1852, Richfield Center, FRANCES A. ANDRUS, aged 2. [2/13]
Feb. 11, 1852, Richfield, Mrs. LUCY VEBER, aged 73. [2/27]
Jan. 25, 1852, Westford, Mrs. PHEBE JACKSON, aged 89. [2/27]
Jan. 8, 1852, Springfield, MARIETTE HOLT, aged 31. [2/27]
Feb. 28, 1852, Otsego, TIMOTHY BABCOCK, aged 71. [3/5]
Feb. 24, 1852, Butternuts, JOHN BREWER, aged 67. [3/5]
Feb. 23, 1852, Otsego, HELEN FITCH, aged 18. [3/12]
March 9, 1852, Hartwick, NATHAN FIELD, aged 85. [3/12]
March 1, 1852, Otsego, EMER AMANDA KINNEY, aged 6. [3/12]
Feb. 5, 1852, Garrattsville, HENRY STEPHENS, aged 61. [3/12]
Feb. 19, 1852, Cherry Valley, ASA RICH, aged 74. [3/12]
March 6, 1852, Cherry Valley, MARY IDA WOODBURN, aged 5. [3/12]
March 4, 1852, Maryland, ANDREW J. BURNSIDE, aged 23. [3/12]
Feb. 22, 1852, Edmeston, CALEB PERKINS, aged 75. [3/19]
March 5, 1852, Pittsfield, SIMEON B. GALLUP, aged 51. [3/19]
Feb. 23, 1852, Morris, THOMAS SHAW, aged 51. [3/19]
Feb. 27, 1852, Exeter, SELDOM M. ROSE, aged 12. [3/19]
April 8, 1852, Otsego, Mrs. MARY L. SMITH, aged 61. [4/16]
April 5, 1852, Middlefield, Mrs. LUCY PARSHALL, aged 72. [4/23]
April 12, 1852, W. Hartwick, Mrs. ANNA ALWORTH, aged 87. [4/23]
April 12, 1852, Hartwick, WILLIAM EDDY, aged 67. [4/23]

April 22, 1852, Otsego, NOYES LEWIS, aged 36. [4/30]
April 28, 1852, Clarksville, Otsego Co., EDWIN V. HOLLISTER, infant. [5/7]
Feb. 2, 1852, Waterville, DAVID BELKNAP, aged 60. [5/7]
May 2, 1852, Waterville, Mrs. HARRIET BELKNAP, aged 55. [5/7]
May 9, 1852, Westford, AARON BREESE, aged 71. [5/15]
April 16, 1852, Exeter, SARAH B. ANGELL, aged 59. [5/21]
May 21, 1852, Cherry Valley, DANIEL R. BURNETT, aged 19. [5/28]
Feb. 26, 1852, Fly Creek, SILAS WILLIAMS, aged 81. [6/11]
June 5, 1852, Fly Creek, JOHN C. WILLIAMS, aged 49. [6/11]
June 19, 1852, Cooperstown, CAROLINE SMITH, aged 40. [6/25]
July 4, 1852, Laurens, HIRAM H. KEYES, aged 12. [7/9]
June 22, 1852, Oneonta, ROE MC DONALD, aged 25. [7/9]

Balance of this year (1852) newspapers missing;
also beginning of 1853.

Aug. 10, 1853, Hartwick, Mrs. SARAH ANN CRAFTS, aged 36. [8/19]
July 23, 1853, Milford, E. SPENCER BAKER, aged 44. [8/19]
Aug. 23, 1853, Schuyler's Lake, Mrs. AMANDA GARRATT, aged 40. [9/2]
July 30, 1853, Laurens, WILLIAM D. WARD, aged 28. [9/2]
Aug. 12, 1853, New Lisbon, DALLAS J. HOLLAND of N.Y.C., aged 16. [9/9]
Aug. 30, 1853, New Lisbon, EBENEZER NEARING, aged 71. [9/9]
Aug. 29, 1853, New Lisbon, EDMUND MICKEL, aged 27. [9/9]
Sept. 16, 1853, Morris, Mrs. CHARITY JACKSON, aged 74. [9/23]
Sept. 15, 1853, Otsego, MATILDA FREEMAN, aged 27. [9/30]
Sept. 25, 1853, Unadilla, Hon. SHERMAN PAGE, aged 75. [10/7]
Sept. 13, 1853, Milford, Mrs. LETITIA WILCOX, aged 66. [10/7]
Sept. 14, 1853, Springfield, MORTIMER E. HOLT, aged 27. [10/14]
Sept. 25, 1853, Springfield, ANDREW ALDEN, aged 68. [10/14]
Oct. 9, 1853, W. Hartwick, Mrs. ELIZA HUTCHINS, aged 25. [10/21]
Oct. 19, 1853, Otsego, TIMOTHY WATERMAN, aged 69. [10/21]
[No date] Springfield, JOHN WINSLOW, aged 69. [10/28]
Oct. 18, 1853, Hartwick, FRANK B. RAPALIE, of Milo, Pa., infant. [10/28]
Oct. 27, 1853, Cooperstown, FRANCES A. TANNER, infant. [11/4]
Nov. 7, 1853, Hartwick, Mrs. DANIEL MOTT, aged 69. [11/18]
Oct. 27, 1853, Laurens, WILLIAM C. JOHNSON, aged 60. [11/18]
Nov. 8, 1853, Burlington, Mrs. LAURA A. GORHAM, aged 31. [11/25]

Nov. 20, 1853, Portlandville, CHARLES W. LATIMER, 1 year. [11/25]
Nov. 20, 1853, Fly Creek, Mrs. MARY BROWNELL. [12/2]
Nov. 26, 1853, Cooperstown, Mrs. HARRIET DRAKE, aged 42. [12/2]
Nov. 22, 1853, Otsego, HEZEKIAH W. LYON, aged 63. [12/2]
Dec. 6, 1853, Middlefield, LEWIS SMITH DAVIS, aged 33. [12/16]
Feb. --, ---, Pittsfield, Mrs. PHEBE STRAIGHT, aged 84. [12/23]
Dec. 21, 1853, Cooperstown, NATHAN WEEKS, aged 59. [12/30]
Dec. 22, 1853, Cooperstown, Mrs. HENRY MILLER, aged 45. [1/6/1854]
Jan. 9, 1854, Butternuts, AMBROSE WARD, aged 77. [1/13]
Jan. 2, 1854, Morris, ELIJAH BUTTS, aged 75. [1/13]
Feb. 1, 1854, Cooperstown, MARGARET S. ROBINSON, aged 19. [2/3]
Jan. 30, 1854, Westford, HENRY A. KELSO, aged 18. [2/10]
Feb. 2, 1854, Westford, Mrs. NANCY WRIGHT, aged 75. [2/10]
Jan. 31, 1854, W. Hartwick, Mrs. MARY BENJAMIN, aged 69. [2/10]
Feb. 4, 1854, Springfield, Dea. MOSES FRANKLIN, aged 91. [2/17]
Feb. 5, 1854, Middlefield, EMER D. BROOKS, aged 18 months. [2/17]
Dec. 27, 1853, Cherry Valley, HARRIET WEBSTER, aged 16. [2/24/1854]
Jan. 15, 1854, Cherry Valley, Mrs. ANNA COSSART, aged 37. [2/24]
Feb. 11, 1854, Morris, LEMUEL S. BROOKS, aged 27. [3/3]
Feb. 20, 1854, New Berlin, FRANCIS THOMAS, aged 84. [3/3]
Feb. 23, 1854, Morris, Dea. URI JACKSON, aged 75. [3/3]
Feb. 28, 1854, Richfield, DANIEL MC COLLUM, aged 82. [3/10]
March 5, 1854, Middlefield, Mrs. ELIZABETH RHINEES, aged 28. [3/17]
March 7, 1854, Butternuts, HAWLEY SWARTWOUT, aged 25. [3/17]
Feb. 24, 1854, Burlington, NATHAN W. MATTERSON, aged 58. [3/17]
March 5, 1854, Otsego, Mrs. PHEBE M. SEAVER, aged 36. [3/17]
March 9, 1854, Middlefield, Mrs. MARY CAMPBELL PARSHALL, aged 52. [3/17]
March 11, 1854, Middlefield, Mrs. POLLY THORP, aged 71. [3/17]
March 18, 1854, Cooperstown, JACOB SNYDER, aged 68. [3/24]
Feb. 24, 1854, New Berlin, GARDNER POTTER, aged 50. [3/24]
March 31, 1854, Pierstown, SEYMOUR J. LENT, aged 25.
April 1, 1854, Cooperstown, Dr. C. G. HALL, aged 63. [4/14]
March 11, 1854, Laurens, HENRY L. ELDRED, aged 80. [4/14]
March 29, 1854, Toddsville, Mrs. CATHERINE TODD, aged 63. [4/14]
March 25, 1854, Burlington, Mrs. ISABEL FITCH, aged 82. [4/14]
April 29, 1854, Burlington, HENRY FITCH, aged 83. [4/14]
April 6, 1854, Otego, ABRAHAM BLAKELEY, aged 92. [4/14]
April 15, 1854, Morris, Mrs. MARIA R. HUDSON, aged 28. [4/21]
April 16, 1854, Springfield, Mrs. SARAH INGALLS, aged 99. [4/21]
Oct. 22, 1853, Pittsfield, Mrs. MIRIAM SISSON, aged 30. [4/21/1854]

April 6, 1854, Unadilla, CHARLES C. SISSON, son of above. [4/21]
April 14, 1854, Oneonta, WILLIAM FAIRCHILD, aged 74. [4/21]
April 15, 1854, Butternuts, GEORGE H. LUCE, aged 18. [4/21]
April 24, 1854, Clarksville, GEORGE A. POWERS, aged 13. [4/28]
April 13, 1854, Springfield, Mrs. HANNAH DOLLAWAY, aged 76. [5/5]
March 5, 1854, New Lisbon, C. W. T. TAYLOR, aged 16. [5/5]
April 12, 1854, Middlefield, Mrs. RACHEL RULOFSON, aged 78. [5/5]
May 12, 1854, Cooperstown, CHARLES B. BALL, aged 17. [5/19]
May 21, 1854, Morris, TRUMAN BLADIN, aged 82. [5/19]
May 12, 1854, Hartwick, EDGAR J. OLENDORF, aged 22. [5/26]
April 14, 1854, Middlefield, Mrs. EFFIE SIMISON, aged 68. [5/26]
May 19, 1854, Otsego, Mrs. NAOMI NEAL, aged 62. [6/2]
April 4, 1854, Milford, Mrs. ELIZABETH MANN, aged 79. [6/2]
April 16, 1854, Otsego, DAN. B. PIER, aged 8. [6/2]
June 4, 1854, Cooperstown, JOHN T. PHINNEY, aged 25. [6/9]
May 15, 1854, Laurens, TIMOTHY FLETCHER, aged 59. [6/16]
June 3, 1854, Westford, GEORGE SNYDER, aged 65. [6/16]
June 11, 1854, Springfield, ARTHUR E. HOKE, aged 1 year. [6/23]
June 16, 1854, Cooperstown, Col. PETER MEGHAR, aged 80. [6/23]
June 16, 1854, Cooperstown, Mrs. SARAH STEWART of N.Y.C. [6/23]
May 16, 1854, Cooperstown, Mrs. SARAH ANN DAVIS, aged 45. [6/23]
June 21, 1854, Middlefield, ELLEN SMITH, aged 3. [6/30]
May 20, 1854, S. Worcester, Mrs. PHALLY STRAIN, aged 65. [6/30]
April 13, 1854, Richfield, WILLIAM EDDY, aged 95. [6/30]
June 13, 1854, Hartwick, GEORGE W. SMITH, aged 23. [6/30]
June 26, 1854, Worcester, Mrs. MARY CARYL. [7/7]
July 12, 1854, S. Worcester, CHRISTIAN MULTER, aged 68. [7/21]
June 9, 1854, Burlington, ISAAC BOLTON, aged 53. [7/28]
July 17, 1854, Butternuts, ELLA J. BENTLEY, aged 4. [7/28]
Juy 26, 1854, Cherry Valley, Mrs. JANE KIRBY, aged 46. [7/28]
Aug. 1, 1854, Cooperstown, FLAVIL BEADLE, aged 66. [8/4]
July 28, 1854, Otsego, REUBEN HINDS, aged 86. [8/4]
July 27, 1854, Worcester, Mrs. HANNAH GRANT, aged 67. [8/11]
July 25, 1854, Hartwick, ALEX. MURDOCK, aged 59. [8/11]
Aug. 2, 1854, Springfield, ELIZA P. HOLT, aged 21. [8/11]
Aug. 6, 1854, Otsego, Mrs. ANNA FISH, aged 69. [8/18]
Aug. 8, 1854, Hartwick, HARRIET ALLEN, aged 21. [8/18]
July 27, 1854, Otsego, Mrs. LYDIA FULLER, aged 64. [8/18]
Aug. 22, 1854, Cooperstown, Mrs. C. DORRANCE, aged 79. [9/1]
Aug. 26, 1854, Burlington, Mrs. POLLY SENA DIMOCK, aged 78. [9/22]
Sept 24, 1854, Oneonta, HENRY H. MILLER, aged 62. [9/29]

Sept. 27, 1854, MARIA WHITWELL, infant. [10/6]
Sept. 23, 1854, Cherry Valley, RINEAR BECKER, aged 82. [10/6]
Sept. 26, 1854, Burlington, GEORGE S. RITTER, aged 46. [10/6]
Oct. 6, 1854, W. Burlington, SAMUEL SIMMONS, aged 64. [10/13]
Sept. 11, 1854, Exeter, JOHN ROSE, aged 53. [10/13]
Sept. 20, 1854, Otsego, RICHARD A. FREEMAN, aged 64. [10/13]
Sept. 6, 1854, Unadilla Forks, Mrs. EUNICE BABCOCK, aged 74. [10/13]
Aug. 17, 1854, Otsego, Mrs. MARY E. HOLT, aged 27. [10/13]
Oct. 7, 1854, Laurens, Mrs. SALLY E. CATHCART, aged 82. [10/20]
Sept. 25, 1854, Pittsfield, Mrs. MARY A. HINDS, aged 34. [10/20]
Oct. 13, 1854, Burlington, HANNAH C. PRICE, aged 7. [10/27]
Oct. 22, 1854, Martland, Mrs. ELECTA BOYNTON, aged 68. [11/3]
Oct. 19, 1854, Morris, NATHANIEL GIFFORD, aged 60. [11/3]
Oct. 13, 1854, New Lisbon, Mrs. POLLY BUNDY, aged 68. [11/3]
Oct. 14, 1854, Laurens, Mrs. NATHAN ELDRED, aged 59. [11/3]
Oct. 26, 1854, Springfield, Mrs. MARY STANSEL, aged 61. [11/10]
Oct. 24, 1854, Burlington, Mrs. OLIVE THOMPSON, aged 75. [11/17]
Nov. 13, 1854, Cooperstown, WILLIAM S. MARVIN, aged 2. [11/24]
Nov. 16, 1854, Burlington, Mrs. PHEBE S. DIMOCK, aged 34. [12/1]
Nov. 25, 1854, Richfield Spa, BENJAMIN R. ELWOOD, aged 68. [12/8]
Dec. 5, 1854, Middlefield, DEWITT C. PARSHALL, aged 29. [12/15]
Dec. 10, 1854, Cooperstown, STEPHEN CLARK, aged 28. [12/15]
Dec. 21, 1854, Cooperstown, DAVID WILLARD, aged 42. [12/22]
Dec. 16, 1854, Little Falls, ELIZABETH A. COLTIS of Fly Creek, aged 32. [12/22]
Dec. 3, 1854, Decatur, POLLY TRIPP, aged 61. [12/22]
Dec. 18, 1854, Exeter, Mrs. CATHERINE HERKIMER, aged 86. [12/22]
[No date] Roseboom, HENRY MC DAVY, aged 41. [12/29/1854]
Dec. 17, 1854, Exeter, EMELINE M. HART, aged 14. [12/29]
Dec. 27, 1854, Cooperstown, MORTIMER HINMAN, aged 20. [12/29]
Dec. 24, 1854, Otsego, OSCAR WHIPPLE. [12/29]
Dec. 9, 1854, Middlefield, Mrs. TAVANCHA BAILEY. [12/29]
Dec. 26, 1854, Middlefield, HARVEY WATERMAN, aged 33. [1/5/1855]
Jan. 3, 1855, Hartwick, ELVENA A. TAYLOR, aged 21. [1/5]
Dec. 11, 1854, Gilbertsville, LOWELL B. LUCE, aged 55. [1/5/1855]
Oct. 31, 1854, Hartwick, HANNAH ROBINSON, aged 60. [1/5/1855]
Dec. 29, 1854, Mrs. HANNAH NILES, aged 82. [1/11/1855]
Jan. 6, 1855, W. Hartwick, MARGARET A. MC INTOSH, aged 17. [1/19]
Dec. 28, 1854, S. Hartwick, Mrs. CLARISSA WILCOX, aged 46. [1/19/1855]

Jan. 3, 1855, Milford, ABIJAH ROBERTS, aged 21. [1/19]
Jan. 19, 1855, Cooperstown, HIRAM D. MALLORY, aged 28. [1/26]
Jan. 19, 1855, Oneonta, LOUISA A. WATKINS, aged 29. [1/26]
Jan. 27, 1855, Portlandville, Mrs. CATHERINE DOOLITTLE PHILLIPS, aged 24. [2/16]
Feb. 17, 1855, Fly Creek, DAVID MARVIN, aged 84. [2/23]
Feb. 14, 1855, Springfield Center, HENRY S. WOOD, aged 25. [2/23]
Feb. 16, 1855, Otsego, FRANCES D. JOHNSON, aged 31. [3/2]
Feb. 21, 1855, Otsego, NELSON RUSSELL, aged 39. [3/2]
Feb. 19, 1855, Roseville (?), Dr. JOSEPH CARPENTER, aged 72. [3/2]
Feb. 21, 1855, Hartwick, EMMA S. CONKLIN, infant. [3/2]
Feb. 4, 1855, Exeter, Mrs. JULIA L. FAY, aged 22. [3/9]
March 2, 1855, Cooperstown, Mrs. CATHERINE ERNST, aged 72. [3/9]
March 1, 1855, Oneonta, WILLIS T. CARPENTER, aged 2. [3/9]
March 8, 1855, Cooperstown, Mrs. LORAINE GAGE, aged 26. [3/16]
March 11, 1855, E. Springfield, Mrs. ALMIRA GRAY, aged 34. [3/16]
March 16, 1855, Hartwick Sem., Mrs. HULDAH C. HAZELINE. [3/23]
March 16, 1855, New Lisbon, LUCIUS ADAMS, aged 55. [3/30]
March 24, 1855, E. Springfield, ISAAC WOODWARD, aged 93. [3/30]
March 27, 1855, New Lisbon, RANDALL WELLS, aged 78. [4/6]
March 28, 1855, Burlington, Mrs. LOIS STORY, aged 92. [4/6]
Feb. 23, 1855, Richfield, MOSES JAQUES, aged 63. [4/13]
March 27, 1855, Middlefield, FRANCES CRUSH, aged 103. [4/13]
April 11, 1855, Otsego, Mrs. MARION TISDALE, aged 18. [4/20]
April 7, 1855, Middlefield, CHRISTOPHER ELLIS, aged 73. [4/20]
April 25, 1855, Hartwick, ASA INGALSBE, aged 80. [5/4]
April 20, 1855, Fly Creek, Mrs. MARY BRAMAN, aged 49. [5/4]
April 30, 1855, Otsego, Mrs. ESTHER KELLOGG, aged 70. [5/4]
May 4, 1855, Cooperstown, JAMES STOWELL, aged 68. [5/11]
May 1, 1855, Laurens, HENRY HOPKINS, aged 30. [5/11]
May 4, 1855, Hartwick, Mrs. MARY HOLBROOK, aged 86. [5/18]
May 13, 1855, Laurens, RUTH T. ROBERTS, aged 18. [6/1]
May 20, 1855, Hartwick, SARAH SCOTT, aged 91. [6/1]
June 8, 1855, Cooperstown, JENAS CHAPMAN, aged 86. [6/15]
June 8, 1855, Otsego, RUFUS TISDALE, infant, 9 mos. [6/29]
June 20, 1855, Burlington, AMOS HOLLISTER, aged 80. [6/29]
May 8, 1855, Butternuts, DAVID WALKER, aged 80. [7/6]
July 6, 1855, Springfield, MORTIMER WHITE, aged 43. [7/13]
July 5, 1855, Hartwick, GEORGE W. STILLMAN, aged 70. [7/3]
July 14, 1855, Otego, JOHN BLAKLY, aged 73. [7/20]
July 20, 1855, Cooperstown, Dr. JOHN B. BERESFORD, aged 46. [7/27]

Aug. 8, 1855, Cooperstown, Dr. JAMES M. PEAKE, aged 47. [8/10]
July 13, 1855, Springfield, Mrs. SARAH BUEL, aged 74. [8/10]
Aug. 6, 1855, Milford, Mrs. AMOS WATERS, aged 74. [8/10]
Aug. 9, 1855, New Lisbon, Mrs. ELNAH DUROE, aged 68. [8/17]
Aug. 18, 1855, Otego, JAMES W. CARR, aged 54. [8/24]
Aug. 18, 1855, Cherry Valley, JABEZ D. HAMMOND, aged 77. [8/24]
Aug. 29, 1855, Cooperstown, Mrs. ELIZABETH A. MARVIN, aged 27. [8/31]
Aug. 24, 1855, JACOB W. MORRIS, aged 63. [8/31]
Aug. 27, 1855, Hartwick, JOS. E. FAULKNER, infant, 17 mos. [9/7]
Aug. 30, 1855, Morris, PASCHAL FRANCHOT, aged 82. [9/7]
Sept. 12, 1855, Cooperstown, FRANKIE DOUBLEDAY, infant. [9/14]
Sept. 5, 1855, Westford, JOHN COSSART, aged 35. [9/14]
Sept. 2, 1855, Maryland, MARY A. RISEDORPH, aged 23. [9/21]
Sept. 16, 1855, Cooperstown, RANSOM GAGE, aged 4. [9/21]
Sept. 26, 1855, Hartwick Sem., JOHN DAVISON, aged 15. [9/28]
Sept. 16, 1855, Middlefield, Mrs. CLARISSA CLARK, age 30. [9/28]
Sept. 11, 1855, Pittsfield, Mrs. SARAH M. BEARDSLEY, aged 42. [9/28]
Sept. 6, 1855, Pittsfield, AMBER YATES, aged 11. [10/12]
Sept. 29, 1855, Richfield, STEPHEN F. EDSON, aged 79. [10/12]
Oct. 14, 1855, Gilbertsville, Mrs. CORNELIA A. BABCOCK, aged 35. [10/19]
Oct. 12, 1855, Cooperstown, Mrs. SALLY STARR, aged 80. [10/19]
Oct. 17, 1855, Toddsville, Mrs. MARY CARD, aged 26. [10/26]
Oct. 17, 1855, Hartwick Sem., JOSEPH RUSSELL, aged 54. [10/26]
Oct. 17, 1855, Springfield Cen., Mrs. MARY E. PARSHALL, aged 22. [11/2]
Oct. 28, 1855, Burlington, Mrs. LYDIA GARDNER, aged 66. [11/9]
Oct. 28, 1855, Otsego, STEPHEN EDDY, aged 55. [11/9]
Oct. 4, 1855, Oneonta, Mrs. HENRIETTA CARPENTER, aged 54. [11/23]
Nov. 27, 1855, Otsego, HARRIET GILL SMITH, aged 22. [12/7]
Nov. 29, 1855, Otsego, WILLIAM HIGBY, aged 70. [12/7]
Nov. 30, 1855, Fly Creek, CHARLIES [sic] E. BADGER, aged 4. [12/7]
Dec. 19, 1855, ELECTA WILLIAMS BROWNELL, aged 12. [12/28]
Dec. 25, 1855, Cooperstown, Mrs. HARVEY PERKINS, aged 44. [12/28]
Dec. 27, 1855, Fly Creek, Mrs. PHEBE WILLIAMS, aged 69. [1/4/1856]
Dec. 30, 1855, Hartwick, Mrs. LUCY KELLY, aged 78. [1/11/1856]
Sept. 13, 1855, New Lisbon, SALLY HARRIS, aged 72. [1/11/1856]
Jan. 15, 1856, Toddsville, ELLEN M. STEERE, aged 9. [1/18]
Jan. 12, 1856, Cooperstown, Mrs. REBECCA L. LAMB, aged 29. [1/18]

Dec. 24, 1855, New Lisbon, JOHN HUME, aged 83. [1/25/1856]
Jan. 29, 1856, Exeter, Mrs. CAROLINE M. CRIPPEN, aged 28. [2/1]
Feb. 16, 1856, Oneonta, HARRIET HOPKINS, aged 19. [2/22]
Feb. 7, 1856, Middlefield, JOHN WOODRUFF, aged 71. [2/22]
Feb. 22, 1856, Exeter, STEPHEN RYDER, aged 88. [2/29]
Feb. 26, 1856, Springfield, Mrs. ELIZABETH M. BARRETT, aged 38. [3/7]
Feb. 26, 1856, Fly Creek, Mrs. ELIZA OLENDORF, aged 57. [3/7]
Feb. 24, 1856, Hornelsville, NY, PETER OLENDORF, aged 63. [3/7]
Feb. 26, 1856, Springfield, BALTIS LOSEE, aged 72. [3/14]
Feb. 29, 1856, Springfield Center, CYRUS BROWN, aged 69. [3/14]
Feb. 26, 1856, Fly Creek, MATILDA TAYLOR, aged 32. [3/14]
March 17, 1856, Cherry Valley, HORACE RIPLEY, aged 83. [3/21]
March 8, 1856, San Jacinto, TX, WM. BRISTOL, late of Cooperstown, aged 45. [3/28]
April 1, 1856, Cooperstown, CHARLES SMITH, aged 73. [4/11]
March 26, 1856, Otsego, Mrs. MARTHA POTTER, aged 87. [4/18]
April 11, 1856, Laurens, OLIVER MYERS, aged 77. [4/18]
April 18, 1856, Schenevus, Mrs. MARY A. SLINGERLAND, aged 56. [4/25]
April 27, 1856, Otsego, SAMUEL LENT, aged 38. [5/2]
April 26, 1856, Cooperstown, RUSSELL S. VAN NORT, aged 9. [5/2]
April 12, 1856, New Lisbon, Mrs. EMELINE DEWEY, aged 29. [5/2]
April 30, 1856, Otsego, Mrs. LYDIA M. SMITH, aged 26. [5/2]
May 6, 1856, Middlefield, GEORGE D. GANOM, aged 24. [5/9]
May 9, 1856, Cooperstown, ELIJAH H. METCALF, aged 40. [5/16]
May 31, 1856, Otsego, ROSWELL P. WILLIAMS, aged 34. [6/6]
April 16, 1856, New Lisbon, Mrs. MARTHA NICHOLS, aged 90. [6/6]
May 10, 1856, New Lisbon, LEMUEL CHAPIN, aged 54. [6/6]
May 17, 1856, New Lisbon, STANTON BARTON, aged 24. [6/6]
May 30, 1856, New Lisbon, Mrs. CYNTHIA G. GREGORY, aged 43. [6/6]
April 23, 1856, Middlefield, HENRY F. BROWN, aged 13. [6/6]
May 24, 1856, Springfield, DORLISCA COOK, aged 2. [6/6]
May 28, 1856, Middlefield, JOSEPH SHIPWAY, aged 52. [6/6]
June 11, 1856, Springfield, Mrs. ANNA C. SHELDON. [6/20]
June 14, 1856, Butternuts, E. R. BREWER, aged 52. [6/27]
June 2, 1856, Burlington, Mrs. TEMPERANCE SMITH, aged 89. [7/4]
June 21, 1856, Middlefield, Mrs. ARSULA CONGDON, aged 24. [7/4]
June 14, 1856, Gilbertsville, EZRA R. BREWER, aged 53. [7/4]
July 3, 1856, Cooperstown, DANIEL MARVIN, aged 68. [7/11]

July 8, 1856, New Lisbon, Mrs. LUCINA GIBSON, aged 35. [7/18]
Sept. 26, 1856, Pittsfield, DELIA A. HALL, aged 18. [10/3]
Sept. 30, 1856, Cooperstown, Mrs. POLLY CLARK, aged 76. [10/3]
Oct. 1, 1856, E. Hartwick, Mrs. REBECCA MOORE, aged 88. [10/10]
Oct. 3, 1856, Milford, ADELAIDE BULSON, aged 18. [10/10]
Oct. 3, 1856, New Lisbon, TABITHA GARDNER, aged 37. [10/10]
Oct. 2, 1856, Cooperstown, CORA A. HEWES, aged 25. [10/17]
Oct. 5, 1856, Burlington, Mrs. ANN WRIGHT, aged 66. [10/17]
Oct. 2, 1856, Milford, Mrs. ABIGAIL BATES, aged 69. [10/24]
Oct. 8, 1856, Maryland, Mrs. DEBORAH WIGHTMAN, aged 40. [10/24]
Oct. 10, 1856, Butternuts, NATHAN TANNER, aged 75. [10/24]
Oct. 7, 1856, Laurens, Mrs. HANNAH UPHAM, aged 52. [10/24]
Nov. 1, 1856, W. Burlington, Mrs. HARRIET W. GAIGE, aged 34. [11/14]
Oct. 23, 1856, Middlefield, DANIEL NORTH, aged 79. [11/14]
Nov. 9, 1856, Springfield, THOMAS PEGG, aged 6 7. [11/21]
Nov. 14, 1856, Middlefield, BENJAMIN NORTH, aged 85. [11/21]
Nov. 16, 1856, Cooperstown, WINFIELD E. BEADLE, aged 4. [11/21]
Nov. 8, 1856, Springfield, ALBERT E. SHERMAN, aged 13. [11/21]
Nov. 2, 1856, Butternuts, Mrs. ERUTHA WARD, aged 76. [11/28]
Nov. 19, 1856, New Lisbon, ELMORE WAKEFIELD, aged 76. [11/28]
Nov. 22, 1856, New Lisbon, HUBBARD CHURCH, aged 84. [11/28]
Dec. 3, 1856, Mrs. RACHEL CAMPBELL, aged 76. [12/5]
Nov. 20, 1856, Hartwick, NATHAN CHAPPELL, aged 68. [12/5]
Nov. 24, 1856, Roseboom, MARVIN S. MATTISON, aged 30. [12/5]
Dec. 3, 1856, Springfield, MARY M. MILLER, aged 66. [12/5]
Nov. 26, 1856, Richfield Spa, MOSES WHEELER, Jr., aged 29. [12/5]
Nov. 18, 1856, Middlefield, Mrs. POLLY HASKINS, aged 72. [12/12]
Nov. 28, 1856, Hartwick, Mrs. ADELINE ALGER, aged 31. [12/19]
Nov. 5, 1856, Toddsville, STEPHEN BOLLES, aged 64. [12/19]
Dec. 9, 1856, Richfield Spa, Mrs. CATHERINE M. WALTER, aged 27. [12/19]
Dec. 11, 1856, Exeter, PAMELIA UNDERWOOD, aged 19. [12/26]
Dec. 15, 1856, Pittsfield, Dr. WILLIAM G. HALL, aged 71. [1/2/1857]
Oct. 12, 1856, Worcester, Mrs. ANGELICA VAN PATTEN, aged 88. [1/2/1857]
Dec. 5, 1856, Fly Creek, ERASTUS TAYLOR, aged 85. [1/2/1857]
Jan. 1, 1857, EDWARD O. ELWELL, aged 31. [1/9]
Jan. 12, 1857, Middlefield, Mrs. LAURA HAYDEN, aged 26. [1/16]
Jan. 5, 1857, Middlefield, JOSIAH JUTKINS, aged 82. [1/16]
Jan. 14, 1857, Hartwick, GEORGE PROCTOR, aged 22. [1/16]

Jan. 7, 1857, New Lisbon, Capt. LEMUEL PATTENGILL, aged 82. [1/23]
Jan. 11, 1857, Otsego, LOIS LEE, aged 88. [1/23]
Jan. 3, 1857, Milford, Mrs. PATIENCE SWEET, aged 72. [1/23]
Dec. 25, 1856, W. Hartwick, HIRAM WHITE of New Lisbon, aged 60. [1/23/1857]
Jan. 14, 1857, New Lisbon, JOHN JOHNSON, aged 46. [1/23]
Dec. 4, 1856, Edmeston, Mrs. NANCY LEONARD, aged 57. [1/30/1857]
Feb. 1, 1857, Cooperstown, Mrs. SUSAN BOLLES, aged 30. [2/6]
Jan. 23, 1857, Burlington, EDWARD POPE, aged 87. [2/6]
Jan. 24, 1857, Springfield, IRA JAMISON, aged 3. [2/6]
Feb. 7, 1857, Hartwick, JOHN LUTHER, aged 31. [2/13]
Feb. 6, 1857, Otsego, Mrs. CATHERINE PICKENS, aged 55. [2/20]
Feb. 12, 1857, Cooperstown, Mrs. OLIVE THAYER, aged 54. [2/20]
Feb. 7, 1857, Middlefield, SMITH MURPHY, aged 78. [2/20]
Feb. 6, 1857, New Lisbon, ORSON MUMFORD, aged 45. [2/20]
Feb. 13, 1857, New Lisbon, ROBERT BARTON, aged 84. [2/20]
Feb. 18, 1857, Springfield, HARMANUS VEDDER, aged 99. [2/27]
March 3, 1857, Cooperstown, THOMAS FLINT, aged 88. [3/6]
Feb. 21, 1857, Otsego, Mrs. ASENATH F. EDGETT, aged 33. [3/6]
Feb. 28, 1857, New Lisbon, HORACE GARDNER, aged 44. [3/6]
Oct. 3, 1856, New Lisbon, Mrs. HORACE GARDNER. [3/6/1857]
Feb. 28, 1857, Cooperstown, Mrs. ABIGAIL SMITH, aged 70. [3/6]
Feb. 27, 1857, Middlefield, MARY ANN INGALLS, aged 70. [3/6]
March 6, 1857, E. Worcester, Mrs. ANNA CHASE, aged 71. [3/13]
[No date] Hartwick, ALLEN SHUMWAY, aged 79. [3/13]
Feb. 28, 1857, Milford, LEVERETT STICKNEY, aged 21. [3/20]
Feb. 24, 1857, Edmeston, BENAJAH CHAPIN, aged 55. [3/27]
March 13, 1857, Burlington, JANE HUME, aged 42. [4/3]
March 27, 1857, Hartwick, Capt. ABNER ADAMS, aged 85. [4/3]
March 28, 1857, Morris, Mrs. POLLY WALLACE, aged 58. [4/10]
April 2, 1857, New Lisbon, GEORGE BINGHAM, aged 68. [4/10]
April 19, 1857, Cooperstown, JAMES A. KENYON, aged 14. [4/24]
April 21, 1857, Cooperstown, JAMES BODEN HEWS, aged 23. [4/24]
April 7, 1857, Oaksville, GEORGE W. BALDWIN, aged 31. [4/24]
April 5, 1857, New Lisbon, CLARK NORTHRUP, aged 16. [5/1]
April 25, 1857, Laurens, Mrs. JANE JOHNSON of New Lisbon, aged 50. [5/1]
April 25, 1857, Springfield, Mrs. SARAH HOLT, aged 58. [5/1]
May 3, 1857, Middlefield, EVERETT HINMAN, aged 63. [5/8]
April 30, 1857, New Lisbon, PERCIVAL G. WEBSTER, aged 21. [5/8]
April 29, 1857, New Lisbon, EVERETT WHEELER, aged 4. [5/15]

April 27, 1857, ZENAS WASHBURN, aged 67. [5/22]
April 29, 1857, Clarksville, ANNA C. HORTON, aged 4. [5/22]
May 4, 1857, Milford, ALICE M. EDDY, aged 9. [5/22]
May 10, 1857, New Lisbon, EPHRAIM MANN, aged 51. [5/22]
May 13, 1857, New Lisbon, Mrs. JANE HUME RATHBONE, aged 35. [5/22]
May 10, 1857, Otsego, Mrs. ANNIE REXFORD, aged 85. [5/22]
May 26, 1857, Boston, Dr. CAMPBELL L. TURNER of Cooperstown, aged 26. [5/29]
May 19, 1857, New Lisbon, Mrs. POLLY NEARING, aged 65. [5/29]
May 22, 1857, New Lisbon, ELISHA ADAMS, aged 1 year. [5/29]
May 30, 1857, Morris, HORATIO P. JOHNSON, aged 29. [6/5]
April 13, 1857, Burlington, Mrs. HANNAH CARD, aged 94. [6/5]
May 13, 1857, New Lisbon, Mrs. JANE E. RATHBUN, aged 31. [6/5]
May 28, 1857, New Lisbon, JOHN DAVIDSON, aged 22. [6/5]
May 25, 1857, Burlington, NATHAN FISK, aged 85. [8/14]
July 22, 1857, Fly Creek, SAMUEL PICKENS, aged 97. [8/28]
Aug. 26, 1857, New Lisbon, Mrs. NANCY GREGORY, aged 67. [9/4]
Aug. 29, 1857, New Lisbon, Mrs. SAMANTHA WALLACE, aged 48. [9/4]
Aug. 27, 1857, Fly Creek, Mrs. NABBY WILLIAMS, aged 51. [9/4]
Sept. 8, 1857, Laurens, THOMAS W. RATHBONE, aged 41. [9/18]
Aug. 14, 1857, Edmeston, SHEFFIELD BENNETT, aged 62. [9/18]
Aug. 28, 1857, W. Burlington, HARMON MAY, aged 80. [9/18]
Sept. 2, 1857, Springfield, Rev. GERRISH BARRETT, aged 60. [9/18]
Oct. 20, 1857, Laurens, GEORGE GRIFFITH, aged 77. [10/30]
[No date] Maryland, PELEG CHAMBERLAIN, aged 77. [10/30]
Oct. 9, 1857, Unadilla Forks, JOSHUA BABCOCK, aged 83. [10/30]
Nov. 27, 1857, Morris, Mrs. ROXIE SMITH, aged 78. [12/11]
Dec. 5, 1857, Otsego, THOMAS RUSSELL, aged 58. [12/11]
Dec. 11, 1857, Cooperstown, MARY A. BROWN, aged 4. [12/18]
Dec. 13, 1857, New Lisbon, Mrs. ANNA GROSS, aged 89. [12/18]
Dec. 18, 1857, Gilbertsville, MARY E. BABCOCK, aged 15. [12/25]
Dec. 22, 1857, Springfield, SAMUEL COLEMAN, aged 96. [1/1/1858]
Dec. 20, 1857, Laurens, DEWITT WALBY, aged 3. [1/8/1858]
Jan. 13, 1858, Middlefield, WILLIAM O. SMITH, aged 31. [1/22]
Jan. 20, 1858, Milford, Mrs. OLIVE BABCOCK, aged 73. [1/29]
Jan. 23, 1858, Otsego, RUFUS PETERS, aged 33. [1/29]
Jan. 23, 1858, Laurens, MARCUS O. WALBY, aged 11 months. [2/5]
Jan. 25, 1858, New Lisbon, RALPH ROCKWELL, aged 74. [2/5]
Jan. 19, 1858, Middlefield, Mrs. MIRIAM REYNOLDS. [2/5]
Jan. 25, 1858, New Lisbon, JOSEPH COMBS, aged 79. [2/12]

Feb. 13, 1858, Cooperstown, CUTTER FIELD, aged 49. [2/19]
Feb. 24, 1858, Cooperstown, EMILY STEWART BOWERS, aged 3. [2/26]
Feb. 22, 1858, Jacksonville, PHILIP GARDNER, aged 81. [3/4]
[No date] Oneonta, SARAH ANN COOLEY, aged 39. [3/4]
March 7, 1858, Otsego, CHARLES EDWIN DOUBLEDAY, aged 8 months. [3/12]
Feb. 11, 1858, Edmeston, WILLIAM GREEN, aged 90. [3/12]
Feb. 12, 1858, Otsego, CHARLES F. TORRY, aged 1. [3/12]
Feb. 28, 1858, Otsego, Mrs. THANKFUL C. RUSSELL, aged 57. [3/12]
March 7, 1858, New Lisbon, JOS. SEARGENT, aged 56. [3/12]
March 15, 1858, Westford, ALFRED B. KAPLE, aged 26. [3/26]
March 13, 1858, Richfield, SAMUEL COLWELL, aged 77. [3/26]
March 22, 1858, Hartwick, Mrs. ESTHER CHAPPEL. [3/26]
March 16, 1858, Middlefield, JAMES CHASE, aged 86. [3/26]
March 26, 1858, Otego, Mrs. SUSAN A. SHEPHERD, aged 19. [4/2]
Feb. 13, 1858, d. on board D. S. John L. Stepkins, OLIVER B. BRANCH (E. Springfield), aged 26. [4/2]
March 30, 1858, New Lisbon, Mrs. SARAH KELLOGG, aged 72. [4/9]
April 4, 1858, New Lisbon, ZARA WATSON, aged 72. [4/9]
March 30, 1858, New Lisbon, ELIAS CUMMINGS, Esq. [4/9]
April 4, 1858, Otego, DAVID S. BUNDY, aged 67. [4/9]
April 9, 1858, Cooperstown, KATE TURNER KEESE, infant. [4/16]
April 11, 1858, Maryland, EPHRAIM BURNSIDE, aged 84. [4/16]
April 3, 1858, Burlington, EZRA BOLTON, aged 56. [4/16]
April 5, 1858, Green Bay, Wisc., Mrs. CATHERINE COOPER CUTHWAITE. [4/16]
April 15, 1858, Cooperstown, EDWIN F. DOUBLEDAY, aged 4 months. [4/23]
April 13, 1858, Middlefield, SARAH O. LENT, aged 4. [4/23]
May 5, 1858, Hartwick, MARY TUCKER, aged 7. [5/14]
May 15, 1858, Middlefield, NATHAN CLAYTON LESTER, aged 13. [5/21]
May 6, 1858, Richfield, JOHN W. TUNNICLIFF, aged 74. [5/21]
March 16, 1858, Hartwick, DANIEL MOTT, aged 72. [5/28]
May 18, 1858, Hartwick, JULIA NICKERSON, aged 32. [5/28]
May 24, 1858, Burlington Flats, FRANK PERKINS, aged 1. [5/28]
March 20, 1858, Burr Oak "in the west," GEORGE THAYER, aged 40. [5/28]
April 18, 1858, New Lisbon, NATHANIEL GARDNER, aged 70. [6/4]
May 25, 1858, Pittsfield, Mrs. ESTHER C. WILLIAMS, aged 46. [6/4]
April 30, 1858, New Lisbon, WILLIAM EMMET ALGER, aged 15. [6/11]

June 26, 1858, Cooperstown, ALICE E. ROBINSON, aged 12. [7/2]
June 16, 1858, Springfield, Mrs. MARY RATHBUN, aged 59. [7/2]
June 31, 1858, Oneonta, ABRAHAM N. BATES, aged 62. [7/2]
June 29, 1858, Middlefield, ROBERT BATES, aged 81. [7/2]
June 20, 1858, Garratsville, JOHN ROBERTS, aged 71. [7/9]
July 3, 1858, Burlington, ELIJAH H. CHAPIN, aged 53. [7/23]
June 18, 1858, Hartwick, THOMAS D. WRIGHT, aged 44. [8/6]
July 22, 1858, Cherry Valley, Mrs. ELIZABETH JUDD, aged 74. [8/6]
Aug. 8, 1858, Morris, JOHN DAVIS, aged 52. [8/13]
Aug. 6, 1858, Laurens, Mrs. AMY SHOVE, aged 69. [8/20]
July 27, 1858, New Lisbon, RISPAH J. PATTER, aged 6. [8/20]
Sept. 5, 1858, Cooperstown, FANNY E. WINSLOW, aged 5. [9/10]
[No date] Oaksville, DORE P. SEATON, aged 5. [9/10]
Aug. 28, 1858, Hartwick, WILLIAM BISHOP, aged 26. [9/10]
Sept. 8, 1858, Cooperstown, WILLIAM H. BAIGRIE, aged 1. [9/17]
Sept. 27, 1858, Cooperstown, THEODORE KEESE, Esq., aged 58. [10/1]
Sept. 16, 1858, Springfield, MARGARET M. GILCHRIST, aged 73. [10/1]
Aug. 26, 1858, Schenevus, Mrs. LOVINA HOWE, aged 68. [10/8]
Oct. 3, 1858, Middlefield, DAVID P. BENNETT, aged 28. [10/8]
Oct. 5, 1858, Garratsville, THOMAS W. HUME, aged 2. [10/15]
Oct. 3, 1858, Richfield, Mrs. FRANCES PLAMER, aged 61. [10/15]
Sept. 8, 1858, Middlefield, MOSES RICH, aged 65. [10/22]
Oct. 17, 1858, Cooperstown, Mrs. KATHERINE METCALF, aged 75. [10/22]
Oct. 15, 1858, Richfield Spa, Mrs. ANN E. CONKLIN, aged 83. [10/22]
Oct. 27, 1853, Cooperstown, ADELAIDE A. LIVERMORE, aged 3. [11/5]
Oct. 21, 1858, Middlefield, CATHERINE GREEN, aged 56. [11/5]
Aug. 23, 1858, Hartwick, Mrs. CLARISSA LUTHER, aged 58. [11/5]
Oct. 30, 1858, Middlefield, Dr. JEREMIAH B. NORTH, aged 24. [11/12]
Nov. 4, 1858, Schenevus, Mrs. NANCY GRAY, aged 68. [11/12]
Nov. 9, 1858, Pierstown, Mrs. ESTHER TEFFT, aged 79. [11/12]
Nov. 9, 1858, Otsego, JANE MC KEEN, aged 63. [11/19]
Oct. 30, 1858, Middlefield, CARRIE L. BATES, aged 1. [11/26]
Nov. 18, 1858, Hartwick, BENJAMIN MOREHOUSE, aged 74. [11/26]
Nov. 19, 1858, Milford, AMOS WATERS, aged 78. [11/26]
Nov. 22, 1858, Middlefield Center, Mrs. HELEN WILSON, aged 96. [12/3]
Nov. 28, 1858, Middlefield Center, Mrs. ESTHER S. HANDY, aged 64. [12/10]
Nov. 19, 1858, Williams, Mich., ELISHA BRADFORD (Otsego Co.), aged 50. [12/10]

Dec. 14, 1858, Decatur, CHAUNCEY PARKER, aged 75. [12/17]
Dec. 11, 1858, Pierstown, MARY FRANCES SHEPARD, aged 3. [12/24]
Dec. 18, 1858, E. Springfield, CHARLES ALVIN GENTER, infant. [12/31]
Dec. 25, 1858, Milford, WILLIAM STEVENS, aged 87. [1/7/1859]
Jan. 8, 1859, Laurens, Mrs. HULDAH PRIEST, aged 82. [1/14]
Jan. 4, 1859, Laurens, SUSAN HELLSINGER, aged 49. [1/14]
Jan. 10, 1859, Otsego, Mrs. SARAH A. QUAIL, aged 31. [1/14]
Jan. 2, 1859, Milford, RICE PRATT, aged 72. [1/14]
Jan. 17, 1859, Cherry Valley, DAVID WOODBURN, Sr., aged 80. [1/28]
Jan. 24, 1859, Portlandville, MOREY SMITH, aged 78. [2/4]
Dec. 15, 1858, Richfield Spa, SARAH P. WALKER, aged 19. [2/4]
Jan. 28, 1859, Portlandville, Mrs. LAVANTHA LANE, aged 25. [2/11]
Feb. 2, 1859, Mrs. AMELIA SHERMAN, Otsego, aged 71. [2/11]
Feb. 14, 1859, Cooperstown, ALFRED COOPER, aged 4. [2/18]
Jan. 10, 1859, Milford, LORENZO BATES, aged 73. [2/18]
Feb. 22, 1859, Cooperstown, ISAAC WATTS FAIRMAN, aged 22. [2/25]
Feb. 13, 1859, New Lisbon, ORLAND GREGORY, aged 1 year. [2/25]
March 4, 1859, Maryland, JOHN S. GARNEY, aged 34. [3/11]
Feb. 21, 1859, S. Edmeston, DENTON GAYLAY, aged 73. [3/11]
March 16, 1859, Otsego, WILLIAM RUSSELL, aged 73. [3/18]
Feb. 19, 1859, New Lisbon, Mrs. POLLY STANTON, aged 74. [3/18]
March 3, 1859, Corning, JOS. ROBINSON (Toddsville), aged 50. [3/18]
March 27, 1859, Hartwick Sem., HAMILTON DAVISON, aged 2. [4/1]
March 8, 1859, Middlefield, Mrs. SARAH MURPHY, aged 77. [4/1]
March 25, 1859, Morris, JANE R. WING, aged 48. [4/1]
[No date] Cooperstown, Mrs. FANNY WATERMAN, aged 86. [4/8]
Feb. 25, 1859, Hartwick, Mrs. NANCY PERRY, aged 68. [4/8]
March 28, 1859, W. Burlington, Mrs. MARY SHOLES, aged 52. [4/8]
April 10, 1859, Exeter, CORNELIUS JONES, Esq., aged 82. [4/22]
April 10, 1859, Westford, Deacon JAMES COSSART, aged 66. [4/22]
May 2, 1859, Otsego, Mrs. LUCY KELLOGG, aged 71. [4/29]
March 3, 1859, India, Rev. WILLIAM E. SNYDER. [4/29]
May 2, 1859, Hartwick, ROBERT CARR, aged 76. [5/20]
May 6, 1859, Decatur, JAMES STAFFORD, aged 44. [5/20]
April 28, 1859, Milford, Mrs. HANNAH R. JEWELL, aged 63. [5/27]
April 25, 1859, Hartwick, Mrs. ALTHEDA ROBINSON, aged 72. [5/27]
May 20, 1859, New Lisbon, Mrs. POLLY ROCKWELL, aged 28. [5/27]
April 27, 1859, Hartwick, EDWARD BORO, aged 79. [6/10]
June 5, 1859, Hartwick, ANNA INGALSBE, aged 41. [6/10]
June 9, 1859, Cooperstown, HELEN LOUISE BROWN, aged 22. [6/17]

June 9, 1859, Jacksonville, Mrs. TAMER SARGENT, aged 89. [6/17]
June 31 [sic], 1859, Middlefield, Mrs. MARTHA FLING, aged 2 [sic]. [6/17]
June 16, 1859, Cooperstown, FANNY E. WALRADT, infant. [6/24]
May 23, 1859, Springfield, WILLIAM FRASIER, aged 42. [6/24]
June 17, 1859, Unadilla, WILLIAM CARMICHAEL, aged 85. [6/24]
March 21, 1859, Bennington, MI, DOLLY RATHBURN [sic] (Springfield, N.Y.), aged 83. [6/24]
March 26, 1859, Bennington, MI, JOHN DUTCHER (Springfield), aged 62. [6/24]
April 5, 1859, Bennington, MI, FERNANDO C. RATHBUN (Springfield), aged 53. [6/24]
June 18, 1859, Worcester, JOHN CARROLL, aged 67. [7/1]
July 4, 1859, Cooperstown, Mrs. CATHERINE MC INTOSH, Jr., aged 44. [7/8]
July 4,1859, New Lisbon, ASA F. ROCKWELL, aged 10. [7/8]
June 28, 1859, Middlefield, SOPHRONIA J. ANDREWS, aged 15. [7/22]
June 11, 1859, New Lisbon, JANE HUME, aged 47. [7/22]
July 31, 1859, Morris, Rev. G. STARR BAILEY, aged 31. [8/12]
Aug. 14, 1859, Milford, JOSEPH WESTCOTT, aged 76. [8/26]
Aug. 23, 1859, Cooperstown, MICHAEL DUNN, aged 56. [8/26]
Aug. 23, 1859, Edmeston, ALBERT CHAMBERLAIN, aged 3. [9/2]
Aug. 25, 1859, Pierstown, JOHN W. CLARK, aged 52. [9/9]
Aug. 24, 1859, Hartwick, JONAS PERRY, aged 70. [9/9]
June 18, 1859, ELIJAH HUBBARD, aged 30. [9/16]
Sept. 9, 1859, Cooperstown, CHARLES B. TOMLINSON, infant. [9/16]
Sept. 17, 1859, Cooperstown, DAVID WILLIS BALL, aged 24. [9/23]
Sept. 16, 1859, Exeter Center, FRANCES E. ANGELL, aged 14. [9/23]
Sept. 11, 1859, Laurens, ADAM J. GRIFFITH, aged 35. [9/30]
Sept. 28, 1859, Schuyler's Lake, JANETTE SUTHERLAND, aged 27. [10/7]
Sept. 4, 1859, Otsego, Mrs. MARY ROBERTS, aged 75. [10/14]
Oct. 15, 1859, S. Worcester, Mrs. MARY BECKER, aged 60. [10/21]
Oct. 14, 1859, Exeter, ASA MATTISON, aged 47. [10/28]
Oct. 16, 1859, Springfield Center, MARY A. GAMWELL, aged 46. [10/28]
Oct. 16, 1859, Milford, THOMAS EDDY, aged 52. [11/4]
Oct. 12, 1859, Morris, Capt. DAN. SMITH, aged 86. [11/4]
Nov. 9, 1859, Cooperstown, Mrs. ABIGAIL MORSE, aged 64. [11/11]
Oct. 27, 1859, Hartwick, URSULA M. GREEN, aged 19. [11/11]
Nov. 1, 1859, Hartwick, ADALAIDE ROBINSON, aged 17. [11/11]

Nov. 12, 1859, Cooperstown, Mrs. AMY BEADLE, aged 58. [11/18]
Oct. 8, 1859, Milford, ADELMER D. NORTH, M.D., aged 33. [11/25]
Nov. 27, 1859, Cooperstown, OLIVER H. LEE, aged 17. [12/2]
Nov. 18, 1859, Richfield, THOMAS AUSTIN, aged 87. [12/2]
Nov. 25, 1859, Hartwick, Mrs. POLLY ALLEN, aged 7 5. [12/16]
Nov. 23, 1859, Milford, ANDREW SPENCER, aged 56. [12/16]
Dec. 20, 1859, Cooperstown, JACKSON SNYDER, aged 44. [12/30]
Jan. 1, 1860, Middlefield, SAMUEL S. CAMPBELL, aged 82. [1/20]
Nov. 11, 1859, W. Burlington, PHEBE RUSSELL, aged 89. [1/20/1860]
Jan. 6, 1860, Hartwick, NOYES EDWIN LEWIS, aged 3. [1/20]
Jan. 9, 1860, Hartwick, CHARLES E. LEWIS, aged 3. [1/20]
Jan. 19, 1860, Burlington, Mrs. HEPSIBAH SILL, aged 86. [1/27]
Jan. 28, 1860, Cooperstown, ALFRED VARR, aged 56. [2/3]
Jan. 5, 1860, Albany, WHEELER PALMER of Richfield, aged 69. [2/3]
Jan. 27, 1860, Burlington, Mrs. THERESA D. MATHER, aged 44. [2/3]
Feb. 2, 1860, Otsego, Dea. ELEAZER JOSLYN, aged 64. [2/10]
Feb. 1, 1860, Otsego, Mrs. POLLY LINCOLN, aged 69. [2/10]
Jan. 13, 1860, New Lisbon, Mrs. HULDAH A. ADAMS, aged 59. [2/10]
Feb. 4, 1860, Cherry Valley, Mrs. ELIZABETH STERNS, aged 74. [2/10]
Feb. 9, 1860, Middlefield, Mrs. HANNAH NORTH, aged 85. [2/10]
Feb. 7, 1860, Otego, ANNA EDSON, aged 95. [2/17]
Feb. 16, 1860, Hartwick, Mrs. REBECCA S. TUCKER, aged 39. [2/24]
Feb. 15, 1860, Chaseville, Dr. WILLIAM PRICE, aged 39. [2/24]
Feb. 13, 1860, Roseboom, CORTLAND J. COLE, aged 30. [2/24]
March 6, 1860, Westford, ROBERT BARNARD, aged 51. [3/9]
March 13, 1860, Westford, SARAH ADELIA ALLEN, aged 17. [3/16]
March 6, 1860, Laurens, JOSEPH R. FASSETT, aged 37. [3/16]
March 13, 1860, Burlington, JAMES MARKS, aged 61. [3/23]
Feb. 19, 1860, Rome, Italy, EDWARD LOERAINE CLARK, aged 21. [3/23]
March 27, 1860, Laurens, HENRY SEGENDORF, aged 17. [3/30]
March 22, 1860, Otsego, Mrs. SUSANNA KELLEY, aged 69. [3/30]
March 8, 1860, Westford, OLIVE LEONARD, 4 years. [3/30]
March 1, 1860, Laurens, Mrs. HANNAH BUTTS, aged 90. [3/30]
March 7, 1860, Portlandville, SARAH A. BISHOP, 1-(?) years. [3/30]
Feb. 19, 1860, Milford, WILLIAM SCOTT, aged 84. [3/30]
March 29, 1860, Otsego, Mrs. LAURA DOUBLEDAY, aged 59. [4/6]
March 9, 1860, New Lisbon, TABITHA POTTER, aged 76. [4/6]
March 26, 1860, Farmington, IL, CYRUS W. NEWTON (Burlington), aged 26. [4/13]
Feb. 26, 1860, Edmeston, OBEDIAH HALL, aged 78. [4/13]

March 9, 1860, Hartwick, HELEN A. BURLINGHAM, aged 17. [4/20]
April 10, 1860, Unadilla, JEDEDIAH JOHNSON, aged 76. [4/20]
April 13, 1860, Middlefield, WANDAL RHINES, aged 74. [4/20]
April 12, 1860, Burlington, MINER SHOLES, aged 62. [4/20]
March 30, 1860, Oneonta, RICHARD CLARK, aged 63. [4/20]
April 18, 1860, Laurens, MORRIS GILBERT, aged 65. [4/27]
April 20, 1860, Otego, LUCY COOK, aged 69. [4/27]
April 30, 1860, Maryland, Mrs. EMILY A. FERRY, aged 27. [5/4]
April 12, 1860, Worcester, JOEL CARYL, aged 36. [5/4]
May 22, 1860, Westford, BELA J. KAPLE, aged 53. [5/25]
May 6, 1860, Springfield, Mrs. MARY SEEBER, aged 76. [5/25]
May 11, 1860, Otsego, Mrs. AMANDA EDDY, aged 61. [6/1]
April 23, 1860, Portlandville, OLIVE DANA MANNING, aged 1 year. [6/1]
May 16, 1860, Cooperstown, PHILIP A. BRIMMER, aged 30. [6/8]
May 28, 1860, Milford, ALBRO D. HOAG, aged 12. [6/8]
May 11, 1860, Otsego, Mrs. MANDANA EDDY, aged 61 or 62. [6/15]
June 7, 1860, Middlefield, HARVEY S. EGGLESTON, aged 52. [6/15]
--- 1860, MARY ANN COOPER of Cooperstown, aged 22. [6/22]
June 6, 1860, Burlington, LEVI PIERSON, aged 56. [6/22]
June 12, 1860, Unadilla Forks, Mrs. CATHERINE M. BROWN, aged 53. [6/22]
May 25, 1860, Otsego, ARTHUR M. HOLT, aged 1. [6/29]
June 1, 1860, Springfield, JESSE A. AYRES, aged 36. [6/29]
June 9, 1860, Milford, GEORGE D. MANN, aged 89. [6/29]
June 12, 1860, Otsego, HIRAM W. BIRDSALL, aged 22. [7/6]
June 28, 1860, Burlington, Mrs. JOANNAH PARKER, aged 83. [7/6]
June 2, 1860, Morris, ENOS LAWRENCE, aged 78. [7/6]
July 11, 1860, Otsego, ALGENE L. CONNROD, aged 10. [7/20]
July 15, 1860, Burlington, ABNER GILBERT, Jr., aged 66. [7/20]
July 18, 1860, Fly Creek, Mrs. ANNA HAWKINS, aged 35. [7/27]
July 28, 1860, Cooperstown, PAUL K. TUCKER, infant. [7/27 sic]
June 9, 1860, Fly Creek, Mrs. RACHEL ANDERSON, aged 93. [8/3]
July 7, 1860, Jacksonville, Mrs. BETSEY GARDNER, aged 71. [8/3]
July 14, 1860, Hartwick, LUCY GROVER, aged 22. [8/3]
July 19, 1860, Burlington, Mrs. MARY G. TIFFANY, aged 43. [8/3]
July 30, 1860, Cherry Valley, Mrs. ESTHER RIPLEY, aged 82. [8/10]
July 8, 1860, Burlington, MARY RUTHERFORD, aged 26. [8/10]
July 22, 1860, New Lisbon, SIMEON BUNDY, aged 73. [8/17]
Aug. 18, 1860, Fly Creek, JENNY V. CLARK, infant. [8/17]
July 19, 1860, Morris, JANE THOMAS, aged 85. [9/7]

July 25, 1860, Springfield, ABBE ELLY, aged 23. [9/7]
Aug. 3, 1860, Springfield, Mrs. AMANDA MC RORIE, aged 27. [9/7]
Aug. 3, 1860, Otsego, CATHERINE CASBY, aged 18. [9/7]
July 30, 1860, Hartwick, MARY ANN LUTHER, aged 21. [9/7]
Aug. 29, 1860, Hartwick, Mrs. MATTIE AUGUR, aged 75. [9/7]
Aug. 6, 1860, New Lisbon, ADELINE DUNBAR, aged 12. [9/14]
Aug. 13, 1860, Milford, JAMES MUMFORD, aged 48. [9/14]
April 8, 1860, Portlandville, FREDDIE LANE, aged 1. [9/14]
Sept. 5, 1860, FLORIE LANE, aged 7 months. [9/14]
Sept. 17, 1860, Unadilla, MARY LOMIS, aged 28. [9/20]
Sept. 1, 1860, Roseboom, CLARA BUTLER, aged 5. [9/20]
Sept. 28, 1860, Portlandville, ELISHA SPAFFORD, aged 76. [10/5]
Sept. 22, 1860, Pittsfield, Mrs. HELEN HALL, aged 33. [10/5]
Aug. 7, 1860, Otsego, Mrs. RACHEL WIKOFF, aged 52.
Oct. 24, 1860, Cooperstown, Mrs. JERUSHA W. BODEN, aged 42. [11/2]
Nov. 1, 1860, Cooperstown, ISAAC TUCKER, aged 55. [11/9]
Nov. 2, 1860, Springfield, DANIEL BASINGER, aged 72. [11/9]
Sept. 26, 1860, Toddsville, MARYETTE BUTTS, aged 33. [11/9]
Nov. 1, 1860, Toddsville, LUTHER BUTTS, aged 78. [11/9]
[no date], Hartwick, Mrs. ROSANNA SMITH, aged 73. [11/23]
Oct. 12, 1860, S. Hart., BENJAMIN CAMP, aged 98. [12/7]
Nov. 22, 1860, Burlington, ELIJAH HUBBELL, aged 72. [12/7]
Nov. 1, 1860, Middlefield, DAVID F. OLENDORF, aged 37. [12/7]
Sept. 16, 1860, Maryland, JOHN HINMAN, aged 32. [12/14]
Oct. 7, 1860, Maryland, Mrs. ORCELIA A. HINMAN, aged 22. [12/14]
Nov. 28, 1860, Springfield, CYNTHIA TARPENNING, aged 85. [1/4/1861]
Dec. 18, 1860, Milford, DELEVAN ROSE, aged 28. [1/4/1861]
Dec. 23, 1860, Cooperstown, Mrs. MARY SHORT, aged 85. [1/11/1861]
Jan. 18, 1861, Otsego, Mrs. ABILENE KIBBY, aged 94. [1/25]
Jan. 15, 1861, Richfield Springs, DANIEL BROWN, aged 87. [1/25]
Sept. 19, 1860, Burr Oak, IA, Capt. EPHRAIM THAYER (Springfield), aged 79. [1/25/1860]
Jan. 12, 1861, Morris, IRVING W. COOK, aged 21. [1/25]
Jan. 23, 1861, Otsego, JAMES C. ALLEN, aged 3. [2/1]
Jan. 23, 1861, Otsego, LAURA E. ALLEN, aged 1 year, 11 months. [2/1]
Jan. 10, 1861, Springfield, GEORGE SNYDER, aged 75. [2/1]
Jan. 24, 1861, Cooperstown, JACOB HARDY, aged 74. [2/1]
Dec. 26, 1860, Morris, RICHARD JOHNSON, aged 81. [2/8/1861]
Jan. 30, 1861, Morris, DANIEL SMITH, aged 67. [2/8]
Jan. 1, 1861, Maryland, Mrs. LOVINA KENYON, aged 26. [2/8]

Feb. 8, 1861, New Lisbon, Mrs. CATHERINE M. WEDDERSPOON, aged 35. [2/15]
Feb. 18, 1861, Cooperstown, JOHN BREWER, aged 64. [2/22]
Feb. 21, 1861, Cooperstown, SILAS ROOT, aged 84. [2/22]
Feb. 4, 1861, Laurens, JAMES HOAG, aged 75. [2/22]
Feb. 2, 1861, Milford, BENJAMIN AYLESWORTH, aged 87. [2/22]
Jan. 3, 1861, Hartwick, Mrs. JERUSHA CHASE, aged 87. [2/22]
Jan. 4, 1861, Hartwick, Mrs. ALVIRA SALISBURY, aged 20. [2/22]
Feb. 7, 1861, Philadelphia, HANSON WRIGHT (Westford), aged 47. [2/22]
Jan. 30, 1861, Springfield, MARY JANE ACKLER, aged 6. [2/22]
Feb. 15, 1861, ALICE CASLER, aged 9. [2/22]
Feb. 17, 1861, Stewarts Patent, LORENZO MC RORIE, aged 9. [2/22]
Feb. 19, 1861, Unadilla, Mrs. POLLY HEATH, aged 78. [3/1]
Feb. 15, 1861, New Lisbon, Dea. URIAH GREGORY, aged 72. [3/1]
Feb. 19, 1861, Exeter, GEORGE NORTHRUP, aged 32. [3/1]
Feb. 26, 1861, New Lisbon, NATHANIEL HARRINGTON, aged 78. [3/1]
--- 1861, Plainfield, VARNUM C. CRUMB, aged 65. [3/1]
Feb. 10, 1861, Otsego, Mrs. ALMIRA KASLEY, aged 39. [3/8]
Feb. 13, 1861, Worcester, JOHN RAND, aged 88. [3/8]
Feb. 26, 1861, New Lisbon, Mrs. SABRA GARDNER, aged 71. [3/8]
Feb. 28, 1861, New Lisbon, Mrs. NANCY GREGORY, aged 48. [3/8]
March 11, 1861, Middlefield, MIAL PIERCE, aged 95. [3/15]
Feb. 8, 1861, Middlefield Cen., Mrs. ANGELINE DUTCHER, aged 28. [3/22]
March 8, 1861, Middlefield Cen., Mrs. ABIGAIL E. BAILEY, aged 77. [3/22]
March 11, 1861, Burlington, GEORGE COLEMAN, aged 21. [3/22]
Feb. 21, 1861, Laurens, HENRY HOPKINS, aged 68. [3/22]
March 7, 1861, Cherry Valley, Mrs. SOPHIA BATES, aged 53. [3/22]
March 9, 1861, Oneonta, Mrs. HEZEKIAH WATKINS, aged 71. [3/22]
March 20, 1861, Cooperstown, LUCY WOOD, aged 69. [3/29]
Feb. 18, 1861, Exeter, GILBERT C. WATSON, aged 6. [3/29]
March 25, 1861, Westford, HORACE M. TYLER, aged 59. [4/5]
March 25, 1861, Milford, infant son of EDGAR AYLESWORTH, aged 3 months. [4/5]
March 30, 1861, Hartwick, MARY A. REDFORD, aged 16. [4/5]
March 31, 1861, Hartwick, CORA E. SMITH, aged 17. [4/5]
March 29, 1861, Laurens, Mrs. TRYPEHNA HOLLISTER, 77 years. [4/12]

March 20, 1861, Milford, LEONARD BAKER, aged 69. [4/12]
March 17, 1861, New Lisbon, Mrs. POLLY SHUMAKER, aged 67. [4/19]
March 27, 1861, New Lisbon, Mrs. LYDIA CHAPIN, 95 years. [4/19]
April 14, 1861, Cooperstown, HOSEA F. ANTISDEL, 48 years. [4/26]
April 18, 1861, Cooperstown, Mrs. SUSAN ADAMS, 60 years. [4/26]
April 20, 1861, Schenevus, EMORY A. MULKINS, 23 years. [4/26]
April 14, 1861, Middlefield, WILLIAM PATTEN, 74 years. [4/26]
April 23, 1861, Otsego, ANSON ROCKWELL, 78 years. [5/3]
April 23, 1861, Hartwick, EMMA A. MURDOCK, 1 year 6 mos. [5/3]
April 14, 1861, Richfield, Dea. JASPER BRAMAN, 87 years. [5/10]
May 7, 1861, Oneonta, ELIOT GILL, 17 years. [5/10]
April 21, 1861, Hartwick, JACOB M. LUCE, 55 years. [5/17]
May 8, 1861, Otsego, MARY E. PIERCE, 7 years. [5/17]
May 17, 1861, Cooperstown, Mrs. SALLY ROOT, 78 years. [5/24]
May 16, 1861, Otsego, JAMES KELLEY, 75 years. [5/24]
May 9, 1861, Cleveland, WILLIAM ARVELL CARTER, 2 years. [5/24]
April 11, 1861, Otsego, JOHN LUMLEY, 87 years. [5/31]
May 28, 1861, Springfield Center, DANIEL M. HOKE, 30 years. [6/7]
June 13, 1861, Schuylers Lake, MARGARET L. WESTCOTT, 8 years. [6/21]
June 12, 1861, Hartwick, DANIEL MURDOCK, 68 years. [6/21]
May 24, 1861, Otsego, KATIE THAYER, 8 years. [6/21]
June 28, 1861, Cooperstown, THOMAS MC INTOSH, 70 years. [6/28]
June 26, 1861, Cooperstown, Col. JOHN PRENTISS, 78 years. [6/28]
June 21, 1861, New Berlin, RUSSELL B. BURCH, M.D., 55 years. [6/28]
June 24, 1861, Otsego, MATHEW VAN HORNE, 61 years. [6/28]
June 13, 1861, Oaksville, BENJAMIN J. LENT, 44 years. [6/28]
June 16, 1861, Milford, ESTHER HARDY, 15 years. [6/28]
June 2, 1861, Milford, WILLIAM R. AYLESWORTH, 3 years. [6/28]
April 24, 1861, Fly Creek, WILLIAM B. SULLIVAN, infant 7 mos. [6/28]
June 9, 861, Hartwick, Mrs. SOPHIA ARNOLD, 78 years. [6/28]
June 16, 1861, Hartwick, COMFORT CHASE, 89 years. [7/5]
June 12, 1861, Roseboom, DANIEL W. WINNE, 68 years. [7/5]
June 14, 1861, Otego, JOSEPH HOPKINS, 35 years. [7/5]
July 6, 1861, Westford, AMEU BADEAU, 63 years. [7/12]
July 21, 1861, Springfield, JOSIAH W. GROUT, 52 years. [7/12]
July 3, 1861, Maryland, GLOUD T. BURNSIDE, 82 years. [7/12]
July 9, 1861, Hartwick, Mrs. LUCY MORGAN, 95 years. [7/12]
June 30, 1861, Springfield, LUCIA BROWN, 20 years. [7/19]
July 21, 1861, Cooperstown, AURELIA E. SMITH, 8 years. [7/26]
June 3, 1861, Westford, HENRY GARDNER, 26 years. [7/26]

July 26, 1861, Cooperstown, MARYETT ROOT, 41 years. [8/2]
[no date] Cooperstown, JAMES JOHNSON, 4 years. [8/2]
July 16, 1861, New Lisbon, TRUMAN NEARING, 81 years. [8/2]
July 24, 1861, Richfield, Capt. OLCOTT C. CHAMBERLAIN, 67 years. [8/9]
July 8, 1861, Morris, Mrs. ANNA BALDWIN, 85 years. [8/9]
July 25, 1861, Middlefield, Mrs. HARRIET BALDWIN, 74 years. [8/9]
July 3, 1861, Cooperstown, WILLIAM W. SMITH, 3 years. [8/9]
July 15, 1861, Edmeston, Mrs. PATIENCE PARKER, 66 years. [8/9]
Aug. 18, 1861, Cooperstown, Mrs. EPPA GRAVES, 61 years. [8/23]
July 9, 1861, Fly Creek, Mrs. POLLY V. C. BADGER, 62 years. [8/23]
July 18, 1861, Hartwick, IRA STEERE, 68 years. [9/6]
Sept. --, 1861, Otsego, Mrs. IRA STEERE, 67 years. [9/6]
Sept. 8, 1861, Cooperstown, LYMAN B. BALL, 8 years. [9/13]
Aug. 17, 1861, Milford, IDA DEETTE STILL, 7 years. [9/13]
Aug. 28, 1861, Milford, CHARLES CEYLON STILL, 8 years. [9/13]
Sept. 3, 1861, Milford, HERBERT STILL, 2 years. [9/13]
July 23, 1861, Otsego, WILLIAM J. TORRY, 3 years. [9/20]
Sept. 18, 1861, Cherry Valley, ORRIN THOMPSON, 53 years. [9/27]
Oct. 2, 1861, Hartwick Sem., Mrs. POLLY DAVISON, 65 years. [10/4]
Aug. 20, 1861, New Lisbon, MARY J. BROWNELL, 30 years. [10/18]
Sept. 14, 1861, Hartwick, Mrs. ELECTA COMFORT, 58 years. [10/18]
Oct. 23, 1861, Cooperstown, JANE W. SMITH, infant. [10/25]
Oct. 1, 1861, New Lisbon, EUGENE REED, 3 years. [10/25]
Oct. 7, 1861, Otsego, ISABELLE C. WEDDERSPOON, 7 years. [10/25]
Sept. 1, 1861, Burlington, ELIAS D. FITCH, 19 years. [10/25]
Oct. 1, 1861, East Worcester, ROSMAN K. HOLLENBECK, 10 years. [10/25]
Oct. 30, 1861, Cooperstown, ELVIRA WINSLOW, 46 years. [11/1]
Oct. 8, 1861, Hartwick, WATERMAN ELDRED, 57 years. [11/8]
Oct. 20, 1861, New Lisbon, HANNAH M. MYERS, 14 years. [11/8]
Oct. 21, 1861, New Liston, LORENZO ADAMS, 15 years. [11/8]
Oct. 20, 1861, New Lisbon, WELCOME ADAMS, 24 years. [11/8]
Oct. 29, 1861, Pittsfield, Mrs. HULDAH A. CHASE, 47 years. [11/8]
Oct. 31, 1861, Morris, EDSON AVERY BABCOCK, 1 year. [11/15]
Nov. 6, 1861, Morris, Mrs. MARY JANE BABCOCK, 28 years. [11/15]
Nov. 10, 1861, Morris, LUCINDA BAKER, 30 years. [11/15]
Oct. 31, 1861, Otsego, Mrs. HENRIETTA VAN HORNE, 42 years. [11/15]
Oct. 26, 1861, Fly Creek, DAVID PATTEN, 36 years. [11/15]
Oct. 22, 1861, Exeter, JARVIS S. SMITH. [11/15]

Oct. 24, 1861, Hartwick, Mrs. ADELIADE (ADELIA) G. SMITH, 45 years. [11/22]
Nov. 3, 1861, New Lisbon, Mrs. ROSANNA C. JANES, 43 years. [11/22]
Nov. 10, 1861, Laurens, NOEL GARDNER, 79 years. [11/22]
Nov. 8, 1861, Cooperstown, EMELINE SPENCER, 27 years. [11/22]
Nov. 8, 1861, Otsego, EDGAR C. WEDDERSPOON, 2 years. [11/22]
Nov. 14, 1861, Otsego, FLORA PARSHALL. [11/22]
Nov. 19, 1861, Cooperstown, F. M.BURNETT, 40 years. [11/22]
Nov. 27, 1861, Cooperstown, FLORENCE V. COLE, 8 years. [11/22]
Nov. 24, 1861, Burlington, JAMES R. BALCOM, 9 years. [12/13]
Dec. 5, 1861, Milford, LEGRANDERSON PECK, 63 years. [12/13]
Dec. 9, 1861, Exeter Center, JOHN PHILIPS, 63 years. [12/13]
Dec. 1, 1861, Burlington, WEBSTER BALCOM, 6 years. [12/13]
Nov. 20, 1861, Burlington, CHARLES R. BALCOM, 27 years. [12/13]
Dec. 1, 1861, Springfield, PETER FRINK, 64 years. [12/13]
Dec. 15, 1861, Fly Creek, Mrs. MARY WILLIAMS, 64 years. [12/20]
Dec. 24, 1861, Cooperstown, GEORGE POMEROY, 83 years. [12/27]
Dec. 9, 1861, Westford, RUSSELL GROVER, 74 years. [12/27]
Dec. 19, 1861, Otsego, AMBROSE PARSHALL, 5 years. [12/27]
Dec. 25, 1861, Cooperstown, Mrs. JANE SMITH, 30 years. [1/3/1862]
Dec. 28, 1861, Roseboom, PERMILLA ALLEN, 14 years. [1/10/1862]
Dec. 20, 1861, Campe Bates, Md., ZIBA H. BROWN, Co. D, 23 years. [1/10/1862]
Jan. 8, 1862, Exeter, EUNICE V. WALRATH, 5 years. [1/17]
Jan. 12, 1862, Morris, Mrs. DEBORAH FRANCHOT, 75 years. [1/17]
Jan. 10, 1862, E. Springfield, Mrs. HANNAH GRAY, 78 years. [1/17]
Jan. 21, 1862, Cooperstown, Mrs. BETSEY HALL, 66 years. [1/24]
Jan. 15, 1862, Otsego, JOHN KELLOGG, 72 years. [1/24]
Dec. 22, 1861, Springfield, ALMON WHITE, 80 years. [1/24/1862]
Jan. 18, 1862, Middlefield, BARKLEY W. YOUNG, 4 years. [1/24]
Jan. 12, 1862, Hartwick, JEROME MOAK NASH, 8 years. [1/24]
Jan. 17, 1862, Clarksville, JAMES VAN ALLEN, 47 years. [1/24]
Jan. 10, 1862, E. Springfield, Mrs. HANNAH GRAY, 77 years. [1/24]
Jan. 12, 1862, Otsego, Mrs. CAROLINE HOWE, 75 years. [1/31]
Jan. 15, 1862, NY City, Mrs. ELIZA O. WHITE (Cherry Valley), 67 years. [1/31]
Jan. 27, 1862, Camp Newton, FAIRFIELD M. WILSON, 32nd Regt., 23 years. [2/7]
[no date] Oaksville, JOHN BALDWIN, 73 years. [2/7]
Jan. 1, 1862, Richfield, Mrs. LOIS HAWKS, 89 years. [2/7]
Jan. 12, 1862, Schuyler's Lake, ROBERT M. DURFY. [2/7]

Feb. 7, 1862, Laurens, JOSEPHINE GILBERT, 9 years. [2/14]
Feb. 8, 1862, Annandale (?) nr. Cooperstown, LOUIS M. JOHNSTON, 2 years. [2/21]
Feb. 10, 1862, Morris, H. N. MC COLLOM, 53 years. [2/21]
[no date] Hancock, Md., EMERSON D. PIER, Co. D, 19th Regt., 17 years. [2/28]
Jan. 27, 1862, Pittsfield, Mrs. LUCRETIA PATRICK, 28 years. [2/28]
Jan. 25, 1862, Otego, NATHAN BIRDSALL, 69 years. [3/7]
[no date] Morris, Mrs. FRANCES ROOD, 47 years. [3/7]
March 8, 1862, Otsego, WILLIAM THAYER, 89 years. [3/14]
March 8, 1862, Richfield Spa, Mrs. MARY A. CARY, 62 years. [3/14]
March 10, 1862, Cherry Valley, Mrs. NANCY CLARK, 92 years. [3/21]
March 12, 1862, Otsego, Mrs. JANNETT WHIPPLE, 49 years. [3/28]
March 24, 1862, Otsego, ROXY GIBBS, 54 years. [3/28]
Feb. 23, 1862, Morris, ABBIE PERINE, 1 year. [4/4]
April 7, 1862, Springfield, ELIZABETH MILLER, 70 years. [4/11]
April 4, 1862, Decatur, ROBERT BABCOCK, 89 years. [4/11]
April 1, 1862, Cooperstown, FANNIE PITCHER, 2 years. [4/11]
April 16, 1862, Cooperstown, JOHN BAILEY, 71 years. [4/18]
April 14, 1862, Otsego, JAMES FOLLETT, 62 years. [4/25]
April 23, 1862, New Lisbon, ORRA HARRIS, 68 years. [5/2]
March 6, 1862, Evansville, Ind., D. W. GROSS of Garratsville, Co B., 49th Reg., 35 years. [5/2]
April 13, 1862, Hartwick, SUSAN WHEELER, 74 years. [5/2]
April 22, 1862, Fortress Monroe, CYRUS S. RIPLEY of Cooperstown, 18 years (Ellsworth Regt.). [5/2]
May 6, 1862, Cooperstown, GEORGE AUGUSTUS BROWN, 16 years. [5/9]
April 25, 1862, Otsego, DEMAS A. DOUBLEDAY, 71 years. [5/9]
[no date] New Lisbon, HARRIET D. THAYER, 1 year. [5/9]
April 28, 1862, Otsego, ISAAC STOCKER, 71 years. [5/9]
May 2, 1862, Springfield, MARY A. YOUNG, 11 years. [5/9]
May 1, 1862, Cooperstown, EDWARD OMAR BODEN, infant. [5/16]
May 18, 1862, Cooperstown, Mrs. ANN POMEROY CRIPPEN, 51 years. [5/23]
May 9, 1862, New Lisbon, Mrs. SALLY WATSON, 66 years. [5/23]
May 15, 1862, Middlefield, SIMEON C. AMES, 64 years. [5/23]
May 7, 1862, Cooperstown, Mrs. MARIA PAUL. [5/23]
May 7, 1862, Fly Creek, Mrs. OLIVE A. ROSE, 28 years. [5/23]
May 24, 1862, Westford, JENNIE E. GLEDHILL, infant. [5/30]
May 30, 1862, Otsego, JEFFERSON PIERCE, 1 year. [6/6]

May 4, 1862, Morris, AMOS BURLINGAME, 74 years. [6/13]
June 13, 1862, Cooperstown, ALICE RAY, infant. [6/20]
June 12, 1862, Milford, Mrs. ABIGAIL AYLESWORTH, 25 years. [6/20]
June 8, 1862, Mrs. LOUISA M. SERGENT, 38 years. [6/20]
June 14, 1862, Otsego, JOHN M. ELWELL, 5 years. [6/27]
June 26, 1862, Oneonta, SELINA G. LOW, 22 years. [7/4]
July 3, 1862, Garrattsville, EMMET HOAG, 2 years. [7/11]
Feb. 9, 1862, Portlandville, Mrs. MARGARET LANE, 71 years. [7/11]
May 8, 1862, Burlington, JOSEPH NEFF, 92 years. [7/11]
July 4, 1862, E. Springfield, JENNIE E. RATHBUN, 7 years. [7/18]
June 20, 1862, Newbern, NC, JAMES F. WEEKS of Hartwick, 3rd NY Artillery Hospital. [7/18]
July 22, 1862, Cooperstown, HORACE LATHROP, 76 years. [7/25]
June 29, 1862, New Lisbon, JOSEPH GARDNER, 28 years. [7/25]
July 14, 1862, Hartwick Sem., Mrs. ELIZA CRAFTS, 55 years. [8/1]
Aug. 1, 1862, Cooperstown, HENRY P. COOLEY, 40 years. [8/8]
Aug. 1, 1862, Milford, MOSES LUTHER, 70 years. [8/8]
Aug. 7, 1862, Middlefield, LEVI WOOD, 5 years. [8/15]
Aug. 7, 1862, Washington, JOHN C. CLARK of Pierstown, a soldier. [8/15]
Aug. 2, 1862, Bellevue Hospital NY City, M. JEROME ESMAY, 61st Reg., (E. Worcester), 18 years. [8/15]
Aug. 7, 1862, Cooperstown, WILLIAM L. BENTON, 2 years. [8/15]
Aug. 8, 1862, Oneonta, COLIN D. STRONG, 1 year. [8/22]
Aug. 10, 1862, Oneonta, ROBERT L. STRONG, 1 year. [8/22]
Aug. 8, 1862, Hartwick, CORNELIA A. KIRBY, 2 years. [8/22]
Aug. 12, 1862, Edmeston, SARAH E. SMITH, 3 years. [8/22]
[date not given] Newbern, NC, HYLER D. PRINDLE, 51st Regt. Co. I, 21 years. [8/22]
Aug. 5, 1862, Middlefield Center, Mrs. SALLY SMITH, 63 years. [8/29]
[no date] Westford, GEORGE H. PLATNER, 2 years. [9/29]
Sept. 3, 1862, Cooperstown, Mrs. SARAH A. BEABEE, 58 years. [9/5]

DEATHS FROM SEPT. 19, 1862 - DEC. 30, 1875 TAKEN FROM THE *OTSEGO HERALD & WESTERN ADVERTISER* AND *FREEMAN'S JOURNAL*

VOLUME III

Compiled by Gertrude A. Barber

Aug. 28, 1862, Cooperstown, AGNES LUCY MC NAMEE, 6 years. (no issue given)

Aug. 26, 1862, Otsego, NATHANIEL MOTT, 77 years. (no issue given)

Sept. 12, 1862, Middlefield, WILLIAM A. METCALF, 10 years. [9/19]

[no date] Cooperstown, Mrs. LUCY S. CRAFTS. [9/26/1862]

Sept. 10, 1862, New Lisbon, JARED GARDNER, 82 years. [9/26]

Sept. 13, 1862, Richfield, Mrs. ABIGAIL WILDER, 78 years. [9/26]

July 22, 1862, Hartwick, JOHN WINDSOR, 79 years. [9/26]

Sept. 18, 1862, Middlefield, KATE M. BROOKS, 6 years. [9/26]

Sept. 23, 1862, Middlefield, Mrs. BETSEY ALLEN COOPER, 68 years. [10/3]

Sept. 24, 1862, Toddsville, MERCY O. CAMP, 30 years. [10/3]

Sept. 26, 1862, Morris, Mrs. ABIGAIL JARVIS, 92 years. [10/3]

Sept. 1, 1862, Hartwick, DANIEL A. KENYON, 12 years. [10/3]

Sept. 17, 1862, Hartwick, MARY JANE KENYON, 9 years. [10/3]

Sept. 28, 1862, Edmeston, J. M. BURDICK, 24 years. [10/10]

Sept. 14, 1862, Morris, ADELLA S. BALDWIN, 8 years. [10/10]

Sept. 20, 1862, Maryland, ELIZABETH M. MC KOWN, 7 years. [10/10]

Sept. 28, 1862, Alexandria, Corpl. JOHN J. COOK, Co. D., 51st Regt., 23 years. [10/10]

Sept. 28, 1862, Butternuts, Mrs. ASENATH COSS, 56 years. [10/10]

Oct. 8, 1862, Cooperstown, CHARLES PAUL COOPER, 18 months, son of RICHARD COOPER. [10/17]

Aug. 24, 1862, Otsego, JOHN PIERCE, 71 years. [10/17]

Sept. 3, 1862, Key West, FL, JOHN P. TERWILLIGER, Co. A, 90th Regt., 29 years. [10/17]

Oct. 9, 1862, W. Burlington, PHEBE CUSHMAN, 20 years. [10/17]

[no date given] Roanoke, NC, THEO. E. PECK (soldier), 31 years. [10/24]

Oct. 1, 1862, Hartwick, MARY J. RUSSELL, 32 years. [10/24]

Oct. 20, 1862, W. Burlington, W. AUGUSTUS GETOHELL, 10 years. [10/31]

Oct. 4, 1862, Richfield, STEVEN L. VAN BUREN, 9 years. [10/31]
Oct. 10, 1862, Richfield, EVA O. VAN BUREN, 6 years. [10/31]
Oct. 12, 1862, Richfield Spa, WILLIAM HARVEY REED, 19 years. [10/31]
Jan. 24, 1862, Richfield, Mrs. LUCY ADAMS, 40 years. [10/31]
[no date], Burketsville, MD, DAVID BUSHNELL (a soldier) of Worcester, 20 years. [10/31]
Oct. 4, 1862, Richfield, STEVEN L. VAN CUREN, 9 years. [11/7]
Oct. 16, 1862, Hartwick, JULIA PICKENS, 27 years. [11/7]
Nov. 5, 1862, Middlefield, WILLIAM COMPTON, 85 years. [11/14]
Nov. 1, 1862, Laurens, STEPHEN D. BROWN, 8 months. [11/14]
Nov. 11, 1862, Edmeston Center, Mrs. POLLY BOOTMAN, 63 years. [11/21]
Nov. 12, 1862, Cooperstown, LEVERETT SECOR, 20 years. [11/21]
Oct. 20, 1862, Springfield, Mrs. JEAN FERGUSON, 96 years. [12/5]
Nov. 25, 1862, Milford, AMOS L. MANCHESTER, 5 years. [12/5]
Nov. 17, 1862, Middlefield, JUDSON FAULKNER, 43 years. [12/5]
Nov. 29, 1862, Hartwick, HELEN C. VAN BUREN, 14 years. [12/5]
Dec. 9, 1862, Laurens, Mrs. HARRIET R. BARTON, 55 years. [12/12]
Nov. 23, 1862, Richfield, JOHN WOODBURY, 85 years. [12/12]
Dec. 1, 1862, Middlefield, HORACE ECKLER, 24 years. [12/12]
Dec. 6, 1862, Edmeston, DAVID N. CASPRUS, 11 years. [12/12]
Dec. 4, 1862, Middlefield, MORRIS J. BAILEY, 23 years. [12/12]
Dec. 4, 1862, NYC, Mrs. J. ELIZ. NELSON WHITE, 34 years. [12/12]
Dec. 16, 1862, NY, RICHARD COOPER of Cooperstown, 54 years. [12/19]
Nov. 14, 1862, Cooperstown, PETER BROOKHAM, 45 years. [12/19]
Nov. 5, 1862, Chaseville, HUDSON BURNSIDE, 58 years. [12/19]
Oct. 28, 1862, E. Worcester, ISAAC L. LA MOURE, 50 years. [12/19]
Dec. 3, 1862, E. Worcester, JAMES B. COOLEY. [12/19]
Dec. 2, 1862, Fort Pennsylvania, DC, RUSSELL DORR ASHLEY of Clarksville, 20 years. [12/19]
Dec. 6, 1862, Milford, ZETEELLA GAGE, infant. [12/26]
Dec. 15, 1862, Burlington, CLARA JANE BENJAMIN, 3 years. [12/26]
Dec. 18, 1862, Warren Hill, Otsego, Mrs. HARRIET E. CHAPIN WARREN, 60 years. [12/26]
Dec. 28, 1862, Cooperstown, HENRY D. BURDITT, 23 years. [1/2/1863]
Dec. 26, 1862, Cooperstown, PAUL B. BODEN, 20 years. [1/2/1863]
Nov. 30, 1862, Westville, RICHARD P. FERRIS, 101st Regt., 20 years. [1/2/1863]
Nov 27,1862, Oaksville, Mrs. ESTHER PRESTON, 94 years. [1/9/1863]

Dec. 1, 1862, Mitcheville, TN, JOHN F. MILLER, Esq. of 4th MI Cav., 30 years. [1/9/1863]
Jan. 12, 1863, Cooperstown, Mrs. JENNIE STORRS WORTHINGTON, 20 years. [1/16]
Jan. 8, 1863, Milford, REUBEN WESTCOTT, 62 years. [1/16]
Dec. 27, 1862, Fredericksburg, EDGAR RUSSELL of Hartwick, 22 years. [1/16]
Jan. 2, 1863, Butternuts, FRANCES HEBE TAYLOR, 3 years. [1/16]
Jan. 7, 1863, Butternuts, ORIN KEPLER TAYLOR, 20 months. [1/16]
Jan. 7, 1863, Fly Creek, WILLIAM WILLIAMS, 1 year. [1/16]
Jan. 14, 1863, Worcester, Mrs. HARRIET GRANT, 43 years. [1/23]
Jan. 26, 1863, Cooperstown, ELIHU PHINNEY, 77 years. [1/30]
Dec. 7, 1862, Milford, Mrs. ANNIS SHUTE, 73 years. [1/30/1863]
Jan. 20, 1863, Westville, Mrs. MERCY M. NEWTON, 52 years. [1/30]
Jan. 25, 1863, Otsego, MARY JANE FREEMAN, 7 years. [1/30]
Jan. 30, 1863, Fly Creek, SARAH E. MARVIN, infant. [2/6]
Jan. 7, 1863, Laurens, Mrs. MARGARET BROWN, 55 years. [2/6]
Jan. 24, 1863, Hartwick, LAURA INGALSBE, 48 years. [2/6]
Jan. 21, 1863, Burlington, JEREMIAH PRATT, 99 years. [2/13]
Jan. 30, 1863, Hartwick, MARY M. PERRY, 37 years. [2/13]
Feb. 13, 1863, Morris, G. W. NEWELL, 4 years. [2/20]
Jan. 12, 1863, Maryland, NATHANIEL CARPENTER, 84 years. [2/20]
Jan. 17, 1863, New Lisbon, Mrs. ELEANOR TIFFANY, 88 years. [2/20]
Jan. 9, 1863, Middlefield, HORACE C. PRATT, 32 years. [2/27]
Dec. 13, 1862, Hartwick, JOHN E. PAINE, 8 years. [2/27/1863]
Feb. 16, 1863, Middlefield, HELEN L. KAPLE, 22 years. [2/27]
Feb. 22, 1863, Middlefield, ADA MARY PARSHALL, 9 months. [2/27]
Feb. 27, 1863, Cooperstown, Mrs. HANNAH COOPER WESSELS, 48 years. [3/6]
March 2, 1863, Laurens, Mrs. ABIGAIL STRAIGHT, 59 years. [3/6]
Feb. 23, 1863, Worcester, JOHN HURD, 68 years. [3/6]
Jan. 29, 1863, Falmouth, VA, ALBERT J. CHASE (soldier), 20 years. [3/6]
Feb. 7, 1863, Aquia Creek, VA, LAWINE INGLSBEE (soldier), 30 years. [3/6]
Dec. 28, 1862, White Oak Creek, VA, WILLIAM J. ELLIOTT of Burlington, 19 years. [3/6]
Jan. 26, 1863, White Oak Creek, VA, ANDREW CHISHOLM of Burlington, 23 years. [3/6]
Jan. 21, 1863, Springfield, Mrs. LUCY CLARK, 86 years. [3/6]
March 2, 1863, Hartwick, GEORGIANA SILVERNAIL, infant. [3/13]
Feb. 17, 1863, Richfield, WILLIAM COLE, 96 years. [3/13]

March 1, 1863, White Oak Creek, VA, JAMES H. BAILEY, 20 years, Co. F. 121st Regt. NYV. [3/13]
March 5, 1863, Otsego, LAURA E. BEACH, 15 months. [3/13]
Feb. 24, 1863, Otsego, JOHN D. FREEMAN, 10 years. [3/13]
Feb. 26, 1863, Fly Creek, GEORGE W. ANDREWS, 44 years. [3/13]
Feb. 19, 1863, Springfield, WILLIE BROOKS CASLER, 5 years. [3/20]
Feb. 9, 1863, Leonardsville, WARD CRUMB, 18 years. [3/20]
March 3, 1863, Leonardsville, FRANCIS V. CRUMB, 16 years. [3/20]
March 4, 1863, Jacksonville, WILLIAM M. GARDNER (Laurens), 44 years. [3/20]
March 3, 1863, Otsego, CHARLES ELWELL, 7 mos. [3/20]
March 18, 1863, Springfield, Mrs. POLLY DEAN, 88 years. [3/27]
March 23, 1863, ALVAN POTTER, 71 years. [3/27]
March 20, 1863, Colliersville, Mrs. ELIZABETH COLLIER, 80 years. [3/27]
March 26, 1863, Pierstown, ERASTUS W. SQUIRES, 4 years. [4/3]
March 12, 1863, Fly Creek, OLNEY Z. ANDREWS, 66 years. [4/3]
March 25, 1863, Toddsville, MARY E. PECK, infant. [4/3]
March 25, 1863, Hartwick, MARY JANE HOUSE, 10 years. [4/3]
March 22, 1863, E. Springfield, EUNICE HARDY, 10 years. [4/3]
April 8, 1863, Cooperstown, Mrs. SABRA TUCKER, 53 years. [4/10]
March 30,1863, Garratsville, LORENZO D. WATSON, 27 years. [4/10]
March 26, 1863, Fly Creek, EDGAR R. REXFORD, 2 years. [4/10]
March 27, 1863, White Oaks Church, VA, PETER CROUSE of Roseboom, 19 years. [4/10]
March 23, 1863, Schuylers Lake, SAMUEL BROWN, 83 years. [4/10]
March 7, 1863, Edmeston, MARY TEN BROECK, 90 years. [4/10]
April 10, 1863, Cooperstown, HORACE W. LATHROP, 16 months. [4/17]
April 10, 1863, Edmeston, Mrs. ABIGAIL PEET, 69 years. [4/17]
March 19, 1863, Springfield, MARY ELIZA ALLEN, 2 years. [4/17]
Feb. 20, 1863, Springfield, MARTHA E. SEEBER, 15 years. [4/17]
April 6, 1863, Middlefield, MARY CLARK WALKER, 15 months. [4/17]
March 29, 1863, Unadilla Forks, FRANK IRVING BABCOCK, 7 years. [4/17]
April 14, 1863, Westford, PETER ROSEBOOM, 77 years. [4/17]
April 11, 1863, Fly Creek, THOMAS TAYLOR, 83 years. [4/17]
April 13, 1863, Cooperstown, ELIZABETH WILLIAMS, 52 years. [4/24]
April 14, 1863, Butternuts, PHILIP FOSTER, 62 years. [4/24]
April 13, 1863, Pierstown, METTIE A. SQUIRES, 6 years. [4/24]
April 12, 1863, Cooperstown, FANNIE B. BOLLES, infant. [4/24]

April 3, 1863, Hartwick Sem., JOHN PAUL CLINTON, 2 years. [4/24]
April 18, 1863, Hartwick Sem., MARY J. CLINTON, 6 years. [4/24]
April 13, 1863, E. Springfield, MINNIE E. FOWLER, 3 years. [4/24]
April 12, 1863, Clintonville, PETER J. CARR, 1 year. [4/24]
March 10, 1863, Washington, DC, SOLOMON A. GREEN of Otego, 20 years. [5/1]
May 6, 1863, Cooperstown, EMMA J. CARR, 19 years. [5/8]
April 25, 1863, Otsego, ANDREW SHAW, 82 years. [5/8]
May 1, 1863, Otsego, M. FAIRFIELD WILSON, 59 years. [5/8]
April 22, 1863, Otsego, LEONARD VAN SLYKE, 13 years. [5/8]
Dec. 18, 1862, Falmouth, VA, LORENZO D. CHAMBERLAIN of Maryland, 22 years. [5/8/1863]
April 24, 1863, Morris, Mrs. MARANDA HARRINGTON, 72 years. [5/8]
May 19, 1865, Cooperstown, EMERY M. ROBINSON, 16 years. [5/22]
April 24, 1865, Milford Center, VERNET LEE SEEGER, 10 months. [5/22]
April 25, 1865, Milford Center, ALVIN A. SEEGER, 6 years. [5/22]
May 1, 1863, Hartwick, FRANCES A. MERCER, 11 years. [5/22]
May 5, 1863, Otsego, CHARLES MOAK CARD, 2 years. [5/29]
May 22, 1863, Otsego, ELLA M. CARD, 10 months. [5/29]
June 1, 1863, Edmeston, HELEN L. GATES, 37 years. [6/12]
March 24, 1863, Edmeston, JAMES P. DENNISON, 50 years. [6/12]
June 6, 1863, Hartwick, LOENSKI BOTSFORD, 16 years. [6/12]
May 31, 1863, Westford, RUFUS TRIPP, 57 years. [6/12]
June 5, 1863, Middlefield, ELIAS ISMOND, 87 years. [6/19]
June 12, 1863, Burlington, HANNAH M. BONNAR, 8 years. [6/19]
June 2, 1863, New Lisbon, Mrs. AMY GARDNER, 75 years. [6/19]
June 4, 1863, Oneonta, HELEN M. FORD, 29 years. [6/19]
May 21, 1863, Osego, ZIBA BURCH, 75 years. [6/26]
June 4, 1863, Fly Creek, Mrs. MARYETTE REXFORD of Burlington, 37 years. [7/3]
May 26, 1863, Laurens, Mrs. DEBORAH COOLEY, 78 years. [7/3]
June 20, 1863, Otego, Dea. ELIAS ARNOLD, 79 years. [7/10]
June 22, 1863, Cooperstown, EDWARD J. COX, 3 years. [7/10]
June 18, 1863, Burlington Green, ELIZABETH OLIVER, 34 years. [7/17]
[no date] Fly Creek, GEORGE W. PECK, 7 years. [7/17]
June 29, 1863, W. Springfield, ABRAHAM MAXFIELD, 51 years. [7/17]
June 22, 1863, Milford, VIOLA S. DURHAM, 9 years. [7/17]
July 20, 1863, Chicago, ALICE GRAY PEAKE, formerly of Cooperstown, 24 years. [7/31]
July 24, 1863, Chicago, JAMIE D. PEAKE, 5 months. [7/31]

June 16, 1865, Middlefield, Mrs. PHEBE E. REYNOLDS, 47 years. [7/31]
July 29, 1863, Garratsville, HERBERT GORTON, 2 years. [8/7]
July 28, 1863, Garratsville, GEORGE C. GORTON, 1 year. [8/7]
Aug. 3, 1863, Laurens, MARY HERRING, 10 years. [8/7]
July 24, 1863, Gettysburg [PA], Corp. TRACEY KELLOGG of Otsego, 21 years. [8/14]
Aug. 7, 1863, Laurens, NANCY WRIGHT, 21 years. [8/14]
July 16, 1863, Unadilla, Mrs. SUSAN E. WATSON. [8/14]
July 31, 1863, Exeter, FREDDY E. FAY, 16 months. [8/21]
Aug. 11, 1863, ELIZA SNYDER STROBEL, 19 years. [8/21]
Aug. 9, 1863, Garratsville, JOHN B. COOK, 37 years. [8/21]
Aug. 10, 1863, Hartwick, ROMEYN C. GARDNER, 1 year. [8/21]
Aug. 7, 1863, Springfield, Mrs. MARIA CALE, 74 years. [8/21]
Aug. 3, 1863, Middlefield, MYRON H. SHERMAN, 1 year. [8/21]
July 28, 1863, Cherry Valley, Capt. DANIEL GILCHRIST, 82 years. [8/28]
Aug. 26, 1863, Cooperstown, NANCY HENRY of Nashville, TN. [8/28]
Aug. 18, 1863, Westford, Mrs. HARRIET KINGSLEY, 36 years. [9/4]
Sept. 8, 1863, Cooperstown, Mrs. POLLY M. HINMAN, 61 years. [9/11]
Sept. 14, 1863, Oaksville, FRANK A. PRESTON, 6 years. [9/18]
Aug. 20, 1863, Cooperstown, JAMES R. JOHNSON, 28 years. [9/25]
Sept. 28, 1863, Cooperstown, HOLDER CORY, 63 years. [10/2]
Oct. 3, 1863, Laurens, HANNAH MAY KENYON, 1 year. [10/9]
Oct. 2, 1863, Cooperstown, Mrs. ELLEN S. MAYNARD of Washington. [10/16]
Sept. 23, 1863, Unadilla Forks, EUNICE C. BABCOCK, 5 years. [10/16]
Oct. 19, 1863, Otsego, MARY JANE GARDNER, 4 years. [10/23]
Oct. 17, 1863, Westford, MYRA A. PITCHER, 7 years. [10/30]
Oct. 17, 1863, Milford, Mrs. CLARISSA R. WAITE, 73 years. [11/6]
Oct. 23, 1863, Middlefield, LORENZO D. HUBBARD, 23 years. [11/6]
Oct. 30, 1863, New Lisbon, FRANCELIA A. POTTER, 18 years. [11/6]
Sept. 24, 1863, Laurens, BENJAMIN MILLER, 99 years. [11/6]
Nov. 2, 1863, Westford, HORACE ROBERTS, 66 years. [11/28]
Sept. 22, 1863, Schuylers Lake, CLARA E. MOTT, 17 years. [11/28]
Nov. 7, 1863, Hartwick, Mrs. JANE INGALSBE, 83 years. [11/28]
Nov. 13, 1863, Roseboom, JAMES M. MARSH, 22 years. [11/27]
Nov. 13, 1863, Decatur, FRANK POTTER, 11 years. [11/27]
Nov. 18, 1863, Middlefield Center, SARAH WHITE, 95 years. [11/27]
Dec. 4, 1863, Clarksville, Mrs. MARY SOULES, 43 years. [12/11]
Dec. 8, 1863, Toddsville, Mrs. LUCY A. MILLER of Franklin, 35 years. [12/11]

Nov. 18, 1863, Otsego, Mrs. HARRIET L. SMITH, 33 years. [12/18]
Dec. 1, 1863, Springfield Center, GEORGE A. PEGG, 35 years. [12/18]
Dec. 11, 1863, Decatur, Mrs. REBECCA JOHNSON, 70 years. [12/25]
[no date], Milford, JOHN S. COOPER, 41 years. [12/25]
Aug. 18, 1863, Newbern, NC, HERBERT L. WAID, soldier, age 24. [12/25]
Dec. 14, 1862 [sic], Middlefield Center, H. ESTHER WHITE, 60 years. [12/25]
Aug. 26 (?), Laurens, HENRY M. GARDNER, 16 years. [12/25]
Sept. 13 (?), Laurens, DANIEL GARDNER, 11 years. [12/25]
Sept. 26 (?), Laurens, CHAUNCEY GARDNER, 8 years. [12/25]
Oct. 22 (?), Laurens, CORDELIA GARDNER, 15 years. [12/25]
Nov. 13, 1863, Decatur, FRANK POTTER, 11 years. [1/1/1864]
Dec. 20, 1863, Decatur, CHARLES H. POTTER, 8 years. [1/1/1864]
Jan. 5, 1864, Cooperstown, JOHN F. FAIRCHILD, 78 years. [1/8]
Nov. 24, 1863, Edmeston, Mrs. POLLY ST. JOHN, 60 years. [1/8/1864]
Dec. 13, 1863, Edmeston, JOHN BILYEA, 68 years. [1/8/1864]
Dec. 26, 1863, Burlington, EMMA ADELIA CLOCK, 6 years. [1/8/1864]
Dec. 17, 1863, Middlefield, JULIA E. GRIGGS, 12 years. [1/8/1864]
Dec. 29, 1863, Westford, FRANCELIA HILL, 18 years. [1/8/1864]
Jan. 4, 1864, Hartwick, REUBEN HUBBARD, 80 years. [1/8/1864]
Jan. 9, 1864, Hartwick, Capt. JEROME CLARK, 84 years. [1/15]
Jan. 7, 1864, Hartwick, Maj. GEORGE H. DERBYSHIRE, 79 years. [1/15]
Jan. 7, 1864, Otsego, CHARLES H. WARREN, 14 years. [1/15]
Jan. 5, 1864, Burlington, ALONZO V. HUMPHREY, 10 years. [1/15]
Jan. 4, 1864, Burlington, B. F. DELONG, 52 years. [1/15]
Jan. 4, 1864, Oneonta, MARY J. BROWNELL, of New Lisbon, 5 years. [1/15]
Jan. 14, 1864, Rome, JAMES D. VAUGHN of Richfield, 53 years. [1/22]
Dec. 7, 1863, Cooperstown, ASHBEL GRAVES, 73 years. [1/22]
Jan. 8, 1864, Hartwick, MARTHA A. BECKLEY, 16 years. [1/22]
Dec. 24, 1863, E. Springfield, Mrs. H. F. STOCKER, 35 years. [1/22/1864]
Jan. 17, 1864, Westford, SARAH ASHLEY, 9 years. [1/22]
Jan. 17, 1864, Morris, MARTHA SOPHIA PERRY, 1 year. [1/22]
Jan. 16, 1864, Morris, JENNIE M. & CORA E. COLTON, aged 4 & 5 years. [1/29]
Jan. 23, 1864, Cooperstown, HELEN M. MILLER, 19 years. [1/29]
Jan. 12, 1864, Hartwick Sem., JOHN C. JONES, 62 years. [1/29]
Jan. 20, 1864, Mt. Given, CARRIE L. OLENDORF, 4 years. [2/5]

Feb. 3, 1864, MARY E. OLENDORF, 8 years. [2/5]
Jan. 7, 1864, Springfield, Mrs. NANCY COLMAN, 68 years. [2/5]
Dec. 29, 1863, Oaksville, OLIVE ANN PERKINS, 10 years. [2/12/1864]
Dec. 30, 1863, Oaksville, ELLA JANE PERKINS, 6 years. [2/12/1864]
Jan. 30, 1864, Springfield Center, FLORA S. NILES, 15 years. [2/12]
Feb. 8, 1864, Oaksville, MARTHA ANN NILES, 24 years. [2/12]
Feb. 14, 1864, Exeter Cen., Mrs. EVELINA HALE JONES, 51 years. [2/19]
Feb. 12, 1864, Cooperstown, CHARLES J. WALRADT, 6 years. [2/19]
Feb. 7, 1864, Otsego, CHARLES VAN HORNE, 18 years. [2/19]
Feb. 11, 1864, Westford, JAMES CUMMINGS, 76 years. [2/26]
Feb. 17, 1864, Cooperstown, Mrs. SUSAN DAVIS BUNYAN, 31 years. [2/26]
Feb. 19, 1864, Pittsfield, WILLIAM JACKSON, 45 years. [2/26]
Feb. 12, 1864, Springfield Cen., Mrs. SOPHRONIA W. SHIPMAN. [3/4]
Feb. 20, 1864, Cooperstown, Mrs. MARY JANE STENSON, 30 years. [3/4]
Feb. 20, 1864, Richfield Spa, JENNIE HORTON, 15 years. [3/4]
March 2, 1864, S. Worcester, ABRAHAM BECKER, 5 years. [3/4]
March 1, 1864, Otsego, JOHN DELONG, 84 years. [3/11]
March 2, 1864, Roseboom, Mrs. RUTH ROSEBOOM, 85 years. [3/11]
March 10, 1864, Cooperstown, Major W. BACON, 59 years. [3/11]
Feb. 5, 1864, Westford, CLARK ALDRICH, 33 years. [3/18]
Feb. 19, 1864, Middlefield, JAMES OTTAWAY, 38 years. [3/18]
Feb. 12, 1864, Hart, SAMUEL KING, 87 years. [3/18]
March 14, 1864, Portlandville, Mrs. CLARISSA Y. PACKER, 58 years. [3/18]
March 15, 1864, Middlefield, WILLIAM PAGE, 19 years. [3/18]
March 8, 1864, Westford, BARNARD SALISBURY, 2 years. [3/25]
March 23, 1864, Springfield, Mrs. GERTRUDE SIMONSON, 56 years. [4/1]
March 28, 1864, Springfield, NETTIE CASLER, 1 year. [4/1]
March 21, 1864, Locust Grove, Otsego Co., Mrs. HANNAH THAYER, 57 years. [4/1]
March 6, 1864, N. Lisbon, MELVIN GARDNER POTTER, 6 years. [4/1]
March 11, 1864, N. Lisbon, ELLEN VIRGINIA POTTER, 10 years. [4/1]
March 20, 1864, Canesteo, NY, SCHUYLER SOUTHWORTH, 62 years. [4/1]
March 25, 1864, Middlefield, ALFRED M. CLARK, 15 years. [4/1]
March 10, 1864, Hart, PETER ANGUR, 78 years. [4/1]
Feb. 23, 1864, Mrs. JEMIMA GEER, aged 83 years. [4/1]

Feb. 13, 1864, ORLU V. WELDON, 1 years. [4/1]
March 20, 1864, Decatur, Mrs. SALLY M. ROE, 58 years. [4/1]
April 2, 1864, Cooperstown, HARVEY MARVIN, 43 years. [4/8]
March 8, 1864, Middlefield, LEWIS G. PARSHALL, 1 year. [4/8]
March 30, 1864, Maryland, EBENEZER BOYNTON, 82 years. [4/8]
March 4, 1864, Toddsville, JOSIAH GIBSON, 41 years. [4/8]
March 2, 1864, Toddsville, Mrs. RUBY BENJAMIN, 41 years. [4/8]
April 2, 1864, Hartwick, JOHN HORACE BISSELL, 11 months. [4/8]
April 4, 1864, Milford, JOSHUA HART, 72 years. [4/15]
April --, 1864, Maryland, SARAH E. MC KOWN, 6 years. [4/15]
April 10, 1864, ANNA MC KOWN, 13 years. [4/15]
March 18, 1864, Worcester, PORTER M. SEWARD, 8 years. [4/15]
March 21, 1864, Burlington, CLARENCE M. PRATT, 8 years. [4/22]
April 21, 1864, Cooperstown, JAMES COCKETT, 43 years. [4/22]
April 14, 1864, Roseboom, Dr. ABRAHAM A. HOWLAND, 73 years. [4/22]
April 11, 1864, Davids Is., ALMON H. JOHNSON, soldier, 23 years. [4/22]
March 16, 1864, Laurens, Mrs. AMY STANTON, 52 years. [4/22]
March 30, 1864, Westford, Mrs. PHEBE T. BIDLAKE, 53 years. [4/22]
March 30, 1864, Schenevus, WILLIAM R. BRONK, 45 years. [4/22]
April 9, 1864, Otsego, NETTIE BYARD, 1 year. [4/29]
April 7, 1864, Bowerstown, DAVID REED, 63 years. [5/6]
April 27, 1864, Middlefield, MORRIS B. FAULKNER, 14 years. [5/13]
May 7, 1864, Middlefield, Mrs. CAROLINE ISMOND, 57 years. [5/13]
May 8, 1864, Richfield, PROSPER FITCH, 74 years. [4/13]
May 4, 1864, Clarksville, ALEX. LLOYD, 55 years. [5/20]
April 10, 1864, Toddsville, Mrs. PERCY VAN SLYKE, 54 years. [5/27]
May 10, 1864, Burlington Flats, Mrs. LUCY C. BROWN, 55 years. [5/27]
May 31, 1864, Davenport, IA, BYRON W. BURDITT of Cooperstown, 34 years. [6/3]
May 13, 1864, Spottsylvania, VA, Lieut. SILAS E. PIERCE, 20 years. [6/3]
May 13, 1864, Memphis TN, Dr. SEELEY BROWNELL of Hartwick. [6/3]
May 5, 1864, Battle of Wilderness, Corp. JOHN E. BUSH, Co. F. 121st Regt., 20 years. [6/3]
May 4, 1864, Morris, Mrs. SARAH J. NILES, 28 years. [6/3]
June 3, 1864, Hospital in Washington, TITUS SAVAGE of Cooperstown, 21 years. [6/10]
May 30, 1864, Clarksville, Mrs. SALLY S. DAVIS, 71 years. [6/10]
[no date], Milford, Lieut. DAVID MEAD, 34 years. [6/17]

May 6, 1864, Battle of Wilderness, FENIMORE LEWIS of Cooperstown. [6/17]
June 8, 1864, Hospital in Alexandria, JAMES H. DUTCHER, 26 years. [6/17]
May 20, 1864, Fredericksburg, ALFRED WELCH of Richfield Spa. [6/17]
June 9, 1864, Washington, GEORGE BELCHER of Laurens, 18 years. [6/24]
June 17, 1864, Unadilla, ABBIE NORTON. [6/24]
June 17, 1864, Middlefield, JENNIE O. ANEY, 4 years. [7/1]
June 12, 1864, Springfield, FENIMORE C. CAREY, 25 years. [7/1]
June 7, 1864, Pittsfield, Mrs. LOUISA PERRY, 37 years. [7/8]
July 12, 1864, Otsego, JAMES O. FREEMAN, 14 years. [7/15]
July 4, 1864, Middlefield, ODELL MANCHESTER, 10 years. [7/22]
June 16, 1864, ALBERT DEVILLE WALKER, 3 years. [7/22]
July 26, 1864, Cooperstown, JOEL W. STONE, 35 years. [7/29]
June 28, 1864, Milford, MATHIAS LANE, 65 years. [7/29]
June 25, 1864, Milford, Mrs. CYNTHIA LANE, 64 years. [7/29]
June 19, 1864, Middlefield, Mrs. LUCY COFFIN, 80 years. [7/29]
[no date], Otsego, WILLIAM PIERCE, infant. [8/1]
July 30, 1864, Otego, Mrs. HELEN A. HOGOBOOM, 27 years. [8/1]
July 5, 1864, Pittsburg, PA, J. LEVI KINNE of Morris, 23 years. [8/5]
June 29, 1864, Maryland, CHARLES H. SEWARD, 39 years. [8/5]
July 19, 1864, Cooperstown, CHARLES E. MERRIHEW, 22 years. [8/12]
Aug. 6, 1864, Middlefield, ANTHONY LINES, 74 years. [8/12]
Aug. 3, 1864, Milford, POLLY STOCKER, 74 years. [8/12]
Aug. 5, 1864, Pittsfield, CAROLINE R. CARD, 13 years. [8/19]
Aug. 11, 1864, Pittsfield, HENRY ELLIS GROSS, 7 years. [8/19]
July 15, 1864, Middlefield, Mrs. CYNTHIA BOWEN, 82 years. [8/19]
Aug. 14, 1864, Exeter, Mrs. POLLY CASE, 61 years. [8/26]
Aug. 18, 1864, Edmeston, Mrs. LOVINA B. BOOTMAN, 28 years. [8/26]
Aug. 21, 1864, Edmeston, ROBERT E. RUSSELL, 75 years. [8/26]
Sept. 11, 1864, Westford, HARRIET PLATNER, 2 years. [9/16]
Sept. 19, 1864, Cooperstown, SIMEON WATERMAN, 89 years. [9/23]
Sept. 19, 1864, Cooperstown, SAMUEL M. INGALS, 85 years. [9/30]
Sept. 16, 1864, Fly Creek, RUTH LEONTINE, 25 years. [9/30]
Sept. 21, 1864, Pittsfield, Mrs. ARVILLA A. FRY, 45 years. [10/7]
Sept. 20, 1864, Middlefield, LUCIUS PALMER, 77 years. [10/14]
[no date] City Point, VA, RANDOLPH FIELDS of Schenevus, 27 years. [10/14]
Oct. 15, 1864, Fly Creek, ROB E. WILLIAMS, 10 mos. [10/21]
Oct. 12, 1864, Richfield, JAMES WILSIE, 39 years. [10/21]

Oct. 20, 1864, Hart. Sem., ALICE LOUISA DERBYSHIRE, 3 years. [10/28]
Oct. 10, 1864, Cooperstown, JAMES I. COATS, 23 years. [10/28]
Oct. 9, 1864, Otsego, Mrs. SOPHIA HURD, 62 years. [10/28]
Sept. 29, 1864, Springfield, MA, JOHN BUSH of Exeter (soldier), 36 years. [10/28]
Oct. 20, 1864, Newtown, VA, Lt. ISAAC B. BURCH of Cooperstown, 26 years. [11/4]
Oct. 18, 1864, Morris, ASIA T. HOLBROOK, 58 years. [11/4]
Oct. 16, 1864, Spooner's Corners, URSULA SPOONER, 72 years. [11/4]
May 5, 1864, Milford, Mrs. ESTHER STEVENS, 87 years. [11/4]
Oct. 29, 1864, Springfield, Mrs. HANNAH FIELD, 84 years. [11/11]
Oct. 14, 1864, Hartwick, SQUIRE CAMP, 68 years. [11/11]
Sept. 19, 1864, Memphis, TN, Capt. PAUL A. QUEAL of Worcester, 31 years. [11/11]
Oct. 19, 1864, Cooperstown, GEORGE FITCH, soldier. [11/18]
Aug. 7, 1864, Lt. JOS. HINDS. [11/18]
Nov. 8, 1864, Middlefield Cen., BILLINGS BURLINGHAM, 82 years. [11/25]
[no date] Middlefield Cent., Mrs. ESTHER SAXTON, 86 years. [12/2]
Nov. 17, 1864, Westford, Mrs. DOLLY TYLER, 82 years. [12/2]
Nov. 23, 1864, Cooperstown, Dr. W. WEBBER RYDER, 30 years. [12/2]
Nov. 30, 1864, Roseboom, DEETTE PIERCE, 10 years. [12/16]
Dec. 17, 1864, Westford, BENJAMIN WESTCOTT, 49 years. [12/23]
Dec. 17, 1864, Otego, NICHOLAS HOGOBOOM, 75 years. [12/23]
Nov. 19, 1864, Richfield Spa, DAVE BROWN, 68 years. [12/30]
Dec. 24, 1864, Hartwick, WILLIAM HARRINGTON, 58 years. [12/30]
Jan. 7, 1865, Cooperstown, Mrs. HARRIET T. MERCHANT, 23 years. [1/13]
Jan. 10, 1865, Otsego, JOHN EDDY, 7 years. [1/13]
Nov. 18, 1864, E. Springfield, BENJAMIN STOCKER, 74 years. [1/13/1865]
Dec. 6, 1864, Chattanooga, JAMES H. WATERS (Utica), 23 years. [1/13/1865]
Dec. 15, 1864, Anoka, Minn., HENRY RUSSELL (Hartwick), 29 years. [1/13/1865]
Dec. 17, 1864, Otsego, Mrs. SUSANNAH CUNNINGHAM, 65 years. [1/20/1865]
Jan. 7, 1865, Hartwick Sem., Mrs. EIETHEA [?] DERBYSHIRE, 74 years. [1/20/1865]
Sept. 8, 1864, Milford, Mrs. DELIA G. BARNARD, 55 years. [1/20/1865]

Dec. 15, 1864, New Lisbon, Mrs. LIZA GLEDHILL, 62 years. [1/27/1865]
Dec. 1, 1864, Springhill, VA, Capt. C. ALPHONSO PARSHALL, formerly of Middlefield, 25 years. [1/27/1865]
Jan. 15, 1865, Oneonta, Mrs. ELECTA LUTHER, 72 years. [1/27]
Jan. 26, 1865, Otego, AARON WOOD, 55 years. [2/3]
Feb. 1, 1865, Butternuts, RICHARD MORRIS, 82 years. [2/10]
Feb. 5, 1865, Hartwick Sem., Mrs. ANN E. MILLER, 42 years. [2/10]
Jan. 25, 1865, Fly Creek, Mrs. FANNY M. NORTHRUP, 66 years. [2/10]
Feb. 1, 1864 [sic], Pierstown, MC KEAN T. ALLEN, 10 years. [2/10/1865]
Sept. 26, 1864, Florence, SC, GEORGE T. ADAMS (Middlefield), 32 years. [2/10]
[no date] Decatur, RICHARD IDE HARTWELL, 16 years. [2/10]
Nov. 22, 1864, Cherry Valley, ALICE M. MC RORIE, 1 year. [2/17]
Aug. 9, 1864, City Point, VA, GEORGE H. RYNDERS, Otsego, 29 years. [2/17/1865]
Feb. 2, 1865, Middlefield, JOHN DENTON, 85 years. [2/17]
Feb. 16, 1865, Schenevus, Lt. S. B. KELLEY, 23 years. [2/24]
Feb. 12, 1865, Westford, Mrs. FRANCES M. SNYDER, 34 years. [2/24]
Jan. 17, 1865, New Lisbon, LEONARD THAYER, 64 years. [2/24]
Feb. 16, 1865, Burlington, ASA MEACHAM, 72 years. [2/24]
Feb. 17, 1865, Cooperstown, CLARINDA REED, 51 years. [3/3]
Jan. 25, 1865, Hartwick, WILLIAM H. AUGUR, 45 years. [3/3]
Feb. 17, 1865, Hartwick, Mrs. JULIA A. TOMPSON, 54 years. [3/3]
Jan. 20, 1865, Lovettsville, VA, LEWIS SHELMAN, 21 years. [3/3]
Feb. 7, 1865, Springfield, JENNIE CASLER, 5 years. [3/10]
March 7, 1865, Westford, JOHN R. GRIGGS, 59 years. [3/24]
March 10, 1865, Springfield Cen., J. CLELLIE WOOD, 1 year. [3/24]
March 20, 1865, Schenevus, Mrs. SARAH STEVER, 66 years. [3/31]
Feb. 23, 1865, Otego, MARION TRASK, 23 years. [4/7]
March 25, 1865, E. Springfield, THOMAS FRANCIS, 56 years. [4/7]
March 17, 1865, Westford, Mrs. DOTHE BIRGE. [4/7]
March 11, 1865, Laurens, LLOYD BROWN, 20 years. [4/7]
March 31, 1865, Laurens, Capt. JAMES RATHBUN, 78 years. [4/14]
April 11, 1865, Toddsville, HARRIET B. BURCH, 43 years. [4/14]
April 17, 1865, Clarksville, FANNY WARREN, 4 years. [4/28]
April 4, 1865, Hartwick, HARVEY TUCKER, 45 years. [4/28]
April 8, 1865, Cooperstown, MARY L. RAY, 3 years. [4/28]
April 23, 1865, Oneonta, HENRY E. CARPENTER, 32 years. [5/5]
April 12, 1865, Burlington, HORACE ALGER, 66 years. [5/5]

April 28, 1865, Otsego, JOHN R. RICHARDS, 70 years. [5/5]
April 12, 1865, Fly Creek, ASAHEL B. DAVIDSON, 81 years. [5/5]
April 27, 1865, Roseboom, GURNSEY D. HUBBARD, 24 years. [5/12]
May 9, 1865, Pierstown, JOHN C. COLE, 72 years. [5/19]
May 15, 1865, Cooperstown, ALBERT R. ALVERSON, Hounsfield, NY, 72 years. [5/19]
May 13, 1865, Springfield, Mrs. HANNAH SLITER, 59 years. [5/19]
May 10, 1865, Clarksville, Mrs. JANE GRIFFIN (Westford), 65 years. [5/26]
[no date] Springfield, JOHN MONK, 68 years. [5/26]
April 9, 1865, Burlington, ROBERT LOUGH, 46 years. [5/26]
May 25, 1865, Hartwick, JAMES STEERE, 74 years. [6/2]
May 19, 1865, Cherry Valley, JACOB LIVINGSTON, 85 years. [6/2]
March 19, 1865, Cherry Valley, Mrs. MARIA ROSE, 79 years. [6/2]
June 12, 1865, Cooperstown, LOOMIS BROWN, 50 years. [6/16]
June 3, 1865, Cooperstown, THOMAS BUNYAN, 27 years. [6/16]
June 8, 1865, Edmeston, THOMAS RICHARDS, 40 years. [6/16]
June 18, 1865, Edmeston, EPHRAIM CHAMBERLAIN, 67 years. [6/23]
May 14, 1865, New Lisbon, Mrs. ALEXA STANTON, 25 years. [6/30]
June 21, 1865, Cooperstown, ALMA ANN FAULKNER, 8 years. [7/7]
July 11, 1865, Otego, GEORGE SCRAMLING, 50 years. [7/21]
July 26, 1865, Morris, CHAUNCEY MOORE, 61 years. [8/4]
July 16, 1865, New Lisbon, JOEL GROVER, 62 years. [8/4]
Aug. 1, 1865, Clarksville, JOSEPH W. REYNOLDS, 71 years. [8/11]
July 29, 1865, Burlington, JAMES BONNER, 47 years. [8/11]
July 20, 1865, Middlefield, THOMAS T. BROWN, 81 years. [8/11]
July 17, 1865, Milford, DEXTER WEELMAN, 33 years. [8/11]
July 22, 1865, Cooperstown, Mrs. ELIZA ADAMS, 59 years. [8/11]
June 24, 1865, Plainfield, HARLON P. CUMMINGS. [8/18]
June 20, 1865, Otego, RUFUS POPE, 67 years. [9/8]
Aug. --, 1865, Westville, ASA DENTON, 76 years. [9/8]
Sept. 10, 1865, Otsego, MELVIN GIBBS, 11 years. [9/15]
Sept. 7, 1865, Wilmot, Wis., Mrs. TIMOTHY COOK, Milford, 44 years. [9/15]
Sept. 27, 1865, Cooperstown, KATE FULLER BARROWS, 26 years. [9/29]
Sept. 16, 1865, Middlefield, Mrs. EVELINE BICE, 58 years. [9/29]
Sept. 10, 1865, Oneonta, WILLIAM MOFFAT, infant.
Sept. 15, 1865, Unadilla, GEORGE F. WOOD, Carmichael, 3 years. [9/29]
Sept. 9, 1865, Springfield, Dea. RICHARD B. SYKES, 65 years. [9/29]

Oct. 4, 1865, Jersey City, Mrs. KATE WORTHINGTON GREGORY, 23 years. [10/6]
Oct. 20, 1865, Unadilla, ERASTUS KINGSLEY, [10/6]
Oct. 3, 1865, Otsego, JOEL L. SQUIRES, 48 years. [10/6]
Sept. 22, 1865, Otsego, Mrs. JULIA A. WHEELER, 48 years. [10/6]
Sept. 22, 1865, Otsego, FRED R. WHEELER, 1 year. [10/6]
Sept. 29, 1865, Richfield Spa, WILLIAM TUNNICLIFF, 41 years. [10/6]
Sept. 30, 1865, Westford, Mrs. EMILY BIDLAKE, 41 years. [10/6]
Sept. 4, 1865, Morris, JAMES ROOD, 85 years. [10/13]
June 14, 1865, Pittsfield, ELIAS ROOD, 60 years. [10/13]
Sept. 29, 1865, S. Hartwick, Mrs. SALLY BROOKS, 78 years. [10/13]
Oct. 20, 1865, Middlefield, MARTHA STICKLES, 12 years. [10/13]
Nov. 14, 1865, Cooperstown, IRCINE M. PERSONS, 38 years. [11/17]
Oct. 16, 1865, Hartwick Sem., Mrs. CORNELIA MERCER, 43 years. [11/24]
Nov. 19, 1865, Milford, MALINE HARDY, 24 years. [11/24]
Nov. 24, 1865, Cooperstown, Mrs. GEORGIANN KEESE, 59 years. [12/1]
Nov. 22, 1865, Clarkville, ELLEN A. GREEN, 23 years. [12/1]
Nov. 4, 1865, Hartwick, Dea. SOLOMON ROBINSON, 84 years. [12/1]
Nov. 27, 1865, Otego, WALTER C. FOLLETT, infant. [12/15]
Nov. 17, 1865, Springfield, Mrs. LAURA ECKERT, 78 years. [12/15]
Nov. 26, 1865, Maryland, STEPHEN PLATT, 69 years. [12/15]
Nov. 29, 1865, Exeter, ADELAIDE S. WILLMARTH, 22 years. [12/15]
Dec. 24, 1865, Cooperstown, JOHN SHORT, 12 years. [12/29]
Jan. 3, 1866, Cooperstown, WILLIAM G. S. HALL, 43 years. [1/5]
Oct. 19, 1865, Exeter, OTTO M. DAUCHY, 20 years. [1/5/1866]
Dec. 30, 1865, Milford, S. LOOMIS RUSSELL, 42 years. [1/5/1866]
Dec. 26, 1865, Milford, ELIZABETH DONNELLY, 77 years. [1/5/1866]
Jan. 11, 1866, Morris, Mrs. HARRIET F. MATTESON, 26 years. [1/19]
Jan. 17, 1866, Cooperstown, Mrs. MARY CRANDAL, 70 years. [1/19]
Jan. 20, 1866, Otsego, Mrs. HANNAH KELLOGG, 73 years. [1/26]
Jan. 18, 1866, Cooperstown, Mrs. JULIA KEYES TUCKER, 32 years. [1/26]
Oct. 8, 1865, Fly Creek, LUZERNE B. SCOTT, 11 years. [2/1]
Feb. 3, 1866, Cooperstown, FRANK S. HOOKER, 11 years. [2/9]
Feb. 13, 1866, Milford, Mrs. SARAH BAKER, 34 years. [3/2]
Feb. 20, 1866, Oaksville, Mrs. EMMA KNOWLTON, 52 years. [3/2]
Feb. 6, 1866, Westville, Mrs. SARAH DENTON, 57 years. [3/2]
March 6, 1866, Cooperstown, SETH DOUBLEDAY, 72 years. [3/9]
March 7, 1866, Cooperstown, Rev. F. MC CURRY, 30 years. [3/9]

March 7, 1866, Cooperstown, JAMES FENIMORE COOPER, s[on] RICHARD, 13 years. [3/9]
March 6, 1866, Cooperstown, GEORGE BENJAMIN GRANT, 7 years. [3/9]
March 1, 1866, Exeter, Mrs. EUNICE WHITE, 73 years. [3/9]
March 12, 1866, Cooperstown, LOUISA A. GRAVES, 24 years. [3/16]
March 13, 1866, Cooperstown, ANNIE GRACE SCOTT, 9 years. [3/16]
March 10, 1866, Cooperstown, CHARLES WADSWORTH, 6 years. [3/16]
March 6, 1866, Westford, LOUISA HULL, 39 years. [3/16]
March 1, 1866, Milford, LESLIE E. CLARK, infant. [3/16]
Feb. 22, 1866, Springfield, MARTIN YOUNG, 50 years. [3/16]
March 9, 1866, Hartwick, Mrs. ABIGAIL MUMFORD, 39 years. [3/16]
March 19, 1866, Cooperstown, Mrs. LOIS E. BABCOCK, 48 years. [3/23]
March 18, 1866, Cooperstown, NELLIE NEWELL, 11 years. [3/23]
March 19, 1866, Middlefield, CLARENCE J. WOOD, 16 years. [3/23]
March 6, 1866, S. Valley, WALLACE PRATT, 8 years. [3/23]
March 19, 1866, Otsego, Mrs. HANNAH LEWIS, 40 years. [3/23]
March 19, 1866, Middlefield, NAOMI J. ADAMS, 28 years. [3/23]
March 1, 1866, Worcester, MARY M. GRANT, 21 years. [3/23]
March 8, 1866, New Lisbon, EBER HINMAN, 73 years. [3/23]
March 21, 1866, Westford, EMILY M. TYLER, 20 years. [3/30]
March 24, 1866, Cooperstown, MINNIE E. GILBERT, 6 years. [3/30]
March 25, 1866, Cooperstown, GEORGE D. ALLEN, 2 years. [3/30]
March 27, 1866, Cooperstown, JAMES W. BROCKHAM, 6 years. [3/30]
March 2, 1866, Morris, Mrs. ELINA J. LULL, 20 years. [3/30]
March 31, 1866, Cooperstown, DAVID BALL, 61 years. [4/6]
Feb. 24, 1866, Oaksville, EDGAR C. FITCH, 22 years. [4/6]
Feb. 26, 1866, Oaksville, Mrs. MARY C. FITCH, 42 years. [4/6]
Feb. 25, 1866, Middlefield, ALVIN ECKLER, 33 years. [4/6]
April 6, 1866, Cooperstown, ANNA BLUNK, 5 years. [4/13]
March 23, 1866, Otsego, MARY J. WHITWILL, 21 years. [4/13]
[no date], Hartwick, Mrs. ANN E. GREEN, 36 years. [4/13]
March 31, 1866, Richfield, JESSIE K. LEWIS, 5 years. [4/13]
April 11, 1866, Cooperstown, ARTHUR H. RUSSELL, 18 mos. [4/20]
April 9, 1866, Laurens, THANKFUL HARRINGTON, 78 years. [4/20]
April 19, 1866, Cooperstown, MARY A. LEWIS, 13 years. [4/27]
April 23, 1866, Cooperstown, MARY A. SPENCER, 24 years. [4/27]
April 21, 1866, Hartwick, Mrs. MINERVA N. KING, 37 years. [4/27]
April 11, 1866, Summit, Wis., Mrs. SOPHIA PHINNEY KING, 77 years. [4/27]

April 29, 1866, Cooperstown, CYRUS LEWIS, 37 years. [5/11]
March 30, 1866, Toddsville, JOHN I. HOUCK, 77 years. [5/11]
April 30, 1866, Richfield Spa, MAJOR W. LEWIS, 2 years. [5/11]
May 11, 1866, Cooperstown, Mrs. MARCIA MC NAMEE, 81 years. [5/18]
May 11, 1866, Cooperstown, GEORGE E. MISSON, 5 years. [5/18]
May 5, 1866, Toddsville, Mrs. SARAH A. MURDOCK, 46 years. [5/18]
May 26, 1866, Cooperstown, GEORGE L. BOWNE, 49 years. [6/1]
May 27, 1866, Burlington, ELISHA DORR SILL, 68 years. [6/1]
May 23, 1866, Butternuts, MARIA E. STEWART, 21 years. [6/1]
April 14, 1866, Burlington, JAMES E. CLARK, 20 years. [6/8]
May 31, 1866, Middlefield, Mrs. CHARITY HOOSE, 70 years. [6/15]
June 6, 1866, Cooperstown, ROBERT H. SMITH, 14 years. [6/22]
June 10, 1866, Cooperstown, MARY A. CLARK, 47 years. [6/22]
June 21, 1866, Cooperstown, Mrs. CHARLOTTE SWARTWOUT, 44 years. [6/22]
June 11, 1866, Cooperstown, CHARLES A. ROBINSON, 18 years. [6/22]
June 14, 1866, Otsego, Mrs. SARAH A. SABIN, 49 years. [6/22]
June 7, 1866, Middlefield, Mrs. LOIS HINMAN, 64 years. [6/22]
June 3, 1866, Middlefield, ANN ELIZA PEASLEE, 20 years. [6/29]
July 4, 1866, Cooperstown, DON F. LIDELL, 32 years. [7/6]
July 3, 1866, Cooperstown, JOHN S. OLIVE, 84 years. [7/6]
June 20, 1866, Butternuts, HELEN E. HOLLIS, 27 years. [7/6]
June 20, 1866, Hartwick, ANN CHASE, 15 years. [7/6]
May 14, 1866, Oaksville, CORNELIUS C. FISH, 58 years. [7/13]
July 8, 1866, Milford, CORA M. WESTCOTT, 9 years. [7/20]
July 19, 1866, Otsego, Mrs. BETSEY ALLEN, 28 years. [8/3]
Aug. 2, 1866, Otsego, JULIUS WARREN, 81 years. [8/10]
July 31, 1866, Oneonta, SAMUEL B. BEACH, 80 years. [8/10]
July 21, 1866, Otsego, WILLIAM HULL, 90 years. [8/10]
July 22, 1866, Middlefield, AMOS D. WICKWIRE, infant. [8/10]
July 12, 1866, Burlington Green, HIRAM SOULES, 31 years. [8/10]
Aug. 6, 1866, New Lisbon, ELIJAH C. PERRY, 27 years. [8/17]
Aug. 15, 1866, Phoenix Mills, FREDERICK C. WOOD, 2 years. [8/24]
Aug. 17, 1866, Cooperstown, THOMAS M. CLARKE, 18 years. [8/31]
Aug. 17, 1866, Cooperstown, Mrs. MARIA M. FITCH, 63 years. [8/31]
Aug. 27, 1866, Toddsville, GRACE P. STEERE, 6 years. [8/31]
Sept. 18, 1866, Cooperstown, Mrs. E. M. BINGHAM, 42 years. [9/31]
Sept. 7, 1866, Cooperstown, BELLE SIVER, 6 years. [9/21]
Sept. 14, 1866, Laurens, DANIEL DUNBAR, 90 years. [9/28]
Sept. 22, 1866, Cooperstown, WILLIAM WILSON, 77 years. [10/5]

Aug. 16, 1866, Middlefield, HARVEY R. SHORT, 28 years. [10/5]
Sept. 28, 1866, Schenevus, JENETTE R. MORSE, 29 years. [10/12]
Oct. 5, 1866, Clarksville, Mrs. HANNAH PARSHALL, 58 years. [10/12]
Oct. 5, 1866, Hartwick, JOANNA LYONS, 42 years. [10/26]
Oct. 4, 1866, Edmeston, Mrs. FREELOVE PEET, 43 years. [10/26]
Oct. 12, 1866, Laurens, ALLIDA M. FERGUSON, 46 years. [10/26]
Oct. 14, 1866, Westford, PETER L. NELLIS, 77 years. [10/26]
Oct. 3, 1866, Otsego, SAMUEL W. WILSON, 26 years. [11/2]
Oct. 13, 1866, Fly Creek, Mrs. ELIZABETH BROWN, 75 years. [11/2]
Oct. 26, 1866, SAMUEL B. LEWIS, 26 years. [11/2]
Nov. 19, 1866, Cooperstown, FLORA TEMPLE, 8 years. [11/23]
Nov. 7, 1866, Cooperstown, Mrs. ANNIS BURKE, 90 years. [11/23]
Nov. 13, 1866, Otsego, Mrs. LYDIA WILLIAMS, 84 years. [11/23]
Nov. 12, 1866, Decatur, DANIEL SHARP, 49 years. [11/23]
Oct. 25, 1866, Morris, HARRIET N. ROOD, 51 years. [11/30]
Nov. 27, 1866, Hartwick Sem., Mrs. ABBY T. DAVISON, 64 years. [11/30]
Nov. 12, 1866, Middlefield, JAMES S. MURPHY, 3 years. [12/7]
Dec. 7, 1866, Cooperstown, LYMAN J. WALWORTH, 65 years. [12/14]
Nov. 27, 1866, Burlington, Mrs. MARY PARKER, 21 years. [12/14]
Dec. 29, 1866, Fly Creek, Mrs. MARY E. METCALF, 21 years. [1/4/1867]
Jan. 1, 1867, Cooperstown, ABRAM LAMBERT, 55 years. [1/4]
Jan. 4, 1867, Fly Creek, Rev. MARTIN MARVIN, 66 years. [1/11]
Dec. 25, 1866, Richfield, Mrs. NELLIE A. MC RORIE, 20 years. [1/11/1867]
Dec. 15, 1866, Springfield, Mrs. LUCY ALLEN, 63 years. [1/18/1867]
Dec. 29, 1866, Cooperstown, GRACE B. NEWELL, 4 years. [1/18]
[no date] Springfield, DANIEL WILES, 65 years. [1/25]
Nov. 30, 1866, Milford, Mrs. LAVINA AYLESWORTH, 66 years. [1/25/1867]
Dec. 30, 1866, Hartwick, DAVIS WARD, 69 years. [1/25/1867]
Jan. 22, 1867, Cooperstown, LAVIRA EDDY, 19 years. [1/25]
Jan. 18, 1867, Middlefield, Mrs. LUCY D. GRIFFIN, 60 years. [1/25]
Jan. 23, 1867, Cooperstown, Mrs. HANNAH M. RICH, 24 years. [1/25]
Jan. 15, 1867, Unadilla, Mrs. MARY BALESTIER, 25 years. [1/25]
Feb. 1, 1867, Cherry Valley, GILBERT VAN ALSTYNE, 90 years. [1/25]
Dec. 5, 1866, Cherry Valley, SQUIRE BRIGGS, 89 years. [1/25/1867]
Jan. 17, 1867, Pittsfield, HENRY MOORE, 62 years. [1/25]
Jan. 28, 1867, Richfield Spa, MARY LOUISE HORTON, 17 years. [2/8]
Jan. 27, 1867, Hartwick, AMOS MAPLES, 62 years. [2/8]
Feb. 1, 1867, Middlefield, L. MAUDE SAXTON, 1 year. [2/8]

Feb. 11, 1867, Cooperstown, Mrs. IMOGENE CORY, 26 years. [2/15]
Feb. 9, 1867, Cooperstown, JOHN C. MOAK, 29 years. [2/15]
Jan. 24, 1867, Hartwick, CHESTER PHILLIPS, 7 years. [2/15]
Jan. 27, 1867, Unadilla, FRANCES ODELL, 18 years. [2/15]
Jan. 31, 1867, East Worcester, JOHN CHAMPION, 64 years. [2/22]
Jan. 31, 1867, Cooperstown, EDWARD CHILDS, infant. [2/22]
Feb. 8, 1867, Hartwick, SAMUEL H. HUCHINS, 39 years. [2/22]
Jan. 29, 1867, Morris, ANSON TURNER, 63 years. [3/1]
Feb. 16, 1867, Hartwick, ADELBERT JACOBS, 23 years. [3/1]
Feb. 18, 1867, Laurens, Mrs. CHADDEN, 73 years. [3/1]
Feb. 22, 1867, Oneonta, WILLIAM H. HUDSON, 26 years. [3/1]
Feb. 15, 1867, Otego, Mrs. C. M. HUBBARD, 30 years. [3/1]
Feb. 21, 1867, Otego, Mrs. E. A. PARLIN, 44 years. [3/1]
Feb. 25, 1867, Hartwick, CHAUNCEY T. SMITH, 52 years. [3/8]
Feb. 19, 1867, Milford, Mrs. EREXENE DINGMAN, 36 years. [3/8]
March 5, 1867, Hartwick, ISAAC TUCKER, 19 years. [3/8]
March 4, 1867, Cooperstown, ANDREW B. BOGUE, 22 years. [3/8]
March 1, 1867, Morris, ANDREW G. WASHBURN, 78 years. [3/8]
March 10, 1867, Middlefield, MATTIE FLING, 2 years. [3/15]
March 9, 1867, Hartwick, GEORGIANNA FITCH, infant. [3/15]
March 7, 1867, Westford, Mrs. AMANDA M. SALISBURY, 40 years. [3/15]
March 7, 1867, Burlington, THEODORE L. SMITH, 90 years. [3/15]
March 16, 1867, Cooperstown, MARY JACKSON, 29 years. [3/15]
Feb. 28, 1867, Cooperstown, JOHN BRIMMER, 67 years. [3/15]
Feb. 27, 1867, Laurens, Mrs. HARRIET FIELDS, 47 years. [3/15]
March 30, 1867, Milford Center, Mrs. MARY RUSSELL, 64 years. [4/5]
March 31, 1867, Milford, THOMAS HOAG, 79 years. [4/12]
Sept. 30, 1866, Edmeston, Mrs. ABIGAIL SPENCER, 77 years. [4/19/1867]
April 1, 1867, Edmeston, Mrs. LUCY J. SPENCER, 39 years. [4/19]
April 7, 1867, Laurens, CLARA E. STANTON, 1 year. [4/19]
April 21, 1867, Cooperstown, STEPHEN GREGORY, 77 years. [4/26]
Feb. 16, 1867, Middlefield, EMMA ECKLER, infant. [4/26]
April 12, 1867, Unadilla, CARRINGTON F. NOBLE, 39 years. [4/26]
April 11, 1867, Canville, KS, CEYLON O. LIPPITT of Cooperstown, 34 years. [5/3]
April 13, 1867, Garratsville, Mrs. MARY SHOVE, 60 years. [5/10]
May 12, 1867, Cooperstown, JENNIE LEWIS of Oneonta, 16 years. [5/17]
May 14, 1867, Cooperstown, EUGENE PECK, 17 years. [5/17]
April 20, 1867, Hartwick, CORA E. HOLDRIDGE, 1 year. [5/17]

April 28, 1867, Otsego, Mrs. NANCY M. HOUSE, 73 years. [5/17]
May 15, 1867, Milford Center, Capt. WILLIAM L. WRIGHT, 88 years. [5/24]
April 3, 1867, Springfield, JAMES YOUNG, 77 years. [5/24]
May 14, 1867, Cooperstown, Mrs. CANDACE B. ANGELL, 65 years. [5/24]
May 23, 1867, Hartwick, Mrs. OLIVE HOWE, 58 years. [5/31]
May 28, 1867, Morris, JOHN BOWNE, 9 years. [5/31]
June 3, 1867, Cooperstown, CHAUNCEY M. CHAPMAN, 69 years. [6/7]
May 25, 1867, Exeter, WILLIAM FITCH of Milford, 79 years. [6/7]
April 28, 1867, Unadilla Forks, EDITH M. BABCOCK, 2 years. [6/21]
June 27, 1867, Cooperstown, Mrs. ALMIRA LUCE, 67 years. [7/5]
June 11, 1867, New Lisbon, LEROY S. PORTER, 21 years. [7/5]
July 1, 1867, Hartwick, ALBA ADAMS, 67 years. [7/5]
July 8, 1867, Springfield, Mrs. DEBORAH HENDRYX, 78 years. [7/12]
July 3, 1867, Springfield, JAMES D. SCOLLARD, 67 years. [7/12]
June 9, 1867, Springfield, JOHN C. SCOLLARD, infant. [7/12]
July 5, 1867, Westford, FREDERICK L. SPAFFORD, 22 years. [7/19]
July 11, 1867, Springfield, THOMAS COOK, 37 years. [7/26]
July 7, 1867, Oaksville, Mrs. ARTEMESIA KNOWLTON, 67 years. [7/26]
July 15, 1867, Otsego, Mrs. BETSEY KANE, 80 years. [7/26]
July 5, 1867, New Lisbon, ZEBULON BARTON, 39 years. [7/26]
July 2, 1867, Laurens, RENSSELAER KENYON, 54 years. [8/2]
June 1, 1867, Roseboom, HIRAM BARTON, 63 years. [8/9]
July 19, 1867, Toddsville, JUDSON D. WHEELER, 28 years. [8/9]
Aug. 5, 1867, Hartwick, STEPHEN CRONKHITE, 77 years. [8/16]
Aug. 2, 1867, Otsego, Mrs. SARAH B. PADDEN, 55 years. [8/16]
[no date] Westford, Mrs. ANN BEDEAU, 64 years. [8/16]
Aug. 9, 1867, Morris, NELSON BALLARD, 59 years. [8/16]
Aug. 9, 1867, Cooperstown, Mrs. MARY MC LEAN, 55 years. [8/23]
Aug. 12, 1867, Richfield, LAURA CARY, 47 years. [8/23]
Aug. 17, 1867, Otego, HEZEKIAH M. COLE, 37 years. [8/23]
Aug. 16, 1867, Oneonta, ANDREW PARRISH, 84 years. [8/23]
Aug. 17, 1867, W. Laurens, NELLIE D. BENNETT, 18 years. [8/23]
Aug. 17, 1867, Otsego, Mrs. CLARISSA ELDRED, 69 years. [8/30]
July 6, 1867, Westford, Mrs. ANN M. BROWN, 19 years. [8/30]
Aug. 17, 1867, Roseboom, EMELINE BARTON, 28 years. [8/30]
Aug. 5, 1867, W. Burlington, GEORGE R. BROOKS, 39 years. [9/67]
Aug. 28, 1867, Middlefield Cen., Mrs. BETHANY CLYDE, 57 years. [9/6]
Sept. 16, 1867, Cooperstown, Mrs. JILPHA BABCOCK, 90 years. [9/20]
Sept. 2, 1867, Hartwick, DELILAH BLANCHARD, 13 years. [9/20]

Sept. 6, 1867, Toddsville, IRA WHEELER, 78 years. [9/20]
Sept. 6, 1867, Butternuts, Mrs. ELIZABETH KNAPP, 74 years. [9/20]
Sept. 1, 1867, Hartwick, Dea. JOHN L. LATTIN, 61 years. [9/27]
Sept. 19, 1867, Milford, Mrs. CORNELIA PEASLEE, 72 years. [10/4]
Oct. 7, 1867, Cooperstown, Mrs. EMILY SHORT, 49 years. [10/11]
Oct. 5, 1867, Pierstown, CHARLES KELLOGG, 81 years. [10/11]
Aug. 9, 1867, Morris, NELSON BALLARD, 57 years. [10/11]
Oct. 20, 1867, Cooperstown, DANIEL P. TEMPLE, 33 years. [10/25]
Oct. 19, 1867, Burlington, Mrs. LUCINDA HUBBELL, 67 years. [10/25]
Nov. 6, 1867, Cooperstown, WILLIAM K. BINGHAM, 49 years. [11/8]
Oct. 28, 1867, Pittsfield, Mrs. ELEANOR HALL, 66 years. [11/8]
Oct. 9, 1867, Westford, ANN ASHLEY, 20 years. [11/15]
Nov. 1, 1867, Springfield Center, JAMES THAYER, 46 years. [11/15]
Nov. 19, 1867, Cooperstown, Mrs. SOPHIA TEMPLE, 41 years. [11/22]
Nov. 15, 1867, Cooperstown, ARIEL THAYER, 82 years. [11/22]
Nov. 15, 1867, Cooperstown, CHARLES W. MARSHALL, 35 years. [11/22]
Nov. 16, 1867, Cooperstown, B. SILAS HOWE, 63 years. [11/22]
Nov. 20, 1867, Otsego, Mrs. ABIGAIL OLMSTEAD, 74 years. [11/22]
Nov. 21, 1867, Cooperstown, EDWARD S. HICKLING, infant. [11/29]
Nov. 23, 1867, Cooperstown, Mrs. MARY A. HARPER, 48 years. [11/29]
Oct. 25, 1867, Byron, Wis., CARLTON J. MUMFORD, 23 years. [12/13]
Dec. 15, 1867, Hartwick, E. C. AVERY, 46 years. [12/20]
Dec. 25, 1867, Cooperstown, MARY BOWERS, 14 years. [12/20 sic]
Oct. 26, 1867, Fly Creek, IRA HYDE, 54 years. [12/20]
Dec. 16, 1867, Exeter Center, Mrs. MINERVA COUNRAD, 56 years. [12/20]
Dec. 3, 1867, Jacksonville, Mrs. HARRIET GARDNER, 47 years. [1/3/1868]
Dec. 27, 1867, Middlefield, Mrs. ELIZABETH VUNK, 67 years. [1/3/1868]
Nov. 8, 1867, Morris, EDWIN MAYNARD, 44 years. [1/17/1868]
Jan. 9, 1868, Middlefield, ASENATH BATES, 86 years. [1/24]
Jan. 9, 1868, Cherry Valley, Mrs. MARY ANN O'CONNELL, 50 years. [1/24]
Jan. 2, 1868, Hartwick, Mrs. RHODA ROBINSON, 57 years. [1/24]
Dec. 12, 1867, New Lisbon, ELIZA B. SMITH, 56 years. [1/24/1868]
Dec. 31, 1867, Clarksville, HIRAM ISMOND, 60 years. [1/31/1868]
Jan. 14, 1868, W. Burlington, PAULINE GARRETT, 65 years. [2/14]
Feb. 10, 1868, Hartwick, ELIZABETH T. FERGUSON, 17 years. [2/14]
Dec. 12, 1868, Toddsville, CYRUS DAGGETT, 11 years. [2/14/1868]

Feb. 18, 1868, Cherry Valley, CHARLES BOTSFORD, 19 years. [2/14]
Feb. 12, 1868, Exeter, Mrs. CORNELIA G. LEWIS, 62 years. [2/14]
Feb. 11, 1868, New Lisbon, Mrs. ELLEN LAIDLER, 59 years. [2/28]
Feb. 5, 1868, Fly Creek, STEPHEN R. WELSH, 76 years. [2/28]
Feb. 20, 1868, Cooperstown, HIRAM S. BABCOCK, 57 years. [2/28]
Feb. 4, 1868, Burlington, ABRAM PARKER, 73 years. [2/28]
Feb. 21, 1868, Butternuts, JAMES H. TRUMAN, 3 years. [3/6]
Feb. 20, 1868, Butternuts, NATHAN TRUMAN, 2 years. [3/6]
March 1, 1868, Oaksville, EVERETT D. PRESTON, 35 years. [3/6]
March 8, 1868, Cooperstown, Mrs. MARY SCHROM, 79 years. [3/13]
Feb. 7, 1868, Hartwick, Mrs. HULDAH CAULKINS, 55 years. [3/13]
March 3, 1868, Milford, JUSTICE SEEGAR, 16 years. [3/13]
March 1, 1868, Milford, CHARLES WARD, 2 years. [3/13]
Feb. 22, 1868, Middlefield, ERASTUS S. STERLING, 64 years. [3/20]
March 9, 1868, Middlefield, JOHN T. JOSLIN, 76 years. [3/20]
March 20, 1868, Fly Creek, MARIETTE TAYLOR, 27 years. [3/27]
March 23, 1868, Hartwick, ANDREW J. EDMUNDS, 20 years. [4/3]
March 11, 1868, Otsego, WILLIAM COOPER JARVIS, 18 years. [4/3]
March 28, 1868, Fly Creek, LEWIS DOUBLEDAY, 72 years. [4/3]
March 24, 1868, Oneonta, Mrs. CAROLINE B. WINSLOW, 34 years. [4/3]
March 23, 1868, S. Worcester, JOSIAH DORWIN, 79 years. [4/3]
March 29, 1868, Otego, CHARLES L. COBURN, 10 years. [4/3]
April 4, 1868, New Lisbon, Mrs. ZILPHA M. BROWNELL, 56 years. [4/10]
March 30, 1868, Morris, ELEAZER H. WARNER, 23 years. [4/10]
April 7, 1868, New Lisbon, WILLIS E. POTTER, 58 years. [4/10]
April 13, 1868, Cooperstown, STEPHEN L. WILLIAMS, 53 years. [4/17]
April 18, 1868, Cooperstown, Mrs. ALICE M. PARKER, 24 years. [4/24]
Jan. 18, 1868, Burlington, Mrs. LYDIA R. YEOMAN, 79 years. [5/1]
April 28, 1868, Chicago, MARTHA B. BRADFORD. [5/1]
March 13, 1868, Otsego, CYNTHIA WHITNEY, 75 years. [5/8]
May 4, 1868, New Lisbon, HANNAH THAYER, 63 years. [5/22]
May 8, 1868, Milford, Mrs. MARY A. DINGMAN, 31 years. [5/22]
May 12, 1868, Unadilla, Dr. JOHN COLWELL. [5/22]
April 24, 1868, Exeter, LODOWICK MOTT, 43 years. [5/5]
June 3, 1868, Hartwick, SYLVA ADAMS, 59 years. [6/12]
June 5, 1868, Milford Center, SUSAN MORRIS, 20 years. [6/12]
June 13, 1868, Richfield Spa, SOLOMON PIPER, 51 years. [6/19]
May 24, 1868, Sing Sing, Mrs. SARAH LULL, 32 years. [6/19]
June 19, 1868, Hartwick Sem., CHARLOTTE M. MITLER [sic] [6/26]

May 18, 1868, Morris, NATHANIEL BEERS, 79 years. [6/26]
June 8, 1868, Toddsville, ABRAM COON, 40 years. [6/26]
June 26, 1868, Cooperstown, ALICE M. SYNNOTT, infant. [7/3]
July 7, 1868, Cooperstown, Mrs. SALLY GREEN, 68 years. [7/10]
July 7, 1868, Otsego, BUCKINGHAM FITCH, 84 years. [7/10]
July 13, 1868, Cooperstown, BENJAMIN B. JOHNSTON, 8 years. [7/24]
July 13, 1868, Middlefield, Mrs. ELIZABETH GILBERT, 55 years. [7/24]
July 23, 1868, Otsego, Mrs. DAPHNE JARVIS, 75 years. [7/31]
July 19, 1868, New Lisbon, JENNIE JONES, 5 years. [7/31]
Aug. 1, 1868, Portlandville, Mrs. MALINDA DAVIS, 68 years. [8/7]
Aug. 2, 1868, Cooperstown, GEORGE M. LITTLE, infant. [8/21]
Aug. 2, 1868, New Lisbon, Mrs. BETSEY FITCH, 87 years. [8/21]
Aug. 20, 1868, Oneona, NANCY BURNSIDE, 70 years. [8/28]
Aug. 21, 1868, Milford Center, Mrs. SARAH ROSE, 24 years. [8/28]
[no date] Oneonta, MARTHA I. BREWER, 17 years. [8/28]
Aug. 11, 1868, Westford, WILLIAM HARRISON GROFF, 49 years. [9/4]
Sept. 7, 1868, Cooperstown, Dea. ALFRED ROBINSON, 53 years. [9/11]
Sept. 3, 1868, Cooperstown, WILLIAM NICHOLS, 82 years. [9/11]
Aug. 28, 1868, Hartwick, AARON LUTHER, 84 years. [9/11]
Sept. 11, 1868, Westford, Mrs. NANCY GRIGGS, 56 years. [9/25]
Sept. 16, 1868, Schenevus, WICKHAM GRISWOLD, 82 years. [9/25]
Sept. 19, 1868, Chaseville, Mrs. DANIEL HOUGHTON, 95 years. [9/25]
Aug. 24, 1868, Middlefield, JANE PRATT, 35 years. [10/2]
Sept. 16, 1868, Milford, PETER CLINE, 82 years. [10/2]
Sept. 7, 1868, Milford, NORMAN BISSELL, 85 years. [10/2]
Sept. 23, 1868, Milford, Mrs. ANN BARNARD, 74 years. [10/2]
Sept. 21, 1868, New Lisbon, Mrs. POLLY M. PECK, 75 years. [10/9]
Oct. 1, 1868, Middlefield, EDWIN D. NEWELL, 29 years. [10/9]
Oct. 16, 1868, Cooperstown, ALEXANDER P. BALL, 27 years. [10/23]
Oct. 6, 1868, Cooperstown, Mrs. ELIZA B. WELLMAN, 70 years. [10/23]
Sept. 19, 1868, Burlington, JAMES OLIVER, 86 years. [10/23]
Oct. 17, 1868, Springfield, ADOLPHUS SEEBER, 64 years. [10/30]
Oct. 21, 1868, Middlefield, ORRIS J. CUMMINGS, 27 years. [10/30]
Nov. 8, 1868, Cooperstown, CHARLES C. MC NELLY, 31 years. [11/13]
Nov. 10, 1868, Cooperstown, JACKSON MC NAMEE, 40 years. [11/13]
Oct. 31, 1868, Middlefield, HANNAH LYNES, 78 years. [11/13]
Nov. 5, 1868, Maryland, Mrs. SARAH W. IRISH, 52 years. [11/13]
Oct. 28, 1868, Huntsville, Ala., Col. ADDISON M. SMITH of Morris, 51 years. [11/13]
Nov 20, 1868, Otsego, LOUISA ST. JOHN, 42 years. [11/20]
Nov 20, 1868, Hartwick, ABBIE BELLE HARDY, 3 years. [11/20]

Nov. 29, 1868, New Lisbon, THOMAS EDMUNDS, 78 years. [12/11]
Nov. 5, 1868, Toddsville, Dr. WALTER ALMY, 83 years. [12/11]
Dec. 11, 1868, Otsego, Mrs. PAMELIA REED, 79 years. [12/25]
Dec. 21, 1868, Middlefield, ADDIE SPRINGSTEED, 4 years. [1/1/1869]
Dec. 24, 1868, Middlefield, JOSIAH SPRINGSTEED, 1 year. [1/1/1869]
Dec. 16, 1868, Cherry Valley, JOHN D. GROSS, 36 years. [1/1/1869]
Dec. 29, 1868, Hartwick, EZRA PEMBLETON, 43 years. [1/15/1869]
Jan. 20, 1869, Cooperstown, HENRY P. METCALF, 62 years. [1/22]
Oct. 24, 1868, Edmeston, PERRY POPE, 73 years. [1/29/1869]
Jan. 3, 1869, Cooperstown, Mrs. HARRIET E. GRANT, 45 years. [2/5]
Dec. 31, 1868, Otsego, Mrs. EMELINE WHITWELL, 59 years. [2/5/1869]
Jan. 27, 1869, Oneonta, Mrs. JULIA A. KROMER SNOW, 54 years. [2/5]
Jan. 21, 1869, Middlefield, JAMES C. BRATT, 37 years. [2/5]
Jan. 31, 1869, Otsego, Mrs. LEVINA DUGGLESBY, 24 years. [2/12]
Jan. 27, 1869, Exeter, DAN DARBY. [2/12]
Feb. 4, 1869, Westford, DAVID NASH ALLEN, 62 years. [2/12]
Feb. 13, 1869, Cooperstown, MARY ANN BODEN, 72 years. [2/19]
Feb. 11, 1869, Mt. Vision, JESSIE B. KEYON, 63 years. [2/19]
Feb. 12, 1869, Hartwick, GEORGE H. STUART, 71 years. [2/19]
Feb. 19, 1869, Otsego, MATTIE DUGGLEBY, infant. [2/26]
Feb. 6, 1869, Cherry Valley, Mrs. MARY ANN SPRAKER, 54 years. [3/5]
Feb. 22, 1869, S. Hartwick, FRANCES C. ELDRED, 13 years. [3/5]
March 1, 1869, Middlefield, LINN B. BROWN, 5 years. [3/5]
Feb. 21, 1869, Roseboom, Mrs. REBECCA D. POPE, 83 years. [3/5]
Feb. 14, 1869, Clifton, Ill., HENRY SILL of Burlington, NY, 83 years. [3/5]
March 10, 1869, Cooperstown, ABEL S. BABCOCK, 62 years. [3/12]
March 9, 1869, Cooperstown, GRAHAM STEWART LEE, 4 years. [3/12]
March 5, 1869, Middlefield Cen., Mrs. ALMERETTA TRIPP, 39 years. [3/12]
March 7, 1869, Middlefield Cen., FLORA E. BROWN, 3 years. [3/12]
March 6, 1869, Cherry Valley, WILLIAM LEANING, 73 years. [3/12]
Feb. 28, 1869, N. Lisbon, Mrs. SOPHIA EDMUNDS, 79 years. [3/12]
Feb. 17, 1869, Portlandville, OLIVER NEWELL, 50 years. [3/12]
Jan. 17, 1869, N. Lisbon, NATHAN JOHNSON, 59 years. [3/12]
March 10, 1869, Cooperstown, ABEL S. BABCOCK, 62 years. [3/19]
March 7, 1869, S. Worcester, JOHN STRAIN, 79 years. [3/19]
March 10, 1869, Oneonta, Mrs. MELISSA PERKINS, 55 years. [3/19]
Feb. 10, 1869, Oneonta, EZRA G. POTTER, 28 years. [3/19]
March 8, 1869, Oneonta, Mrs. MARIA DOOLITTLE, 44 years. [3/19]

Feb. 25, 1869, W. Laurens, Mrs. MARY D. BRIGGS, 24 years. [3/19]
March 17, 1869, Cooperstown, WILLIAM COOPER, 64 years. [3/26]
March 9, 1869, Otsego, Mrs. CATHERINE HERRICK, 84 years. [3/26]
March 18, 1869, Otsdawa, JAMES WEATHING, 58 years. [3/26]
March 21, 1869, Otsdawa, Mrs. SARAH M. OSBORN, 50 years. [3/26]
March 12, 1869, Otsdawa, Mrs. CATHERINE MARTIN, 79 years. [3/26]
March 13, 1869, Cooperstown, Mrs. SALLY ADAMS, 67 years. [4/2]
March 19, 1869, Decatur, S. A. DOUGLAS FERN, 6 years. [4/2]
March 19, 1869, Middlefield Cen., Rev. ALVAN PERMLEE, 66 years. [4/2]
March 20, 1869, Westford, M. CALVIN HOLMES, 73 years. [4/6]
March 24, 1869, Westford, Mrs. PETER ROSEBOOM, 70 years. [4/6]
March 29, 1869, Westford, PHILIP SALISBURY, 70 years. [4/6]
March 17, 1869, Brooklyn, BRIDGET KELLEY of Otsego, 24 years. [4/6]
March 24, 1869, Richfield Spa, Mrs. AURELIUS TUNNICLIFF, 55 years. [4/6]
April 5, 1869, Hartwick Sem., Rev. GEORGE B. MILLER, 73 years. [4/6]
March 21, 1869, N. Lisbon, WILLIS E. GARDNER, 54 years. [4/6]
March 25, 1869, Laurens, MATIE WINSOR, 3 years. [4/6]
March 15, 1869, New Lisbon, Mrs. ELIZABETH WHITE, 81 years. [4/6]
March 30, 1869, Westford, Mrs. MARIA SAULISBURY, 76 years. [4/16]
March 21, 1869, Otsdawa, Mrs. SARAH M. OSBORN, 50 years. [4/23]
April 21, 1869, Cooperstown, Mrs. MARIA MC GOWN, 73 years. [4/30]
April 24, 1869, Middlefield, RUSSELL SMITH, 95 years. [4/30]
April 14, 1869, Butternuts, Mrs. CAROLINE PETERS. [4/30]
April 22, 1869, Springfield, Mrs. JENNIE C. LAWLESS, 27 years. [4/30]
April 20, 1869, Sidney, Del. Co., STEPHEN ADAMS of Middlefield, 69 years. [4/30]
May 2, 1869, Cooperstown, MARIUS B. ANGELL, 38 years. [5/7]
May 7, 1869, Cooperstown, FREDERICK A. MURDOCK, 13 years. [5/14]
May 2, 1869, Worcester, Mrs. MARY W. ROGERS, 28 years. [5/14]
April 30, 1869, Middlefield, WILLIAM R. NEWTON, 34 years. [5/14]
May 6, 1869, Laurens, ELIZA M. HARRIS, 28 years. [5/14]
April 21, 1869, Oneonta, STEPHEN BARNES, 76 years. [5/14]
April 10, 1869, Oneonta, JOHN BEAMS, 82 years. [5/14]
April 23, 1869, Oneonta, Mrs. ELIZ. BEAMS, 85 years. [5/14]
May 26, 1869, Cooperstown, Mrs. SARAH W. WALKER, 66 years. [5/28]
May 21, 1869, Otsego, Mrs. OLIVE PERKINS, 82 years. [5/28]
May 31, 1869, Cooperstown, Mrs. SARAH W. WALKER, 66 years. [6/4]
May 31, 1869, Cooperstown, Mrs. MARY POTTER, 66 years. [6/4]

May 29, 1869, Garratsville, Mrs. URIAH GREGORY, 82 years. [6/11]
June 2, 1869, Morris, ALICE HOLLISTER, 17 years. [6/11]
June 2, 1869, Mt. Vision, Mrs. HATTIE C. BURNSIDE, 31 years. [6/11]
May 27, 1869, Springfield, FRANCES M. RATHBUN, 37 years. [6/11]
May 7, 1869, Otego, WILLIAM BAKER, 61 years. [6/11]
May 31, 1869, Laurens, S. C. FENTON, 72 years. [6/11]
June 1, 1869, Springfield, THOMAS I. THOMPSON, 77 years. [6/18]
June 15, 1869, Springfield, Mrs. NANCY SCOLLARD, 72 years. [6/18]
May 31, 1869, Laurens, SAMUEL C. FENTON, 72 years. [6/18]
June 13, 1869, Laurens, HERBERT S. ALLEN, 5 years. [6/18]
June 17, 1869, Cooperstown, GRACE SCOTT ERNST, 2 years. [6/25]
July 30, 1869, Morris, Mrs. ESTHER GIFFORD, 70 years. [6/25]
Sept. 5, 1869, Otsego, PATRICK BYRNELL, 58 years. [9/10]
Aug. 31, 1869, Exeter, Mrs. ROXANIA MATTISON, 58 years. [9/10]
Sept. 4, 1869, Middlefield, GEORGE W. CLYDE, 32 years. [9/17]
Sept. 12, 1869, Worcester, ROSWELL WATERMAN, 76 years. [9/17]
Sept. 13, 1869, Maryland, Mrs. CYNTHIA WIGHTMAN, 41 years. [9/17]
Sept. 25, 1869, Cooperstown, HIRAM KINNE [HINNE?], 71 years. [10/1]
Sept. 27, 1869, Cooperstown, VOADICEA L. POTTER. [10/1]
Sept. 21, 1869, Burlington, AMASA AVERY, 68 years. [10/1]
Sept. 27, 1869, Otsego, Mrs. POLLY WILLIAMS, 71 years. [10/1]
Sept. 22, 1869, Maryland, BENJAMIN GURNEY, 76 years. [10/1]
Sept. 26, 1869, Maryland, Mrs. MERIBAH GURNEY, 76 years. [10/1]
Sept. 25, 1869, Cooperstown, JAMES COX, 92 years. [10/8]
Sept. 25, 1869, N. Lisbon, ICHABOD W. DUNNING, 66 years. [10/8]
Oct. --, 1869, Edmeston, THOMAS SOUTHWORTH, 78 years. [10/8]
Sept. 27, 1869, Laurens, JOSEPH G. JENKS, 69 years. [10/15]
Oct. 2, 1869, Oneonta, ALGERON L. SABIN, 30 years. [10/15]
Sept. 30, 1869, Worcester, Mrs. ELVIRA ATKINS, 26 years. [10/15]
Sept. 22, 1869, Fly Creek, Mrs. MARY M. BABCOCK, 25 years. [10/22]
Oct. 5, 1869, Westford, Mrs. MARY J. PANK, 27 years. [10/22]
Sept. 18, 1869, Garrettsville, LOTTIE D. EMERSON, 14 years. [10/22]
Oct. 7, 1869, Otego, Mrs. JULIA WARD, 51 years. [10/22]
[no date], Otego, Mrs. WM. O. SMITH, 25 years. [10/22]
Oct. 14, 1869, Morris, Mrs. LOUISA VALENTINE, 40 years. [10/22]
Oct. 3, 1869, Edmeston, THOMAS SOUTHWORTH, 78 years. [10/22]
Oct. 22, 1869, Cooperstown, FANNIE M. FELLOWS, 16 years. [10/29]
Oct. 23, 1869, Springfield, ALFRED CLARKE, 57 years. [10/29]
Oct. 17, 1869, Laurens, PETER MARLETT, 90 years. [10/29]
Nov. 7, 1869, Pierstown, MINNIE A. BEADLE, 6 months. [11/12]
Nov. 6, 1869, Cooperstown, CANDACE HEWS, 64 years. [11/18]

Nov. 6, 1869, Otsego, ALICE D. (I.?) EDDY, 10 years. [11/18]
Oct. 8, 1869, Cherry Valley, JOHN I. MOORE, 96 years. [11/18]
Nov. 23, 1869, Cooperstown, NELSON HERDMAN, 57 years. [11/25]
Nov. 18, 1869, Hartwick Sem., RICHARD SWARTWOUTH, 91 years. [11/25]
Nov. 21, 1869, Hartwick, Mrs. CELINDA GREEN PHILLIPS, 35 years. [12/2]
Nov. 17, 1869, Hartwick, ASA GARDNER, 79 years. [12/2]
Nov. 13, 1869, Pittsfield, STEPHEN GOODSPEED, 93 years. [12/2]
Dec. 8, 1869, Cooperstown, CALVIN H. DAVIS, 62 years. [12/9]
Nov. 14, 1869, Middlefield, ANSON N. GREEN, 30 years. [12/16]
Dec. 29, 1869, Cooperstown, Mrs. GEORGE NEWELL, 38 years. [12/30]
Dec. 29, 1869, Middlefield, GEORGE PARSHALL, 72 years. [1/6/1870]
Jan. 1, 1870, Hartwick, Mrs. ANNA KING, 44 years. [1/13]
Dec. 28, 1869, Burlington, JOSEPH CLARK, 79 years. [1/13/1870]
Jan. 6, 1870, Fly Creek, MARGARET WILLIAMS, 64 years. [1/13]
Jan. 10, 1870, Otsego, JOHN WILLIAMS, 80 years. [1/13]
Jan. 4, 1870, Schuyler's Lake, Mrs. JANE TAYLOR, 52 years. [1/20]
Jan. 15, 1870, Cooperstown, Mrs. PETER BICE, 75 years. [1/27]
Jan. 15, 1870, Otsego, NEHEMIAH HINDS, 85 years. [1/27]
Jan. 28, 1870, Middlefield, SAM. H. HUNTER, 65 years. [2/3]
Feb. 5, 1870, Cooperstown, ABIJAH BARNUM, 76 years. [2/10]
Feb. 8, 1870, Cooperstown, ALMEDA BARNUM, 48 years. [2/10]
Dec. 24, 1869, Otsego, WILLIAM CARROL, 30 years. [2/10/1870]
Jan. 29, 1870, Butternuts, WILLIAM CALVIN LEET, 11 years. [2/17]
Jan. 28, 1870, E. Worcester, ROSWELL POWERS, 77 years. [2/17]
Feb. 7, 1870, Laurens, Mrs. SARAH J. STRONG, 31 years. [2/17]
Jan. 27, 1870, E. Springfield, FRED CURTISS FOWLER, 1 year. [2/24]
Feb. 24, 1870, Cherry Valley, Mrs. ELIZABETH STORY, 71 years. [3/10]
Feb. 27, 1870, Unadilla, Rev. A. V. H. POWELL, 60 years. [3/17]
Feb. 27, 1870, Worcester, MARY CAMPAIGN, 77 years. [3/17]
Feb. 28, 1870, S. Worcester, Mrs. POLLY TAYLOR CLARK, 40 years. [3/17]
March 19, 1870, Pierstown, Mrs. RUTH J. WARREN, 44 years. [3/24]
March 24, 1870, Cooperstown, LEVI WOOD, 81 years. [3/31]
March 23, 1870, Otsego, Mrs. KATHERINE SHAUL, 53 years. [4/7]
March 26, 1870, DEWI H. C. PARSHALL, age 2. [4/7]
April 7, 1870, Cooperstown, Mrs. ANN COOPER POMEROY, 87 years. [4/14]
April 11, 1870, Cooperstown, Mrs. LORINDA STURGES, 77 years. [4/14]
April 2, 1870, Burlington, SHELDON FISK, 71 years. [4/14]

[no date] Middlefield, WILLIAM JARVIS, 17 years. [4/14]
April 11, 1870, Clintonville, Mrs. MARY CLINYON [sic], 79 years. [4/21]
Feb. 17, 1870, Hartwick, Mrs. LOUISA BLISS, 61 years. [4/21]
Feb. 24, 1870, Hartwick, ASA INGALSBE, 60 years. [4/21]
March 30, 1870, Harwick, LINY SMITH, infant. [4/21]
April 11, 1870, Springfield, SEFRENES BASINGER, 79 years. [4/21]
April 21, 1870, Hyde Park, Hartwick, ETTIE M. TEACHOUT, 8 years. [4/28]
April 19, 1870, Richfield, Mrs. LUCY ST. JOHN, 60 years. [4/28]
April 7, 1870, Jacksonville, KATE G. MURDOCK, 1 year. [4/28]
April 6, 1870, Hartwick, JOSIAH JONES, 71 years. [4/28]
April 17, 1870, W. Oneonta, THERON BABBITT, 16 years. [4/28]
April 4, 1870, Springfield, LAVINA W. ELY, 1 year. [5/5]
April 24, 1870, Edmeston, HALSEY SPENCER, M.D., 80 years. [5/12]
May 15, 1870, Cooperstown, MARIA L. SHORT, 24 years. [5/19]
May 4, 1870, Otsego, JOHN LUMLEY, 60 years. [5/19]
May 9, 1870, Toddsville, Mrs. MARTHA BOTSFORD, 91 years. [5/19]
May 13, 1870, Cooperstown, FREDK. R. STARKWEATHER, infant. [5/26]
May 4, 1870, Garrettsville, Mrs. ISAVELLE HUME, 83 years. [5/26]
May 10, 1870, E. Springfield, ANNIE FEDDEN GENTER, 13 years. [5/26]
May 12, 1870, Laurens, HENRY C. WOOD, 24 years. [5/26]
April 26, 1870, Unadilla, DAVID C. FOSTER, 44 years. [5/26]
May 14, 1870, Morris, Mrs. MARY BROWNELL, 70 years. [5/26]
May 19, 1870, Otego, Mrs. MARY M. HUNT, 18 years. [5/26]
May 21, 1870, Fly Creek, Mrs. SARAH MURPHY, 44 years. [6/2]
May 20, 1870, Exeter, JAMES AUSTIN, 75 years. [6/2]
May 26, 1870, Laurens, Mrs. SARAH P. CUTLER, 46 years. [6/2]
May 29, 1870, Edmeston, Mrs. CATHERINE S. ANGER, 43 years. [6/9]
June 10, 1870, Mrs. SARAH A. BABCOCK. [6/16]
June 18, 1870, Middlefield, Mrs. MARGARET LENT, 78 years. [6/23]
June 16, 1870, Cooperstown, Mrs. ELIZA C. MOREHOUSE, 72 years. [6/23]
June 14, 1870, Cooperstown, MARY FOWLER, 84 years. [6/23]
June 12, 1870, Hartwick, JANE GATES, 89 years. [6/23]
June 24, 1870, Cooperstown, Mrs. MARY A. DOUBLEDAY, 63 years. [6/30]
June 19, 1870, New Lisbon, Mrs. SUSAN BRIMMER, 64 years. [6/30]
June 12, 1870, Schuyler's Lake, KATE T. DURFY, 29 years. [6/30]
June 15, 1870, Burlington Green, Mrs. MARY A. SILL, age 61. [7/7]

July 9, 1870, Cooperstown, JENNIE PALMER, 25 years. [7/14]
July 1, 1870, New Orleans, ELIZABETH MOREHOUSE DAVIS, infant. [7/14]
July 12, 1870, Otego, Mrs. CHLOE FRINK, 34 years. [7/21]
July 25, 1870, Cooperstown, Mrs. ESTHER LIPPITT, 65 years. [7/28]
July 20, 1870, Middlefield, BENJAMIN PIERCE, 65 years. [7/28]
July 19, 1870, Milford, DELLA WARD, infant. [7/28]
July 20, 1870, Burlington, SYLVESTER REED, 66 years. [7/28] & [8/4]
July 14, 1870, Schuyler's Lake, ALVAN BROOKS, 79 years. [8/4]
July 23, 1870, Oneonta, ANNA SHORT, 14 years. [8/4]
July 23, 1870, Mt. Vision, FRANK MATTERSON, 14 years. [8/4]
July 27, 1870, Hartwick, NELLIE HYDE, infant. [8/11]
Aug. 9, 1870, Cooperstown, FREDERICK BARTLETT, infant. [8/18]
Aug. 9, 1870, Roseboom, HENRY RURY, 72 years. [8/18]
July 14, 1870, Edmeston, Mrs. MALINDA NELSON, 68 years. [8/18]
Aug. 5, 1870, Burlington, Mrs. MANCRON BOLTON, 63 years. [8/18]
Aug. 5, 1870, Burlington, Mrs. MINERVA BOLTON, 61 years. [8/25]
July 29, 1870, Springfield, HENRY P. KRUM, 77 years. [9/1]
Aug. 16, 1870, Cherry Valley, JOHN ROSEBOOM, 25 years. [9/1]
Aug. 24, 1870, Paines Hollow, Mrs. HANNAH BUSH, 70 years. [9/1]
Aug. 17, 1870, Burlington, Mrs. SUSAN REED, 67 years. [9/1]
July 27, 1870, Milford, FREDERICK N. REYNOLDS, 1 year. [9/1]
Sept. 1, 1870, Cooperstown, LEVERETT C. STOWELL, 59 years. [9/8]
Sept. 1, 1870, Pittsfield, Mrs. SUSAN RATHBON, 62 years. [9/8]
Sept. 12, 1870, Fly Creek, CHESTER DAVIDSON, 52 years. [9/15]
Sept. 5, 1870, Milford, HIRAM VAN BUREN, 38 years. [9/15]
July 11, 1870, Burlington Flats, Mrs. ABIGAIL ADKINS, 73 years. [9/15]
Sept. 12, 1870, Middlefield, HETTIE M. CUMMINGS, 1 year. [9/22]
Sept. 8, 1870, Pittsfield, Mrs. SARAH HALL, 79 years. [9/29]
Sept. 15, 1870, Oakville, CHARLES HARVEY STEERE, 2 years. [9/29]
Sept. 4, 1870, Middlefield, ELIAS PARSHALL, 76 years. [9/29]
Sept. 19, 1870, New Lisbon, Mrs. DELOS POTTER, 28 years. [9/29]
Sept. 6, 1870, EDMUND & EDWIN MURDOCK, infant twins. [10/13]
Oct. 14, 1870, Cooperstown, JAMES MC GOWN, 74 years. [10/20]
June 26, 1870, Plainfield, GEORGE BROWN, 50 years. [10/20]
Sept. 19, 1870, Otsdawa, Mrs. JULIA A. HUNT BEERS, 39 years. [10/20]
Oct. 15, 1870, Otego, Mrs. PHEBE A. WILLIAMS, 39 years. [10/20]
Nov. 2, 1870, Colliersville, SOPHIA E. GUNN, 15 years. [11/17]
Oct. 30, 1870, Westford, Mrs. TILLHA BENTLEY, 80 years. [11/17]
Nov 9, 1870, Oneonta, TRACEY COHN, 37 years. [11/17]

Nov. 4, 1870, Unadilla, Dea. ITHAMER A. SPENCER, 89 years. [11/17]
Nov. 3, 1870, Milford Center, WALLACE MUMFORD, 33 years. [11/24]
Nov. 30, 1870, Cooperstown, Mrs. ANNE E. ROGERS NORTON of Chicago. [12/1]
Dec. 2, 1870, Cooperstown, CHARLES THURSTON, 91 years. [12/1]
Dec. 11, 1870, Cooperstown, GRACE COX, 7 years. [12/15]
Oct. 31, 1870, Fly Creek, CHESTER TAYLOR, 90 years. [12/15]
Nov. 24, 1870, Fly Creek, THOMAS TAYLOR, 70 years. [12/15]
Dec. 14, 1870, Cooperstown, CHARLES S. STEWART, 75 years. [12/22]
Dec. 13, 1870, Oneonta, PETER W. SWART, 68 years. [12/22]
Nov. 27, 1870, Butternuts, Mrs. NARCISSA HENDRIX, 83 years. [12/22]
Dec. 11, 1870, Morris, Mrs. MARY FOOTE, 39 years. [12/22]
Dec. 7, 1870, Laurens, JOHN A. WINDSOR. [12/22]
Nov. 8, 1870, Schuyler's Lake, Mrs. SARAH BREWER, 82 years. [12/22]
Dec. 27, 1870, Harwick, JANE WOOD, 21 years. [12/29]
Dec. 20, 1870, Springfield Cen., JAMES JENNINGS, 33 years. [12/29]
Dec. 15, 1870, Schuyler's Lake, DOLLY GARLICK, 8 years. [12/29]
Dec. 20, 1870, Butternuts, Mrs. MARY L. LUCE, 65 years. [1/5/1871]
Dec. 23, 1870, Oneonta, Mrs. H. H. ALLEN, 34 years. [1/5/1871]
Dec. 24, 1870, Chaseville, WILLIAM BOWISH, 72 years. [1/5/1871]
Dec. 22, 1870, Butternuts, WILLIAM BROWN, 72 years. [1/5/1871]
Dec. 8, 1870, Fly Creek, SAMUEL W. CHENEY, 69 years. [1/12/1871]
Dec. 31, 1870, Fly Creek, CEYLON N. CHENEY, 25 years. [1/12/1871]
Dec. 1, 1870, Decatur, J. H. DEVENPECK, 44 years. [1/12/1871]
Jan. 11, 1871, Cooperstown, Mrs. MARGARET THURSTON, 84 years. [1/19]
Jan. 11, 1871, Springfield, ANN WOOD, 64 years. [1/19]
Jan. 5, 1871, Oneonta, JOHN VAN WOERT, 90 years. [1/19]
Jan. 6, 1871, Unadilla, Col. A. WILLIAMS, 69 years. [1/19]
Jan. 16, 1871, Springfield, SCHUYLER HEWES, infant of 10 months. [1/26]
Jan. 28, 1871, Middlefield, AARON BROWN, 83 years. [2/2]
Jan. 22, 1871, Middlefield, PELEG COFFIN, 86 years. [2/2]
Jan. 25, 1871, Westford, DAVID KELSO, 69 years. [2/2]
Jan. 28, 1871, Cherry Valley, GEORGE W. ROBERTS, 73 years. [2/2]
Jan. 13, 1871, W. Oneonta, Mrs. ESTER CULVER, 45 years. [2/2]
Jan. 25, 1871, W. Oneonta, Mrs. ELIZABETH WILLIAMS, 74 years. [2/2]
Jan. 13, 1871, Middlefield, Mrs. FANNY BLISS, 74 years. [2/2]
Jan. 25, 1871, Unadilla, Mrs. BETSEY BOWEN, 62 years. [2/2]
Jan. 14, 1871, Unadilla, Mrs. HANNAH A. CRANE, 56 years. [2/2]

Jan. 26, 1871, Oneonta, ISAAC PEET, 82 years. [2/9]
Feb. 7, 1871, Cooperstown, GEORGE CHAPMAN, 34 years. [2/9]
Feb. 9, 1871, Cooperstown, Mrs. AMELIA D. BYRAM, 57 years. [2/16]
Feb. 3, 1871, S. New Berlin, MARION K. BABCOCK, 1 year. [2/16]
Feb. 10, 1871, Fly Creek, HORACE TAYLOR, 68 years. [2/23]
Feb. 17, 1871, Richfield, Mrs. VIOLETT WOODBURY, 82 years. [3/2]
Feb. 12, 1871, Richfield, Mrs. REBECCA AMES, 58 years. [3/2]
Feb. 16, 1871, Burlington, Mrs. AMELIA PALMER WALEY. [3/2]
Feb. 19, 1871, Richfield, STEPHEN THORNTON. [3/2]
Jan. 31, 1871, Milford, KATE S. HARDY, infant. [3/2]
Feb. 22, 1871, Richfield, DANIEL LOOMIS, 38 years. [3/9]
Feb. 2, 1871, Schuyler's Lake, Mrs. LUCRETIA PALMER, 74 years. [3/9]
Feb. 21, 1871, Laurens, JAMES MEAD, 66 years. [3/9]
Feb. 19, 1871, Butternuts, Mrs. EMILY VOLE, 80 years. [3/9]
Feb. 20, 1871, Butternuts, ANDREW DARROCH, 50 years. [3/9]
Feb. 27, 1871, Cherry Valley, MARQUIS DUTCHER, 75 years. [3/16]
March 3, 1871, Cherry Valley, JAMES GEORGE, 43 years. [3/16]
March 8, 1871, Cherry Valley, Mrs. MARY E. SWAN, 48 years. [3/16]
March 13, 1817, Cherry Valley, CHARLES SWAN, 20 years. [3/16]
March 10, 1871, Cherry Valley, JOHN CORY, 71 years. [3/16]
March 10, 1871, Pittsfield, Mrs. ELIZABETH PECK, 63 years. [3/23]
Feb. 22, 1871, Richfield, MASON CORBIN, 77 years. [3/23]
March 23, 1871, Cooperstown, HARVEY HOLLISTER, 66 years. [3/30]
March 24, 1871, Hartwick, OLNEY WELLS, 87 years. [3/30]
March 15, 1871, W. Laurens, WILLIAM STETSON, 77 years. [3/30]
March 8, 1871, W. Oneonta, WILLIAM OLIN, age 68 years. [3/30]
March 21, 1871, Laurens, HENRY HOWE, 44 years. [3/30]
March 18, 1871, Morris, Mrs. LUCINDA P. LIGHT, 40 years. [3/30]
March 16, 1871, Oneonta, CHARLES HAND, 79 years. [3/30]
March 16, 1871, Worcester, JOSEPH G. EARL, 34 years. [3/30]
April 4, 1871, Cooperstown, JOSHUA H. STORY, 53 years. [4/6]
March 17, 1871, Burlington Flats, SOLOMON HUESTIS, 40 years. [4/6]
March 17, 1871, Hartwick, Mrs. SALLY M. TUCKER, 74 years. [4/6]
March 3, 1871, Schuyler's Lake, Mrs. HARMONY BURRELL, 40 years. [4/6]
March 30, 1871, Richfield Spa, CHARLES MONROE BADGER, 14 years. [4/6]
April 7, 1871, Cooperstown, ALVER KENYON, 53 years. [4/13]
Feb 25, 1871, Exeter, BENJAMIN DAVENPORT, 66 years. [4/13]
April 8, 1871, Otsego, LEWIS MALLORY, 66 years. [4/20]
Apr 6, 1871, Edmeston, SIDNEY HOPKINS, 63 years. [4/20]

April 15, 1871, Edmeston, JAMES O'BRIEN, 48 years. [4/20]
April 4, 1871, Cherry Valley, Mrs. BETSEY SUTLIFF, 87 years. [4/20]
April 16, 1871, Hartwick, SYLVESTER B. LUTHER, 64 years. [4/20]
April 11, 1871, Hartwick, ABNER AUGUR, 14 years. [4/27]
March 8, 1871, Otsego, Mrs. JANE GARLOCK PERRY, 23 years. [5/4]
April 23, 1871, Hartwick, PHILLIPS M. ADAMS, infant. [5/4]
April 10, 1871, New Lisbon, SAMUEL KEMBALL, 54 years. [5/4]
April 9, 1871, Otsdawa, Mrs. CORNELIA SCRAMLING, 31 years. [5/4]
May 6, 1871, Hinman Hollow, JULIA M. HOWE, 35 years. [5/11]
May 3, 1871, E. Worcester, HARRY GOTT, 4 years. [5/11]
April 23, 1871, Middlefield, STEPHEN REYNOLDS, 47 years. [5/11]
April 13, 1871, Richfield, CORNELIUS LOSEE, 60 years. [5/11]
May 3, 1871, Oneonta, Mrs. MIRIAM H. REYNOLDS, 52 years. [5/11]
April 29, 1871, Butternuts, DANIEL BEARDSLEY, 92 years. [5/11]
April 27, 1871, Cherry Valley, JESSIE BRONSON, 52 years. [5/11]
May 1, 1871, N. Lisbon, JOSEPH PECK, 82 years. [5/11]
May 1, 1871, Butternuts, AMOS COLEGROVE, 39 years. [5/11]
May 9, 1871, Burlington Flats, CHARLES N. BURROWS, 3 years. [5/18]
May 9, 1871, Butternuts, Mrs. LORETTA F. TRUMAN, 60 years. [5/18]
April 23, 1871, Hartwick, PHILIP M. ANDRUS, 10 months. [5/18]
May 19, 1871, New Lisbon, Mrs. HANNAH BEERS, 77 years. [6/1]
May 18, 1871, Maryland Hill, ALTON BENTON, 19 years. [6/1]
May 18, 1871, Worcester, CHESTER WRIGHT, 66 years. [6/1]
June 3, 1871, Cooperstown, Mrs. EMMA E. ROBINSON, 46 years. [6/8]
May 27, 1871, Burlington Flats, GEORGE ALGER, 75 years. [6/8]
June 10, 1871, Cooperstown, KITTIE SUNDAY (colored), 2 years. [6/15]
June 4, 1871, Richfield Spa, Mrs. MARY OWENS, 87 years. [6/15]
June 5, 1871, Richfield Spa, MICHAEL MC NAMARA, 54 years. [6/15]
May 29, 1871, Butternuts, GEORGE GADSBY, 72 years. [6/15]
June 1, 1871, Unadilla, Mrs. ANNIS DEVOL, 72 years. [6/15]
May 31, 1871, Plainfield, OLIVER WILCOX, 60 years. [6/22]
June 4, 1871, Richfield Spa, Mrs. MARY OWENS, 87 years. [6/22]
June 10, 1871, Morris, Mrs. PHINEAS C. BALL, 71 years. [6/22]
June 10, 1871, Otsego, HARLEY T. WILLIAMS, 44 years. [6/29]
June 1, 1871, W. Burlington, Mrs. PERMELIA LINES, 78 years. [6/29]
June 21, 1871, Richfield Spa, WILLIAM P. JOHNSON, 61 years. [6/29]
June 27, 1871, Pittsfield, Mrs. LYDIA HARRINGTON, 68 years. [7/13]
July 4, 1871, Garratsville, ARTHUR C. HERRICK, 38 years. [7/13]
July 4, 1871, Otego, GEORGE M. COLE, 52 years. [7/13]
July 12, 1871, Cooperstown, BURDETT D. KING, 22 years. [7/20]
July 14, 1871, Otego, Mrs. LUCY M. COBURN, 50 years. [7/20]

July 17, 1871, Toddsville, Dr. E. J. ALMY, 59 years. [7/20]
June 27, 1871, Pittsfield, Mrs. LYDIA HARRINGTON, 68 years. [7/27]
June 23, 1871, Milford, GEORGE W. SAYRE, 59 years. [7/27]
June 25, 1871, Fly Creek, Mrs. ELLA M. PATTIN SEEBER, 21 years. [8/3]
July 29, 1871, Otsego, Mrs. MARIA WARREN, 68 years. [8/3]
July 26, 1871, W. Laurens, Mrs. LUCINDA S. HAY, 17 years. [8/3]
July 24, 1871, Morris, NORMAN NEWELL, 68 years. [8/3]
July 10, 1871, Otsego, Mrs. ABIGAIL PLUMB, 73 years. [8/10]
July 28, 1871, Springfield, Mrs. DAVID BAIRD. [8/10]
Aug. 1, 1871, Hartwick, SALLY NICKERSON, 54 years. [8/10]
Aug. 6, 1871, Oneonta, Mrs. SOPHIA WEIDMAN, 80 years. [8/17]
Aug. 14, 1871, Worcester, Mrs. POLLY PRESTON, 78 years. [8/31]
Aug. 16, 1871, Schenevus, LIBBIE HASWELL, infant. [8/31]
Aug. 16, 1871, Chaseville, GEORGE W. CHASE, 10 years. [8/31]
Aug. 26, 1871, Fly Creek, HARVEY BIRGE, 56 years. [9/7]
Sept. 3, 1871, Portlandville, JOHN S. LATIMER, 85 years. [9/14]
Aug. 26, 1871, Burlington, ZARA COMSTOCK, 73 years. [9/14]
Sept. 3, 1871, New Lisbon, Mrs. MARY E. PORTER SLOAN, 24 years. [9/14]
Aug. 26, 1871, Fly Creek, HARVEY BIRGE, 55 years. [9/14]
Sept. 12, 1871, Oneonta, JOSEPH WHITNEY, 76 years. [9/21]
Sept. 3, 1871, Morris, DORA R. MATTESON, 11 years. [9/21]
Sept. 9, 1871, Morris, NATHANIEL STEVENSON, 61 years. [9/21]
Sept. 4, 1871, Westford, Mrs. MARY L. WILSON, 52 years. [9/21]
Aug. 26, 1871, Mrs. REBECCA WILBER, 72 years. [9/21]
Sept. 18, 1871, Oaksville, HARVEY KENYON STEERE, infant. [9/28]
Sept. 26, 1871, Garratsville, EZRA MATHER, 57 years. [9/28]
Sept. 12, 1871, Maryland, IRA O. TALLMADGE, 2 years. [9/28]
Aug. 25, 1871, New Lisbon, WALTER C. CRUNDEL, 78 years. [9/28]
Sept. 22, 1871, Pierstown, E. JOSEPHINE SWARTOUT, 29 years. [10/5]
Sept. 29, 1871, Cooperstown, WILLIAM COOLEY, 38 years. [10/5]
Sept. 11, 1871, NY City, THOMAS SHANKLAND (Otsego), 66 years. [10/5]
Sept. 20, 1871, Worcester, Mrs. ELVIRA DAY, 42 years. [10/5]
Sept. 28, 1871, Springfield, JOHN WILES, 42 years. [10/5]
Oct. 7, 1871, Cooperstown, THOMAS CLARKE, 63 years. [10/12]
Sept. 15, 1871, S. Valley [sic], EMMA C. ALLEN, 7 years. [10/12]
Oct. 9, 1871, N. Lisbon, Mrs. LUCINDA STEVENS, 34 years. [10/19]
Oct. 15, 1871, E. Worcester, Col. LIONEL SHELDON, 85 years. [10/19]
Sept. 21, 1871, Morris, NANCY WEATHERBY, 30 years. [10/19]

Sept. 23, 1871, W. Oneonta, EPHRAIM H. SLEEPER, 84 years. [10/23]
Oct. 2, 1871, Otego, GEORGE T. NORTHRUP, 87 years. [10/26]
Oct. 31, 1871, Cooperstown, Mrs. ELLA E. JOHNSON NOBLE. [11/2]
Oct. 31, 1871, Sidney Cen., Mrs. ELIZABETH MC RORIE, 60 years. [11/9]
Nov. 1, 1871, Oneonta, Mrs. RODNEY EMMONS, 41 years. [11/9]
Oct. 29, 1871, W. Laurens, EZRA BLANCHARD, 48 years. [11/9]
Nov. 7, 1871, Springfield, Capt. LINDEL H. SLITER, 72 years. [11/16]
Oct. 29, 1871, Otsego, JUDIAH S. ELLSWORTH, 52 years. [11/16]
Oct. 15, 1871, Springfield, Mrs. CATHERINE ORMISTON, 96 years. [11/16]
Oct. 31, 1871, Roseboom, Mrs. CHRISTIAN S. BELL, 74 years. [11/16]
Oct. 29, 1871, Mrs. RHODA H. SPENCER, 42 years. [11/16]
Nov. 9, 1871, Otego, LOUISE E. BIRDSALL, 17 years. [11/23]
Nov. 15, 1871, Cooperstown, HARVEY M. SMITH, 2 years. [11/23]
Nov. 13, 1871, Toddsville, MARY HORTH MURDOCK, 23 years. [11/23]
Nov. 11, 1871, Colliersville, Mrs. HORACE D. SPENCER, 59 years. [11/23]
Oct. 20, 1871, Unadilla, Mrs. RHOAD [sic] H. SPENCER, 42 years. [11/23]
Nov. 4, 1871, Chaseville, SIMON B. SHUTTS, 51 [?81] years. [11/23]
Nov. 2, 1871, Maryland, SALLY HUNT, 81 years. [11/23]
Nov. 23, 1871, Cooperstown, Dr. WILLIAM A. COMSTOCK, 62 years. [11/30]
Oct. 27, 1871, New Lisbon, ELIAS GREGORY, 80 years. [11/30]
Nov. 25, 1871, Burlington, Hon. JAMES C. WALWORTH, 75 years. [11/30]
Nov. 16, 1871, Richfield, CHRISTOPHER H. BENEDICT, 82 years. [11/30]
Nov. 10, 1871, Otego, MARY DAVIS, 16 years. [11/30]
Nov. 14, 1871, Otego, LEVI B. PACKARD, 72 years. [11/30]
Nov. 11, 1871, Colliersville, Mrs. HORACE D. SPENCER, 59 years. [11/30]
Nov. 19, 1871, Morris, Mrs. SUSAN CARD, 76 years. [11/30]
Nov. 18, 1871, Morris, JONAH DAVIS, 68 years. [11/30]
Nov. 21, 1871, Burlington, Mrs. LUCINDA JENKS, 67 years. [12/7]
Dec. 5, 1871, Cooperstown, Mrs. MARGARET MC INTOSH, 75 years. [12/14]
Dec. 7, 1871, Oaksville, Mrs. MARY BROOKS, 74 years. [12/14]
Nov. 8, 1871, Otego, EDMUND P. EMMONS, 84 years. [12/14]

Dec. 2, 1871, Unadilla, HYATT FOOTE, 67 years. [12/14]
Nov. 20, 1871, Westford, CROSBY VAN DEVEER, 47 years. [12/14]
Nov. 29, 1871, Middlefield, RENSSELAER BUTLER, 68 years. [12/21]
Dec. 17, 1871, Hart. Sem., LUTHER I. BURDITT, infant. [12/21]
Sept. 20, 1871, Westford, CHARLES HANES, 84 years. [12/28]
Dec. 20, 1871, Westford, MARY HANES, 83 years. [12/28]
Dec. 13, 1871, Springfield Cen., Mrs. ELSEY WOOD HEWES, 76 years. [1/4/1872]
Dec. 26, 1871, Springfield Cen., Mrs. MARY A. SMITH, 73 years. [1/4/1872]
Nov. 12, 1871, Schuylers Lake, DAVID BREWER, 83 years. [1/4/1872]
[no date] Laurens, GEORGE BRIGHTMAN, 73 years. [1/11/1872]
Dec. 1, 1871, Otsego, IRA HYDE, 93 years. [1/11/1872]
Dec. 26, 1871, Springfield Center, Mrs. MARY A. SMITH, 73 years. [1/11/1872]
Dec. 23, 1871, EDWIN PICKENS, 34 years. [1/11/1872]
Dec. 19, 1871, Pierstown, Mrs. MARTHA SQUIER, 74 years. [1/18/1872]
Jan. 12, 1872, Cooperstown, JAMES BROMFIELD, 66 years. [1/18]
Dec. 28, 1871, Cherry Valley, Mrs. ELIZABETH FLINT, 69 years. [1/18/1872]
Jan. 8, 1872, Oneonta Plains, JOSEPH D. BRISACK, 77 years. [1/18]
Jan. 13, 1872, Middlefield Center, JOHN PARSHALL, 89 years. [1/18]
Jan. 18, 1873, Pierstown, Mrs. ABBY WARREN, 85 years. [1/25]
Jan. 23, 1872, Cooperstown, JOHN COLLAR, 65 years. [1/25]
Jan. 28, 1872, Cooperstown, ORSEMUS REYNOLDS, 43 years. [2/1]
Jan. 26, 1872, Cooperstown, GEORGE STOWEL KENYON, 21 years. [2/1]
Jan. 21, 1872, N. Lisbon, CHRISTOPHER BELL, 82 years. [2/1]
Jan. 17, 1872, Cooperstown, Mrs. EUNICE FANCHER, 69 years. [2/1]
Jan. 21, 1872, Hartwick, Mrs. POLLY WHIPPLE, 75 years. [2/1]
Jan. 26, 1872, Middlefield, ELIAS ECKLER, 26 years. [2/1]
Feb. 6, 1872, Cooperstown, Mrs. MARGARETTA M. S. BOWERS, 94 years. [2/8]
Feb. 6, 1872, Cooperstown, Mrs. DEBORAH CARR, 61 years. [2/8]
Jan. 19, 1872, N. Lisbon, Mrs. ANNA SPRAGUE, 91 years. [2/8]
Jan. 22, 1872, S. Hartwick, Mrs. CHESTER WRIGHT, 86 years. [2/8]
Feb. 2, 1872, Middlefield, JAMES ADSIT, 88 years. [2/8]
Jan. 30, 1872, Otego, Mrs. PRUDENCE BUNDY, 80 years. [2/8]
Jan. 26, 1872, Westford, BARLEY PATRICK, 70 years. [2/8]
Feb. 6, 1872, Oaksville, PHILO W. PERKINS, 60 years. [2/15]
Feb. 4, 1872, Otsego, Mrs. ELIZABETH SHEPARD, 73 years. [2/22]
Feb 25, 1872, Cherry Valley, Mrs. LUCY SHANNON, 55 years. [2/29]

Feb. 10, 1872, Decatur, Mrs. MARY M. SHELLAND, 29 years. [2/29]
[no date], Morris, ELIZA SIMMON, 21 years. [2/29/1872]
Feb. 10, 1872, Laurens, JENNIE S. STANTON, 8 years. [2/29]
March 1, 1872, Cooperstown, Hon. SCHUYLER CRIPPEN, 77 years. [3/7]
March 2, 1872, Cooperstown, RUTH BOWEN, 2 years. [3/7]
Feb. 6, 1872, Otsego, PHILO CAMP, 59 years. [3/7]
Feb. 24, 1872, Pittsfield, JOSEPH SMITH, 62 years. [3/7]
Jan. 27, 1872, Otego, Mrs. HOPEY COLE, 83 years. [3/7]
Feb. 14, 1872, Butternuts, Mrs. HARRIET L. HOAG, 44 years. [3/7]
Feb. 28, 1872, Richfield Springs, JOHN N. HANNAHS, 41 years. [3/7]
Feb. 26, 1872, S. Worcester, Mrs. NANCY YOUNG, 68 years. [3/7]
Feb. 14, 1872, Unadilla, RUFUS PLACE, 70 years. [3/7]
Jan. 27, 1872, Laurens, Mrs. BETSEY FULLER, 80 years. [3/7]
Feb. 10, 1872, Laurens, JENNIE S. STANTON, 8 years. [3/7]
March 13, 1872, Richfield Spa, NORMAN K. RANSOM. [3/14]
Feb. 24, 1872, Clarksville, DAN E. BELKNAP, M.D., 35 years. [3/14]
March 2, 1872, Hartwick, SEWARD FORD SMITH, 2 years. [3/14]
Feb. 24, 1872, Morris, JOSEPH SMITH, 67 years. [3/14]
March 14, 1872, Cooperstown, Dea. LEWIS HINMAN, 75 years. [3/21]
March 10, 1872, Cooperstown, Mrs. MARIA KENYON, 56 years. [3/21]
March 13, 1872, Cherry Valley, WILLIAM KIRBY, 75 years. [3/21]
March 4, 1872, Milford, BENAJAH AYLESWORTH, 76 years. [3/21]
March 3, 1872, Burlington Flats, GEORGE HENRY DIGNAN, 15 years. [3/21]
Feb. 23, 1872, Middlefield, ANNA E. CLYDE, 31 years. [3/21]
Feb. 28, 1872, Middlefield, Mrs. JANE M. BLAIR, 61 years. [3/21]
Feb. 29, 1872, Oneonta, MORRIS COOLEY, 71 years. [3/21]
March 12, 1872, Laurens, FRANK M. FISHER, 17 years. [3/21]
March 1, 1872, W. Oneonta, Mrs. SARAH D. WALTERS, 86 years. [3/21]
March 9, 1872, Schuyler's Lake, GEORGE MAY, 7 years. [3/21]
March 12, 1872, Milford, Mrs. DOLLY A. MOORE WELLMAN, 53 years. [3/21]
March 19, 1872, Milford, THOMAS J. COLBURN, 64 years. [3/28]
March 9, 1872, Butternuts, DAVID HURD, 80 years. [3/28]
March 17, 1872, Pittsfield, RICHARD SMITH, 76 years. [3/28]
March 20, 1872, Springfield, ROBERT WOOD, 68 years. [3/28]
March 20, 1872, Middlefield, Mrs. EKIZA ANDREWS, 73 years. [4/4]
March 22, 1872, Schenevus, Mrs. BETSEY SNYDER, 81 years. [4/4]
March 24, 1872, N. Lisbon, JONATHAN JOHNSON, 62 years. [4/4]
March 30, 1872, Otsego, SYLVIA BENNETT, 82 years. [4/11]

March 29, 1872, Morris, ENOS J. FORD, 66 years. [4/11]
March 25, 1872, Worcester, CLARENCE WATERMAN. [4/11]
March 30, 1872, Maryland, STEPHEN BROWN, 80 years. [4/11]
April 1, 1872, Milford, WILLIAM QUEAL, 80 years. [4/11]
March 31, 1872, Hartwick, ADDIE M. HACKLEY, 14 years. [4/18]
April 3, 1872, Hartwick, CHAUNCY GARDNER, 56 years. [4/18]
April 15, 1872, Otsego, THOMAS DUGGLEBY, infant. [4/18]
April 7, 1872, Middlefield, JEREMIAH HOPKINS, 81 years. [4/18]
March 30, 1872, Otego, Mrs. MARIA GOODRICH, 75 years. [4/18]
March 14, 1872, Laurens, Mrs. BETSEY GARDNER, 85 years. [4/18]
March 17, 1872, Oaksville, Mrs. NANCY HIGBY, 73 years. [4/18]
April 10, 1872, Springfield, JOHN GILCHRIST, 82 years. [4/25]
March 30, 1872, Maryland, STEPHEN BROWN, 80 years. [4/25]
April 13, 1872, Morris, Mrs. MARIA BEERS, 60 years. [4/25]
April 14, 1872, Maryland, Mrs. JANE JOHNSON, 55 years. [4/25]
April 17, 1872, Worcester, HARRIET HUNTINGTON, 72 years. [4/25]
April 6, 1872, Burlington Flats, LEBBEUS LOOMIS, 64 years. [4/25]
April 27, 1872, Otsego, MINER SMITH, 69 years. [5/2]
March 26, 1872, N. Exeter, MARVIN D. MONK, 2 years. [5/2]
April 17, 1872, Morris, ASAHEL AVERY, 78 years. [5/2]
March 31, 1872, Unadilla Center, Mrs. HANNAH M. MOODY, 43 years. [5/2]
April 7, 1872, Unadilla, HORACE P. SEARLES, 3 years. [5/2]
April 16, 1872, Butternuts, BRADFORD LILLIE, 81 years. [5/2]
April 17, 1872, Otego, Mrs. CATHARINE COLE, 82 years. [5/2]
April 10, 1872, Hartwick, ADNA HOUSE, 13 years. [5/9]
April 26, 1872, Schenevus, PHILIP CRIPPEN, 84 years. [5/16]
April 22, 1872, Undailla, GEORGE RAITT, 82 years. [5/16]
April 27, 1872, Maryland, LEVI BOARDMAN, 41 years. [5/16]
May 3, 1872, Cooperstown, FRANK H. NEAL of Cherry Valley, 1 year 9 months. [5/16]
[no date] Morris, ROBERT GARDNER of Hartwick, 45 years. [5/16]
May 4, 1872, N. Lisbon, ALBEGENCE PERRY, 69 years. [5/23]
May 10, 1872, Unadilla, RUFUS P. GREEN, 71 years. [5/23]
May 11, 1827, Richfield Springs, Mrs. MARTHA WEEKS SEELEY, 30 years. [5/23]
May 27, 1872, Otsego, Mrs. NANCY CLARK, 65 years. [5/30]
May 10, 1872, Unadilla, RUFUS P. GREEN, 71 years. [5/30]
May 6, 1872, Laurens, Mrs. ELIZA A. STEERE, 70 years. [5/30]
May 7, 1872, Oneonta, THOMAS HORTON, 45 years. [5/30]
May 4, 1872, Oneonta, Mrs. POLLY WALRADT, 76 years. [5/30]

June 2, 1872, Cooperstown, Mrs. LUCINDA M. GRISWOLD, 34 years. [6/6]
June 3, 1872, Cooperstown, Mrs. HANNAH FRANKLIN, 86 years. [6/6]
April 18, 1872, Hartwick, Mrs. POLLY TUCKER, 78 years. [6/6]
May 26, 1872, Fly Creek, MARY A. BAILEY, 72 years. [6/6]
June 8, 1872, Middlefield, JOHN F. MARKS, 82 years. [6/13]
May 31, 1872, Cherry Valley, JAMES MC GARITY, 86 years. [6/13]
May 18, 1872, Worcester, Mrs. SARAH L. ROBINS, 41 years. [6/13]
June 7, 1872, Morris, Mrs. ENOCH LAWRENCE, 84 years. [6/13]
June 14, 1872, Morris, Mrs. EMILY T. SCUDDER, 62 years. [6/20]
June 11, 1872, Unadilla, JOHN F. HUDSON, 36 years. [6/20]
June 7, 1872, Unadilla, JOSHUA G. HUTTALEN, 78 years. [6/20]
June 11, 1872, New Lisbon, DELOS M. BROWN, 42 years. [6/20]
May 10, 1872, Middlefield Center, Mrs. ELVIRA BRYANT, 33 years. [6/20]
June 10, 1872, Hartwick, Mrs. LOUISA M. EDMUNDS, 34 years. [6/20]
June 6, 1872, Cooperstown, HELEN V. STOCKING, 23 years. [6/27]
June 21, 1872, Hartwick, DANIEL WINSOR, 78 years. [6/27]
June 29, 1872, Cooperstown, J. RUSSELL POTTER, 65 years. [7/4]
[no date] Richfield Spa, WILLIS FRAZIER, 20 years. [7/4]
April 24, 1872, Otego, CHARLES A. MILLER, 7 years. [7/4]
July 4, 1872, Cooperstown, HARRY BOWEN, infant. [7/11]
June 14, 1872, Fly Creek, Mrs. CYNTHIA HIGBY, 59 years. [7/11]
July 4, 1872, Otsego, ELIAS VAN BENSCHOTEN, 56 years. [7/11]
June 28, 1872, Oneonta, WILLIAM JOHNSTON, 44 years. [7/11]
June 7, 1872, Middlefield, LORETTA HASKINS, 66 years. [7/11]
July 4, 1872, Otsego, DORCAS WESTCOTT, 81 years. [8/1]
July 26, 1872, Middlefield, HENRY ECKLER, 18 years. [8/1]
July 20, 1872, Fly Creek, JOHN POST, 72 years. [8/1]
Aug. 3, 1872, Cooperstown, Dr. A. H. FISH, 44 years. [8/8]
Aug. 1, 1872, Fly Creek, Mrs. GEORGIANNA CHAPMAN, 22 years. [8/8]
Aug. 1, 1872, Cooperstown, DANIEL LAMB, 87 years. [8/8]
July 20, 1872, Fly Creek, Mrs. MARY NEWELL, 61 years. [8/15]
Aug. 7, 1872, Cherry Valley, Mrs. JANE SMITH, 75 years. [8/15]
Aug. 15, 1872, Milford, Mrs. DELIA PARSHALL, 53 years. [8/22]
Aug. 8, 1872, Springfield, LINDEL TEN EYCK, 59 years. [8/22]
Aug. 14, 1872, Toddsville, Mrs. ALICE A. DENTON, 27 years. [8/22]
Aug. 2, 1872, Maryland, Mrs. ABIGAIL CADY, 60 years. [8/22]
Aug. 3, 1872, Maryland, Mrs. PHEBE WAYMAN, 55 years. [8/22]
Aug. 16, 1872, Cooperstown, Mrs. MARY THOMPSON, 56 years. [8/29]

Aug. 20, 1872, Middlefield, Mrs. PERLEY M. PAGE, 21 years. [8/29]
Aug. 19, 1872, Otego, WILLIAM VAN NAMEE, 87 years. [8/29]
Aug. 25, 1872, Hartwick, TORRY J. LUCE, 75 years. [9/5]
Aug. 20, 1872, Otsego, Mrs. ABRAM VAN HORNE, 87 years. [9/5]
Aug. 31, 1872, Springfield, LEWIS W. WINNE, infant. [9/5]
Sept. 10, 1872, Cooperstown, JOHN A. KEMP, 20 years. [9/12]
Sept. 5, 1872, Cooperstown, PATRICK HEWES, 67 years. [9/12]
Aug. 8, 1872, Laurens, DANIEL GILE, 79 years. [9/12]
Aug. 26, 1872, Oneonta, ANDREW GILE, 78 years. [9/12]
Sept. 2, 1872, Butternuts, P. K. MORRIS, 48 years. [9/12]
Sept. 7, 1872, Hartwick, Mrs. ELVA J. SMITH, 19 years. [9/12]
Aug. 12, 1872, S. Edmeston, Mrs. AURILLA CHURCH, 77 years. [9/19]
Sept. 19, 1872, Otsego, JARED BRAINARD, 63 years. [9/26]
Sept. 3, 1872, Schenevus, JOHN D. SMALLWOOD, 75 years. [9/26]
Sept. 16, 1872, Hartwick, Mrs. LOUISA M. WARD, 44 years. [10/3]
Sept. 19, 1872, Westford, GEORGE W. HART, 59 years. [10/3]
Sept. 23, 1872, Edmeston, Col. ERI DEMING, 71 years. [10/3]
Oct. 1, 1872, Hartwick, DAVID GARDNER, 47 years. [10/10]
Sept. 30, 1872, New Lisbon, NEHEMIAH DANIEL, 77 years. [10/10]
Oct. 6, 1872, Westford, JOSEPH PNAH, 28 years. [10/10]
Sept. 29, 1872, Hartwick, EDWIN G. JACOBS, 13 years. [10/10]
Oct. 7, 1872, Hartwick, Mrs. JULIA T. GARDNER, 65 years. [10/17]
Sept. 20, 1872, Burlington, THOMAS J. PRATT, 72 years. [10/17]
Oct. 24, 1872, Oneonta, Mrs. ADELIZA KEYES, 30 years. [10/31]
Oct. 13, 1872, Westford, Mrs. MARY F. LANSING. [10/31]
Oct. 16, 1872, W. Burlington, CALVIN PRIEST, 67 years. [11/7]
Oct. 29, 1872, Milford, Mrs. MARDULA S. SAULSBURY, 51 years. [11/7]
Oct. 8, 1872, Mrs. PHILENA M. DENTON, 37 years. [11/7]
Nov. 14, 1872, Middlefield, ALBERT COATS, 69 years. [11/21]
Nov. 5, 1872, W. Laurens, PERRY BENNETT, 75 years. [11/21]
Nov. 7,1872, Garrattsville, Mrs. ROXIE M. HERRICK, 36 years. [11/21]
Oct. 23, 1872, Middlefield, Mrs. PHEBE TEMPLE, 75 years. [11/21]
Nov. 1, 1872, Burlington, Mrs. ANGELETTA L. WELCH, 23 years. [11/21]
Nov. 3, 1872, Franklin, Del. Co., HATTIE B. DENTON of Westford, age 17. [11/21]
Nov. 4, 1872, Pittsfield, ARLINE MC INTYRE, 21 years. [11/28]
Oct. 29, 1872, Milford, Mrs. MARDULA S. SAULSBURY, 81 years. [11/28] (Note: Previous entry gives age as 51 years.)
Nov 16, 1872, Morris, JARED PATRICK, 93 years. [11/28]

Nov. 21, 1872, Westford, ANDREW BICE, 69 years. [11/28]
Nov. 25, 1872, Westford, HARVEY E. SAXTON, 40 years. [12/5]
Nov. 6, 1872, N. Lisbon, MARBLE BUTTS, 69 years. [12/5]
Oct. 21, 1872, Otsego, Mrs. ANNA ALLEN, 79 years. [12/5]
Dec. 1, 1872, Springfield, MARIETTE DELONG, 30 years. [12/12]
Nov. 14, 1872, Springfield, Mrs. MARTHA TAYLOR FRISBIE, 30 years. [12/12]
Nov. 22, 1872, Colliersville, ELLA JENKS. [12/12]
Nov. 29, 1872, Cherry Valley, LIZZIE FONDA, 27 years. [12/12]
Nov. 19, 1872, Oneonta, Mrs. POLLY RICHARDS, 72 years. [12/12]
Nov. 19, 1872, Otego, GILBERT BUNDY, 73 years. [12/12]
Dec. 15, 1872, Cooperstown, Mrs. POLLY NILES, 65 years. [12/19]
Dec. 17, 1872, Middlefield, WILLARD GRIFFIN, 82 years. [12/19]
Nov. 14, 1872, New Berlin Center, Mrs. POLLY ADAMS, 87 years. [12/19]
Sept. 17, 1872, Laurens, NORRIS BUTTS, 72 years. [12/19]
Dec. 9, 1872, Middlefield, FRANK EGGLESTON, child. [12/19]
Nov. 22, 1872, Burlington, Mrs. E. D. HICKS, 32 years. [12/19]
Dec. 30, 1872, Cooperstown, JOHN C. EASTON, 79 years. [12/26]
Dec. 14, 1872, Toddsville, WILLIAM C. GIFFORD, M.D., 25 years. [12/26]
Dec. 24, 1872, Cooperstown, Mrs. MATILDA BARNEY, 78 years. [1/2/1873]
Dec. 30, 1872, Cooperstown, THOMAS WILSON, 72 years. [1/2/1873]
Jan. 2, 1873, Cooperstown, Mrs. ZADY THOMPSON, 34 years. [1/9]
Jan. 2, 1873, Cooperstown, Rev. JOHN WALLACE, 70 years. [1/9]
Dec. 31, 1872, Cooperstown, Mrs. ROSALLE BERRY, 21 years. [1/9/1873]
Dec. 7, 1872, Springfield, HIRAM FUNK, 48 years. [1/9/1873]
Dec. 6, 1872, Otsego, Mrs. PHILENA G. S. SCRIBNER, 42 years. [1/9/1873]
Dec. 27, 1872, Springfield, JOHN GETMAN, 72 years. [1/9/1873]
Jan. 5, 1873, Fly Creek, CAROLINE M. GIFFORD, 52 years. [1/16]
Jan. 13, 1873, Toddsville, NANCY TEMPLE, 51 years. [1/16]
Jan. 2, 1873, Burlington Flats, Mrs. PHEBE HUBBARD, 100 years. [1/16]
Jan. 13, 1873, Hartwick, Mrs. BETSEY FIELD, 81 years. [1/16]
[no date] Otsego, Mrs. LOVINA MILLER, 67 years. [1/23]
Dec. 19, 1872, Milford, Mrs. LYDIA AYLESWORTH, 83 yars. [1/23]
Jan. 9, 1873, Morris, Mrs. HARRIET DAVIS, 39 years. [1/23]
Jan. 9, 1873, Springfield, Mrs. ABBY GALPIN LAY, 52 years. [1/23]
Jan. 30, 1873, Cooperstown, JAMES A. MURDOCK, 8 years. [2/6]

Feb. 4, 1873, Cooperstown, CHARLES M. LIPPITT, 1 year. [2/6]
Jan. 31, 1873, Springfield, ELIZABETH HOKE, 57 years. [2/6]
Jan. 21, 1873, Snowden Hill, Otsego Co., Mrs. EMILY BUNN, 79 years. [2/6]
March 3, 1873, Otsego, LURINDA HUBBELL, 89 years. [3/6]
March 11, 1873, Hartwick Sem., CLARK DAVISON, 78 years. [3/13]
March 4, 1873, Middlefield, Mrs. HANNAH SNYDER, 83 years. [3/13]
March 9, 1873, New Lisbon, Mrs. DAVID HARD, 81 years. [3/13]
March 4, 1873, Otsego, MARIA BERRY, 11 years. [3/13]
Feb. 25, 1873, Otsdawa, HENRY DAVIS, 22 years. [3/13]
March 6, 1873, Butternuts, SETH D. RICHMOND, 73 years. [3/20]
March 9, 1873, Springfield, ORA ELY, 83 years. [3/20]
March 9, 1873, Otego, W. S. WILLIAMS, 44 years. [3/20]
March 2, 1873, Oneonta, CHANDLER BURGIN, 40 years. [3/20]
March 5, 1873, Coneonta, MICHAEL YAGER, 65 years. [3/20]
March 8, 1873, Oneonta, Mrs. JOHN M. FERREL, 45 years. [3/20]
March 13, 1873, New Lisbon, JOEL PORTER, 81 years. [3/20]
March 19, 1873, Hartwick, PETER CONKLIN, 70 years. [3/27]
March 18, 1873, Hartwick, FREDERICK CALKINS, 12 years. [3/27]
March 13, 1873, Otego, Mrs. DESIRE WOOD, 60 years. [3/27]
March 19, 1873, Cherry Valley, Mrs. ANNA NELSON, 73 years. [3/27]
March 6, 1873, Richfield Spa, ISAAC K. BEACH, 73 years. [3/27]
March 18, 1873, Unadilla, Mrs. SARAH WILLIAMS, 69 years. [3/27]
March 27, 1873, Fly Creek, JOHN CLARK, 82 years. [4/3]
March 7, 1873, Edmeston, Mrs. MELISSA CLARK, 24 years. [4/3]
March 20, 1873, Fly Creek, Mrs. CYNTHIA T. COATS, 62 years. [4/3]
April 2, 1873, Cooperstown, Mrs. LUCY C. SAXTON, 82 years. [4/10]
March 28, 1873, Middlefield Cen., DARIUS GATES, 70 years. [4/10]
March 29, 1873, Hartwick, EVERETT G. BISHOP, 19 years. [4/10]
April 2, 1873, Toddsville, FRANCIS ALLISON, 64 years. [4/10]
April 13, 1873, Cooperstown, HENRY KASEBY, 53 years. [4/17]
April 6, 1873, Unadilla Cen., IRA BRIANT, 64 years. [4/17]
April 7, 1873, Edmeston, Mrs. JULIA A. SPRAGUE, 58 years. [4/17]
April 16, 1873, Cooperstown, DANIEL W. CHAPMAN, 55 years. [4/24]
March 20, 1873, Middlefield, AMOS F. WICKWIRE, 1 year. [4/24]
April 15, 1873, New Lisbon, WILLIAM BUNDY, 47 years. [4/24]
April 8, 1873, Burlington, Mrs. MARGARET HOOD, 81 years. [4/24]
April 8, 1873, Westford, CHRISTOPHER SNYDER, 76 years. [4/24]
April 17, 1873, Middlefield, MARY WINNEGAR, 61 years. [4/24]
April 6, 1873, Oneonta, Mrs. OPHELIA DEAN, 31 years. [4/24]
April 24, 1873, Cooperstown, ELLEN KELLEY, 27 years. [5/1]

April 6, 1873, Unadilla Cen., IRA BRIANT, 64 years. [5/1]
April 7, 1873, Edmeston, Mrs. JULIA A. SPRAGUE, 58 years. [5/1]
May 4, 1873, Cooperstown, infant son of GEORGE M. JARVIS. [5/8]
April 29, 1873, Oaksville, THOMAS POTTS, 40 years. [5/8]
April 18, 1873, Milford, Capt. JOSEPH STILL, 62 years. [5/8]
April 30, 1873, Hartwick, SEYMOUR G. SHAUL. [5/8]
April 24, 1873, Decatur, Mrs. ELIZA TRIPP. [5/8]
May 2, 1873, Middlefield, Mrs. NEOMA REED, 74 years. [5/8]
April 23, 1873, Burlington Flats, CLARK M. HUESTIS, 36 years. [5/8]
March 19, 1873, New Lisbon, Mrs. SALLY PIERCE, 87 years. [5/15]
March 11, 1873, Exeter, Mrs. SARAH NICKERSON, 76 years. [5/22]
April 26, 1873, Cooperstown, Dr. ISAAC BURNETT, 68 years. [5/29]
May 26, 1873, Hyde Park, Mrs. LYDIA MC COLLUM, 82 years. [5/29]
May 19, 1873, New Lisbon, Mrs. ELSIE YOUNG, 66 years. [6/5]
May 26, 1873, Richfield, Mrs. SALLY MARTIN, 77 years. [6/5]
May 25, 1873, Cherry Valley, Mrs. KATE HERDMAN, 38 years. [6/5]
June 4, 1873, Otsego, GEORGE T. LOUGH, infant. [6/12]
May 26, 1873, Pittsfield, HARVEY LAIGHT, 73 years. [6/12]
May 21, 1873, Westford, Mrs. ELIZA GROFF, 37 years. [6/12]
June 9, 1873, Roseboom, DORTHA FELLOWS, 64 years. [6/19]
June 8, 1873, Oneonta, DAVID F. CLARK, 69 years. [6/19]
May 26, 1873, W. Laurens, Mrs. EMMA A. SMITH, 22 years. [6/19]
June 8, 1873, Middlefield, Mrs. ELIZABETH M. HALLIDAY, 45 years. [6/19]
June 7, 1873, Milford, ELLA DINGMAN, 15 years. [6/19]
June 8, 1873, Springfield, ELIZA M. DAVY, 14 years. [6/19]
June 22, 1873, Cooperstown, Mrs. HANNAH I. BEGGS, 53 years. [6/26]
June 16, 1873, New Lisbon, Mrs. ELSIE W. BALLARD, 69 years. [6/26]
July 5, 1873, Hartwick, Mrs. ROSEY GREEN, 41 years. [7/10]
June 28, 1873, Morris, JONATHAN ANGELL, 82 years. [7/10]
June 19, 1873, Middlefield, ESTELLA HANNAH, 19 years. [7/10]
July 11, 1873, Hartwick, ALBERT WHIPPLE, 48 years. [7/17]
June 29, 1873, New Lisbon, ISAAC C. KEMBELL, 58 years. [7/17]
June 2, 1873, Otego, Mrs. EMILY HALE, 72 years. [7/17]
July 25, 1873, Middlefield, Mrs. ELVIRA A. WINEGAR, 39 years. [7/31]
July 12, 1873, Springfield Cen., Mrs. MARY W. HITCHCOCK, 50 years. [7/31]
July 26, 1873, Springfield Cen., Mrs. SARAH STEWART, 75 years. [7/31]
July 14, 1873, Morris, JAMES R. ANGELL, 79 years. [8/7]
Aug. 3, 1873, Hartwick Sem., MINER C. PARSHALL, 67 years. [8/7]
Aug. 12, 1873, Cooperstown, HOWARD E. MC FARREN, infant. [8/14]

Aug. 6, 1873, Fly Creek, Mrs. SOPHIA GREEN, 77 years. [8/14]
Aug. 1, 1873, Westford, Mrs. PARMELIA PLATNER, 86 years. [8/14]
July 31, 1873, Morris, WILLIAM TURNER, 48 years. [8/14]
Aug. 17, 1873, Cooperstown, WILLIAM H. AVERELL, 79 years. [8/21]
Aug. 16, 1873, Cooperstown, Mrs. HARRIET L. PALMER, 46 years. [8/21]
Aug. 17, 1873, Oneonta, Mrs. THOMAS MAYNARD, 30 years. [8/28]
Aug. 16, 1873, Burlington, ELLA F. SLOAN, 9 years. [9/4]
Aug. 5, 1873, Edmeston, EMILY F. WRIGHT, 20 years. [9/11]
Sept. 1, 1873, Hartwick, Mrs. MARY A. SIBLEY, 38 years. [9/11]
Sept. 12, 1873, Laurens, Hon. HARVEY STRONG, 74 years. [9/18]
Sept. 13, 1873, Milford, Mrs. HANNAH SMITH, 91 years. [9/18]
Sept. 3, 1873, Hartwick, Mrs. ELIZABETH KENYON, 46 years. [9/18]
Sept. 10, 1873, Springfield, Mrs. CHARLOTTE E. OVERACRE, 30 years. [9/18]
Sept. 18, 1873, Otsego, Mrs. MARTHA R. PALMER, 25 years. [9/25]
Sept. 12, 1873, Oneonta, Mrs. SUSAN MC GINLEY, 60 years. [9/25]
Sept. 9, 1873, Colliersville, EMELINE V. WRIGHT. [9/25]
Sept. 17, 1873, Burlington, NEVA A. TALBOT, 1 year. [9/25]
Sept. 13, 1873, Milford, Mrs. HANNAH SMITH, 92 years. [10/2]
Sept. 21, 1873, Garrattsville, ANSEL TULLER, 67 years. [10/2]
[no date] Cooperstown, WESTCOT H. COOKE, infant. [10/9]
Sept. 22, 1873, Otsego, Mrs. ALEX. H. CARR, 66 years. [10/9]
Sept. 22, 1873, Unadilla, Mrs. POLLY STEBBINS, 55 years. [10/9]
Sept. 27, 1873, New Lisbon, EMILY A. NEARING, 47 years. [10/9]
Sept. 26, 1873, Maryland, LUCY PALMATIEE, 21 years. [10/9]
Oct. 1, 1873, Maryland, E. W. BENTON, 55 years. [10/9]
Sept. 9, 1873, Westford, MERRITT KNAPP, 29 years. [10/9]
Oct. 14, 1873, Cooperstown, FANNY E. FIELD, 23 years. [10/16]
Sept. 24, 1873, Springfield, DAVID SCABLARD, 82 years. [10/16]
Oct. 16, 1873, Cooperstown, Mrs. MARY A. MORRIS COOPER, 90 years. [10/23]
Oct. 21, 1873, Cooperstown, EDWARD EDWARDS, 56 years. [10/23]
Sept. 20, 1873, Richfield, HAMILTON BAKER, 67 years. [10/23]
Oct. 20, 1873, Hartwick, LYMAN VAN SLYKE, 35 years. [10/23]
Sept. 30, 1873, Springfield, ELLA WOOD, 3 years. [10/23]
Oct. 9, 1873, Worcester, Mrs. HANNAH WINEGARD, 58 years. [10/23]
Oct. 23, 1873, New Lisbon, JONATHAN GARDNER, 85 years. [10/30]
Oct. 16, 1873, Butternuts, EDWARD BURR, 60 years. [10/30]
Oct. 16, 1873, Morris, HENRY D. LEWIS, 32 years. [10/30]
Oct. 30, 1873, Springfield, THOMAS B. ROOT, 31 years. [11/6]

Nov. 5, 1873, Mt. Vision, Mrs. CLARISSA BUNN, 27 years. [11/13]
Nov. 5, 1873, Springfield, JOHN WIRES, 96 years. [11/13]
Oct. 26, 1873, Middlefield, MARY M. WALDBY, 46 years. [11/13]
Nov. 4, 1873, Hartwick, DAVID B. ANDRUS, 1 year. [11/13]
Nov. 5, 1873, Otego, DAVID WEDDERSPOON, 54 years. [11/13]
Nov. 12, 1873, Oneonta, Mrs. LESTER STEWART, 74 years. [11/20]
Oct. 31, 1873, Oneonta, Mrs. LILLIE REYNOLDS, 26 years. [11/20]
Nov. 19, 1873, Hartwick, STEPHEN W. TIFFANY, 63 years. [11/27]
Nov. 21, 1873, Middlefield, Mrs. ELIZABETH OTTAWAY, 81 years. [11/27]
Nov. 12, 1873, Cherry Valley, HUGH R. THOMPSON, 73 years. [11/27]
Nov. 23, 1873, Richfield Spa, HELEN GETMAN, 27 years. [12/4]
[no date] Exeter Cen., ARMINDA ADKINS, 55 years. [12/4]
Dec. 3, 1873, Cooperstown, JOHN KELLY, 57 yars. [12/11]
Nov. 4, 1873, Hartwick, Mrs. IRENA LATTIN, 67 years. [12/11]
Nov. 6, 1873, Otego, Mrs. EMILY C. COUSE, 46 years. [12/11]
Dec. 1, 1873, Springfield, Mrs. RUTH C. VAN HORNE, 38 years. [12/11]
Dec. 8, 1873, Springfield, Mrs. SARAH E. MARVIN. [12/11]
Nov. 28, 1873, Cherry Valley, EDWIN JUDD, 68 years. [12/11]
Nov. 27, 1873, Cherry Valley, Mrs. MARY DIELL, 94 years. [12/11]
Nov. 17, 1873, Cherry Valley, Mrs. ROSA MC GARRITY, 65 years. [12/11]
Nov. 22, 1873, Unadilla, PALMER OSBORN, 18 years. [12/11]
Dec. 13, 1873, Cooperstown, Hon. SAMUEL NELSON, 81 years. [12/18]
Nov. 26, 1873, Otego, ASA W. LAMB, 68 years. [12/18]
Dec. 19, 1873, Cooperstown, HENRY SCOTT, 81 years. [12/25]
Dec. 17, 1873, Cooperstown, EMELINE J. BALDWIN, 19 years. [12/25]
Dec. 17, 1873, Otsego, Mrs. SARAH HINDS, 82 years. [12/25]
Dec. 14, 1873, New Lisbon, WILLIAM REED, 73 years. [12/25]
Dec. 14, 1873, Milford Cen., CLIFFORD TARBOX, 18 years. [12/25]
Dec. 20, 1873, Morris, HARLEY SEARGENT, 67 years. [1/1/1874]
Dec. 23, 1873, Middlefield, JACOB VAN HUSEN, 86 years. [1/1/1874]
Nov. 19, 1873, Burlington, FREDK. R. CUSHMAN, 7 years. [1/1/1874]
Dec. 6, 1873, Burlington, NETTIE A. CUSHMAN, 3 years. [1/1/1874]
Dec. 25, 1873, Otsego, Mrs. MIRANDA S. ALLEN, 61 years. [1/8/1874]
Jan. 6, 1874, Cooperstown, EMMA FULLER, 79 years. [1/15]
Jan. 2, 1874, Hartwick, MICHAEL RICH, 54 years. [1/15]
Jan. 1, 1874, Maryland, HUMPHREY WILBER, 77 years. [1/15]
Dec. 18, 1873, Morris, Mrs. SYLVINA TILLSON, 45 years. [1/15/1874]
Dec. 31, 1873, New Lisbon, Mrs. LUCY BUTTS, 69 years. [1/15/1874]

Jan. 3, 1874, Butternuts, Mrs. JANE MILLER, 58 years. [1/15]
Jan. 19, 1874, Cooperstown, NELSON V. CARR, 36 years. [1/22]
Jan. 14, 1874, Cooperstown, LAURA C. DAVIS, 19 years. [1/22]
Jan. 18, 1874, Otsego, Mrs. SALLY CARR, 81 years. [1/22]
Jan. --, 1874, Hartwick, HENRY R. HOWE, 53 years. [1/22]
Jan. 12, 1874, Cherry Valley, SAMUEL D. BURTON, 63 years. [1/22]
Jan. 10, 1874, Cherry Valley, Mrs. JANE BELKNAP, 76 years. [1/22]
[NOTE: The following 5 entries are probably from issue of 1/29/1874 & not 1/22/1874.]
Jan. 22, 1874, Cooperstown, ELLERY CORY, 80 years. [1/22-sic]
Jan. 25, 1874, Cooperstown, MARGARET HUNTER, 8 years. [1/22-sic]
Jan. 19, 1874, Maryland, A. H. MANZER, 38 years. [1/22]
Jan. 19, 1874, Morris, FRANCES ROTCH. [1/22]
Jan. 19, 1874, Oneonta, Mrs. VESTA M. BALLARD. [1/22]
Feb. 9, 1874, Cooperstown, WILLIAM H. RUGGLES, 53 years. [2/12]
Feb. 6, 1874, Middlefield, JOHN HUTCHINGS, 78 years. [2/18]
Feb. 25, 1874, Cooperstown, FREDK. PEARSE, 11 years. [2/26]
Feb. 23, 1874, Cooperstown, ARCHIBALD HARVEY, 10 years. [2/26]
Feb. 18, 1874, Milford, MARY LEANING, 76 years. [2/26]
Feb. 23, 1874, Middlefield, HENRY SNEDEKER, 29 years. [2/26]
Feb. 25, 1874, Cooperstown, Mrs. MARY CUPPERNULL, 74 years. [3/5]
Feb. 28, 1874, Cooperstown, ELLEN MANDEVILLE, 53 years. [3/5]
March 1, 1874, Middlefield, JOSEPH A. BROWN, 74 years. [3/5]
March 2, 1874, New Lisbon, Mrs. SUSY A. BUNDY, 23 years. [3/5]
Feb. 25, 1874, Otsego, IRA TANNER, 18 years. [3/5]
Feb. 14, 1874, New Lisbon, JOHN YOUNG, 64 years. [3/5]
Jan. 11, 1874, Westford, FREDK. J. GREEN, 4 years. [3/5]
Dec. 27, 1874, Springfield, WILLIAM DRYDEN, 62 years. [3/5]
Jan. 14, 1874, Unadilla, MARY L. HYER, 17 years. [3/5]
March 6, 1874, Cooperstown, JESSE BICE, 3 years. [3/12]
March 8, 1874, Cooperstown, MARY DUNN, 72 years. [3/12]
Feb. 22, 1874, Clarksville, PETER RENO, 67 years. [3/12]
Feb. 13, 1874, Roseboom, PHEBE GREEN, 66 years. [3/12]
March 12, 1874, Cooperstown, JAMES D. CORWIN, 5 years. [3/12]
March 7, 1874, Cooperstown, Mrs. HARVEY MERIHEW, 64 years. [3/12]
March 14, 1874, Cooperstown, infant of ED. BARRETT. [3/12]
Feb. 27, 1874, Unadilla, ALBERT D. AYLESWORTH, 31 years. [3/12]
March 5, 1874, Cherry Valley, ELIZABETH FLINT, 36 years. [3/12]
March 22, 1874, Cooperstown, SAMUEL BINGHAM NEWELL, infant. [3/26]
March 21, 1874, Middlefield, JAMES C. KELLY, 78 years. [3/26]

March 9, 1874, Middlefield, JESSIE JONES, 1 years. [3/26]
March 13, 1874, Cherry Valley, Mrs. SARAH A. TEAKINS, 56 years. [3/26]
March 14, 1874, Richfield Spa, Mrs. JANE SMITH, 38 years. [3/26]
March 11, 1874, Oneonta Plains, CLOVIS STEERS, 75 years. [3/26]
March 26, 1874, Cooperstown, SETH T. WINSLOW, 63 years. [4/2]
March 29, 1874, Otsego, Mrs. ELIZABETH LEWIS, 90 years. [4/2]
March 30, 1874, Toddsville, ELIZABETH PECK, 1 year. [4/2]
March 4, 1874, Milford, NELLIE C. WARD, infant. [4/2]
April 2, 1874, Cooperstown, Mrs. EMMA S. THAYAER, 43 years. [4/9]
April 2, 1874, Hartwick, ISAAC WILBER, 83 years. [4/9]
April 5, 1874, Otsego, EDWIN LYNCH, infant. [4/9]
April 5, 1874, Middlefield, Mrs. ELIZABETH BANISTER, 76 years. [4/9]
April 1, 1874, Exeter, DANIEL VAN COURT, 84 years. [4/9]
April 1, 1874, Hartwick, HORACE CHASE, 65 years. [4/9]
March 29, 1874, Otego, Mrs. LAVISA [sic] TOLLET. [4/9]
March 31, 1874, New Lisbon, AMASA ALDRICH, 77 years. [4/9]
March 15, 1874, Mrs. ESTHER WINSOR, 69 years. [4/9]
April 12, 1874, Oneonta, Mrs. MARY A. GRAVES, 67 years. [4/16]
April 13, 1874, Middlefield, MYRTLE SMITH, infant. [4/16]
March 31, 1874, Laurens, Mrs. SALLY ELDRED, 92 years. [4/16]
April 9, 1874, Middlefield, HARRY D. CLARK, 1 year. [4/16]
April 10, 1874, Middlefield, FRANK GRIDLEY, 14 years. [4/16]
April 14, 1874, Toddsville, Mrs. SOPHIA M. GATES, 85 years. [4/23]
March 7,1874, Otego, MARY D. HOGEBOOM, 81 years. [4/23]
April 19, 1874, Maryland, WILLIAM RAY, 68 years. [4/23]
April 20, 1874, Middlefield, SALLY VUNK, 66 years. [4/23]
April 19, 1874, Middlefield, ALBERT MURDOCK, 7 years. [4/23]
April 27, 1874, Cooperstown, Mrs. SALLY DOUBLEDAY, 82 years. [4/30]
April 27, 1874, Springfield Cen., Mrs. MINERVA E. WOOD, 34 years. [4/30]
April 28, 1874, Springfield Cen., Dr. ALFRED VAN HORNE, 47 years. [4/30]
April 20, 1874, Cherry Valley, Mrs. MARGARET HARDENDORF, 62 years. [4/30]
April 3, 1874, Unadilla, WILLIAM D. SPENCER, 80 years. [4/30]
May 5, 1874, Cooperstown, CORA B. SIVER, 4 years. [5/7]
April 24, 1874, Otsego, PATRICK HAGGERTY, 72 years. [5/7]
April 27, 1874, Fly Creek, Mrs. CATHERINE GARDNER, 75 years. [5/7]
April 28, 1874, Toddsville, JANE SNYDER, 15 years. [5/7]
May 2, 1874, Milford, LYMAN BROOKS, 80 years. [5/7]

May 9, 1874, Cooperstown, TRUMAN DEWEY, 73 years. [5/14]
May 10, 1874, New Lisbon, Dr. JOHN F. MATHER, 70 years. [5/14]
April 25, 1874, Exeter, HATTIE M. HOLLISTER, 14 years. [5/21]
March 8, 1874, West Laurens, Mrs. COMFORT MOSIER, 79 years. [5/21]
April 29, 1874, Unadilla, BETSEY INGRAHAM, 72 years. [5/21]
May 25, 1874, Cooperstown, MARIA COOPER, 1 year. [5/28]
May 13, 1874, Otsego, THOMAS MC EWEN, 80 years. [5/28]
May 16, 1874, S. Hartwick, GEORGE ELDRED, 19 years. [5/28]
May 30, 1874, Portlandville, Mrs. CYNTHIA BECKLEY, 50 years. [6/4]
May 30, 1874, Springfield, WILLIAM W. TEN EYCK, 48 years. [6/11]
May 24, 1874, Schenevus, Mrs. NELLIE BALDWIN, 34 years. [6/11]
May 30, 1874, Springfield, WILLIAM W. TEN EYCK, 48 years. [6/11]
May 30, 1874, Laurens, AMOS JOHNSON, 78 years. [6/11]
May 22, 1874, Portlandville, CHARLES A. QUACKENBUSH, 7 years. [6/11]
June 5, 1874, Milford, JAMES HUNT, 84 years. [6/18]
May 26, 1874, Otsego, MARY S. NILES, 29 years. [6/25]
June 14, 1874, Oneonta, FANNY J. MAC DONALD, 16 years. [6/25]
June 9, 1874, Maryland, MARGARET E. BENNETT, 4 years. [6/25]
June 5, 1874, Garrattsville, RICHARD EMERSON, 75 years. [6/25]
June 27, 1874, Cooperstown, CAROLINE JORDAN CLARK, 59 years. [7/2]
June 18, 1874, Cooperstown, SUSAN CUMMINGS, 15 years. [7/2]
July 6, 1874, Cooperstown, ALEX. M. DAVIS, infant. [7/9]
July 6, 1874, Cooperstown, Mrs. SARAH G. DAVIS. [7/9]
June 5, 1874, Garrattsville, RICHARD EMERSON, 75 years. [7/9]
July 3, 1874, Cherry Valley, Mrs. JOHN DIELL, 70 years. [7/16]
July 7, 1874, Hartwick, WILLIAM JONES, 23 years. [7/23]
July 24, 1874, Otsego, JOHN D. KELLOGG, 1 year. [7/30]
July 6, 1874, New Lisbon, FAITHFUL SMITH, 73 years. [7/30]
June 28, 1874, New Lisbon, JOHN NEARING, 77 years. [7/30]
July 12, 1874, Morris, HORACE M. PERRY, 65 years. [7/30]
June 20, 1874, W. Burlington, DAVID SUMMERS, 20 years. [7/30]
July 15, 1874, Worcester, Mrs. EUNICE IVES, 40 years. [7/30]
Aug. 10, 1874, Hartwick, Dr. C. E. ISMOND, 33 years. [8/13]
Aug. 20, 1874, Cooperstown, Mrs. JULIA WILSON, 78 years. [8/13]
Aug. 12, 1874, Laurens, FRANCES CHENEY, 30 years. [8/13]
Aug. 9, 1874, New Lisbon, Mrs. POLLY PERKINS, 85 years. [8/13]
Aug. 5, 1874, Worcester, LEWIS UTTER, 59 years. [8/13]
Aug. 10, 1874, S. Worcester, Mrs. LUCY OLMSTEAD, 74 years. [8/13]

Aug. 20, 1874, Cooperstown, Mrs. SYLVIA EATON, 68 years. [8/27]
Aug. 6, 1874, Cooperstown, MARGARET CARY, infant. [8/27]
Aug. 13, 1874, Cooperstown, NELSON K. HOOSE, infant. [8/27]
Aug. 14, 1874, Butternuts, Mrs. JENNIE JENKS, 22 years. [8/27]
Aug. 30, 1874, Cooperstown, BELLE ROBINSON, infant. [9/3]
Aug. 27, 1874, Westford, NATHANIEL GROFF, 72 years. [9/3]
Aug. 23, 1874, Garrattsville, E. G. RICKLAND, 75 years. [9/3]
Sept. 6, 1874, Schuyler's Lake, CHARLES SHUMWAY, 24 years. [9/10]
Sept. 2, 1874, Hartwick, Mrs. IDA S. JENKS, 22 years. [9/10]
Sept. 8, 1874, Richfield Spa, ISAAC S. FORD, 74 years. [9/10]
Sept. 11, 1874, Burlington, ARTHUR C. FAY, 21 years. [9/17]
Sept. 10, 1874, Hartwick, ALVAH P. CONVERSE, 68 years. [9/17]
Sept. 14, 1874, Hartwick, CORNELIUS TEACHOUT, 75 years. [9/17]
Sept. 8, 1874, Portlandville, THOMAS L. WAKEFIELD, 82 years. [9/17]
Sept. 17, 1874, Cooperstown, GEORGE KNAPP, infant. [9/24]
Sept. 21, 1874, Springfield Cen., ELSCEY A. WOOD, infant. [9/24]
Sept. 14, 1874, Burlington, Mrs. LUCY BALCOM, 49 years. [9/24]
Aug. 29, 1874, Milford Cen., JESSIE ROSE, 17 years. [9/24]
Sept. 13, 1874, Burlington, ADDIE JOSLIN, 8 years. [9/24]
Sept. 26, 1874, Cooperstown, WILLIAM D. LONGTON, 2 years. [10/1]
Sept. 18, 1874, Cooperstown, MAUD RUSSELL, 1 year. [10/1]
Sept. 26, 1874, Edmeston, SAMUEL C. BILYEA, 46 years. [10/1]
Sept. 15, 1874, W. Oneonta, NARCISSA HODGE, 19 years. [10/1]
Sept. 9, 1874, Oneonta Plains, Mrs. SARAH M. BURRELL, 32 years. [10/1]
Sept. 15, 1874, W. Oneonta, NANCY MORRISON, 19 years. [10/1]
Sept. 21, 1874, Garrattsville, Mrs. H. B. ARNOLD, 30 years. [10/1]
Sept. 21, 1874, Cherry Valley, AMASA BELKNAP, 88 years. [10/1]
Sept. 22, 1874, Cherry Valley, Mrs. SARAH ALLEN, 86 years. [10/1]
Sept. 10, 1874, Hartwick Sem., ALVAN P. CONVERSE, 68 years. [10/1]
Aug. 24, 1874, Hartwick Sem., JAMIE ALGER, 1 year. [10/1]
Oct. 10, 1874, Hartwick, Mrs. OLIVE TUCKER, 86 years. [10/15]
Oct. 8, 1874, Cooperstown, Mrs. CATHERINE DOYLE, 78 years. [10/15]
Oct. 12, 1874, Cooperstown, CLARA L. JACKSON, 14 years. [10/15]
Oct. 9, 1874, Hartwick, MICHAEL MC CABE, 75 years. [10/15]
Oct. 6, 1874, Springfield, Mrs. DANIEL WHITE, 70 years. [10/15]
Oct. 17, 1874, Cooperstown, Mrs. SARAH CATHCART, 57 years. [10/28]
Oct. 15, 1874, Westford, J. LAVERN SAXTON, 45 years. [10/28]
Oct. 11, 1874, Milford, DANIEL BARNEY, 66 years. [10/29]
Oct. 22, 1874, E. Springfield, Mrs. HENRY A. DAVEY. [10/29]

Oct. 23, 1874, Springfield Cen., Mrs. GEORGE WILLIAMS, 24 years. [10/29]
Oct. 22, 1874, New Lisbon, Mrs. HARRIET F. ADAMS, 47 years. [10/29]
Oct. 23, 1874, Hartwick, WILLIS MYERS, 77 years. [10/29]
Oct. 29, 1874, Cooperstown, JOHN H. ANTHON, 42 years. [11/5]
Oct. 28, 1874, Cooperstown, Mrs. SARAH M. VAN NORMAN of NYC. [11/5]
Nov. 4, 1874, Toddsville, FRED A. SHUMWAY, 22 years. [11/5]
Oct. 28, 1874, Springfield, Mrs. POLLY WIER, 81 years. [11/5]
Oct. 29, 1874, Fly Creek, Mrs. LYDIA CAREY, 89 years. [11/5]
Oct. 22, 1874, E. Springfield, Mrs. MARY TALBOT DAVEY, 41 years. [11/5]
Oct. 30, 1874, E. Springfield, LYMAN DRUSE, 68 years. [11/5]
Nov. 4, 1874, Toddsville, FRED A. SHUMWAY, 22 years. [11/12]
Nov. 7, 1874, Cooperstown, HENRY T. WILLIAMS, 7 years. [11/12]
Nov. 11, 1874, Hartwick, JOHN WILSON, 78 years. [11/19]
Nov. 14, 1874, Cooperstown, MORRIS HOGAN, 67 years. [11/19]
Nov. 16, 1874, Cooperstown, JOHN WILLIAMS, 5 years. [11/19]
Oct. 27, 1874, Hartwick, JOHN D. WEEKS, 71 years. [11/19]
Nov. 22, 1874, Middlefield, ROBERT ROUSE, 59 years. [11/26]
Nov. 20, 1874, Toddsville, ROSA RIPHENBERGH, 1 year. [11/26]
Nov. 26, 1874, Cooperstown, CARRIE WICKS, 3 years. [12/3]
Nov. 29, 1874, Cooperstown, DANIEL SHAY, 3 years. [12/3]
Nov. 30, 1874, Cooperstown, RUSSELL H. SMITH, 43 years. [12/3]
Nov. 22, 1874, Schuyler's Lake, ELISHA G. TOWNE, 33 years. [12/3]
Nov. 24, 1874, Middlefield, Mrs. CANDACE M. MARKS, 84 years. [12/3]
Nov. 14, 1874, Burlington, ORIGEN CHURCH, 93 years. [12/10]
Dec. 2, 1874, Oaksville, ADDIE F. SMITH, 2 years. [12/10]
Dec. 11, 1874, Westville, ROBERT DUTTON, 85 years. [12/17]
Dec. 8, 1874, Unadilla, CLARISSA L. BIDWELL, 65 years. [12/17]
Nov. 27, 1874, Butternuts, DAVID SHAW, 97 years. [12/24]
Dec. 28, 1874, Middlefield, RAYMOND W. EGGLESTON, 52 years. [12/31]
Jan. 5, 1875, Cooperstown, DANIEL PECK, 74 years. [1/7]
Dec. 10, 1874, Morris, CHRISTOPER GIFFORD, 78 years. [1/7/1875]
Dec. 19, 1874, Burlington Flats, Mrs. E. A. HOLLOWAY, 74 years. [1/7/1875]
Jan. 1, 1875, Worcester, JAMES MC MULLEN, 50 years. [1/7]
Dec. 25, 1874, Morris, NELSON BURDICK, 60 years. [1/7/1875]
Jan. 12, 1875, Cooperstown, Mrs. ELMIRA DEWEY, 70 years. [1/14]

Jan. 7, 1875, Index, EVA M. MC INTYRE, 7 years. [1/14]
Dec. 30, 1874, Burlington, JAMES TREWHIT, 73 years. [1/14/1775]
Jan. 2, 1875, Oneonta, ALANSON BENEDICT, 72 years. [1/14]
Jan. 3, 1875, Morris, Mrs. HENRIETTA T. HARRISON, 73 years. [1/14]
Dec. 19, 1874, New Lisbon, Mrs. JULIA GARDNER, 55 years. [1/14/1875]
[no date] E. Springfield, Mrs. CHRISTOPHER DUTCHER, 91 years. [1/14/1875]
Dec. 19, 1874, Burlington Flats, Mrs. E. A. HOLLOWAY, 74 years. [1/14/1875]
Jan. 11, 1875, Exeter, CAROLINE BREZEE, infant. [1/28]
Jan. 21, 1875, Cooperstown, JENNIE E. JOHNSON, 9 years. [1/28]
Jan. 28, 1875, Hartwick, Mrs. SARAH FISK, 80 years. [2/4]
Jan. 25, 1875, Burlington, CHAD R. CHEESEBRO, 70 years. [2/4]
Jan. 26, 1875, Fly Creek, Mrs. AURELIA PATTEN, 89 years. [2/4]
Feb. 3, 1875, Cooperstown, JAMES S. MACKEY, 54 years. [2/11]
Feb. 3, 1875, Otsego, WALTER TURNBULL, 72 years. [2/11]
Feb. 7, 1875, Otsego, POTTER ROSE, 70 years. [2/11]
Feb. 4, 1875, Laurens, Mrs. JANE E. HARRIS, 73 years. [2/11]
Jan. 17, 1875, Cherry Valley, Mrs. CATHERINE MICHAELS, 65 years. [2/11]
Feb. 15, 1875, Cooperstown, NOAH W. RIPLEY, 77 years. [2/18]
Feb. 13, 1875, Middlefield, HARRISON H. NORTH, 55 years. [2/18]
Feb. 12, 1875, Springfield, CLARA E. TAFF, 7 years. [2/18]
Feb. 13, 1875, Middlefield, ELMER MORRELL, 48 years. [2/18]
Feb. 23, 1875, Cooperstown, WILLIAM NICHOLS, 86 years. [2/25]
Feb. 18, 1875, Cooperstown, Mrs. ESTHER S. LEWIS, 82 years. [2/25]
Feb. 22, 1875, Cooperstown, Mrs. HELEN S. LITTLE, 36 years. [2/25]
Feb. 12, 1875, Cherry Valley, Mrs. SYBIL KIRBY, 68 years. [2/25]
Feb. 16, 1875, Hartwick, EUNICE WALBY, 75 years. [2/25]
Jan. 30, 1875, Middlefield, Mrs. CATHERINE PITTS, 67 years. [2/25]
Feb. 20, 1875, Hartwick, Mrs. WAITEY POTTER, 74 years. [2/25]
Feb. 18, 1875, Oneonta, HEZEKIAH WARNER, 66 years. [2/25]
Feb. 25, 1875, Cooperstown, ELLEN CONNELLY, 66 years. [3/4]
March 1, 1875, Cooperstown, THOMAS CONLISS, 31 years. [3/4]
Feb. 8, 1875, Pittsfield, SAMUEL ATWELL, 77 years. [3/4]
Feb. 13, 1875, Butternuts, ELISHA LILLIE, 85 years. [3/4]
Feb. 19, 1875, Morris, Mrs. SAWTELLE, 80 years. [3/4]
Feb. 19, 1875, Morris, Mrs. LUCY BABCOCK, 77 years. [3/4]
March 1, 1875, Schuyler Lake, Mrs. POLLY BEADLE, 83 years. [3/4]

Feb. 22, 1875, Schuyler Lake, Mrs. RHODA VAN COURT, 83 years. [3/4]
Feb. 27, 1875, Schuyler Lake, Mrs. RUTH SMITH, 79 years. [3/4]
March 6, 1875, Cooperstown, MICHAEL SHAY, 54 years. [3/11]
March 7, 1875, Otsego, WILLIAM BABCOCK, 2 years. [3/11]
Feb. 26, 1875, Hartwick, AMELIA L. BISHOP, 9 years. [3/11]
March 2, 1875, Hartwick Sem., Mrs. HATTIE BROOKS, 29 years. [3/11]
March 10, 1875, Chicago, CORRINE E. GILLMAN of Cooperstown, 16 years. [3/18]
March 14, 1875, Milford Cen., Mrs. LUCY M. WRIGHT, 92 years. [3/18]
March 12, 1875, Toddsville, WILLIAM F. ALPAUGH, 25 years. [3/18]
March 18, 1875, Cooperstown, HENRY GOULD, 69 years. [3/25]
March 24, 1875, Cooperstown, HANNAH RAY, 83 years. [3/25]
May 21, 1875, Cooperstown, Mrs. CATHERINE GILLON, 35 years. [3/25]
March 17, 1875, Otsego, JOHN REYNOLDS, 45 years. [3/25]
March 19, 1875, Middlefield, EDWARD O'CONNELL, 2 years. [3/25]
March 22, 1875, Middlefield, Mrs. BETSEY BROWN, 85 years. [3/25]
March 21, 1875, Middlefield, MARY SKINION, 20 years. [3/25]
March 16, 1875, Burlington Flats, Mrs. BETSEY HUBBELL, 83 years. [3/25]
March 24, 1875, Middlefield, HENRY BICE, 70 years. [4/1]
March 27, 1875, Otsego, SARAH ANN TRACEY, 75 years. [4/1]
March 6, 1875, Unadilla Forks, LEROY SPENCER, 62 years. [4/1]
March 7, 1875, Unadilla Forks, Mrs. DORCAS CHAPMAN, 75 years. [4/1]
April 7, 1875, Cooperstown, MARY P. SCHROM, infant. [4/8]
April 1, 1875, Otsego, CARRIE B. VAN HORNE, infant. [4/8]
April 3, 1875, Middlefield, FRANCES ANDREWS, 63 years. [4/8]
March 27, 1875, Middlefield, Mrs. SARAH E. PRATT, 49 years. [4/8]
March 20, 1875, Mt. Vision, Mrs. WILLIAM CHENEY, 59 years. [4/8]
March 27, 1875, Unadilla, PHELPS LOOMIS, infant. [4/8]
March 13, 1875, Butternuts, JOHN WETMORE, 81 years. [4/8]
April 9, 1875, Cooperstown, Mrs. CATHERINE A. NELSON, 70 years. [4/15]
April 12, 1875, Cooperstown, Mrs. ELIZABETH MC DONALD, 85 years. [4/15]
April 12, 1875, Fly Creek, BETSEY ROCKWELL, 80 years. [4/15]
April 17, 1875, Cooperstown, ALFRED BROCKWAY, 92 years. [4/22]
April 9, 1875, New Lisbon, Mrs. MARY M. JACKSON, 27 years. [4/22]
March 1, 1875, Milford, WILLIAM D. MUMFORD, 18 years. [4/22]

March 31, 1875, Milford, WALLACE MUMFORD, 14 months. [4/22]
April 11, 1875, E. Springfield, Mrs. BILLINGS BURLINGAME, 91 years. [4/22]
April 12, 1875, Morris, ELISHA THURSTON, 77 years. [4/22]
April 20, 1875, Richfield Spa, WILLIAM R. RUSSELL, 16 years. [4/29]
April 1, 1875, New Lisbon, MARY H. PATTENGILL, 16 years. [4/29]
May 1, 1875, Cooperstown, HEINRICH DEISLER, 70 years. [5/6]
April 30, 1875, Middlefield, JENNETT ISMOND, 57 years. [5/6]
April 25, 1875, Garrattsville, WILLIAM H. WHITE, 48 years. [5/6]
April 28, 1875, New Lisbon, Mrs. TAMAR TUTTLE, 79 years. [5/6]
May 4, 1875, Otsego, EDGAR SHERMAN, 53 years. [5/13]
May 9, 1875, Hartwick Sem., Mrs. RHODA MONAGHAN, 21 years. [5/13]
April 1, 1875, Westford, GEORGE SKINNER, 82 years. [5/13]
May 16, 1875, Cooperstown, SIMON VAN SICE, 81 years. [5/20]
May 17, 1875, Otsego, EDWARD DUGGLEBY, 2 years. [5/20]
May 18, 1875, Middlefield, CHARLES SNYDER, 15 years. [5/20]
March 25, 1875, Cherry Valley, SALINDA GALT, 78 years. [5/20]
April 22, 1875, Cherry Valley, MATTHEW WINNE, 77 years. [5/20]
April 28, 1875, Springfield, Mrs. SUSAN CONNANT, 84 years. [5/20]
April 30, 1875, Middlefield, Mrs. JOSEPH WEBB, 77 years. [5/20]
May 9, 1875, Schuyler's Lake, KATIE LIDELL, 16 years. [5/20]
May 3, 1875, Hartwick, MARY E. LOUGH, 2 years. [5/27]
May 3, 1875, Hartwick, ELEANOR M. LOUGH, 3 years. [5/27]
May 21, 1875, Hartwick, LUCY E. INGALLS, 2 years. [5/27]
May 18, 1875, Hartwick, CORA E. SPICER, 5 years. [5/27]
May 20, 1875, Hartwick, AMOS H. BOLTON, 28 years. [5/27]
May 20, 1875, Middlefield, MARCIA PIERCE, 34 years. [5/27]
May 12, 1875, Otsego, EDGAR RUSSELL, 11 years. [5/27]
May 30, 1875, Cooperstown, Mrs. ABNER GRAVES, 68 years. [6/3]
May 30, 1875, Richfield Spa, JOHN DANA, 65 years. [6/10]
May 31, 1875, Exeter Cen., CALEB ANGELL, 75 years. [6/10]
June 4, 1875, Hartwick, Mrs. ERASTUS WARD, 22 years. [6/10]
June 22, 1875, Burlington Flats, LILLIE CLARK, 11 years. [7/1]
June 24, 1875, Middlefield, CHARLES P. BEST, 23 years. [7/1]
June 24, 1875, Otsego, Mrs. MARY BYARD, 66 years. [7/1]
June 25, 1875, Fly Creek, Mrs. MILLICENT SIBLEY, 75 years. [7/1]
June 29, 1875, Hartwick, FRANCIS CLARK, 70 years. [7/1]
June 25, 1875, Schuyler Lake, WILLIAM THORNTON, 10 years. [7/1]
June 22, 1875, Hartwick, MARY ALIVE AINSLIE, 8 years. [7/1]
July 2, 1875, Toddsville, FRED A. HANUMN, 6 years. [7/8]

June 22, 1875, Morris, Mrs. HELEN A. DAVIS, 21 years. [7/8]
July 14, 1875, Middlefield Cen., Mrs. MARY A. VUNK, 58 years. [7/22]
May 24, 1875, Hartwick, GEORGE GREEN, 9 years. [7/22]
July 12, 1875, Otsego, JENNIE L. NORTHRUP, 4 years. [7/22]
July 26, 1875, Oaksville, Mrs. MARY BROADWELL, 22 years. [7/29]
July 7, 1875, Hartwick, LILLIAN CURRY, 19 years. [7/29]
July 31, 1875, Morris, JENNIE H. CLINTON, 19 years. [8/5]
July 19, 1875, New Lisbon, LUCY HARRIS, 6 years. [8/5]
July 19, 1875, Morris, Mrs. BETSEY HOWLAND, 75 years. [8/5]
Aug. 1, 1875, Toddsville, WILLIAM A. FINCH, 22 months. [8/5]
July 22, 1875, Springfield, Mrs. ABIGAIL THAYER, 76 years. [8/12]
Aug. 12, 1875, Cooperstown, ROBERT DAVIS, 68 years. [8/19]
Aug. 13, 1875, S. Worcester, Mrs. MARIA D. BECKER, 58 years. [8/19]
Aug. 7, 1875, Morris, Mrs. ANN E. FILER, 74 years. [8/19]
Aug. 11, 1875, Springfield, JOSEPH WOOD, 52 years. [8/19]
Aug. 13, 1875, S. Worcester, Mrs. ABRAHAM BECKER, 58 years. [8/26]
July 25, 1875, Cherry Valley, Mrs. MARIA METCALF, 77 years. [8/26]
[no date] E. Springfield, PAUL COOK, 78 years. [8/26]
Aug. 27, 1875, Otsego, OLIVER FREEMAN, 57 years. [9/2]
Aug. 30, 1875, Oaksville, Mrs. LUCY PRESTON, 71 years. [9/2]
Aug. 29, 1875, Butternuts, Mrs. HANNAH W. DONALDSON, 67 years. [9/9]
Sept. 2, 1875, Otego, WILLIAM D. BLISS, 40 years. [9/9]
Aug. 30, 1875, Carrysville, Mrs. AMANDA C. TOWNSLEY, 45 years. [9/9]
Sept. 10, 1875, Cooperstown, THOMAS H. RUTHERFORD, 70 years. [9/16]
Sept. 14, 1875, Toddsville, WESLEY FINCH, 32 years. [9/23]
Sept. 15, 1875, Hartwick, SAMUEL STEERE, 75 years. [9/23]
Sept. 18, 1875, Otsego, ELISHA P. GARDNER, 58 years. [9/23]
Sept. 23, 1875, Cooperstown, SARAH M. POTTER, 20 years. [9/30]
Sept. 27, 1875, Cooperstown, JEDEDIAH P. SILL, 68 years. [9/30]
Sept. 18, 1875, Gilbertsville, THOMAS STUART, 59 years. [9/30]
Sept. 7, 1875, Middlefield, JOHN PAUL JONES, infant. [9/30]
Sept. 15, 1875, E. Springfield, Mrs. CATHERINE BASINGER, 81 years. [9/30]
Sept. 27, 1875, W. Burlington, Mrs. RELIEF BAILEY, 90 years. [10/14]
Oct. 10, 1875, Chaseville, AMELIA MASTERS, 66 years. [10/21]
Oct. 10, 1875, Worcester, Mrs. ASA BUTLER, 27 years. [10/21]
Oct. 17, 1875, Index, REBECCA NESTLE, 18 years. [10/21]
Oct. 17, 1875, Otsego, JAMES REYNOLDS, 84 years. [10/21]

Oct. 23, 1875, Otsego, Mrs. HANNAH BAILEY, 63 years. [10/28]
Oct. 26, 1875, Middlefield, Mrs. SALLY JONES, 69 years. [10/28]
Oct. 11, 1875, Exeter, Mrs. NANCY DAVENPORT, 73 years. [10/28]
Oct. 11, 1875, Cherry Valley, Mrs. FRANCES LEANING, 79 years. [10/28]
Oct. 19, 1875, Middlefield, JEROME WHITE, 50 years. [10/28]
Oct. 19, 1875, Middlefield, JAMES SHELLAND, 84 years. [10/28]
Oct. 20, 1875, E. Worcester, Exeter [?], FLORA MC BALL, 16 years. [10/28]
Oct. 28, 1875, Cooperstown, HENRY F. PHINNEY, 59 years. [11/4]
Nov. 3, 1875, Cooperstown, CELESTIA M. KENYON, 20 years. [11/4]
Oct. 25, 1875, S. Hartwick, Mrs. ADALINE C. HOWE, 30 years. [11/11]
Nov. 12, 1875, Otsego, Mrs. CATHERINE REYNOLDS, 75 years. [11/18]
Nov. 9, 1875, Schuyler Lake, Mrs. ALECIA PHINNEY, 70 years. [11/18]
Nov. 10, 1875, Maryland, FLORA L. COLE, 17 years. [11/18]
Nov. 4, 1875, Roseboom, AARON BAILEY, 70 years. [11/18]
Oct. 14, 1875, Exeter, Mrs. SOPHIA RYDER, 77 years. [11/18]
Nov. 18, 1875, Middlefield, Mrs. POLLY BECKER, 75 years. [11/25]
Oct. 27, 1875, Otego, Mrs. MARY A. MYERS, 27 years. [11/25]
Oct. 21, 1875, Otego, Mrs. POLLY MUMFORD, 97 years. [11/25]
Nov. 23, 1875, Otsego, Mrs. AMY ANDREWS, 79 years. [12/2]
Nov. 22, 1875, Cherry Valley, MARY WOODBURN, 22 years. [12/2]
Nov. 30, 1875, Otsego, Mrs. EUNICE WHIPPLE, 79 years. [12/9]
Dec. 9, 1875, Cooperstown, LUCIA M. TULLER, 48 years. [12/16]
Dec. 1, 1875, Laurens, AMOS HENRY HAND, 51 years. [12/16]
Dec. 4, 1875, Morris, OLNEY POTTER, 77 years. [12/16]
Nov. 21, 1875, Morris, JERUSHA FAIRCHILD, 49 years. [12/16]
Dec. 24, 1875, Cooperstown, Mrs. ELIZABETH ROGERS, 81 years. [12/30]

INDEX

~ A ~

Abbey, Stephen 48
Abbott, Ebben S. 49
Ackler, Mary Jane 121
Ackley, Calvin 15
Adams, Abner 112
  Alba 145
  Benoni 100
  Betsey 61
  David 50
  Dudley 48
  Elisha 113
  Eliza 139
  Eliza Matilda 48
  George T. 138
  Hannah 51
  Harriet F. 174
  Huldah A. 118
  John 1
  Lewis 57
  Lorenzo 123
  Lucius 108
  Lucy 128
  Naomi J. 141
  Nathan 93
  Phillips M. 157
  Polly 165
  Sally 150
  Stephen 150
  Susan 122
  Sylva 147
  Walter F. 93
  Welcome 123
Addams, Elizabeth 9
  William 77

Adkins, Abigail 154
  Arminda 169
Adsit, James 160
  Noah 93
Ainslie, Mary Alive 177
Alden, Andrew 104
  Jaben 34
  Julia Ann 2, 37
Aldrich, Amasa 171
  Clark 134
  Dennis 76
Alexander, Caleb 35
Alger, Adeline 111
  George 157
  Horace 138
  Jamie 173
  Minerva 3, 38
  Rispa 64
  William Emmet 114
Allen, Amasa 23
  Anna 165
  Benjamin 79
  Betsey 142
  Charlotte 43
  Chloe 51
  Christopher 13
  Cyrus 30
  David 21
  David Nash 149
  Elizabeth 41
  Emma C. 158
  Frederick B. 87
  George D. 141
  H. H. (Mrs.) 155
  Han. 57

Allen, Harriet 106
  Herbert S. 151
  Hosmer 28
  James 47
  James C. 120
  Jared 3, 38, 48
  Laura E. 120
  Lucy 48, 143
  Mary Eliza 130
  McKean T. 138
  Miranda S. 169
  Orlo 73
  Permilla 124
  Polly 118
  Sarah 173
  Sarah Adelia 118
  Stephen 84
  Theodorus 41
  William 15
Allice, Wealthy 33
Allison, Francis 166
Almay, Walter 149
Almy, E. J. 158
  William W. 80
Alpaugh, William F. 176
Alverson, Albert R. 139
  Daniel 34
Alvord, David B. 73
Alworth, Anna 103
  William 64
Ames, Cyrus 38
  Emily 94
  Jotham 1
  Rebecca 156
  Sarah 57

Ames, Simeon C. 125
Anders, Lemuel 84
Anderson, Rachel 119
Andreas, Zatto 64
Andrews, Amy 179
  Ekiza 161
  Frances 176
  George W. 130
  Mary 78
  Olney Z. 130
  Simeon J. 35
  Sophronia J. 117
Andrus, Clarissa 35
  David B. 169
  Desire 57
  Fanny 65
  Frances A. 103
  John H. 46
  Philip M. 157
  Seth B. 51
  Susan 65
Aney, Jennie O. 136
Angel, Amanda 26, 78
  Caleb 12
  Catherine 33
  Eunice 58
  Jeremy R. 12
  Jonathan 65
  Philetus 61
  William 4, 76
  William G. 33
Angell, Caleb 102, 177
  Candace B. 145
  Frances E. 117
  James R. 167
  Jonathan 167
  Marius B. 150

Angell, Sally 32
  Sarah B. 104
  William 42
Anger, Catherine S. 153
Angur, Edward B. 98
  Peter 134
Annas, Volney 94
Anthon, John H. 174
Anthony, Eliza 89
Antisdale, Nathaniel 75
Antisdel, Annie 58
  Elizabeth 87
  Hannah 75
  Hosea F. 122
Antsidel, Dan 90
Aplin, Betsey 1, 11
  Emeline B. 5
  Harvey 3
  Harvey H. 52
  Thankful 27
  William 54
Appleton, Jesse 21
Arkins, Elvira 151
Arnold, Abby 96
  Calphurnia 89
  Catherine C. 66
  Elias 131
  Fluria 29
  Fluvia 24
  George 94
  George W. 62
  H. B. (Mrs.) 173
  Lovina M. 5
  Rodney 29
  Sophia 122
Arold, Benjamin 102
Ashley, Ann 146

Ashley, Elizabeth 40
  James 27
  Russell Dorr 128
  Sarah 133
Aspinwall, Caleb 70
Atherton, Mary 50
Atkins, Samuel 72
Atwell, Samuel 175
Augur, Abner 157
  Mattie 120
  William H. 138
Austick, Mary 51
Austin, Ed. 77
  James 153
  Thomas 118
Averell, James 20, 57
  Jane A. M. 51
  Marcy 53
  William H. 168
Averill, Avery 8
  James 9, 19
  Mary 1
  Mehitable 38
  William 40
Avery, Amasa 151
  Asahel 162
  E. C. 146
Axtell, Henry 38
  Rebecca 38
Aylesworth, Abigail 126
  Albert D. 170
  Benajah 161
  Benjamin 121
  Edgar 121
  Lavina 143
  Lydia 165
  William R. 122
Ayres, Jesse A. 119

~ B ~

Babbit, Christopher 9
Warren 92
Babbitt, Anna 80
Theron 153
Babcock, Abel S. 149
Alonzo 79
Amos (Mrs.) 48
Catherine 66
Charles 3
Charles W. 5, 44
Cornelia A. 109
Cytus 22
Edith M. 145
Edson Avery 123
Eunice 107
Eunice B. 77
Eunice C. 132
Frank Iriving 130
George 80
Hammisson 79
Harvey W. 53
Henry Adams 75
Hiram S. 147
Jilpha 145
Joshua 113
Lois E. 141
Lucy 175
Marion K. 156
Mary E. 113
Mary Jane 56, 123
Mary M. 151
Olive 113
Robert 125
Samuel 58
Sarah 49
Sarah A. 153
Sylvina 90
Babcock, Timothy 103
William 176
William Sidney 95
Bache, Benjamin Franklin 7
Bachelor, Elijah 23
Backus, Asel 17
Bacon, W. 134
Badeau, Ameu 122
Badger, Charles Monroe 156
Charlies E. 109
John 52
Naomi 57
Polly V. C. 123
Baigrie, William H. 115
Bailey, Aaron 179
Abigail E. 121
Charles 32
G. Starr 117
Hannah 179
Herman 63
James 83
James (Mrs.) 84
James H. 130
John 125
Mary A. 163
Morris J. 128
Relief 178
Tavancha 107
Baird, David (Mrs.) 158
Baker, Allen 100
Ann Philles 53
Benjamin 3
Clara W. 64
Clark 99
E. Spencer 104
Hamilton 168
Baker, Henry 58
Isebenda 54
Leonard 122
Lucinda 123
Sarah 140
Thomas 62
William 151
Balard, Olive 51
Balcom, Charles R. 124
James R. 124
Lucy 173
Webster 124
Baldiwn, Lora 14
Baldwin, Aaron 51, 91
Abner 54
Adella S. 127
Anna 123
Emeline J. 169
George W. 112
Harriet 123
Horace 67
John 124
Joseph 88
Lydia 70
Martha 94
Nellie 172
William 20
Balestier, Mary 143
Ball, Alexander F. 148
Charles B. 106
David 141
David Willis 117
Heman 23
Lyman B. 123
Norma 80
Phineas C. (Mrs.) 157

Ballard, Elsie W. 167
  Nelson 145, 146
  Vesta M. 170
Banister, Elizabeth 171
Barid, Olive 69
Barker, Amanda 65
  Samuel N. 78
  Sarah 97
Barnard, Ann 148
  Delia G. 137
  Robert 118
  William 100
Barnes, Isabel
  Lucinda 43
  Lucy Miranda 43
  Moses 14
  Stephen 150
  William 43
Barney, Daniel 173
  Matilda 165
Barnum, Abijah 152
  Almeda 152
  Lewis 77
Barras, Mary 93
Barrett, --- 170
  Ed. 170
  Elizabeth M. 110
  Gerrish 113
  Henry 86
  Lois 78
Barron, Samuel 11
Barrows, Kate Fuller 139
Bartholomew, John C. 84
Bartlett, Atticus A. 78
  Frederick 154
  Rachel 55

Bartlett, Russell 37
Bartling, Charles W. 92
Barton, Emeline 145
  Harriet R. 128
  Hiram 145
  Lydia 95
  Robert 112
  Stanton 110
  Zebulon 145
Basainger, Patty 77
Basinger, Catherine 178
  Daniel 120
  Mary Y. 44
  Safrinus 43
  Sefrenes 153
Bastow, William 7
Bates, Abigail 111
  Abraham N. 115
  Adon W. 46
  Asenath 146
  Carrie L. 115
  Charity 76
  Charles 4, 41
  Lorenzo 116
  Mary M. 82
  Nathan 5, 44
  Rhoda Ann 102
  Robert 115
  Simeon 28
  Sophia 121
  Sovina 83
  Tompkins 78
Beabee, Sarah A. 126
Beach, Isaac K. 166
  Laura E. 130
  Samuel B. 142
Beadle, Amy 118
  Flavil 106
  Henry 60

Beadle, Homer 77
  Minnie A. 151
  Nancy 65
  Polly 175
  Susan 97
  Winfield E. 111
Beal, Flora 66
  Samuel M. 66
Beams, Elizabeth 150
  John 150
Beardsley, Daniel 157
  Eunice 12, 78
  Hannah 64
  Harvey 34
  Morgan Lewis 47
  Nathan 47
  Obadiah 72
  Peter 34
  Sarah M. 109
Bebee, Levi 63
Becker, Abraham 134
  Abraham (Mrs.) 178
  Caroline 87
  Catherine 80
  Hannah 86
  Maria D. 178
  Mary 117
  Mary W. 62
  Polly 179
  Rinear 107
Beckley, Cynthia 172
  John 9
  Martha A. 133
  William L. Marcy 67
Beckwith, Desire 99

Beckwith, Mary 71
  Sarah 60
Bedeau, Ann 145
  David A. 102
Beebe, Elnathan 59
Beebee, Tryphena 76
Beers, Hannah 157
  Julia A. Hunt 154
  Maria 162
  Nathaniel 148
Beggs, Hannah I.
  167
Belcher, George 136
  Moses 70
Belknap, Amasa 173
  Dan E. 161
  David 104
  Harriet 104
  Jane 170
Bell, Christian S.
  (Mrs.) 159
  Christopher 160
  John 6
Bemis, Benjamin 34
  Calvin 27
Benedict, Alanson
  175
  Christopher H.
  159
  David 31
  Elizabeth 66
  Hart 18
  William 41
Benjamin, Clara Jane
  128
  Elizabeth 51, 70
  Mary 105
  Mary E. 46
  Moses G. 50
  Ruby 135
  Russell 103

Bennett, Albert 48
  David P. 115
  Margaret E. 172
  Nellie D. 145
  Perry 164
  Sally 46
  Samantha 65
  Sheffield 113
  Sylvia 161
  Zeruiah 62
Bentley, Ella J. 106
  Harriet E. 74
  Tillha 154
Benton, Alton 157
  Caleb 29
  E. W. 168
  Orlando 14
  William L. 126
Beresford, John B.
  108
Berry, Maria 166
  Rosalle 165
Besancon, Mary J.
  59
  Paschal 69
Best, Charles P. 177
Betts, Daniel 30
  Samuel 71
Bevins, E. 34
  Hannah Lavinia 34
Bibb, W. W. 19
Bice, Andrew 165
  Eveline 139
  Henry 176
  Jesse 170
  Peter 152
Bidlack, Oliver
  (Mrs.) 36
Bidlake, Emily 140
  Phebe T. 135

Bidwell, Clarissa L.
  174
Bieglow, Ezra 17
Bigelow, Bertrand 85
  Henrietta M. 97
  Joshua 55
  Rhoda 47
  Timothy 22
  U. Y. 99
Bills, Christiana 71
  Elisha 83
Bilyea, Electa 63
  John 133
  Samuel C. 173
Bingham, E. M.
  (Mrs.) 142
  George 112
  Jeptha S. 94
  King 6, 46
  Melinda 66
  Ruth 38
  William K. 146
Bird, Richard S. 56
Birdsall, Hiram W.
  119
  Louise E. 159
  Nathan 125
Birge, Dothe 138
  Harvey 158
  James 100
Bishop, Alfred T. 48
  Amelia L. 176
  David 36
  Deborah 29
  Everett G. 166
  John 8
  Matthew O. 98
  Samuel 8
  Sarah A. 118
  William 115
Bissell, Artemas 93

Bissell, Benjamin 1, 57
  Emilius 98
  George 46
  Gilbert 60
  Horace 99
  Huldah 4
  Isaac 26, 72
  John Horace 135
  Maria E. 90
  Martha 71
  Norman 148
  Orange 71
  Sally 68
Bixby, Ira 56
  Sarah 80
Blackman, Mary A. 83
Bladin, Truman 106
Blair, Ann E. 82
  Anna 93
  Gardner 85
  Jane M. 161
  William 3
  William L. 40
Blakeley, Abraham 105
Blakeman, Alfred D. 4, 42
Blakley, Mary 26
Blakly, John 108
Blanchard, Charlotte 81
  Clyde 50
  Delilah 145
  Dolly 9
  Ezra 159
  Joseph 50, 64
  Stelle J. 60
Bliss, Elezer 51
  Fanny 155

Bliss, Louisa 153
  Wayne Collins 44
  Wayne O. 5
  William D. 178
Blood, John 2
Bloom, Isaac 8
Bloomfield, Jonathan 3, 38
  Joseph 26
Bloss, Manassah 39
Blunk, Anna 141
Boardman, Alida 44
  Elijah 26
  Levi 162
Boden, Edward Omar 125
  Jerusha W. 120
  Mary Ann 149
  Omar 81
  Paul B. 128
  Sally 72
Bogue, Andrew B. 144
  Franklin R. 43
Bolles, Emmogene 99
  Fannie B. 130
  Stephen 111
  Susan 112
Bolton, --- (Mrs.) 11
  --- (Rev. Mr.) 11
  Amos H. 177
  Betsey 78
  Daniel 19
  Ezra 114
  Isaac 106
  Lemuel 80
  Mancron (Mrs.) 154
  Minerva 154
  Ruth 78

Bond, Edward 36
Bonnar, Hannah M. 131
Bonner, James 139
Bonney, Luke 10
Bony, Sebastian 67
Boom, Chaney P. 57
  Elman 61
Boorn, Chaney P. 57
Boorne, Harvey 89
Bootman, Lovina B. 136
  Polly 128
Boro, Edward 116
Bostwick, Henry 7
  Samuel 64
Boswell, David 1
Bosworth, Mindwell (Mrs.) 16
Botsford, Alice A. 81
  Charles 147
  Charles G. 81
  Charles McHenry 70
  Harriet McLean 66
  Loenski 131
  Martha 153
Bottsford, Charles 80
Boudinot, Elias 23
Bourne, Daniel 71
  Hannah 97
  Julia 77
Bow, Daniel 15
Bowdish, John R. 92
  W. S. 94
  Wellesley
    Wellington 58
Bowen, Abigail 79
  Alphonso 86
  Betsey 155
  Cynthia 136

Bowen, Elisha 78
  Harry 163
  Henry 96
  Hezekiah 58
  John 52
  Julia E. 91
  Ruth 161
Bowers, Emily
    Stewart 114
  Helen 53
  Henry 7
  John M. 1, 10, 53, 88
  Margaret 1
  Margaretta M. 160
  Mary 146
Bowish, William 155
Bowman, Eliza 99
Bowne, Amy S. 73
  Eliza N. 67
  Emma 71
  George L. 142
  Henry 42
  John 145
  Joseph 95
  Robert L. 22
Boyd, Josephine E. J. 102
  Julia C. 94
  Martha 57
Boyde, James 72
Boynton, Ebenezer 135
  Electa 107
Bradford, Elisha 115
  Esek 73
  George W. 18
  Harvey S. 73
  Helen Maria 18
  Huldah 3
  Martha B. 147

Bradford, Mary 2
  Sally 9
  Sarah 48
Bradley, Stephen 42
  Sylvia 84
Bragg, Ira 71
  Lewis M. 79
Brainard, Jared 164
  Nathan 84
  Salinda 67
Braine, Daniel 96
Braman, Earl P. 96
  Elias 84
  Jasper 122
  Mary 108
Branch, Oliver B. 114
Brant, Catherine 61
  Joseph 61
Brasse, Julia A. 80
Bratt, James C. 149
Brazie, Francis 91
  Ransom E. 95
Breese, Aaron 104
  John 67
  Sarah J. 103
Brewer, David 160
  E. R. 110
  Ezra R. 110
  Hannah 71
  John 103, 121
  Martha I. 148
  Polly 41
  Sarah 155
  Susanna 81
Brezee, Caroline 175
Briant, Ira 166, 167
Bridge, Fidel (Mrs.) 78
Bridgen, Thomas 32
Briggs, Charlotte 61

Briggs, Griffin 93
  Joseph 48
  Mary D. 150
  Patience 96
  Rufus 50
  Squire 143
Brightman, George 160
Brimmer, John 144
  Philip A. 119
  Susan 153
Brisack, Joseph D. 160
Bristol, James 64
  Peter C. 92
  William 110
Broadwell, Mary 178
Brockham, James W. 141
Brockway, Alfred 176
  Harmony 1
  Marilla 27
  Theressa 96
Bromfield, James 160
Bronk, William R. 135
Bronner, Frederick 79
Bronson, Jessie 157
Brookham, Peter 128
Brooks, Alvan 154
  Benjamin 29
  Emer D. 105
  George R. 145
  Hattie 176
  Isaac 51
  Julia A. 102
  Kate M. 127
  Lemuel S. 105

Brooks, Lyman 171
  Mary 159
  Orra 90
  Sally 69, 140
  Thomas 65
Broome, John 11
Brother, Valentine
  19
Brown, Aaron 155
  Ann 85
  Ann M. 145
  Barzilla 81
  Betsey 176
  Caleb 15, 37
  Catherine M. 119
  Cyrus 110
  Daniel 49, 120
  Dave 137
  David 75
  Delevan 37
  Delos M. 163
  Dennison 75
  Eliza L. 101
  Elizabeth 143
  Ephraim 32
  Erexena 72
  Flora E. 149
  George 154
  George Augustus
    125
  Harmon 42
  Harvey 53
  Helen Louise 116
  Henry F. 110
  Isaac 98
  Isaac P. 97
  John 8, 52
  Joseph A. 170
  Linn B. 149
  Lloyd 138
  Loomis 139

Brown, Lucia 122
  Lucina 4
  Lucy C. 135
  Margaret 129
  Mary 52
  Mary A. 113
  Matilda 82
  Mercy A. 93
  Nahum T. 88
  Samuel 8, 130
  Stephen 162
  Stephen D. 128
  Thomas T. 139
  William 77, 155
  Ziba H. 124
Brownel, Almira 3
Brownell, Electa
  Williams 109
  Mary 105, 153
  Mary A. 68
  Mary J. 123, 133
  Seeley 135
  William 41
  Zilpha M. 147
Brownley, Samuel 36
Bruce, Arthur 29
Bruen, Mathias 41
Bryant, Elvira 163
  Moses N. 82
Buckingham,
  Cornelia 96
  Nathan F. 34
Buckley, Mary 35
  Rheda 9
Buel, Sarah 109
Bullis, Alonzo 91
Bulson, Adelaide 111
Bundy, Betsey 72
  David S. 114
  Eliza 92
  Gilbert 165

Bundy, Nathan 89
  Polly 107
  Prudence 160
  Simeon 119
  Susy A. 170
  William 166
Bunn, Clarissa 169
  Emily 166
Bunyan, Susan Davis
  134
  Thomas 139
Burch, Harriet B.
  138
  Isaac 5, 45, 76
  Isaac B. 137
  Mary Ann 60
  Nehemiah 55
  Russell B. 122
  William 78
  Ziba 131
Burdick, Andrew V.
  84
  Francis L. 61
  J. M. 127
  Nelson 174
Burditt, Byron W.
  135
  Henry D. 128
  Luther I. 160
  Wigglesworth 19
Burgess, Gregory 87
  Jane D. 76
  John 52
  Paul 85
  William 69, 70
Burgin, Chandler
  166
Burke, Annis 143
  Patty 46
Burkingham, Naboth
  75

Burlingame, Amos
  126
  Billings (Mrs.) 177
  Harriet E. 99
  Susannah 103
Burlingham, Billings
  137
  Elisha 64
  Ezekiel 14
  Helen 76
  Helen A. 119
  Hopkins 84
  Warren 80
Burlington, James S.
  2
  William 37
Burneson, Nancy 68
Burnett, Daniel R.
  104
  F. M. 124
  Isaac 167
Burnham, Adelbert
  Westley 63
Burnside, Andrew J.
  103
  Ephraim 114
  Gloud T. 122
  Hattie 151
  Hudson 128
  Nancy 148
Burr, Edward 168
Burrell, Harmony
  156
  John 11
  Sarah M. 173
Burrill, James 20
Burrows, Charles N.
  157
Burt, Mercy 91
Burton, Clarinda W.
  75

Burton, Samuel D.
  170
Burwell, Catherine
  A. 55
Bush, Diantha 94
  Hannah 154
  Henry 40
  John 137
  John E. 135
  Martha 101
  William 53
  Zachariah 52
Bushnell, David 128
Butler, Asa (Mrs.)
  178
  Clara 120
  David 75
  Rensselaer 160
Butterfield, James 17
  Nabby 57
  Rachel 94
Button, Elias 27
Butts, Anna 86
  Elijah 105
  Hannah 118
  James 66, 94
  John S. 77
  Lucy 169
  Luther 120
  Marble 165
  Maryette 120
  Norris 165
  Rebecca 86
Byam, Mary 101
Byard, Mary 177
  Nettie 135
Byram, Amelia D.
  156
Byrnell, Patrick 151

~ *C* ~

Cady, Abigail 163
Calder, Harriet A.
  89
  Joseph 86
Cale, Maria 132
Calkin, Clarissa 70
Calkins, Frederick
  166
Camp, Benjamin
  120
  Joseph 101
  Mercy O. 127
  Nicholas 96
  Philo 161
  Sarah 94
  Squire 137
Campaign, Mary
  152
Campbell, Alonzo 70
  David 69
  Deborah 99
  Elenor 88
  Elizabeth 100
  Eugine 99
  Jane 26, 57
  John 86
  Kenneth 74
  Mary 38
  Matthew 85
  Nancy 93
  Oliver 2
  Rachel 111
  Richard 3, 38
  Robert 26, 92
  Sabrina 4, 42
  Samuel 75
  Samuel S. 118
  Theodore 79
  William 66, 83

Campbell, Zurial 31
Canfield, Oliver 35
  Samuel 16
  Timothy 79
Cannon, James 41
Cantine, Moses I. 25
Card, Caroline R. 136
  Charles Moak 131
  Daniel L. 93
  Ella M. 131
  Hannah 113
  Jacob L. 93
  Mary 109
  Nancy A. 83
  Nathaniel L. 78
  Susan 159
Carey, Fenimore C. 136
  Lydia 174
  Theodore 35
Carmichael, William 117
Carpenter, Elenora 85
  Gardner M. 18, 85
  Henrietta 109
  Henry E. 138
  Joseph 108
  Nathaniel 129
  Ruth 93
  Willis T. 108
Carr, Alexander H. (Mrs.) 168
  B. Wheeler 99
  Daniel 93
  Deborah 160
  Emma J. 131
  Isaac 86
  James E. 109
  Josephine 90

Carr, Loisa 60
  Nelson V. 170
  Peter J. 131
  Peter T. 103
  Robert 26, 116
  Sally 170
  Theo. P. 58
Carrier, Livia 70
  Richard 76
Carrington, Edward 11
Carrol, William 152
Carroll, Ezra 80
  John 84, 117
  Linus A. 66
Carter, Desire 9
  Giles 91
  Sally Maria 84
  William Arvell 122
Cary, Ann 45
  Betsey 29
  Cornelius L. 83
  Ezra 49
  Laura 145
  Louisa 2
  Margaret 173
  Mary A. 125
  Richard 9
Caryl, Joel 119
  Mary 106
Casby, Catherine 120
Case, Caroline 41
  Polly 136
  Rufus 99
Casler, Alice 121
  Jennie 138
  Matilda 102
  Nettie 134
  Willie Brooks 130

Casprus, David N. 128
Cassaart, Staley 90
Caswell, Betsey M. 80
  Levi 47
Cathcart, Sally E. 107
  Sarah 173
Caulkins, Abel 14, 81
  Huldah 147
Caye, Lucinda 12
Center, Angeline 90
  James 95
  William L. 82
Chadden, --- (Mrs.) 144
Chaddon, Daniel M. 72
  Sarah H. 92
  Thomas 91
Chaffee, Ezra 60
  Lovici 102
Chamberlain, Albert 117
  Cynthia 99
  Ephraim 90, 139
  Joel M. 88
  John 56
  Julia A. 96
  Lorenzo D. 131
  Olcott C. 123
  Peleg 113
Chamberlin, Cornelia 101
Champion, Eliza 85
  Elizabeth 99
  Harriet 101
  John 144
  Philo J. 96

Champion, Reuben 82
Champlin, Anna B. 87
Chaney, John 92
Chapin, Benajah 112
  David 10, 24
  Elijah H. 115
  Eunice 55
  Joel 86
  Lemuel 110
  Lydia 122
  Nancy 9
  Sophia 83
Chapman, Burr B. 101
  Charles 5, 45
  Chauncey M. 145
  Daniel W. 166
  Dorcas 176
  Elijah 30
  Emeline 101
  Fanny M. 83
  George 156
  Georgianna 163
  Henry 26
  Jenas 108
  Pamela 57
  Whitmore E. 97
Chappel, Amy 43
  Betsey 97
  Esther 114
Chappell, Ada A. 101
  Nathan 111
Chase, Albert J. 129
  Ann 142
  Anna 112
  Celine 77
  Clarissa 37
  Clarrissa 2

Chase, Comfort 122
  Elizabeth 85
  Elvira 24
  George W. 158
  Horace 171
  Huldah A. 123
  Isaac 88
  James 114
  Jerusha 121
  Joshua 74
  Josiah 14
  Marcy 5
  Mary 45
  Olive 67
  Polly 80
  Samuel 63
Chatfield, Mary 65
Cheesebro, Chad R. 175
Cheetham, James 11
Cheles, Melissa 18
Cheney, Ceylon N. 155
  Ebenezer 8
  Frances 172
  Isaac R. 64
  Samuel W. 155
  William (Mrs.) 176
Chesbrew, Bois 36
Chester, John 10
  John E. 79
  Thomas 47
Child, Parker M. 60
Childs, Edward 144
  Oscar W. 101
  Perry G. 55
Chisholm, Andrew 129
Chittenden, David D. 9
Church, Aurilla 164

Church, Hannah R. 52
  Hubbard 111
  Origen 174
  William 4, 43
Chuseman, Ed. 69
Clapp, Julia 50
Clark, Abel 18, 49
  Alfred M. 134
  Amy 9
  Arminda 5, 44
  Arthur 33
  Asabel 57
  Aulina M. 62
  Betsey 18
  Brewster 55
  Caroline Jordan 172
  Catherine Maria 48
  Clarissa 109
  Corlin 89
  Cyrus 24
  Daniel 89
  Daniel A. 15
  David F. 167
  Edward Loeraine 118
  Erastus 2, 30
  Ezekiel 29
  Francis 177
  George 33, 56
  Georgiana 4
  Harry 34
  Harry D. 171
  Isaac 24
  Israel 37
  James E. 142
  Jenny V. 119
  Jerome 100, 133
  John 166
  John C. 126

Clark, John W. 117
  Joseph 152
  Justin 24
  Leslie E. 141
  Lillie 177
  Lucy 129
  Mary A. 142
  Mary Elizabeth 57
  Melissa 166
  Nancy 125, 162
  Orrin 35
  Paul 45
  Perry 33
  Polly 111
  Richard 119
  Solomon 15
  Stephen 107
  William 82
  Xeriah 99
Clarke, Alfred 151
  Ann L. 99
  Anson 21
  Cynthia 101
  George 43
  Georgiana 43
  Lucy 41
  Thomas 158
  Thomas M. 142
  William 39, 74
Cleland, Catherine 57
Cleveland, Lemuel 10
Clifford, Elizabeth 90
  Jenette 91
Cline, Peter 148
Clinton, George 72
  Jennie H. 178
  John Paul 131
  Mariah 17

Clinton, Mary 9
  Mary J. 131
Clinyon, Mary 153
Clock, Emma Adelia 133
Close, John T. 21
Clover, Edward 68
Clyde, Anna E. 161
  Bethany 145
  Catherine 35
  Eleanor C. 88
  George 92, 99
  George W. 151
  Hannah L. 88
  Margaret 3, 39
Coan, Charles 24
Coates, Prudence 71
Coats, Albert 164
  Almira M. 71
  Bartholomew 50
  Betty 38
  Billings 77
  Cynthia T. 166
  James I. 137
  Mary 91
Coburn, Charles L. 147
  Lucy M. 157
  Seymour 2, 37
Cochrane, Walter (Mrs.) 30
Cockett, James 135
  John 59
Coe, John 26
  Jonas 25
Coffin, Caleb 40
  Horace I. 75
  Job 50
  Lucy 136
  Lydia 27
  Noah 29

Coffin, Peleg 155
  Ralph Sherman 102
  Robert J. 35
Cohen, Tracey 154
Colburn, Thomas J. 161
Cole, Catharine 162
  Clarinda 86
  Cortland J. 118
  Flora L. 179
  Florence V. 124
  George M. 157
  Hezekiah M. 34, 145
  Hopey 161
  John C. 139
  William 129
Colegrove, --- (Major) 42
  Amos 157
Coleman, Eliza H. 68
  George 121
  Hannah 27
  Nancy 134
  Samuel 113
Collar, John 160
Collier, Elizabeth 130
  Jacob 66
  Lydia Ann 41
  Peter 87
Collins, Emily Bowers 77
  William A. 73
Colman, Anson 60
Coltis, Elizabeth A. 107
Colton, Cora E. 133
  Jennie M. 133

Colvard, Asa 47
Colwell, John 147
  Samuel 114
Combs, Joseph 113
Comfort, Electa 123
Commick, John 62
Compton, Phebe 84
  William 128
Comstock, Abigail 76
  Daniel 94
  Elizabeth 13
  Jane 100
  Lewis 31
  Lucy 17
  Mary F. 83
  Miles 31
  Salmon 85
  Sarah B. 68
  Sarah Cooper 88
  William 52
  William A. 159
  Zara 158
Cone, Daniel 75
  Joseph O. 14
Congdon, Arsula 110
Conkey, Cornelia 1
  Silas A. 63
Conklin, Ann E. 115
  Emma S. 108
  John (Mrs.) 81
  Peter 166
Conliss, Thomas 175
Connant, Susan 177
Connelly, Ellen 175
Connis, Almira C. 67
Connrod, Algene L. 119

Converse, Alvah P. 173
  Alvan P. 173
  Harriet 47
  Jane A. 67
  John 47
Cook, --- 61
  Abigail 39
  Adeline 91
  Charles 88
  Cyrenus 20
  Dorlisca 110
  Edwin 61
  Eleanor 55
  Henry B. 29
  Hiram 51
  Irving W. 120
  John B. 132
  John J. 127
  Joshua 26
  Lucy 119
  Mary Ann 40
  Noah 86
  Paul 178
  Phonehas 31
  Rebecca 35
  Richard 51
  Sally 8
  Seth 18
  Seth J. 67
  Susan 94
  Susanna 71
  Thomas 145
  Timothy (Mrs.) 139
  William 38
  Zebediah F. 16
Cooke, Elmira 72
  Harriet S. 39
  Jason 90
  Lucy 68

Cooke, Westcot H. 168
Cooley, Deborah 131
  Henry P. 126
  James B. 128
  Morris 161
  Richard 100
  Sarah Ann 114
  William 158
Coon, Abram 148
Coonrod, Abigail 67
  Betsey P. 55
  Henry 72
Cooper, Alfred 116
  Amelia R. 88
  Betsey Allen 127
  Charles Paul 127
  Eliza J. 92
  Elizabeth 12, 13, 17
  Fennimore 26
  Goldsboro 49
  Hannah 17
  Isaac 17
  James 13, 26
  James Fenimore 141
  John S. 133
  Maria 172
  Mary 87
  Mary A. Morris 168
  Mary Ann 119
  Richard 12, 127, 128, 141
  Richard F. 13, 17
  Thomas (Mrs.) 96
  William 1, 11, 18, 20, 48, 150
  William A. 66

Coopernail, James 66
Cope, Julia 65
Copwell, Elizabeth 43
Corbin, Mason 156
Corning, Elisha 32
Cornish, Aaron P. 95
Cornwell, Stephen M. 98
Corwin, James D. 170
Cory, Ellery 32, 34, 53, 170
  George 34
  George A. 53
  Holder 132
  Imogene 144
  James K. 33
  John 156
  Lucia T. 92
  Marcia 81
  Oliver (Mrs.) 47
  Phebe 69
  Philip 4, 41
  William 32
Coss, Asenath 127
Cossart, Anna 105
  James 116
  John 109
Cotes, John 55
Counrad, Minerva 146
Couse, Emily C. 169
  Harriet 72
Cowdery, Loren 42
Cox, Edward J. 131
  Grace 155
  James 151
  William 6
Coye, Asa 65

Cradal, Sophia B. 91
Crafts, Alfred 67
  Alva S. 36
  Eliza 126
  Erastus 102
  George S. 2
  Griffin 56
  Hannah 34
  Joseph 82
  Joseph L. 2, 36
  Lucy S. 127
  Maria A. 2
  Mary 65
  Samuel 96
  Sarah Ann 104
  Walter 47, 83
  William 32
Crandal, Justus 6
  Mary 140
  Mary S. 91
  Samuel 75
Crandall, Abel H. 79
  Henry 82
  Horace M. 51
  Justus 46
Crane, Ezra 5, 46
  Hannah A. 155
  Mary E. 67
  Polly 30
Crippen, Aabrina 77
  Ann Pomeroy 125
  Caroline M. 110
  Daniel 87
  Elizabeth 87
  Hamilton Nish 89
  Paul C. 103
  Philip 162
  S. (Mrs.) 61
  Schuyler 161
  Silas 5, 45

Crocker, Solomon 16
Cronkhite, Stephen 145
Cross, Betsey 95
  Crowell 90
  Erastus 86
  John 49
Crouse, Peter 130
Crumb, Francis V. 130
  Haskell 80
  Julia A. 77
  Varnum C. 121
  Ward 130
Crundel, Walter C. 158
Crush, Frances 108
Cudenard, Henry 21
Culver, Ester 155
Cummings, Daniel 96
  Elias 114
  Elizabeth 97
  Everett 94
  Harlon P. 139
  Hettie M. 154
  Hooper 30
  James 134
  Jasper 28
  Orris J. 148
  Prudence 16
  Susan 172
Cumpton, Edward 29
Cunningham, Susannah 137
Cuppernull, Mary 170
Curliss, Mary 3
Curry, Lillian 178

Curtiss, Ames 54
  Emeline 85
  Mary 40
  Theodotia P. 56
  Zebina 35
Cushman, Abigail 43
  Benjamin 50
  Elizabeth 91
  Frederick R. 169
  Hetta 27
  Nettie A. 169
  Phebe 127
Cuthbert, Lemuel 40
Cuthwaite, Catherine
  Cooper 114
Cutler, Alpheus 12
  Sarah P. 153
Cuyler, Jacob I.
  (Mrs.) 9
  John I. 8

~ **D** ~

Daggett, Cyrus 146
  Ora 17
Dailey, Eben 86
Daily, Thaddeus 54
Dana, John 177
Daniel, Nehemiah
  164
Daniels, Abigail 69
  L. T. 60
  Pamelia 100
Danielson, Alvina A.
  Pier 4
  Avaline A. (Pier)
    43
  Emily 71
  Lucretia 28
  Polly 1
Darby, Dan 149

Darbyshire, Mathew
  17
Darroch, Andrew
  156
Dauchy, Otto M.
  140
Davenport, Benjamin
  156
  Nancy 179
Davey, Henry A.
  (Mrs.) 173
  Mary Talbot 174
Davidson, Amelia
  102
  Asahel B. 139
  Catherine 62
  Chester 154
  John 63, 113
  Mary 83
  Richard 79, 93
  Theodore C. 73
Davis, Alexander M.
  172
  Arthur 79
  Benajah 92
  Calvin H. 152
  Charles 54
  Elizabeth
    Morehouse 154
  Hannah S. 52
  Harriet 165
  Helen A. 178
  Henry 166
  Ichabod 32
  James H. 45
  John 51, 115
  John W. 77
  Jonah 159
  Laura C. 170
  Lewis Smith 105
  Lydia Ann 82

Davis, Malinda 148
  Martha 78
  Mary 159
  Mary E. 81
  Polly 85
  Robert 50, 178
  Sally S. 135
  Sarah Ann 106
  Sarah G. 172
  Solomon 45
  Thomas 76
Davison, Abby T.
  143
  Charles 66
  Clark 166
  Delia Tracy 54
  Emma 51
  Hamilton 116
  John 109
  Nancy 3, 38
  Nathan 22
  Phebe 48
  Polly 123
Davy, Eliza M. 167
  Henry 39
Dawley, Daniel 47
Day, Benjamin F. 46
  Elvira 158
Dayton, Hezekiah 18
Dean, Ezra 73
  Mary 86
  Ophelia 166
  Polly 130
Deans, Sarah M. 72
DeForest, Mary 45
  Susan 15
Deisler, Heinrich
  177
Deitz, Adam 51
  Lydia A. 96
Delancey, John 35

Delong, B. F. 133
  John 134
  Mariette 165
  Oscher C. 99
Demelt, Kezia 100
Deming, Adin 92
  Eri 164
  Martha 93
  Wealthy 96
Dennison, James P. 131
Denslow, Benjamin 102
Denton, Alice A. 163
  Asa 139
  Hannah 80
  Hattie B. 164
  John 138
  Philena M. 164
  Sarah 58, 140
Derby, Julia L. 98
  Rebecca 70
Derbyshire, Alice Louisa 137
  Eiethea 137
  George H. 56, 133
Derrbyshire, Matthew 60
Derthick, John 39
  Moses L. 39
Devenpeck, J. H. 155
Devol, Annis 157
  Silas 90
Dewey, Eliphalet 25
  Eliphlet 59
  Eliza 5
  Elizabeth 13
  Elmira 174
  Emeline 110

Dewey, Henry 46
  J. H. 72
  Martha 13
  Orrin F. 73
  Truman 172
Dewitt, Susan 27
Dickinson, Sybil 20
Dickson, Eleanor 83
  James 69
Diell, John (Mrs.) 172
  Mary 18, 169
Dietz, Anna Elizabeth 32
  Jacob 47
Dignan, George Henry 161
Dillingham, William 49
Dimoch, Ward 22
Dimock, Cook 27
  Cornelia 71
  Eli 92
  Phebe S. 107
  Polly Sena 106
Dingman, Ella 167
  Erexene 144
  Mary A. 147
Dixon, Benjamin 65
  Lois 83
  Mary 76
  Mary O. 4
Dixson, Thomas P. 41
  William C. 58
Dole, James 8
Dollaway, Hannah 106
Dolton, Lucy 94
Donaldson, Hannah W. 178

Donaldson, Timothy 77
Donnelly, Ann 59
  Elizabeth 140
  Joseph 65
Doolittle, Maria 149
Dorr, Russell 27
Dorrance, C. (Mrs.) 106
Dorwin, Josiah 147
Doubleday, Barthena 47
  Charles Edwin 114
  Clarissa 89
  Demas A. 125
  Edwin C. 98
  Edwin F. 114
  Frankie 109
  Laura 118
  Lester C. 103
  Lewis 147
  Mary A. 153
  Mercy 17
  Sally 11, 171
  Seth 11, 59, 140
Dougherty, Thomas 25
Douglass, Asa 12
  Henry W. 86
Dow, Nancy 41
  Samuel 27
Downed, Cyrus 33
Downing, Polly 50
Downs, John Day 50
Dowse, William 10, 12
Doyle, Catherine 173
Drake, Eunice 69
  Harriet 105
  Leonard 22

Drake, Nancy 99
  Perez 53
Draper, Mary 26
  Rufus 23
Druse, Lyman 174
Dryden, William 170
Duane, Mary 22
  Mary Ann 35
Duggleby, Edward 177
  Mattie 149
  Thomas 162
Dugglesby, Levina 149
Dunbar, Adeline 120
  Daniel 142
  Jessie 84
  Laura A. 83
  Rebecca 84
  Susanna 54
Dunham, --- (Mrs.) 42
  Abner 24
  Laura 63
  Obadiah 12
Dunlap, Elizabeth 88
  Mary S. 73
Dunn, Mary 170
  Michael 117
Dunning, Ichabod W. 151
Durfy, Kate T. 153
  Robert M. 124
Durham, Viola S. 131
Duroe, Elnah 109
Dutcher, Angeline 121
  Christopher 87

Dutcher, Christopher (Mrs.) 175
  Elenor 90
  Gabriel 97
  Israel P. 98
  James H. 136
  John 117
  Marquis 156
Dutton, Robert 174
Dwight, Henry E. 29

~ *E* ~

Earl, Joseph G. 156
Easton, John C. 165
  Sophronia 59
Eaton, Ezra 61
  Ezra W. 92
  James 98
  Olive 96
  Rachel Ann 87
  Sarah 21
  Sylvia 173
  Tamson W. 87
  Theophilus 19
  William F. 4
  William Franklin 41
Eckert, Laura 140
Eckler, Alvin 141
  Elias 160
  Emma 144
  Henry 163
  Horace 128
Eddy, Alice D. 152
  Alice I. 152
  Alice M. 113
  Amanda 119
  Asa 91
  Daniel 4, 42

Eddy, Dorcas 91
  Jesse 62
  John 137
  Lavira 143
  Lucina L. 66
  Luther 97
  Lydia 29
  Mandana 119
  Mary 64, 95
  Noah 92
  Stephen 109
  Sybil 82
  Thomas 117
  Willard 29
  William 103, 106
Edgerton, Erastus 10
Edget, Alsina 93
  Delos W. 84
Edgett, Asenath F. 112
Edmunds, Andrew J. 147
  Louisa M. 163
  Samuel 31
  Sophia 149
  Thomas 149
Edson, Abigail 101
  Anna 118
  Benjamin 78
  Elizabeth 57
  Hannah S. 101
  Lydia 75
  Obed 68
  Orimel 52
  Stephen F. 109
  Theodatus 54
  Willis 61
  Wyllis 26
Edwards, --- (Mrs.) 11
  Charlotte M. 102

Edwards, Edward 168
  Harriet 38
  Jonathan 8
  Richard 9
  William G. 103
Eells, John 48
Eggleston, Frank 165
  Harvey S. 119
  Raymond W. 174
Egleston, Jeme 101
  Lydia 53
Eilcox, Eliza 97
Eldred, Almira 50
  Clarissa 145
  Daniel 54
  Elisha 30
  Eunice 55
  Frances C. 149
  George 172
  Henry L. 105
  Mary (Russell) 52
  Mary A. 75
  Naamah (Mrs.) 37
  Nathan 107
  Sally 171
  Solomon 74
  Thomas 90
  Waterman 123
Eldridge, John H. 98
Elemdorf, Edmund 45
  John S. 45
  Peter Edward 55
Elliott, William J. 129
Ellis, Arnos 87
  Christopher 108
Ellison, Francis J. 95
Ellsworth, Judiah S. 159

Ellsworth, Stukely 60
Elly, Abbe 120
Elmendorf, John S. 5
Elwell, Charles 130
  Edward O. 111
  Jerusha 72
  John M. 126
  Samuel 72
Elwood, Benjamin R. 107
  Daniel 28
  Richard 30
Ely, Amanda 53
  Lavina W. 153
  Ora 166
Emerson, Betsey 3
  Lottie D. 151
  Lydia 58
  Richard 39, 172
Emmons, Asa 21, 23
  Edmund P. 159
  Rodney (Mrs.) 159
Emory, Arthur W. 96
Emsworth, Lucy 25
English, Abel 49
Ensign, Harvey P. 70
Ensworth, Sally 69
Ernest, Catherine 108
Ernst, Grace Scott 151
  John F. 5
  John Frederick 9, 44
  John Schoolcraft 90
Esmay, M. Jerome 126

Everett, Oliver H. 43

~ *F* ~

Fairchild, Abijah 101
  Gabriel 31
  Jerusha 179
  John F. 133
  Lucy 24
  William 14, 106
Fairchilds, Eunice 65
Fairman, Anna 50
  Isaac Watts 116
  Richard 23
Fancher, Eunice 160
  Mary 87
Farling, Sally 8
Farmer, Frances M. 47
Farr, Almira 52
Farrar, Salmon 77
Farrington, Desire 89
Fassett, Chester A. 67
  Joseph R. 118
  Martha L. 78
Faulkner, --- (Dr.) 51
  Alma Ann 139
  Elizabeth 89
  Joseph E. 109
  Judson 128
  Morris B. 135
Fay, Arthur C. 173
  Freddy E. 132
  Julia K. 92
  Julia L. 108
Feakins, Sarah Jane 85

Featherstonbaugh,
  Sarah F. 29
Feeter, — (Mrs.) 47
Fellow, Fannie M.
  151
Fellows, Daniel 41
  Dortha 167
  John M. 70
Feltus, Henry J. 36
Fenn, Stephen 51
Fenno, George 39
Fenton, S. C. 151
  Samuel C. 151
Ferguson, Allida M.
  143
  Elizabeth T. 146
  Jean 128
Fern, S. A. Douglas
  150
Ferrel, John M.
  (Mrs.) 166
Ferris, Hannah 95
  Justus 62
  Phebe 86
  Richard P. 128
  Sarah 52
Ferry, Emily A. 119
Few, William 36
Field, Arthur 28
  Betsey 165
  Clarissa 43
  Cutter 114
  Elizabeth 56
  Fanny E. 168
  George P. 74
  Hannah 137
  Mary 89
  Mary A. 77
  Mary Jane 78
  Nathan 103
  Silas 84

Field, Stephen 91
Fields, Erastus 93
  Harriet 144
  Oliver P. 86
  Randolph 136
Filer, Ann E. 178
Filkins, Adeline 82
Finch, Wesley 178
  William A. 178
Fish, A. H. 163
  Anna 106
  Clarinda 58
  Cornelius C. 142
  Frederick 89
  Hannah 97
  Henry C. 83
Fisher, Frank M.
  161
  Margaret A. 64
Fisk, Nathan 113
  Philip 70
  Sarah 175
  Sheldon 152
Fiske, Rufus 71
Fitch, Aaron 21, 32
  Almarader 5
  Betsey 148
  Buckingham 148
  Catherine 1
  Charles 96
  Charles D. 92
  Collins 48
  Delia L. 68
  Edgar C. 141
  Eleazer 6
  Elias D. 123
  Emeline 89
  Erastus 76
  Fenner R. 94
  George 137
  Georgianna 144

Fitch, German C. 68
  Helen 103
  Henry 45, 105
  Isaac 88
  Isabel 105
  James 24, 33
  James E. 97
  Maria M. 142
  Mary C. 141
  Mason 95
  Nancy 98
  Prosper 135
  Rexaville L. 75
  Stephen 3
  Stephen (Mrs.) 1
  William 59, 145
Flagg, Hezekiah 23
Fletcher, Timothy
  106
Fling, David 47
  Martha 117
  Mattie 144
  Susanna 73
Flint, Dorothy 59
  Elizabeth 160, 170
  Hannah 14
  Thomas 112
  Zacheus 54
Floyd, William 23
Follett, James 125
  Walter C. 140
Folts, Melchort 40
Fonda, Henry 37
  Lizzie 165
Foot, Ebenezer 14
Foote, Catherine B.
  3
  Catherine Blacque
  40
  Charles A. 36
  Ebenezer 42

Foote, Elisha 40, 73
  Eliza 3
  Eliza J. 40
  Hyatt 160
  Isaac 74
  Mary 20, 155
  Phebe Steere 96
Ford, Enos J. 162
  Helen M. 131
  Isaac S. 173
  Lucia 69
  Nathan 39
Forrester, John K. 56
Foster, David C. 153
  Jonah 21
  Philip 130
Fowler, Fred Curtiss 152
  Mary 153
  Minnie E. 131
Fowlston, --- (Gen.) 70
  Joel L. 78
Fox, Jabez 28
  James L. 49
  Noah 24
  Sarah 32
Franchot, Catherine 49
  Deborah 124
  Julia A. 61
  Paschal 109
Francis, Thomas 138
Francisco, Henry 20
Franklin, Hannah 163
  Moses 105
Frasier, William 117
Frazier, Willis 163
Freeck, Elizabeth 57
Freedom, Cato 40

Freeman, Elizabeth 34
  Gideon 10
  Helen L. 101
  James O. 136
  John D. 130
  Mary Jane 129
  Matilda 104
  Oliver 178
  Richard A. 107
French, Daniel 44
  Elizabeth 49
  William 12
Frey, Elizabeth 30
  Hendrick 34
Frink, Chloe 154
  Peter 124
Frisbie, Martha Taylor 165
Fry, Arvilla A. 136
  Rhodes 39
Fuller, Amanda 15
  Betsey 161
  Elijah 31
  Elizabeth 58
  Emma 169
  Harriet M. 73
  Harriet S. 31
  Jonathan 74
  Lydia 106
  Nathaniel 30
  Rhoda 74
  Sas 37
  Susan 74
  Thomas 42, 60
  William 68
Funk, Hiram 165
  William 86

~ G ~

Gadsby, George 157
Gage, Loraine 108
  Ransom 109
  Zeteella 128
Gaige, Harriet W. 111
Gallup, Eliza 100
  Hannah M. 82
  Simeon B. 103
Galpin, Huldah 19
  Rhoda 55
Galt, Salinda 177
Gamwell, Mary A. 117
Gano, Ira 76
  Mary 103
Ganom, George D. 110
Gardinier, Barent 23
Gardner, Amy 131
  Asa 152
  Betsey 119, 162
  Catherine 171
  Chauncey 133
  Chauncy 162
  Cordelia 133
  Daniel 133
  David 164
  Elijah 2, 36
  Elisha P. 178
  Harriet 146
  Henry 122
  Henry M. 133
  Horace 112
  Horace (Mrs.) 112
  Isaac 42
  J. Judson 89
  Jared 127
  Jonathan 168

Gardner, Joseph 102, 126
  Julia 175
  Julia T. 164
  Lucinda 79
  Lydia 109
  Mary 75
  Mary Jane 132
  Nathaniel 114
  Noel 124
  Philip 114
  Remeyn C. 132
  Robert 162
  Ruth 23
  Sabria 121
  Sarah 22
  Tabitha 111
  William M. 130
  Willis E. 150
Garlick, Dolly 155
Garney, John S. 116
Garratt, Amanda 104
  George 82
Garrett, John 71
  Lucia 18
  Pauline 146
  William 18
Gaskin, Abigail 29
Gates, Asahel 53
  Calvin 81
  Darius 166
  George 64
  George O. 3
  Helen L. 131
  Jane 153
  Lucia 45
  Sophia M. 171
Gautier, --- (Gen.) 21
Gaylay, Denton 116
Gaylord, Samuel 71

Gaylord, Seymour 75
Gayly, Susannah 53
Gazley, Alexander 53
Geddes, Mary 23
Geer, Jamima 134
Genter, Annie Fedden 153
  Charles Alvin 116
  Maranda 96
  George, James 156
  Georgia, Emma M. 89
Gerrtner, J. P. 39
Getman, Helen 169
  John 165
Getohell, W. Augustus 127
Gholson, Thomas 16
Gibbs, Alice 36
  Melvin 139
  Roxy 125
  Zebulon 86
Gibson, Josiah 135
  Lucina 111
  Samuel 17
Gidney, Hannah Reynolds 60
Gifford, Caroline M. 165
  Christopher 174
  Christopher B. 60
  Esther 151
  Nathaniel 107
  William C. 165
Gilbert, Abigail 25
  Abner 119
  Augustus 82
  Benjamin 35
  Elizabeth 148
  Hannah 43

Gilbert, Josephine 125
  Lloyd 29, 87
  Minnie E. 141
  Morris 119
  Robert C. 84
  Silas 27
  Silas (Mrs.) 27
  Storyes 92
Gilchrist, Daniel 2, 132
  John 162
  Margaret M. 115
  Mary 28, 30
  Peter 62
Gile, Andrew 164
  Daniel 164
  Lucretia 92
Gill, Eliot 122
  Elliott 85
  Moses 7
Gillet, Adeline E. 68
  David 101
  David A. 71
Gillett, Sodeima 77
Gillman, Corrine E. 176
Gillon, Catherine 176
Glazier, Phebe E. 81
Gleason, Jason 62
Gledhill, Jennie E. 125
  Liza 138
Glover, Mable 25
Gnodell, Elizabeth 81
Goff, Morris 40
  Nathan 11
Gold, Thomas R. 35
Goodell, Richard 30

Goodrich, Chauncey 15
  Cornelia 77
  Hannah Y. 78
  Jeremy 42
  John 21
  Joseph H. 54
  Maria 162
  Sarah 82
Goodsell, Deborah 22
  Elizabeth R. 13
  Henry 27
Goodspeed, Stephen 152
Gorham, Abigail 80
  Laura A. 104
Gorton, George C. 132
  Herbert 132
Gott, Ellen R. 85
  Harry 157
  Sarah 7
  Susannah 49
Gould, Ann 60
  Henry 176
  Martha A. 99
Graces, Mary Webb 50
  Moses P. 41
Grady, Patrick 6
Graff, Catherine 75
Graham, Eliza 46
  Elvira 5
  Polly 100
  Ruth 99
Granah, Theodorus V. W. 25
Granger, Gideon 25
Grant, George Benjamin 141

Grant, Hannah 106
  Harriet 129
  Harriet E. 149
  Joshua 30
  Mary M. 141
  Richard 41
Graves, Abner 54
  Abner (Mrs.) 177
  Ashbel 133
  Calvin 32
  Ella F. 102
  Emma Jane 63
  Eppa 123
  Fenimore 54
  Frances Rebecca 32
  George C. 90
  Louisa 66
  Louisa A. 141
  Mary 94
  Mary A. 171
  Moses 37
  Moses P. 4
  Nancy 63
  Recompence 22
  Roxane 22
  Sarah Jane 56
  Susan 13
  Theodore 6, 46
Gray, Almira 108
  Hannah 124
  John H. 91
  Julia 94
  Levi (Mrs.) 53
  Nancy 115
  William 30
Green, Ann E. 141
  Anson N. 152
  Betsey E. 85
  Caroline 49
  Catherine 115
  Ellen A. 140

Green, Frederick J. 170
  George 178
  Isaac 15
  Olive E. 52
  Phebe 170
  Rosey 167
  Rufus P. 162
  Sally 148
  Solomon A. 131
  Sophia 168
  Ursula M. 117
  William 26, 114
Greene, Daniel 85
  David 85
  Elizabeth S. 85
Greenleaf, Thomas 7
Gregory, Anna 28
  Cynthia G. 110
  Delos 24
  Ebenezer 91
  Elias 159
  Hezekiah 74
  John 90
  Kate Worthington 140
  Mary S. 95
  Myra C. 77
  Nancy 113, 121
  Orland 116
  Sophronia 5
  Stephen 5, 24, 49, 144
  Susan 57
  Uriah 121
  Uriah (Mrs.) 151
Gridley, Chloe 74
  Frank 171
Griffen, Sarah 61
Griffin, Hammond 43

Griffin, Harriet 15
  Jane 139
  Joseph 68
  Kirtland 43
  Lucy D. 143
  Nijah 5
  Samuel 19, 65
  Sophia 57
  Vine 12
  Ward 29
  Willard 165
Griffith, Adam J. 117
  Daniel 14
  George 113
  L. 72
  Nijah 45
  Samuel 16
Griggs, Jerusha 83
  John R. 138
  Julia E. 133
  Nancy 148
Griswold, Chester A. 49
  Gaylord 10
  Lucinda M. 163
  Triphena 58
  Wickham 148
Groat, Elias 75
  Harmont 65
  Lois 79
Groff, Eliza 167
  Nathaniel 173
  Paul 72
  William Harrison 148
Gross, Anna 113
  Betsey 94
  D. W. 125
  Henry Ellis 136
  John D. 149

Gross, Marvin H. 100
  Nancy M. 100
Grout, Josiah W. 122
Grover, Joel 139
  Lucy 119
  Russell 124
Guest, Henry 21
Guild, Israel 8
Gunn, Sophia E. 154
Gurney, Benjamin 151
  Meribah 151
Gustin, John 48
Guthrie, Joseph 59

~ *H* ~

Hackley, Addie M. 162
  Polly 93
Haggerty, Hannerett 96
  Patrick 171
Haines, Julius C. 100
Hale, Eleazer 98
  Emily 167
  Hiram W. 3, 40
Hall, Anan 69
  Ann 10
  Benjamin 84
  Betsey 124
  C. G. 105
  Delia A. 111
  Eleanor 146
  Ephraim 45
  Helen 120
  Horace 71

Hall, John C. 57
  Jonathan 7
  Joshua 26
  Martha 59
  Martha M. 62
  Mortimer A. 98
  Obediah 118
  Sarah 154
  Thomas 10
  William G. 111
  William G. S. 140
Halliday, Elizabeth M. 167
Hamilton, Paul 16
Hammond, Jabez D. 109
Hand, Amos Henry 179
  Charles 156
  Elizabeth 96
Handy, Esther S. 115
Hanes, Charles 160
  Mary 160
Hann, James 75
Hannah, Catherine Frances 48
  Estella 167
  J. 48
  Polly 53
Hannahs, Daniel 76
  John N. 161
  Jonas 79
  William 42
Hannay, John 53
  John S. 73
  Julia A. F. 67
  Mary 53
Hanumn, Fred A. 177
Hard, David 166

Hard, Sarah E. 71
Hardendorf,
   Margaret 171
Harding, Salinda 78
Hardy, Abbie Belle
   148
  Esther 122
  Euince 130
  Jacob 120
  Kate S. 156
  Maline 140
  Mary F. 96
Harper, Elizabeth 6
  H. S. 74
  James 6
  Margaret 39
  Mary 38
  Mary A. 146
  Susan 62
Harrington,
  Benjamin 31
  Elizabeth (Scott)
   56
  Job (Mrs.) 51
  Lydia 157, 158
  Lyman 99
  Maranda 131
  Nathaniel 121
  Thankful 141
  William 137
Harris, Abigail 9
  Asa 17
  Eliza M. 150
  James 55
  Jane E. 175
  Lucy 178
  Nathaniel 89
  Orra 125
  Rachel 74
  Sally 109

Harrison, Henrietta
   T. 175
  Salmon 59
Hart, Amanda 69
  Emeline M. 107
  George W. 164
  Joshua 135
Hartshorn, Polly 17
Hartwell, Abraham
   17
  Ann 57
  Luther 44
  Richard Ide 138
Hartwick, John
   Christopher 7
Harvey, Archibald
   170
  Frederick W. 79
Hascall, Ralph 26
Haskell, Sarah Ann
   19
Haskins, Loretta 163
  Polly 111
  William 36
Hastings, Ann 80
  Dier 78
Haswell, Anthony 16
  Libbie 158
Hatch, Daniel L. 31
  Dorastus 81
  Doros 33
  Lucy 76
  Menzo 33
  Samuel 31
  William 76
Hatter, Nicholas 8
Havens, Matilda 83
  Nathaniel 68
Hawkins, Anna 119
  Benjamin 16
  Rufus 9

Hawks, Elizabeth 71
  James 29
  Lois 124
  Nathaniel 50
Hawley, --- (Mrs.) 7
  Joseph C. 84
  Lydia (Eddy) 29
  Philena 31
  Rufus 7
  William 37
Hay, Lucinda S. 158
Hayden, Hezekiah
   25
  Laura 111
Hayes, Sally 36
Haynes, Samuel 86
  William 99
Hayward, Joshua 68
Hazard, Nathaniel
   20, 22
Hazeline, Huldah C.
   108
Hazen, Wealthy 34
Head, Daniel A. 97
  Helen A. 97
Heath, Polly 121
Hellsinger, Susan
   116
Hendrix, Narcissa
   155
Hendryx, Deborah
   145
Henicker, Frances 97
Henn, Bernhart 28
  Hannah Elizabeth
   38
Henniker, Levantia
   102
  Nancy 80
  Polly 87
  Robert 80

Henry, Abigail 21
  Adam 63
  Francis 18
  Hannah 23
  Laura 36
  Mary 73, 85
  Nancy 42, 132
  Priscilla 18
  Robert 16
  Rowetta 40
  Samuel 18, 44
  William 21
Herdman, Kate 167
  Nelson 152
Herick, Lydia 1
Herkimer, Abner M. 84
  Alonzo 77
  Anna 46
  Catherine 107
  George 3, 38
Herrick, Anna 40
  Arthur C. 157
  Catherine 150
  Evan Lewis 67
  Mariette T. 65
  Roxie M. 164
  Ruth 13
Herring, Mary 132
Herrington, Francis 97
Hetherington, James 78
Hewes, Cora A. 111
  Daniel 88
  Elsey Wood 160
  Eunice 101
  Joseph 12
  Patrick 164
  Schuyler 155
Hewit, Amos 33

Hews, Candace 151
  James Boden 112
Hewson, Robert B. 30
Heyward, Isaac 64
Hibbard, Andrew M. 77
Hickling, Edward S. 146
Hicks, E. D. (Mrs.) 165
Hicock, Samuel 88
Hicok, Alanson 54
Higby, Anson 91
  Charles H. 92
  Cynthia 163
  Emily 17
  Eunice 71
  Nancy 162
  William 109
Hildreth, Mathias B. 12
Hill, Francelia 133
  Sarepta 13
Hinds, Eugene 69
  John 19, 21
  Joseph 137
  Juliabeth 85
  Mary 65
  Mary A. 107
  Mary E. 98
  Nehemiah 152
  Polly 69
  Polly M. 84
  Reuben 106
  Sarah 169
Hinman, Anna 9
  Eber 141
  Elizabeth 72
  Everett 112
  John 120

Hinman, Lewis 161
  Lois 142
  Mary 89
  Mortimer 107
  Orcellia A. 120
  Polly M. 132
Hinne, Hiram 151
Hitchcock, Mary W. 167
Hix, Rufus 89
Hoag, Abel 60
  Albro D. 119
  Emmet 126
  Harriet L. 161
  James 121
  Matilda 89
  Sally Ann 36
  Sarah 37
  Sarah Ann 37
  Thomas 37, 144
Hobby, Morris 88
Hodge, Narcissa 173
  Rachel 82
Hodskins, Egber: L. 63
  Jonas 82
Hodson, Martha 73
Hogan, Morris 174
Hogeboom, Lawrence 8
  Mary D. 171
Hogoboom, Helen A. 136
  Nicholas 137
Hoke, Arthur E. 106
  Daniel M. 122
  Elizabeth 166
  Rozeltha A. 92
Holbrook, Asia T. 137
  Mary 108

Holden, Ebenezer
  M. 85
  Stephen (Mrs.) 9
Holdridge, Cora E.
  144
Holland, Dallas J.
  104
  Ivory 21
Hollenbeck, Rosman
  K. 123
Holliday, Gideon 39
Hollis, Helen E. 142
  Thomas 95
Hollister, Alice 151
  Amos 108
  Edwin V. 104
  Harvey 156
  Hattie M. 172
  Trypehna 121
Holloway, E. A.
  (Mrs.) 174, 175
Holman, Thomas 31
Holmes, M. Calvin
  150
  Orren 52
  William 73
Holt, --- (Miss) 28
  Arthur M. 119
  Elijah 32
  Eliza P. 106
  George 67
  Joseph 59
  Joseph (Mrs.) 10
  Lester 28
  Mariette 103
  Martha 68
  Mary 19
  Mary E. 107
  Mortimer E. 104
  Sarah 42, 112
Hood, John 70

Hood, Margaret 166
  Nancy 60
Hoogekerk, Henry
  38
Hooker, Amoret L.
  86
  Frank S. 140
Hooper, Jasper 10
  Sarah Catherine 10
Hoose, Charity 142
  Nelson K. 173
Hopkins, George M.
  93
  Harriet 110
  Henry 108, 121
  Jeremiah 162
  Joseph 122
  Mercy 82
  Roswell 41
  Sarah Ann 102
  Sidney 156
  William 15
Horton, Anna C.
  113
  Jennie 134
  Mary Louise 143
  Mercy 74
  Thomas 162
Houck, John I. 142
  Lydia S. 42
Hough, Betsey 64
  David 72
  Eliza 6, 47
Houghton, Albert 72
  Daniel (Mrs.) 148
House, Adna 162
  Mary Jane 130
  Nancy M. 145
Houseman, --- (Mr.)
  12

Howard, Eliza Ann
  33
  Laura 49
Howe, Adaline C.
  179
  B. Silas 146
  Benjamin 39
  Caroline 124
  Estes 30
  Fanny 18
  Henry 156
  Henry R. 170
  Julia M. 157
  Lazarus 41
  Lovina 115
  Olive 145
Howell, Edward 11
  Harriet E. 101
Howes, Lucinda 40
  Thomas 54
Howland, Abraham
  A. 135
  Betsey 178
  Sarah 80
Hoyt, --- (Mrs.) 52
  Jane 95
Hubbard, C. M.
  (Mrs.) 144
  Christina 29
  Delos 87
  Elijah 117
  Emily 71
  Giles 20
  Griffith 3, 39
  Gurnsey D. 139
  Harvey 16
  John 92
  Joseph 3, 96
  Lorenzo D. 132
  Mary 74
  Phebe 165

Hubbard, Reuben
    133
  Seth 47
Hubbel, Luriania
    (Chapin) 10
  Rebecca 59
Hubbell, Betsey 176
  Elijah 91, 120
  Hannah 61
  Jabez 59
  John A. 68
  Lemuel 84, 85
  Lucinda 146
  Lurinda 166
  Nancy 88
  William O. 88
Hubby, Jonathan 52
Huchins, Samuel H.
    144
Hudson, Barzillai 26
  Ephraim 8, 9
  Hannah 19
  John F. 163
  Maria R. 105
  Mary 46
  Mary Putnam 57
  William H. 144
Huestis, Clark M.
    167
  Solomon 156
Hughes, Hannah K.
    57
  Morris 22
Hull, Louisa 141
  Nathaniel 65
  William 142
Humaston, Charlotte
    79
  Junia 68
  Timothy 78
Hume, Isavelle 153

Hume, Jane 112,
    117
  John 110
  Thomas W. 115
Humiston, Hannah
    81
  Patrick 62
Humphrey, Alonzo
    V. 133
Hunt, Betsey L. 77
  James 172
  Mary M. 153
  Ranson 98
  Sally 159
  Willard 88
Hunter, Margaret
    170
  Samuel H. 152
Huntington, Abigail
    13
  Harriet 162
  Mary J. 21
  Sally 9
  Samuel 57
Huntley, Calvin 52
  Caroline 61
  Patty A. 54
Hurd, --- (Mrs.) 42
  David 161
  John 129
  Sophia 137
Hurlburt, Elizabeth
    44
Husbands, Joseph D.
    50
Huse, Olive 39
Huson, Abigail 89
Hutchings, John 170
Hutchins, Eliza 104
  Harriet 80
  Louisa 68

Hutchins, Matilda
    G. 59
  S. C. 76
  Samuel 37
Hutchinson, Harriet
    D. 68
Hutliff, Henry 89
Huttalen, Joshua G.
    163
Hyatt, Samuel 47
Hyde, Alonzo 48
  Ambrose 75
  Gustavus A. 101
  Ira 146, 160
  James 31
  Nellie 154
Hyer, Mary L. 170

~ I ~

Ingalls, Amos 77
  E. B. 95
  James 13
  Lucy E. 177
  Mary Ann 112
  Orrin 14
  Sarah 45, 105
Ingals, Samuel M.
    136
Ingalsbe, Anna 116
  Asa 108, 153
  Jane 132
  Laura 129
Inglas, Mary 5
Inglsbee, Lawine 129
Ingraham, Betsey
    172
  Eliza D. 4
  John 42
Irish, Isaac S. 1
  Joshua 92

Irish, Sarah W. 148
Irons, Jeremiah 6
  Levi 60
  Reubens 97
  Ruth 74
Ismond, C. E. 172
  Caroline 135
  Elias 131
  Hiram 146
  Jennett 177
Ives, Eunice 172

~ J ~

Jackson, Charity 104
  Charles Bardwell 68
  Clara L. 173
  John 102
  Mary 144
  Mary M. 176
  Nancy 58
  Phebe 103
  Uri 105
  William 134
Jacobs, Adelbert 144
  Behiah 10
  Edwin G. 164
  John W. 101
  Samuel 82
Jacobus, Thomas 58
Jamison, Ira 112
Jan, Silence 86
Janes, Elinor 27
  Rosanna C. 124
Jaques, Moses 108
Jarvis, Abigail 127
  Asahel 26
  Content 4, 43
  Daphne 148
  Francis Griswold 2

Jarvis, George M. 167
  Horace P. 63
  Maria 96
  Mary 8
  William 153
  William Cooper 147
Jay, William 64
Jenkins, Robert 21
Jenks, Ella 165
  Ida S. 173
  Jennie 173
  Joseph G. 151
  Lucinda 159
Jennings, James 155
Jewell, Hannah R. 116
  Whitney 87
Johnson, Adam 26
  Almon H. 135
  Amos 172
  Barakiah 31
  Bela 91
  Benjamin 55
  Clarissa 56
  Daniel 62
  Ezekiel 56
  Frances D. 108
  George 62
  Hannah 73, 78
  Harriet E. 69, 70
  Horatio G. 5, 45
  Horatio P. 113
  Israel 56
  James 123
  James H. 59
  James R. 132
  Jane 112, 162
  Jedediah 119
  Jennie E. 175

Johnson, John 112
  Jonathan 11, 61, 161
  Lois 93
  Lucy M. 81
  Lusina D. 74
  Naaman 79
  Nathan 149
  Orrin 44
  Parley 17
  Rebecca 133
  Richard 120
  Robert 4, 9
  Samuel 29, 51
  Timothy 7
  William 53
  William C. 104
  William L. 77
  William P. 157
  William Samuel 20
Johnston, Benjamin B. 148
  David 93
  Louis M. 125
  Walter 67
  William 163
Jones, Amos 73
  Cornelius 116
  Emeline 48
  Evelina Hale 134
  Henry 73
  Isaac (Mrs.) 48
  Jennie 148
  Jessie 171
  John C. 133
  John Paul 178
  Josiah 153
  Nancy 68
  Polly 21
  Sally 98, 179
  Samuel 21

Jones, Samuel M. 80
  William 172
Jordan, Abigail 96
Joslin, Addie 173
  John T. 147
Joslyn, Eleazer 118
  Mary 68
Judd, Aurelia 74
  Edwin 169
  Elizabeth 115
  Martha L. 88
Jutkins, Josiah 111

~ K ~

Kane, Betsey 145
Kaple, Alfred B. 114
  Bela 99
  Bela J. 119
  Helen L. 129
  Jane 22
Kaseby, Henry 166
Kasley, Almira 121
Kean, Peter 37
Keeler, Hiram H. 84
Keen, Jane 115
Keese, Georgiann 140
  Kate Turner 114
  Theodore 115
Kelley, Bridget 150
  Ellen 166
  James 122
  S. B. 138
  Susanna 118
Kellogg, Amanda 61
  Charles 146
  Esther 108
  Ezekiel 26
  Hannah 140
  John 124

Kellogg, John D. 172
  Lucy 116
  Philotha 63
  Sarah 114
  Sarah S. 95
  Tracey 132
Kelly, James C. 170
  John 169
  Lucy 109
  Mary 89
Kelso, David 155
  David H. 87
  Henry A. 105
  Horace 67
Kemball, Samuel 157
Kembell, Isaac C. 167
Kemp, John A. 164
Kendall, David 94
  Rachel 92
Kent, Moss 63
Kenyon, Alver 156
  Celestia M. 179
  Chester 5, 45
  Daniel 97
  Daniel A. 127
  Elizabeth 168
  George Stowel 160
  Hannah May 132
  Ira 100
  James A. 112
  John 16
  Lovina 120
  Maria 161
  Mary Jane 127
  Rensselaer 145
Ker, Nathan 6
  Oliver L. 6

Kerr, Walter (Mrs.) 69
Keyes, Adeliza 164
  Daniel 83
  Hiram H. 104
  Lester D. 102
  Rachel 85
Keyon, Jessie B. 149
Keys, Eunice 95
  John 27
Kibby, Abilene 120
Kilbourn, Delia Harmony 51
King, Anna 152
  Burdett D. 157
  Cyrus E. 81
  James 71
  James S. 46
  Mary 18
  Minerva N. 141
  Samuel 134
  Sophia Phinney 141
Kingley, Nathan 25
Kingsburg, John 100
Kingsley, Catherine E. 76
  Erastus 140
  Harriet 132
  Lydia 71
Kinne, Hiram 151
  J. Levi 136
Kinney, Emer Amanda 103
Kinsley, Alonzo W. 41
Kirby, Cornelia A. 126
  Electa 93
  George F. 101
  Jane 106

Kirby, Roxy 75
  Sybil 175
  William 161
Kirkland, Cornelia
  G. 46
Kirkpatrick, William 49
Kline, William A. 68
Knapp, Elizabeth 146
  George 173
  Merritt 168
  William 95
Knowlton, Artemesia 145
  Emma 140
  Eunice 50
  Giddem A. 11
  Henry 73
  Louisa 74
  Triphenia 28
Kowlison, Carlton 31
Krake, Caroline 87
  Josiah 87
Krum, Henry P. 154

~ L ~

Ladd, Aurelia 15
Laidler, Ellen 147
Laight, Harvey 167
Lake, Gideon 85
  Olive 103
Lamb, Asa W. 169
  Daniel 163
  Rebecca L. 109
Lambert, Abram 143
  Hannah 100
LaMoure, Isaac L. 128

Lampman, Betsey 91, 97
Landon, Norman 7
Lane, Betsey 76
  Chauncey 76
  Cynthia 136
  Derick 45
  Florie 120
  Freddie 120
  Isaac (Mrs.) 96
  Lavantha 116
  Margaret 126
  Mathias 136
  Sarah A. 98
Lansing, Garrit G. 46
  Mary E. 164
  Sarah M. 102
  Sylvia 88
Latham, Deborah 65
  Samuel 62
Lathrop, --- (Dr.) 86
  Francis 63
  Horace 126
  Horace W. 130
  James 49
  Joseph 22
  Nancy A. 78
  Polly 85
Latimer, Charles W. 104
  John S. 158
Latin, Albert 94
Lattin, Irena 169
  John L. 146
Lawless, Jennie C. 150
Lawrence, Augustus H. 37
  Daniel 63
  Enoch 163

Lawrence, Enos 119
Lawyer, Luther 44
  Nicholas 44
Lay, Abby Galpin 165
  Chloe 102
Leaning, Frances 179
  Francis 81
  Marion A. 81
  Mary 170
  William 149
Lear, Tobias 16
Lee, Arnand 53
  Ezra 23
  Graham Stewart 149
  Jerusha 10
  Lois 2, 112
  Martin 29
  Oliver H. 118
Leet, William Calvin 152
Leib, Michael 25
Lent, Ann Elizabeth 45
  Benjamin J. 122
  David 45, 64
  Henry 45
  Margaret 153
  Phebe 25
  Samuel 110
  Sarah O. 114
  Seymour J. 105
Leo, Rebecca A. 70
Leonard, Nancy 112
  Olive 118
Leontine, Ruth 136
Lerow, John 28
LeRow, Juliette 96
LeRoy, Mercy P. 86

Lester, Nathan
   Clayton 114
Leverett, Theo. 85
Lewis, Betsey 63
   Charles E. 118
   Cornelia G. 147
   Cyrus 142
   Edward 91
   Elizabeth 171
   Esther S. 175
   Fenimore 136
   George 66
   Hannah 141
   Henry D. 168
   Jennie 144
   Jessie K. 141
   John F. 91
   Lucy Noyes 54
   Mary A. 141
   Mary Augusta 20
   Moses 92
   Noyes 104
   Noyes Edwin 118
   Ruby A. 95
   Samuel B. 143
   Stewart 39
   W. 142
   William 76
Lidell, Don F. 142
   Kate 177
Light, Lucinda P.
   156
Lightall, Abraham 47
Lillie, Bradford 162
   Elisha 175
Lincklaen, John 24
Lincoln, James W.
   79
   Polly 118
Lines, Anthony 136
   Permelia 157

Linn, John Blair 8
Lippet, --- (Mrs.) 31
   Abraham 7
Lippitt, Ceylon O.
   144
   Charles M. 166
   Esther 154
Little, Alice 88
   David 49
   George M. 148
   Helen S. 175
   Jonathan 33
Livermore, Adelaide
   A. 115
   Samuel 8
Livingston, Elizabeth
   S. 40
   Henry 37
   Jacob 139
   Robert F. 14
   Robert H. 8
   Robert R. 13
Lloyd, Alexander 135
   Heman 73
   James 27
   Polly 23
Lomis, Mary 120
Longton, William D.
   173
Loomer, Darius 16
Loomis, Abigail 56
   Abraham 17
   Catherine 61
   Daniel 51, 156
   Eleazer 12
   Eliza 26
   Emelin M. 59
   Hannah 68
   Harvey 78
   Huldah 90
   Israel 84

Loomis, Joseph 17
   Lebbeus 162
   Lucy 57
   Maria 78
   Phelps 176
Loop, Mary 89
Lord, Asa 17
Losee, Baltis 110
   Cornelius 157
Lossee, Selah K. 99
Lothrop, John H. 40
Lough, Eleanor M.
   177
   George T. 167
   Mary E. 177
   Robert 139
Loveland, Frances E.
   72
Low, Elizabeth 54
   Selina G. 126
   TenEyck C. 75
Lowcock, John 37
Lowe, Phebe C. 75
   Sarah 23
Lowell, Uriel B. 95
Luce, Almira 145
   Betsey 86
   Cynthia Ann 46
   Dille 63
   George H. 106
   Jacob M. 122
   Joanna 3
   John 86
   Louise 57
   Lowell B. 107
   Lydia 64
   Mary L. 155
   Nathan 17
   Othniel 17
   Torry J. 164
   Uriah 73

Luddington, Stephen 34
Lull, Amy 82
  Elina J. 141
  Joel 86
  Nathan 75
  Sarah 147
Lumley, John 122, 153
Lun, Isabella 101
Luscomb, Sarah A. 90
Lush, Richard 17
  Samuel S. 71
Lusk, Elizabeth 58
  Jane A. 87
  John 87
  William 55
Luther, Aaron 148
  Clarissa 115
  Electa 138
  John 112
  Mary Ann 120
  Moses 126
  Rachel 70
  Sylvester B. 157
  Thirza 56
Luvinstson, Ann 33
Luyscomb, Robert 52
Lyman, Elihu 31
  Joseph 31
  Joseph S. 22
Lynch, Edwin 171
Lynes, Hannah 148
Lyon, Hezekiah W. 105
  Joseph 69
  Samuel 37
Lyons, Joanna 143
  Sarah 15

~ M ~

M'Ardle, John 20
M'Cleary, Daniel 16
M'Collom, Reuben 42
M'Collons, Alexander 42
M'Cumber, Mary 42
M'Dowell, Molly 28
M'Namee, Lawrence 15
MacDonald, Fanny J. 172
Mack, Enoch 3, 39
  Stephen 14
Mackey, James S. 175
Maddill, James R. 95
Madison, William S. 22
Magher, George W. 66
  Jane 55
Main, Reuben P. 75
Maine, Joseph 62
  Sally 73
Mallary, Henry 28
Mallery, Abigail 58
  Isaac 9
  Samuel 58
Mallory, Catharine 88
  Hiram D. 108
  Lewis 156
Malory, Russell 67
Manchester, Amos L. 128
  John 75

Manchester, Joseph 92
M. M. 92
  Odell 136
Mandeville, Ellen 170
Mann, Elizabeth 106
  Ephraim 113
  George D. 119
  Jacob 39
Manning, John 54
  Olive Dana 119
Manzer, A. H. 170
Maples, Amos 143
  David 54
  Jabez 2
  Lois 91
Marble, Earl A. 66
  Elliphalle (Mrs.) 81
Markell, Henry 47
Markham, Elizabeth 81
  James 96
Marks, Candace M. 174
  James 118
  Jerusha 100
  John F. 163
Marlett, Peter 151
Marquisee, Dan L. 99
Marr, Daniel 100
Marsh, James M. 132
Marshall, Charles W. 146
Martin, Catherine 150
  Elizabeth 102
  Sally 167
Marvin, Daniel 110

212

Marvin, David 108
　Elinor 95
　Elizabeth A. 109
　Harvey 135
　Ida R. 94
　John R. 83
　Martin 143
　Nathan 9
　Sabrina 27
　Sarah E. 129, 169
　William 18
　William S. 107
Mason, Darius 49
　John M. 42
Masters, Amelia 178
　Delos 101
　Josiah 25
Mather, Charles 4, 41
　Ezra 158
　John F. 172
　Oliver M. 39
　Theresa D. 118
Mathewson, Abigail 1
Matterson, Frank 154
　Nathan W. 105
　Sophia 84
Matteson, Dora R. 158
　Harriet F. 140
Matthewson, Betsey 71
Mattison, Asa 117
　Marvin S. 111
　Roxania 151
Maxfield, Abraham 131
　Susan 79
Maxim, Harriet 66

Maxson, Lucinda 40
May, George 161
　Harmon 113
　Jennette 100
Mayeen, Ezekiel 32
Maynard, Adaline 42
　Edwin 146
　Ellen S. 132
　Thomas (Mrs.) 168
　William H. 49
McBall, Flora 179
McBrine, Patrick 53
McCabe, Michael 173
McClintock, Ralph 60
McCollom, H. N. 125
　James 94
McCollum, Anna 102
　Daniel 105
　Electa 93
　James 52
　Laurette 90
　Lydia 167
McCurdy, Robert 6
McCurry, F. 140
McDavy, Henry 107
McDonald, Elizabeth 176
　Julia 53
　Roe 104
McEwan, Harriet F. 88
McEwen, Thomas 172
McFarren, Howard E. 167
McGarity, James 163
McGarrity, Rosa 169

McGinley, Susan 168
McGown, James 154
　Maria 150
　Mary 19
McIntosh, Catherine 117
　Margaret 159
　Margaret A. 107
　Thomas 122
McIntyre, Arline 164
　Eva M. 175
　Luke 87
McKean, James 52
　Mary 68
McKeen, Jane 49
McKellip, Archibald 91
McKellup, John 58
McKenney, Matthew 22
McKown, Anna 135
　Elizabeth M. 127
　Sarah E. 135
McLean, George W. 89
　Lois 5
　Mary 145
　William 93
McMullen, James 174
McNamara, Michael 157
McNamee, Agnes
　Lucy 127
　Jackson 148
　John Lawrence 15
　Marcia 142
　Sarah M. 52
McNelly, Charles C. 148

McNelly, Michael 56
McRorica, David 65
McRorie, Alice M. 138
  Amanda 120
  Elizabeth 159
  Lorenzo 121
  Nellie A. 143
McTavish, Jannet 100
Meacham, Asa 138
  Jeremiah 3, 39
Mead, David 135
  James 156
Medbury, Hannah 61
Meghar, Peter 106
Mercer, Cornelia 140
  Frances A. 131
Merchant, Harriet T. 137
Merihew, Harvey (Mrs.) 170
Merrell, Helen M. 55
Merriam, Edward Brown 21
  Joseph 21
Merrihew, Charles E. 136
Mesick, Peter 54
  Peter (Mrs.) 54
Metcalf, Abel 35
  Arunah 95
  Arunah (Mrs.) 80
  Caroline 87
  Elijah H. 110
  Emma A. 91
  Henry P. 149
  Katherine 115

Metcalf, Lois 15
  Lydia 15
  Maria 178
  Mariet 4
  Mary 14
  Mary E. 143
  Sally 77
  Traccy 14
  Wealthy 78
  William A. 127
Michaels, Catherine 175
Mickel, Edmund 104
Miles, Barzillai H. 51
Miller, Alpha 4, 41
  Amasa 3
  Ann E. 138
  Benjamin 132
  Caleb 76
  Charles A. 163
  Clement 44
  Elisha 1, 12
  Elizabeth 125
  George B. 150
  George H. 99
  Helen M. 133
  Henry (Mrs.) 105
  Henry H. 106
  J. R. M. (Mrs.) 36
  Jane 170
  John 76
  John F. 129
  John I. 67
  Lovina 165
  Lucy A. 132
  Margaret 41
  Mary 74
  Mary M. 111
  Morris S. 28

Miller, William Alexis 103
Millington, Jacob 43
Mills, Roger 10
Miner, Daniel 35
Mires, Peter 98
Misson, George E. 142
  John 66
Mitchell, Charles 71
  Hugh 23
  Rowena 56
Mitler, Charlotte M. 147
Mix, Dorothy 14
Moak, John C. 144
Moeller, Juliana Margaret 28
Moffat, William 139
Moffatt, Alexander C. (Mrs.) 75
  Hannah 89
Molther, Augustus 56
  John 47
Monaghan, Rhoda 177
Monk, John 139
  Marvin D. 162
Monroe, Phebe 101
  Sabrina 4
  Sally 38
Montgomery, William Melvin 55
Moody, Hannah M. 162
Moore, A. V. 72
  Alanson 83
  Alfred 11
  Asenath 62

Moore, Chauncey 139
  Henry 143
  John I. 152
  Jonathan (Mrs.) 31
  Rebecca 111
  Roger 35
  Zephaniah Swift 26
Morehouse,
    Benjamin 115
  Charles 8
  Eliza C. 153
Morgan, Cynthia 62
  Lucy 122
  Walter 23
Morrell, Elmer 175
Morris, Caroline E. 70
  Charles Mosley 55
  Charles V. 55
  David Johnston 55
  Elizabeth 1
  Gouverneur 16
  Jacob W. 109
  Lurana 91
  Marcia M. 5
  Marcia Maria 44
  Mary 33
  Monroe C. 97
  P. K. 164
  Richard 138
  Richard V. 69
  Samuel 62
  Susan 147
  Thomas 27
Morrison, Caroline 46
  Nancy 173
Morse, Abel 97
  Abigail 117
  Daniel 46

Morse, Elizabeth 32
  Enoch 35
  Jenette R. 143
  Joshua 38
  Miriam 8
  Nelson 61
  Noble 41
  Patience 10
  Timothy 22
Mosher, Eliphalet 26
Mosier, Comfort 172
Mott, Clara E. 132
  Daniel 114
  Daniel (Mrs.) 104
  Lodowick 147
  Margaret 8
  Maria D. 85
  Mary 96
  Nathaniel 127
  Susan 97
Mudge, Rachel 1
Mulkins, Cathering M. 65
  Emory A. 122
  Sarah A. 79
Multer, Christian 106
Mumford, Abigail 141
  Carlton J. 146
  James 120
  Orson 112
  Polly 179
  Ruth 39
  Thomas 2, 36, 47
  Wallace 155, 177
  William D. 176
Mundy, Betsey Kane 56
Munn, Joseph 54
  Sarah 23

Munroe, Daniel 103
  Deborah 87
Munson, Charles O. 46
  Eunice 63
Murdock, Albert 171
  Alexander 106
  Andrew 50
  Daniel 122
  Edwin 154
  Emma A. 122
  Frederick A. 150
  James A. 165
  John 51
  Kate G. 153
  Luvana 89
  Mary Horth 159
  Sarah A. 142
Murphy, Albert S. 91
  Amy 99
  James 86
  James S. 143
  Sarah 116, 153
  Smith 112
Murray, William 2, 36
  William H. 103
  William N. 82
Musson, Ann 7
  William 9
Myers, Barbara 83
  Hannah M. 123
  Mary A. 179
  Oliver 110
  William 85
  Willis 174
Mygatt, Henry 34, 55
  Orlando 34
Myres, Phebe 81

~ N ~

Narron, Samuel 11
Nash, Daniel 18, 58, 82
  Isaac 9
  Jerome Moak 124
  John F. (Mrs.) 65
  Olive 2, 36
Neal, Elisha S. 95
  Frank H. 162
  Naomi 106
Nearing, Ebenezer 104
  Emily A. 168
  Hannah S. 98
  John 172
  Leander 96
  Polly 113
  Russell 94
  Truman 123
Neff, Joseph 126
  Mary 39
Nellis, Peter I. 143
Nelson, --- (Chief Justice) 66
  Anna 166
  Catherine A. 176
  Halley 66
  John 88
  Malinda 154
  Pamela 66
  Samuel 169
  Samuel Henry 49
  Sarah E. 74
Nesbit, Solomon 19
Nestle, Rebecca 178
Newcomb, Henry 79
  Isaiah 58
Newell, Abigail 27
  Achsah 75

Newell, Edwin D. 148
  G. W. 129
  George (Mrs.) 152
  Grace B. 143
  Helen M. 98
  Mary 163
  Nellie 141
  Norman 158
  Oliver 149
  Penelope 15
  Samuel Bingham 170
  Sirajah 97
Newland, Zeba 83
Newton, Alsa 89
  Cyrus W. 118
  Ithamar 62
  L. 63
  Mercy M. 129
  Mina 31
  William R. 150
Niblet, Solomon 16
Nichols, Martha 110
  Martha F. 90
  William 148, 175
Nicholson, James 8
  John 22
Nickerson, Abigail 2, 35
  Anna 47
  Elisha 80, 93
  Harriet 62
  Julia 114
  Sally 158
  Sarah 167
Niell, Elizabeth 10
Niles, Flora S. 134
  George Carr 81
  Gideon 23
  Hannah 107

Niles, John 1
  Martha Ann 134
  Mary S. 172
  Polly 165
  Sarah J. 135
  William 96
  Zerviah 14
Noble, C. C. 66
  Carrington F. 144
  Curtis 45, 55
  Ella E. Johnson 159
  Elnathan 27
  Frederick A. 95
  George H. 92
  Julia A. 66
  Julia Sophia 45
  Louisa 40
  Martin 62
  Sally 74
Noe, John 38
Norman, William E. 37
North, Adelmer D. 118
  Albert 98
  Benjamin 57, 111
  Cyrus 30
  Daniel 111
  Gabriel 33
  Hannah 118
  Harrison H. 175
  Jeremiah B. 115
  John 44
  Linus 88
  Stephen 52, 73
  Waity 68
Northrup, Clark 112
  Fanny M. 138
  George 121
  George T. 159

Northrup, Jennie L. 178
Josiah 81
Lorena 68
Marvin 60
Sophia 79
Norton, Abbie 136
  Anne E. Rogers 155
  Eunice B. 43
Nowlin, Eliza Jane 42
Noyes, Frances H. 60
Mary 21

~ O ~

O'Brien, James 157
O'Connell, Edward 176
  Mary Ann 146
Oakley, Elizabeth 92
Odell, Frances 144
Ogden, Mary F. 51
Olcott, Timothy 6
Oldendorf, Catherine 33
Olendorf, Betsey Morris 102
  Carrie L. 133
  Daniel 4, 43, 91
  David F. 120
  Edgar J. 106
  Eliza 110
  Garret 61
  Jane 50
  Mary E. 134
  Mary G. 81
  Peter 110
Olin, William 156

Olive, John S. 142
  Marcia 98
  Rebecca 68
Oliver, Andrew 50
  Elizabeth 36, 131
  James 148
  Jane F. 78
  John A. 101
Olmstead, Abigail 146
  Lucy 172
Olmsted, Hannah 52
  Stephen R. 52
Orderson, --- (Mrs.) 61
Ormiston, Catherine 159
Ormston, Robert 61
  William O. 61
Osbon, Jacob 55
Osborn, Henry P. 54
  Palmer 169
  Rebecca 32
  Sally 47
  Sarah M. 150
  Smith S. 79
Osgood, Samuel 13
Ostrander, Moses 14
Otis, John A. 4, 41
Ottaway, Elizabeth 169
  James 134
Overacre, Charlotte E. 168
Ovit, Ellen 58
Owens, Mary 157

~ P ~

Packard, Levi B. 159

Packer, Clarissa Y. 134
Padden, Sarah B. 145
Paddock, Thomas 38
Page, Jared 15
  Perley M. 164
  Sherman 104
  William 134
Paine, Amasa 27
  John E. 129
Palmatiee, Lucy 168
Palmer, Elias S. 23
  Elijah 24, 53
  Gershom 62
  Harriet L. 168
  Ichabod B. 10
  Jennie 154
  Lucius 136
  Lucretia 156
  Martha R. 168
  Vose 32
  Wheeler 118
Pardee, Harriet S. 45
Parish, Elijah 30
Park, Mary J. 151
Parker, Abraham 103
  Abraham B. 103
  Abram 147
  Alexander 84
  Alice M. 147
  Chauncey 116
  Eleazer H. 14
  Franklin 102, 103
  Henry O. 95
  Jason 44
  Joanna 100
  Joannah 119
  Leroy 99
  Mary 143
  Patience 123

Parker, Philip S. 46
  Thomas 7
  Timothy 18
  Washington G. 90
Parlin, E. A. (Mrs.) 144
Parrish, Andrew 145
Parshall, Ada Mary 129
  Alfred D. 84
  Ambrose 124
  Ambrose C. 87
  C. Alphonso 138
  Delia 163
  Dewi H. C. 152
  Dewitt C. 107
  Elias 154
  Elias (Mrs.) 51
  Experience 99
  Flora 124
  George 152
  Hannah 143
  Henrietta M. 101
  Huldah E. 56
  James 75, 100
  John 63, 160
  Lewis G. 135
  Lucy 103
  Mary Campbell 105
  Mary E. 109
  Miner 56
  Miner C. 167
  Minor 85
Parsons, David 25
  Stephen 19
Patchen, Daniel 38
Patchin, Daniel 88
Patrick, Barley 160
  Jared 164
  Lucretia 125

Patten, Aurelia 175
  David 65, 123
  Elmira 72
  George 82
  Joel S. 94
  John 69
  William 122
Pattengill, Lemuel 112
  Mary H. 177
Patter, Rispah J. 115
Patterson, Martha 54
Paul, Cornelius M. 51
  James I. 86
  Maria 125
Peabody, Betsey M. 92
  Charlotte 75
  David 49
  Oliver 49
  Roswell 14
Peak, Caroline C. 55
  Elizabeth 29
  Ephraim 89
  James Arthur 64
  John 93
Peake, Alice Gray 131
  Francis Marion 56
  James M. 109
  Jamie D. 131
Pearsall, Joseph 54
Pearse, Frederick 170
Peaslee, Ann Eliza 142
  Cornelia 146
Peck, Catherine 98
  Charles R. 99
  Daniel 174
  Elizabeth 156, 171

Peck, Eugene 144
  George W. 131
  Helen 24
  Jacob 13
  Jedediah 23
  Joseph 157
  Legranderson 124
  Louisa 84
  Mary E. 130
  Mary M. 99
  Mercy 70
  Polly M. 148
  Rachel Ann 74
  Sophia 48
  Theo. E. 127
Peeso, Lydia 89
Peet, Abigail 130
  Freelove 143
  Isaac 156
Pegg, Ed. H. 76
  George A. 133
  Thomas 111
Pellett, Elias P. 67
Pembleton, Ezra 149
  Jabez 72
Penniman, Chiron 16
  Obadiah 20
Perine, Abbie 125
Perkins, Caleb 103
  Ella Jane 134
  Frank 114
  Harvey 91
  Harvey (Mrs.) 109
  James 83
  John 12
  Joseph 90
  Joseph Tredwell 67
  Melissa 149
  Olive 150
  Olive Ann 134

Perkins, Philo W. 160
  Polly 172
Permlee, Alvan 150
Perry, Albegence 162
  Amos M. 101
  Cynthia 43
  Elijah C. 142
  Henry 63
  Horace M. 172
  Jane Garlock 157
  Jonas 117
  Louisa 136
  Martha Sophia 133
  Mary M. 129
  Nancy 116
  Ruth 71
Persons, Abraham 72
  Elizabeth 58
  Ircine M. 140
Peters, Caroline 150
  Ellen J. 83
  Rufus 72, 113
Peterson, Francis 55
Pette, Louiseanna 36
  Louisianna 2
  Martha 80
Phelon, Roena P. 94
Phelps, Betsey 18
Phenix, Nancy 74
Philips, John 76, 124
Phillips, Catherine Doolittle 108
  Celinda Green 152
  Chester 144
  Mehitable 31
  Tempa 26
Phinney, Alecia 179
  Elihu 13, 129
  Henry 102

Phinney, Henry F. 179
  John T. 106
  Mary 72
  Nancy 96
Pickens, Catherine 112
  Edwin 160
  Julia 128
  Samuel 113
Pickering, Timothy 38
Pier, Abner 11
  Avaline A. 43
  Daniel B. 106
  David 29
  Emerson D. 125
  Ephraim 75
  George 6, 46
  John 1, 11
  Lucy 97
  Martha 15
  Nancy 11
  Polly 1, 11, 48
  Thomas 43
Pierce, Azrikim 10
  Benjamin 154
  Benoni 92
  Catherine 81
  Deette 137
  Edward 60
  Enoch E. 50
  F. Marvin 54
  Francis 81
  Hannah E. 77
  Isabella 88
  Jefferson 125
  John 5, 44, 127
  Levi H. 44
  Marcia 177
  Mariett 68

Pierce, Mary E. 122
  Mial 121
  Nathaniel 54
  Philetus S. 59
  Sally 167
  Silas E. 135
  Thomas 88
  William 136
Pierson, Alanson 71
  Levi 119
  Nathan 25
Piper, Solomon 147
Pitcher, Fannie 125
  Gertrude 84
  Myra A. 132
Pitts, Catherine 175
Pixley, Mary L. 72
Place, Rufus 161
Plamer, Frances 115
Platner, George H. 126
  Harriet 136
  Jacob M. 36
  Parmelia 168
  William 71
Platt, Jonas 52
  Maria 85
  Stephen 140
Plattner, Jacob 2
Plumb, Abigail 158
  Almira 83
Pnah, Joseph 164
Pomeroy, Ann Cooper 152
  Edgar 21
  Ellen 18
  George 18, 21, 124
  Medad 20
  William Cooper 1
Pope, Edward 112
  Gershom 11

Pope, Hannah 4, 42
  Lydia 59
  Nathaniel 59
  Perry 149
  Rebecca D. 149
  Rufus 139
  Sarah S. 94
Popple, Frances 59
  Hiram 51
  John 59
  Louisa 59
Porter, Alford 61
  Joel 166
  Leroy S. 145
  Samuel 23
  Thomas 7
Post, John 163
  Wright 36
Potter, Alvan 130
  Asaph 18
  Augusta Maria 48
  Charles H. 133
  Daniel 35
  Delos (Mrs.) 154
  Ellen Virginia 134
  Ezra G. 149
  Francelia A. 132
  Frank 132, 133
  Gardner 105
  Henry 86
  J. Russell 163
  Joel B. 9
  Jonathan 69
  Lucretia 22
  Martha 110
  Mary 3, 13, 38, 150
  Melvin Gardner 134
  Naomi 35
  Nathan 34

Potter, Olney 179
  Philo 31
  Sarah M. 178
  Tabitha 118
  Voadicea L. 151
  Vossice 64
  Waitey 175
  Willis E. 147
Potts, Thomas 167
Powell, A. V. H. 152
  Eliza S. 96
  George W. 94
Powers, George A. 106
  Roswell 152
  William 6
Pratt, Annie 25
  Clarence M. 135
  David Brainard 33
  Horace C. 129
  Jane 148
  Jeremiah 129
  Mary 76
  Mary E. 76
  Rice 116
  S. 70
  Sarah E. 176
  Thomas 84
  Thomas J. 164
  Wallace 141
Prentiss, Catherine 17
  Daniel 24
  George H. 51
  John 122
  John H. 62, 75
  Lucretia 72
Preston, Daniel 98
  Esther 128
  Everett D. 147

Preston, Frank A. 132
  Lucy 178
  Olive 4, 44
  Otis 62
  Polly 158
Prevost, Augustine 22
  Augustus J. 77
Price, Hannah C. 107
  William 118
Priest, Calvin 164
  Huldah 116
Prindle, --- (Mrs.) 81
  Hyler D. 126
Pringle, John 47
Proctor, George 111
  James 81
Provost, Benjamin B. 72
Pumpelly, Charles 42
Putman, Israel 12
Putnam, Peter Schuyler 35

~ *Q* ~

Quackenbush, Charles A. 172
Quail, Sarah A. 116
Queal, Paul A. 137
  William 162

~ *R* ~

Rabun, William 19
Raitt, George 162
Rand, John 121
Randall, Betsey 74

Randall, Margaret 30
　Perez 64
Ransom, Asa 2
　Joshua 4, 41
　Norman K. 161
　Thomas 36
Rapalie, Frank B.
　104
Rathbon, Susan 154
Rathbone, Jane
　Hume 113
　Thomas W. 113
Rathbun, Daniel 28
　Fernando C. 117
　Frances M. 151
　James 80, 138
　Jane E. 113
　Jennie E. 126
　Louisa 95
　Louisa J. 51
　Mary 115
　Mary E. 100
　Selinda 56
Rathburn, Dolly 117
Ray, Alice 126
　Amos 52
　Cornelius 33
　Hannah 176
　Mary L. 138
　William 171
Raymond, Ann C.
　80
　Laura E. 101
　Levantia E. 63
Reccord, Allen 73
Redfield, Levi 63
Redford, Mary A.
　121
Redington, Meriam
　12
Reed, Ahetable 52

Reed, Clarinda 138
　David 74, 135
　Eugene 123
　Fayette 73
　Franklin 73
　John 55, 62, 92
　Joseph 66
　Laura 60
　Leonard 17
　Mariah L. 4
　Neoma 167
　Oramel S. 86
　Pamela 149
　Shubard 83
　Susan 154
　Sylvester 154
　William 169
　William Harvey
　　128
Reelman, George 20
Reid, John 16
Reno, Peter 170
Rexford, Annie 113
　Edgar R. 130
　Ensign 58
　Hannah 50
　Maryette 131
　Sylvester 95
Reynold, George W.
　92
Reynolds, Catherine
　179
　Eunice L. 87
　Frederick N. 154
　Ira 55
　James 178
　John 176
　John M. 94
　John W. 84
　Joseph W. 139
　Lillie 169

Reynolds, Mary 89
　Miriam 113
　Miriam H. 157
　Orsemus 160
　Phebe E. 132
　Sarah 10
　Stephen 157
　Violet 49
Rhinees, Elizabeth
　105
Rhines, Wandal 119
Rhodes, Eliza 60
Rice, Daniel (Mrs.)
　53
　Eliza 94
　Holden 82
　John 100
　John G. 51
　Joseph 2, 37
　Mary 26
　Morgan H. 49
　Olney 26
　William 53
Rich, Asa 103
　Hannah 79
　Hannah M. 143
　Margaret 86
　Michael 169
　Moses 115
　Moses D. 78
Richards, Betsey 31
　Caroline 32
　Delvan 70
　John R. 139
　Polly 165
　Roderick 90
　Thomas 139
Richardson, Betsey
　　Williams 72
　C. 61
　Clarissa A. 50

Richardson, James 49
  James H. 35
  Leonard 55
  Ruth 34
Richmond, Seth D. 166
Rickland, E. G. 173
Rider, Catherine 52
  Simeon 12
Riggs, Caleb S. 32
Rightor, Catherine 100
Riley, Mary Ann 74
Ringe, Daniel 39
Riphenbergh, Rosa 174
Ripley, Cyrus S. 125
  Esther 119
  Horace 110
  Noah W. 175
Risedorph, Mary A. 109
Ritchie, George 46
Ritter, George S. 107
  Mahitable 41
  Mehitable 4
Rivenburgh, Henry 36
Rivera, Hannah R. 20
Road, Sarah A. 74
Robbins, Julia Ann 35
Robbinson, Mary 67
Roberts, Abijah 108
  Alice 28
  George 79
  George W. 155
  Horace 132

Roberts, Horace K. 79
  James 34
  John 36, 115
  Mary 117
  Mary E. 101
  Rhoda 61
  Ruth T. 108
  Sally Maria 2, 36
Robins, Sarah L. 163
Robinson, Adalaide 117
  Alfred 148
  Alice E. 115
  Altheda 116
  Ann 36
  Belle 173
  Charles A. 142
  Comfort 5, 45
  Emery M. 131
  Emma E. 157
  Florence L. 90
  Hannah 107
  Jane 83
  Jeremiah 44
  Jesse 93
  Jonathan 19
  Joseph 116
  Julia A. 82
  Margaret S. 105
  Mary A. 65
  Mary Ann 85
  O. P. 87
  Octavia Sabrina 34
  Rebecca 28
  Rhoda 146
  Solomon 140
  William V. A. 54
Robison, Helen 4
  Jonathan 20

Rochester, Nathaniel 46
Rockwell, Abner E. 99
  Anson 122
  Asa F. 117
  Betsey 176
  Clark 73
  Elisha G. 96
  Eliza 25
  Emily M. 99
  John 34
  Polly 116
  Ralph 113
Rodgers, Augustus 4, 40
Roe, James B. 46
  Sally M. 135
Rogers, Anna 38, 54
  Armenia 17
  Bartlet 32
  Elizabeth 179
  John 35, 65
  Mary W. 150
  William 27
Roman, Peter 25
Rood, Elias 140
  Elijah 34
  Frances 125
  Harriet N. 143
  James 140
Roof, Melville 84
  Philip A. 68
Root, Charles 38
  Erastus 38, 39
  John W. 86
  Mary 14, 66
  Maryett 123
  Reuben 15
  Ruth 95
  Sally 122

Root, Silas 121
  Thomas B. 168
Rose, Benoni 89
  Delevan 120
  Jessie 173
  John 107
  Josiah 97
  Julia 60
  Maria 139
  Mary Ripley 72
  Olive A. 125
  Peleg 90
  Philena 59
  Potter 175
  Sarah 148
  Sarah T. 65
  Seldom M. 103
Roseboom, Henry 28
  John 65, 154
  John J. 39
  Peter 130
  Peter (Mrs.) 150
  Robert 16
  Ruth 134
Ross, Sally 49
Rotch, Charles M. 67
  Frances 170
Rotto, Christopher 65
Rouse, Robert 174
Rowley, Seth 101
Rowlinson, Helen 43
Rucker, Rebecca S. 118
Rudd, Francis A. 85
  George W. 88
Ruggles, Benjamin 62
  Laura A. 97

Ruggles, Mary 100
  William H. 170
Rulofson, Rachel 106
Rury, Henry 154
Russell, Agnes S. 102
  Armena 91
  Arthur H. 141
  Asa E. 95
  Edgar 129, 177
  Elizabeth 64
  Henry 137
  Isaac 52, 87
  Isaac Newton 93
  John 48, 78
  Joseph 109
  Mary 52, 100, 144
  Mary J. 127
  Maud 173
  Nelson 108
  Olive Wells 3, 40
  Phebe 118
  Rensselaer W. 29
  Robert E. 136
  S. Loomis 140
  Salmon 4
  Sarah 100
  Sarah M. 95
  Selina 83
  Thankful C. 114
  Thomas 113
  Walter J. 98
  William 116
  William R. 177
Rutherford,
  Archibald 85
  Mary 119
  Thomas H. 178
Rutt, Peter 89
Ryder, Sophia 179
  Stephen 110

Ryder, W. Webber 137
Rynders, George H. 138

~ S ~

Sabin, --- (Mrs.) 1
  Algeron L. 151
  Francis Lynde 5, 46
  Frederick 49
  Orrin 49
  Sarah A. 142
  Timothy 58
Salisbury, Alvira 121
  Amanda M. 144
  Barnard 134
  Edward 39
  Mary 42
  Philip 150
Sammons, Cornelius 56
Sampson, Ezra 27
Sands, Maria C. 64
Sanger, Jedediah 40
Sargeant, Lemuel 21
Sargent, Tamer 117
Saulisbury, Maria 150
Saulsbury, Mardula S. 164
Savage, Austin 41
  Luman 34
  Titus 135
Sawin, Eleanor 40
Sawtelle, --- (Mrs.) 175
Saxton, Esther 137
  Harvey E. 165
  J. Lavern 173

Saxton, L. Maude 143
　Lucy C. 166
　Nathaniel Huse 45
　Phicelia 80
　Phidelia 70
　Phidelia L. 95
Sayre, David L. 56
　George W. 158
　Harriet M. 71
　Sarah Ann 10
Scablard, David 168
Schaules, Julian 84
Schofield, Ann 52
　James 48
Schrambling, Eunice 69
　Peter 67
Schrom, Mary 147
　Mary P. 176
Scollard, James D. 145
　John C. 145
　Mary 71
　Nancy 151
Scott, --- (Mis.) 47
　Alice 88
　Annie Grace 141
　Catherine 77
　Charlotte P. 93
　Cornelius 90
　Elizabeth 56
　Henry 3, 38, 169
　John B. 97
　Luzerne B. 140
　Rebecca 90
　Ruamy S. 90
　Ruben 90
　Sarah 77, 108
　Thomas 23
　William 118

Scramling, Cornelia 157
　George 139
Scribner, Andrew 101
　Lucien B. 66
　Orlando 66
　Phebe 91
　Philena G. S. 165
Scudder, Emily T. 163
Seargent, Harley 169
Searles, Horace P. 162
Seaton, Dore P. 115
Seaver, Phebe M. 105
Seaward, Sally 21
Secor, Leverett 128
　Samantha 91
Seeber, Adolphus 148
　Ella M. Pattin 158
　Martha E. 130
　Mary 119
Seegar, Justice 147
Seeger, Alvin A. 131
　Vernet Lee 131
Seeley, Martha Weeks 162
Seelye, Caroline 87
　Isaac 24, 50
　Julia 100
　Theoda H. 36
　William Henry 24
Segar, Edward H. 87
Segendorf, Henry 118
Sergent, Joseph 114
　Louisa M. 126
Sewall, Elizabeth 25

Seward, Charles H. 136
　Porter M. 135
Sewell, Joseph 96
Seymour, Alma M. 54
　Daniel 45
Shadden, Thomas 78
Shankland, Charles F. 76
　Rachel 32
　Thomas 26, 158
Shannon, Lucy 160
Shant, Clarinda 69
Sharp, Daniel 143
Shaul, Katherine 152
　Seymour G. 167
Shaw, Andrew 131
　Ann G. 94
　David 174
　Henry 53
　Jane F. 97
　Roselind 51
　S. D. 53
　Samuel 7
　Thomas 92, 103
Shay, Daniel 174
　Michael 176
Sheldon, Andrew F. 53
　Anna C. 110
　Artemas 6, 31
　E. J. 59
　Lionel 158
　Mary E. 85
Shelland, James 179
　Mary M. 161
Shelman, Lewis 138
Shepard, Alfred C. 91
　Elizabeth 160

Shepard, George 47
  Malvina A. 82
  Mary Frances 116
  William 26
Shepherd, Susan A. 114
Sherman, Albert E. 111
  Amelia 116
  Constant 98
  Edgar 177
  Mary 50
  Myron H. 132
  Samuel 30
Shermnan, Russell 86
Sherwood, George 39
  Jasper 101
  Juliet A. 26
  Melville J. 95
  Samuel 72
Shipboy, John 59
Shipman, David 13
  Menzr. 65
  Ruby 43
  Samuel 25
  Sophronia W. 134
Shipway, Joseph 110
Shoemaker, Rob. 62
  Silas 7
Sholes, Abigail 57
  Clariss 95
  Gurdon A. 78
  James 67
  Mary 116
  Miner 119
  Minor 76
Short, Anna 154
  Emily 146
  Harvey R. 143

Short, John 140
  Maria L. 153
  Mary 120
  Samuel 91
  Uriah (Mrs.) 70
Shove, Amy 115
  Daniel 9
  Mary 144
Shumaker, Polly 122
Shumway, Allen 112
  Charles 173
  Fred A. 174
Shute, Annis 129
  Mayette 80
Shutts, Simon B. 159
Sibley, John 97
  Mary A. 168
  Mary Ann 89
  Millicent 177
Sickles, Margaret 82
  Zachariah W. 6
Sile, Matthew Don 27
Sill, Elisha Dorr 142
  Eliza 27
  Helen T. 27
  Henry 149
  Hepsibah 118
  Jedediah P. 178
  Mary A. 153
  Mathew Dorr 100
Silvernail, Georgiana 129
Simison, Effie 106
Simmon, Eliza 161
Simmons, --- 56
  Phebe 95
  Samuel 107
Simonds, Joseph 9

Simonson, Gertrude 134
Simpson, James 19
Simson, John 57
Sinderling, Augusta Adeline 47
Sisson, Charles C. 106
  Miriam 105
Siver, Belle 142
  Cora B. 171
Skidmore, Russell 28
Skiff, Nancy 10
Skinion, Mary 176
Skinner, Elisha 24
  George 177
  Helen 98
Sleeper, Ephraim H. 159
  Joseph H. 42
  Morris 63
  Thankful Irene 40
Slingerland, Cornelia 49
  Mary A. 110
Sliter, Hannah 139
  Lindel H. 159
Sloan, Eila F. 168
  Mary E. Porter 158
Slocum, Jesse 20
Slocumb, Jesse 22
Slooper, Thankful I. 3
Smallie, Andrew 10
Smallwood, John D. 164
Smith, --- 30
  Abigail 53, 112
  Addie F. 174
  Addison M. 148
  Adelaide 73

Smith, Adelia 124
  Adeliade G. 124
  Ann V. 52
  Anna 94
  Artemas Byron 92
  Aurelia E. 122
  Azubah 77
  Betsey 80
  Caroline 104
  Charles 7, 110
  Chauncey T. 144
  Cora E. 121
  Daniel 33, 117, 120
  David 53
  Dewitt 88
  Egbert 94
  Eliza B. 146
  Elizabeth 11
  Elizabeth L. 92
  Ellen 106
  Elva J. 164
  Emma A. 167
  Faithful 58, 172
  Francis 39
  Frederick 36
  George 59
  George W. 106
  Hannah 168
  Harriet Gill 109
  Harriet L. 133
  Harvey M. 159
  Ichabod 88
  Isaac 102
  Jane 124, 163, 171
  Jane W. 123
  Jarvis S. 123
  Jesse 62
  Joel 34
  John L. 63
  Joseph 161
  Liny 153
  Lydia M. 110
  Martha 64
  Mary A. 54, 81, 160
  Mary L. 103
  Miner 162
  Morey 116
  Moses 65
  Myrtle 171
  Nathaniel 24
  Nathaniel K. 41
  Patty 102
  Peter 30, 91
  Reuben 5, 45, 87
  Richard 161
  Richard R. 1
  Robert H. 142
  Rosanna 120
  Roxie 113
  Russell 150
  Russell G. 58
  Russell H. 174
  Ruth 176
  Sally 126
  Sarah E. 126
  Seth 40
  Seward Ford 161
  Stephen 8
  Sylvania 64
  Temperance 110
  Theodore L. 144
  Thomas 47
  Truman 11
  Urilla 75
  William D. 71
  William H. 98
  William O. 113
  William O. (Mrs.) 151
  William W. 123
Snedeker, Henry 170
Snow, Julia A.
  Kromer 149
Snyder, Betsey 161
  Charles 177
  Christopher 166
  Frances M. 138
  George 106, 120
  Hannah 166
  Jackson 118
  Jacob 105
  Jane 171
  Martha 76
  William E. 116
Soules, Hiram 142
  Mary 132
Southerland, William 86
Southworth, Harriet A. 94
  Mary E. 88
  Schuyler 134
  Thomas 151
Sowle, David 52
Spafford, Caroline 68
  Elisha 120
  Elizabeth H. 73
  Frederick L. 145
Spaford, Airel 83
  Eunice 89
Spalding, Sewall 29
Sparrow, Alice 55
  John J. 3
  Mary 76
Sparrows, Erastus 38
  John J. 38
Spencer, Abigail 144
  Amos 78
  Andrew 118
  Emeline 124

Spencer, Halsey 153
  Horace D. (Mrs.) 159
  Laura 9
  Leroy 176
  Lucy J. 144
  Mary A. 141
  Rhoda H. 159
  William D. 171
Spender, Ithamer A. 155
Spicer, Cora E. 177
  Deborah 89
Spooner, Ruffles 58
  Ursula 137
Sprague, Anna 160
  Esther 98
  Helen 44
  Henry 15
  J. S. 44
  Joseph 18, 57
  Julia A. 166, 167
  Mary Day 15
  Nathaniel 68
  Phillis 14
  Rachel Ann 18
Spraker, Mary Ann 149
Springsteed, Addie 149
  Josiah 149
Spurr, Helen M. 76
Squier, Martha 160
Squires, Chloe 87
  Erastus W. 130
  Joel 83
  Joel L. 140
  Mettie A. 130
St. John, Dianthe 100
  Louisa 148

St. John, Lucy 153
  Polly 133
  Stephen 80
Stacy, Henry (Mrs.) 66
Stafford, James 116
  John 20
Stansel, Mary 107
Stanton, Alexa 139
  Amy 135
  Clara E. 144
  Jennie S. 161
  Polly 116
Starkey, Desire 65
Starkweather, Frederick R. 153
  Jane 30
  Samuel 30
Starr, Eli 82
  Harmon A. 82
  Huldah 60
  Jesse H. 14
  Joshua 62
  Olive 32
  Sally 109
Stebbins, Polly 168
Steele, Elijah W. 37
Steere, Charles Harvey 154
  Eliza A. 162
  Ellen M. 109
  Grace P. 142
  Harvey Kenyon 158
  Ira 123
  Ira (Mrs.) 123
  James 139
  Mary 74
  Nicholas 83
  Phebe A. 93
  Phoebe 16

Steere, Rufus 97
Steers, Clovis 171
Stenson, Mary Jane 134
Stephens, Esther 1
  Henry 103
Sterling, Erastus S. 147
  Stephen V. 95
Sterns, Elizabeth 118
Sterre, Martha 59
  Samuel 178
Stetson, Ezra 1
  Mary Jane 98
  William 156
Stevens, Edward 19
  Eliza Ann 80
  Esther 137
  Lima 59
  Lucinda 158
  Nancy (Pier) 11
  William 116
Stevenson, John 56
  Nathaniel 158
Stever, Catherine 89
  Jacob 62
  Sarah 138
Steward, Susan 65
Stewart, Bradley 28
  Catherine 4, 43
  Charles 56
  Charles S. 155
  Harriet B. 5, 44
  Helen (Bowers) 53
  Lester 169
  Maria E. 142
  Sarah 106, 167
Stickeny, Eliphalet 76
Stickles, Martha 140
  Zachariah W. 46

Stickney, Eliphalet 23
　Leverett 112
Still, Charles Ceylon 123
　Herbert 123
　Ida Deette 123
　Joseph 167
　Sally A. 95
Stillman, Barker 74
　Emma 99
　George W. 108
　Helen Maria 64
　Sarah 44
　Willet 33
Stilwell, John 47
Stocker, Benjamin 137
　H. F. 133
　Isaac 125
　Lucy 77
　Polly 136
Stocking, Helen V. 163
Stockwell, Alcena 94
Stone, Joel W. 136
　Mercy 60
　Stephen 43
　William Young 51
Stoneman, Henry 6
Storm, Stephen 40
Storrs, Samuel 93
Story, Elizabeth 152
　James 77
　Jedediah 29
　Joshua H. 156
　Lois 108
　Unice 83
　William 63
Stowel, James 32
　Phebe 59

Stowel, William 24, 83
Stowell, David 63
　George C. 92
　James 86, 108
　Leverett C. 154
　Ruth 79
Straight, Abigail 129
　Joseph 94
　Maryette 80
　Phebe 105
Strain, John 149
　Phally 106
Stranagan, Farrand 32
Stranahan, Annette 67
　Farrand S. 84
　Sarah S. 27
Strobel, Eliza Snyder 132
Stroble, Emma C. 50
Strong, Caleb 19, 20
　Colin D. 126
　Harvey 168
　Joseph 69
　Robert L. 126
　Sarah J. 152
Stryler, Isaac 61
Stuart, George H. 149
　Thomas 178
Sturges, Coley 89
　Lorinda 152
Sullivan, William B. 122
Summers, David 172
Sunday, Kittie 157
Sutherland, Amy 102
　Janette 117

Sutherland, John 71
　Soloman 8
Sutliff, Betsey 157
Sutphen, Matthew L. 33
Sutton, Mary 11
Swackhamer, Jane 100
Swain, George 31
Swan, Charles 156
　Mary E. 156
Swart, Peter 41
　Peter W. 155
Swartout, Abraham 53
Swartwout, Charlotte 142
　E. Josephine 158
　Hawley 105
Swartwouth, Richard 152
Sweatland, Sibyl 14
Sweet, Lucy 83
　Patience 112
Swift, Ceylina 82
　John 15
Sykes, Francis 60
　Richard B. 139
　Rose 82
Synnott, Alice M. 148

~ T ~

Taff, Clara E. 175
Taft, David (Mrs.) 25
Talbot, Neva A. 168
Tallmadge, Ira O. 158
　Mathias B. 20

Talmadge, Elisha 2
Tanner, Anna 29, 57
  Frances A. 104
  Hannah Elizabeth 66
  Ira 82, 170
  Julia 1
  Mary Ann 66
  Nancy 94
  Nathan 111
  Rhoda 82
  Thomas 17
  Zera 67
Tarbox, Clifford 169
Tarpenning, Cynthia 120
Taylor, Abraham 35
  C. W. T. 106
  Chester 155
  Elisha 15, 40
  Elvena A. 107
  Erastus 111
  Frances Hebe 129
  Horace 156
  Jane 152
  John 45
  Mariette 147
  Matilda 110
  Orin Kepler 129
  Polly 152
  Syntha 65
  Thomas 130, 155
Tazewell, Henry 7
Teachout, Cornelius 173
  Ettie M. 153
Teakins, Sarah A. 171
Tefft, Esther 115
  George A. 74

Temple, Daniel P. 146
  Elizabeth 16
  Flora 143
  Joseph 30
  Nancy 165
  Phebe 164
  Sarah 45
  Sophia 146
TenBroeck, Anna 42
  John 25
  Mary 130
TenBroek, Reoloff 86
TenEyck, Lindel 163
  Maria 28
  William W. 172
Terwilliger, John P. 127
Thayer, Abigail 178
  Ariel 146
  Arminda 58
  Ellery 52
  Emma S. 171
  Ephraim 120
  George 114
  Hannah 134, 147
  Harriet D. 125
  James 146
  Jonathan 95
  Katie 122
  Leonard 138
  Nancy 93, 102
  Olive 112
  Robert E. 53
  William 125
Thomas, Calvin 17
  Jane 119
Thompson, Anna 86
  Asenith 93
  Clarissa 93

Thompson, Francis 105
  Hugh R. 169
  Levi 48
  Mary 163
  Olive 107
  Orrin 123
  Thomas 78
  Thomas I. 151
  Zady 165
Thorn, Olive 72
Thornton, Ezekiel 51
  Peleg 7
  Samuel 7
  Stephen 156
  William 177
Thorp, Charles 34
  Henry C. 48
  John 7
  Polly 105
Thrall, F. G. 55
  George 97
  Roger 81
  Sarralette A. 55
Thurber, Caleb 85
  Isaiah 13
  Polly 19
  Terzy 65
  William 53
Thurstan, Deidama 73
Thurston, Abiel 13
  Billa 72
  Charles 155
  Cyrus 13
  Edward 19
  Elisha 177
  Ira 13
  Jeremiah 3, 39
  Margaret 155
  Maria 32

Thurston, Paulina 69
　Thankful 14
Tiffany, Eleanor 129
　Eli 49
　Ellen 100
　Esther 4, 41
　F. T. 30
　Harriet 74
　Jonathan 99
　Juliaette 99
　Mary G. 119
　Mary Miller 30, 79
　Nancy 43
　Stephen W. 169
　William 16
Tifft, William W. 53
Tift, George 74
Tilden, Esther 22
Tillson, Elizabeth 24
　Ruth 97
　Sylvina 169
Tisdale, Marion 108
　Rufus 108
Titus, Jeremy 36, 71
　Jeremy S. 2
　Jeremy Summers 36
　Jerusha 4, 36, 43
Toby, Lucy 56
　Zacheus 52
Todd, Bede 73
　Benjamin 15
　Catherine 105
　Hannah 58
　Jehiel 76
　Sally 67
Tollet, Lavisa 171
Tomlinson, Charles B. 117
Tompkins, Eleazer 28

Tompkins, Elijah 14
　Jonathan 25
　Sarah 11
Tompson, Julia A. 138
Torry, Charles F. 114
　William J. 123
Towne, Elisha G. 174
Townsend, Jeremiah 70
　Mary 53
Townsley, Amanda C. 178
Tracey, Sarah Ann 176
Tracy, Debba 85
　Julia M. 78
　Phebe 69
　Rufus 71
　Ruth 93
　Sally 79
　William G. 43
　William I. 46
Trask, Marion 138
Traverse, Sarah 98
Treadway, David 72
　Rebecca 61
Treadwell, John 26
Tredwell, Thomas 48
Trewhit, James 175
Tripp, Almeretta 149
　David 37
　Eliza 167
　Emily 69
　Mary Ann 65
　Peleg 18
　Polly 107
　Rufus 131

Trippe, David 3
Trowridge, Achsah 61
Trud, Emma 81
Truman, James H. 147
　Loretta F. 157
　Nathan 147
Trumbull, Benjamin 21
　Jonathan 10
Truxton, Thomas 24
Tubbs, Hannah 7, 8
　Samuel 8
Tucker, Ann 97
　Elizabeth 3, 38
　Harvey 138
　Isaac 120, 144
　Joshua 102
　Julia Keyes 140
　Mary 114
　Olive 76, 173
　Paul K. 119
　Polly 90, 163
　Sabra 130
　Sally M. 156
Tuller, Ansel 168
　Lucia M. 179
　Lydia 82
Tunicliff, Cornelius C. 28
　William 58
Tunnicliff, Aurelius 150
　John W. 114
　William 140
Tunnifcliff, William 33
Turnbull, Walter 175
Turner, Anson 144

Turner, Campbell L. 113
  Rebecca A. 4
  William 168
Tuthill, Olive 59
Tuttle, Delos 90
  Tamar 177
Tyler, Dolly 137
  Emily M. 141
  Horace M. 121

~ U ~

Uhcas, Great 32
Underwood, Pamelia 111
Upham, Hannah 111
Utman, Lanson 90
Utter, Lewis 172

~ V ~

Vail, Abijah 50
  Hannah 54
Valentine, Louisa 151
VanAllen, James 124
VanAlstine, Olive 83
VanAlstyne, Gilbert 143
VanBenschoten, Caroline 29
  Elias 163
  Jane 58
VanBergen, Francis 5
  James 91
  Peter A. 8
VanBooskirk, William 71

VanBoskirk, Samuel 69
VanBunschoten, Jacob 43
VanBuren, Eva O. 128
  Hannah 18
  Helen C. 128
  Hiram 154
  Martin 18
  Steven L. 128
VanCourt, Daniel 171
  Rhoda 176
VanCuren, Steven L. 128
VanDerKemp, Francis Adrian 41
VanDeveer, Crosby 160
VanDyke, Catherine 74
  George 89
VanEtten, Samuel 90
VanHorne, Abram (Mrs.) 164
  Alfred 171
  Carrie B. 176
  Charles 134
  David 7
  Eliza A. 80
  Eugenia E. 77
  Henrietta 123
  James 64
  Julia Ann 101
  Margaret 81
  Mathew 122
  Richard 25
  Ruth C. 169
  Thomas 70

Vanhusen, Helen P. 81
VanHusen, Jacob 169
VanNamee, William 164
VanNess, William (Mrs.) 41
VanNorman, Sarah M. 174
VanNort, Russell S. 110
VanPatten, Angelica 111
  Daniel 95
VanRensselaer, Henry K. 16
  Robert 8
VanSchaick, John 21
VanSice, Simon 177
VanSlyke, James 21
  Leonard 131
  Lyman 168
  Percy (Mrs.) 135
VanVechten, Catherine 20
VanWoert, John 155
Varr, Alfred 118
Vars, Joseph 70
Vaughn, Emeranda M. Sheldon 50
  James D. 133
  Lucy 48
Vebber, Lemuel F. 95
  Mary 41
Veber, Lucy 103
  Polly 68
Vedder, Cornelius B. (Mrs.) 88
  Harmanus 112

231

Verry, William C. 98
Vibbard, Epaphras 56
Viele, John 28
Viver, Eunice 91
Vole, Emily 156
Vosburgh, Abraham 33
Vrooman, Peter I. 7
Vunk, Elizabeth 146
  Mary A. 178
  Sally 171

~ W ~

Wadsworth, Charles 141
Waid, Herbert L. 133
Waine, John 27
Wait, Albert 57
  Charles 93
Waite, Clarissa R. 132
Wakefield, Elizabeth A. 96
  Elmore 111
  Louis (Mrs.) 63
  Thomas L. 173
Walbey, William 30
Walby, Dewitt 113
  Eunice 175
  Marcus O. 113
  Mary 39
  Sarah 39
  William 3
Waldby, Mary M. 169
Waldo, Nathan 30
  Ozias 10

Waldo, Polly 2, 37
Waley, Amelia Palmer 156
Walker, Albert Deville 136
  Asseneth 82
  David 108
  Elizabeth 79
  Hezekiah 45
  Mary 63
  Mary Clark 130
  Sarah P. 116
  Sarah W. 150
  William W. 48
Wall, James 22
  John 75
Wallace, Abigail 56
  John 165
  Polly 112
  Samantha 113
Walley, Eunice 101
Walling, Margaret 5, 46
Walradt, Charles J. 134
  Fanny E. 117
  Polly 162
Walrath, Eunice V. 124
Walsh, Dudley 16
Walshe, Henry W. W. 97
Walter, Catherine M. 111
Walters, Sarah D. 161
Walton, John 12, 34
  Joseph 24
  Sarah S. 24
Walworth, James C. 159

Walworth, Lydia 69
  Lyman J. 143
  Philena 58
Ward, Ambrose 105
  Charles 147
  Davis 143
  Della 154
  Erastus (Mrs.) 177
  Erutha 111
  Julia 151
  Louisa M. 164
  Lucy Ann 98
  Nellie C. 171
  Richard 13
  Robert 13
  Samuel 9
  William D. 104
Warner, Eleazer H. 147
  Freelove 3, 40
  Hezekiah 175
  Laura 30
Warren, --- (Mr.) 11
  Abby 160
  Anna A. 98
  Charles H. 133
  Darius 3, 40
  Fanny 138
  Harriet E. Chapin 128
  Julius 142
  Laura C. 64
  Maria 158
  Mary 57
  Mary Elizabeth 73
  Mercy Ann 57
  Ruth J. 152
  Sophia B. 3, 37
Washbon, Daniel 25
  Helen 64
  Nancy 62

Washbon, Zeba 74
Washburn, Abigail 93
  Andrew G. 144
  Zenas 113
Waterman, Clarence 162
  David 76
  Emily J. 101
  Fanny 116
  Harvey 107
  Lorinda 38
  Lucy 48
  Mary A. 77
  Roswell 151
  Simeon 24, 136
  Timothy 104
Waters, Amos 115
  Amos (Mrs.) 109
  Eunice 49
  James H. 137
Watkins, Hezekiah (Mrs.) 121
  John 4
  Louisa A. 108
Watson, Gilbert C. 121
  Lorenzo D. 130
  Sally 125
  Susan E. 132
  Zara 114
Wattles, Jehiel 33
Way, Nicholas 7
Wayman, Phebe 163
Wayne, Anthony 6
Weatherby, Nancy 158
Weathing, James 150
Weaver, Jonathn 40
  Mary 39
  Priscilla 13

Webb, Ceylon 81
  Elizabeth 32, 103
  John 35
  Joseph (Mrs.) 177
  Samuel 32
  Wheeler 97
Webster, Daniel 35
  Grace 35
  Harriet 105
  Noah 14
  Percival G. 112
  William 22
Wedderspoon, Catherine M. 121
  David 169
  Edgar C. 124
  Isabelle C. 123
Weeks, Anjuline 80
  James 87
  James F. 126
  John D. 174
  Martha B. 100
  Nathan 105
Weelman, Dexter 139
Weidman, Sophia 158
Weinegard, Hannah 168
Welby, William 40
Welch, Alfred 136
  Angeletta L. 164
  Sally 70
Weldon, Elizabeth 71
  Orlu V. 135
  Thomas 64
Weller, Daniel 68
Wellman, Dolly A. Moore 161

Wellman, Eliza B. 148
  Ira 25
Wells, Elizabeth 86
  Fanny 74
  John 74
  Olney 156
  Randall 108
  Ruth 37
  William 11
Welsh, Stephen R. 147
Wentworth, Helen 60
Wessels, Hannah Cooper 129
West, Antoinette E. G. 62
  Fanny 63
  Heman 37
  Prince 2, 36
  Sylvenus 60
Westcott, Benjamin 101, 137
  Cora M. 142
  Dorcas 163
  Joseph 117
  Margaret L. 122
  Reuben 129
Weston, Harrison 52
Wetmore, John 176
Wheeler, Amasa 40
  Charlotte 46
  Daniel 45
  Everett 112
  Fred R. 140
  G. W. P. 46
  Hepsey A. 84
  Hezekiah 35
  Ira 146
  Judson D. 145

Wheeler, Julia A. 140
  Lucy 59
  Mary 35
  Moses 111
  Patty 68
  Silas 37
  Susan 125
Whelpey, Philip M. 28
Whipple, --- (Mrs.) 6
  Albert 167
  Barney 6
  Benajah 13
  Eunice 179
  Irving D. 97
  James 14
  Jannett 125
  Oscar 107
  Polly 160
  Sarah (Wilcox) 7
  Seth 90
Whiston, Esther Ann 44
  William Garret 67
Whitaker, John R. 19
White, Abigail 38
  Almon 124
  Benjamin 63
  Daniel (Mrs.) 173
  Deborah 34
  Delos 55
  Eliza O. 124
  Elizabeth 150
  Elizabeth Nelson 128
  Eunice 141
  H. Ester 133
  Hannah H. 70

White, Hiram 112
  Hugh 12
  Isabel 81
  James F. 18
  Jerome 179
  John 78
  Joseph 48, 53
  Levantia 74
  Mortimer 108
  Noadiah 1
  Sarah 132
  William H. 177
Whiteford, James D. 9
Whitemore, Amos 35
Whiteside, John 77
Whiting, John 24
  Lydia 10
  William B. 6
Whitmarsh, F. B. 65
Whitney, Cynthia 147
  Joseph 158
Whitty, John 12
Whitwell, Emeline 149
  Maria 107
Whitwill, Mary J. 141
Wicks, Carrie 174
Wickwire, Amos D. 142
  Amos F. 166
Wier, Polly 174
Wieting, Jerome A. G. 85
Wightman, Cynthia 151
  Deborah 111
Wikoff, Rachel 120

Wilber, Humphrey 169
  Isaac 171
  Jane 53
  Rebecca 158
  Stephen 93
Wilbur, Henry 94
Wilcox, Alanson 42
  Clarissa 107
  Elijah 7
  Letitia 104
  Mary Elizabeth 63
  Morrison D. 47
  Oliver 157
  Sarah 7
Wilder, Abigail 127
Wiles, Daniel 143
  John 158
Wilkins, George K. 85
Willard, David 107
  Elias 33
  Marcus S. 101
  Samuel 21
Williams, A. 155
  Ann 88
  Bille 29
  David 44
  Eliphalet 17
  Elishaba 91
  Eliza Ann 80
  Elizabeth 130, 155
  Esther C. 114
  Ezra 28
  George (Mrs.) 174
  Grosvenor E. 20
  Harley T. 157
  Henry 44
  Henry T. 174
  Howard 98
  Isaac 15

Williams, James J. 61
John 152, 174
John (Mrs.) 2
John C. 104
Julia 101
Lucia (Garrett) 18
Lucia Lucretia 19
Lydia 143
Marcy 2
Margaret 152
Margaret Elizabeth 28
Marietta 32
Mary 36, 124
Mary E. 54
Nabby 113
Phebe 109
Phebe A. 154
Polly 151
Rensselaer 8
Rob E. 136
Roswell P. 110
Russell 19
Sarah 166
Sherman 34
Silas 104
Sophia 19
Stephen L. 147
Theo. 74
Thomas 13
W. S. 166
William 129
Willmarth, Adelaide S. 140
Wilmot, Ann 80
William 98
Wilsie, James 136
Wilson, Ann 84
Elijah 44
Fairfield M. 124

Wilson, Fidelia 100
Grandus 73
Helen 115
James 90
John 174
Julia 172
Kate 103
M. Fairfield 131
Mary L. 158
Nancy 79
Samuel 58
Samuel W. 143
Seldon 79
Thomas 165
William 62, 142
Winchester, Elkanah 7
Winder, Levin 18
Windsor, Hannah 22
John 127
John A. 155
Winegar, Elvira A. 167
Oliver 15
Wing, Charles 98
Jane R. 116
Winne, Daniel W. 122
Lewis W. 164
Matthew 177
Winnegar, Mary 166
Winslow, Caroline 64
Caroline B. 147
Elvira 123
Fanny E. 115
John 104
Mary 45
Seth T. 171
Winsor, Amos 18
Brown 92

Winsor, Daniel 163
Esther 171
Ezer 52
Matie 150
Winton, Alonzo G. 94
Ambrose D. (Mrs.) 100
Wires, John 169
Wisner, Pollydore B. 15
Withers, Jane 81
Witt, Sally S. 45
Susanna 45
Wolcott, Catherine A. 68
William 4, 42
Wood, Aaron 138
Ann 155
Cary 64
Clarence J. 143
Clark 87
Desire 166
Elizabeth 75
Ella 168
Elscey A. 173
Frederick C. 142
George F. 139
Harriet A. 102
Helen A. 96
Henry C. 153
Henry S. 108
J. Clellie 138
Jane 155
Joseph 61, 178
Levi 126, 152
Lucy 121
Lucy N. 98
Marilla 55
Martha C. 102
Mary 69

Wood, Minerva E. 171
　Naomi 21
　Robert 161
　Sally 24
　Samuel 80
　Sophia 23
Woodard, Simeon 4
Woodburn, Amelia M. 79
　David 116
　John W. 97
　Mary 179
　Mary Ida 103
Woodbury, John 128
　Laura 85
　Violett 156
Woodhouse, Lemuel 28
　Melisant 15
　Phoebe 5
Woodin, Lucy 55
Woodruff, John 110
Woodward, Isaac 108
　James D. 87
　John C. 52
　Phebe 80
　Serepta 64
　Sylvester H. 90

Woolsey, Melancton Lloyd 18
Wooster, Sherman 50
Worcester, Samuel 23
Worden, Pamela 9
Wording, Chauncey 49
Worlay, Aghor 12
Worthington, Jennie Storrs 129
　Ralph 37
Wright, Ann 111
　Bezaleal 19
　Chester 157
　Chester (Mrs.) 160
　Emeline V. 168
　Emily F. 168
　Erastus 52
　Flavel 33
　Hanson 121
　Lucy M. 176
　Mary A. 91
　Nancy 105, 132
　Orril 87
　Roswell 43
　Thomas D. 115
　William L. 145
Wyllys, Samuel 26

Wylwin, John Cushing 13
Wyman, John 47

~ Y ~

Yager, Michael 166
Yates, Amber 109
　John W. 2
Yeoman, Lydia R. 147
Young, Barkley W. 124
　Catherine 100
　Elsie 167
　Henry 60
　James 99, 145
　James C. 31
　John 42, 170
　Lydia 39
　Martin 141
　Mary A. 125
　Nancy 161
　Samuel 29
　Simon 42
Youngs, Dennis 43